Lecture Notes in Computer Scier

Commenced Publication in 1973
Founding and Former Series Editors:
Gerhard Goos, Juris Hartmanis, and Jan van Leeuwen

T0238457

Jens Grabowski   Brian Nielsen (Eds.)

Formal Approaches to Software Testing

4th International Workshop, FATES 2004
Linz, Austria, September 21, 2004
Revised Selected Papers

 Springer

Volume Editors

Jens Grabowski
University of Göttingen
Institute for Informatics
Lotzestr. 16-18, 37083 Göttingen, Germany
E-mail: grabowski@informatik.uni-goettingen.de

Brian Nielsen
Aalborg University
Department of Computer Science
Fredrik Bajersvej 7B, 9220 Aalborg, Denmark
E-mail: bnielsen@cs.auc.dk

Library of Congress Control Number: 2005921470

CR Subject Classification (1998): D.2, D.3, F.3, K.6

ISSN 0302-9743
ISBN 3-540-25109-X Springer Berlin Heidelberg New York

Springer is a part of Springer Science+Business Media

springeronline.com

© Springer-Verlag Berlin Heidelberg 2005
Printed in Germany

Typesetting: Camera-ready by author, data conversion by Scientific Publishing Services, Chennai, India
Printed on acid-free paper   SPIN: 11400752   06/3142   5 4 3 2 1 0

Preface

Testing often accounts for more than 50% of the required effort during system development. The challenge for research is to reduce these costs by providing new methods for the specification and generation of high-quality tests. Experience has shown that the use of formal methods in testing represents a very important means for improving the testing process. Formal methods allow for the analysis and interpretation of models in a rigorous and precise mathematical manner. The use of formal methods is not restricted to system models only. Test models may also be examined. Analyzing system models provides the possibility of generating complete test suites in a systematic and possibly automated manner whereas examining test models allows for the detection of design errors in test suites and their optimization with respect to readability or compilation and execution time. Due to the numerous possibilities for their application, formal methods have become more and more popular in recent years.

The Formal Approaches in Software Testing (FATES) workshop series also benefits from the growing popularity of formal methods. After the workshops in Aalborg (Denmark, 2001), Brno (Czech Republic, 2002) and Montréal (Canada, 2003), FATES 2004 in Linz (Austria) was the fourth workshop of this series. Similar to the workshop in 2003, FATES 2004 was organized in affiliation with the IEEE/ACM Conference on Automated Software Engineering (ASE 2004). FATES 2004 received 41 submissions. Each submission was reviewed by at least three independent reviewers from the Program Committee with the help of some additional reviewers. Based on their evaluations, 14 full papers and one work-in-progress paper from 11 different countries were selected for presentation.

This volume contains revised versions of the presented papers. The revisions reflect the lively discussions among the presenters and participants during the FATES workshop. The papers use different formal methods and languages, e.g., automata, labelled transition systems, TTCN-3 or UPPAAL, and apply them to symbolic test generation, the use of model-checking techniques in testing, the test of nonfunctional properties, and test optimization. This diversity of formal methods and application domains in conjunction with the high number of submissions to and participants of the FATES 2004 workshop emphasize the increased importance attributed to the research on formal approaches in software testing.

We would like to express our gratitude to all authors for their valuable contributions and to the Workshop Organizing Committee of the ASE 2004 conference. In addition, we would like to thank all members of the FATES Program Committee and the additional reviewers, who were given the essential task of reviewing many papers in a short period of time. The individuals who contributed to this effort are listed on the following pages.

December 2004 · Jens Grabowski and Brian Nielsen
Goettingen and Aalborg · Program Chairs
· FATES 2004

Organization

Program Chairs

Jens Grabowski	University of Goettingen, Germany
Brian Nielsen	Aalborg University, Denmark

Program Committee

Rachel Cardell-Oliver	University of Western Australia, Crawley, Australia
Shing-Chi Cheung	Hong Kong University of Science and Technology, Hong Kong, China
Marie-Claude Gaudel	Université de Paris-Sud, France
Wolfgang Grieskamp	Microsoft Research, USA
Robert M. Hierons	Brunel University, UK
Thierry Jron	IRISA/INRIA, France
David Lee	Bell Labs, Beijing, China
Jose Carlos Maldonado	University of Sao Paulo, Brazil
Manuel Nunez	Universidad Complutense de Madrid, Spain
Jeff Offutt	George Mason University, USA
Alexandre Petrenko	Computer Research Institute of Montréal, Canada
Ina Schieferdecker	Fraunhofer FOKUS, Berlin, Germany
Jan Tretmans	Radboud University, Nijmegen, The Netherlands
Andreas Ulrich	Siemens AG, Corporate Technology, Munich, Germany
Carsten Weise	Ericsson Eurolab Deutschland GmbH, Germany
Clay Williams	IBM Research, Thomas J. Watson Research Center, New York, USA

Additional Reviewers

Aynur Abdurazik	George Mason University, USA
Roger Alexander	Colorado State University, USA
Ellen Francine Barbosa	University of Sao Paulo, Brazil
Machiel van der Bijl	University of Twente, The Netherlands
Henrik Bohnenkamp	University of Twente, The Netherlands
Sergiy Boroday	CRIM, Canada
Ricky W.K. Chan	University of Hong Kong, Hong Kong, China
Caixia Chi	Bell Labs, China
Lars Frantzen	Radboud University, Nijmegen, The Netherlands
Tim French	University of Western Australia, Australia
David de Frutos-Escrig	Universidad Complutense de Madrid, Spain
Roland Groz	INPG-ENSIMAG, Canada
Yuri Gurevich	Microsoft Research, Redmond, USA
Cedric S.C. Ho	Hong Kong University of Science and Technology, Hong Kong, China
Jin Bei-Hong	Chinese Academy of Sciences, China
Jia Le Huo	CRIM, Canada
Matthew Kaplan	IBM Research, Thomas J. Watson Research Center, New York, USA
Tim Klinge	IBM Research, Thomas J. Watson Research Center, New York, USA
Pieter Koopman	Radboud University, Nijmegen, The Netherlands
Keqin Li	Bell Labs, China
Zhijun Liu	Ohio State University, USA
Marius Mikucionis	Aalborg University, Denmark
Helmut Neukirchen	University of Goettingen, Germany
Vikram Reddy	Ohio State University, USA
Ismael Rodrguez	Universidad Complutense de Madrid, Spain
Fernando Rubio	Universidad Complutense de Madrid, Spain
Guoqiang Shu	Ohio State University, USA
Arne Skou	Aalborg University, Denmark
Tatiana Sugeta	University of Sao Paulo, Brazil
Nikolai Tillmann	Microsoft Research, Redmond, USA
Margus Veanes	Microsoft Research, Redmond, USA
Auri M.R. Vincenzi	University of Sao Paulo, Brazil
Bijendra Vishal	Ohio State University, USA
Frdric Voisin	LRI, Université de Paris-Sud and CNRS, France
Dong Wang	Bell Labs, China
Edith Werner	University of Goettingen, Germany
Tim Willemse	Radboud University Nijmegen, The Netherlands

Table of Contents

Symbolic Test Generation

Testing Non-functional Properties

Test Development with Model Checking Techniques

Test Optimization

Test Generation Based on
Symbolic Specifications

Lars Frantzen*, Jan Tretmans, and Tim A.C. Willemse**

Nijmegen Institute for Computing and Information Sciences (NIII),
Radboud University Nijmegen – The Netherlands
{lf, tretmans, timw}@cs.ru.nl

Abstract. Classical state-oriented testing approaches are based on simple machine models such as Labelled Transition Systems (LTSs), in which data is represented by concrete values. To implement these theories, data types which have infinite universes have to be cut down to finite variants, which are subsequently enumerated to fit in the model. This leads to an explosion of the state space. Moreover, exploiting the syntactical and/or semantical information of the involved data types is non-trivial after enumeration. To overcome these problems, we lift the family of testing relations $\mathbf{ioco}_\mathcal{F}$ to the level of Symbolic Transition Systems (STSs). We present an algorithm based on STSs, which generates and executes tests on-the-fly on a given system. It is sound and complete for the $\mathbf{ioco}_\mathcal{F}$ testing relations.

1 Introduction

Testing is an important technique to assess the quality of systems. In testing, experiments are conducted with a System Under Test (SUT) to determine whether it behaves as expected. There are many different kinds of testing. We focus on formal, specification based, black box, functionality testing. This basically means that the SUT can only be observed (and controlled) via its external interfaces. Moreover, a mathematical, unambiguous specification of the causal order between (appropriate) inputs and expected outputs of the SUT is the starting point for the generation and the analysis of the test results.

Several (formal) test generation tools have been developed for specification based, black box testing. Most of these tools use (variations of) state machines or transition systems as the underlying model for test generation. We refer to these types of tools as *state oriented* tools. For an overview of such tools see [2]. A problem, often encountered in such tools is the *state space explosion*, which is

---

* Lars Frantzen is supported by the Netherlands Organisation for Scientific Research (NWO) under project: STRESS – Systematic Testing of Realtime Embedded Software Systems.
** Tim Willemse carried out this work as part of the TANGRAM project under the responsibility of the Embedded Systems Institute. Tangram is partially supported by the Netherlands Ministry of Economic Affairs under grant TSIT2026.

J. Grabowski and B. Nielsen (Eds.): FATES 2004, LNCS 3395, pp. 1–15, 2005.

due to the fact that they use an explicit internal representation for the states of the specification. This is particularly true when the specification uses complex data structures with large or infinite data domains, because each value in the data domain potentially leads to another state. Consequently, many tools can only cope with very restricted data structures with finite domains.

Opposed to state oriented tools are *data type oriented* tools, which are tools tailored to deal with test generation for complicated data structures, such as QUICKCHECK [3] and GAST [5]. These tools employ the structure of data types to generate test data. However, they lack a built-in concept of state, which makes them less suited to test, e.g., concurrent systems. The way to handle state in such tools is to explicitly define a data structure that represents a state space, but this is not always satisfactory.

The combination of the state oriented and the data type oriented approaches looks promising, and it is exactly this what we investigate in this paper. As our basis we take a state oriented approach to testing, viz. the **ioco** test theory [8]. To the underlying model of Labelled Transition Systems, we add the concept of location variables, and the concept of data, which can be communicated over gates. Both influence the flow of control, thereby allowing us to specify data-dependent behaviour. We refer to these augmented Labelled Transition Systems as *Symbolic Transition Systems* (STSs). We subsequently lift the **ioco** test theory to STSs. As a result, we obtain a sound and complete test derivation algorithm from specifications expressed as STSs.

The test derivation algorithm for STSs allows to treat data symbolically. Rather than elaborating our approach for a specific data formalism, data types are treated as sets of values (algebras) and first order formulas are used to specify values or predicates. This allows to combine STSs with any formalism of choice (with corresponding test tools) for the specification and manipulation of data. This is further elaborated into a tractable algorithm.

From a theoretical point of view, it is also interesting to give an algorithm which generates *symbolic test cases* (STCs). This requires a purely symbolic version of the **ioco**$_{\mathcal{F}}$ relations. This is depicted in Fig. 1. The front triangle

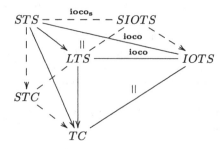

Fig. 1. Classical **ioco** test theory and symbolic **ioco** test theory

represents the classical **ioco** test theory, as presented in [8]. Test cases (TC) are generated out of a specification LTS, and subsequently executed ($\parallel$) on an SUT, assumed to be modelled by an IOTS. The rear triangle consists of a purely symbolic test theory. In this paper, we concentrate on the relation between STSs, LTSs and IOTSs, and on the generation and execution of test cases, i.e. the relation between STSs and TCs. Elaborating on the dashed lines and the corresponding models is another line of research we are pursuing.

Related Work. The idea of combining data type oriented and state oriented approaches is not entirely new in testing. We mention a few noteworthy approaches.

The approach which comes closest to ours is the one described in [7]. There, Input-Output Symbolic Transition Systems (IOSTSs) are used, which are very similar to our STSs. The conformance relation they use corresponds to **ioconf** = **ioco**$_{traces(\mathcal{L})}$, but they do not deal with quiescence. In [7] test purposes are chosen as a way to tackle the state space explosion problem. These are used to compute a subgraph of the IOSTS representing a specific issue of interest. Such test purposes are again (special) IOSTSs. The result is a test case which is still symbolic in the sense that it is a deterministic IOSTS with special states *Pass*, *Fail* and *Inconclusive*. The verdict *Inconclusive* is necessary to judge a behaviour which conforms to a given specification, but does not satisfy the given test purpose. Our approach does not rely on test purposes, even though the set $\mathcal{F}$ which identifies the relation **ioco**$_{\mathcal{F}}$ can be seen as some form of test purpose.

The data-type oriented GAST tool [5] was recently extended in [6] to deal with specifications given as (possibly nondeterministic) Extended Finite State Machines (EFSMs). Such EFSMs are also symbolic specifications, but in some senses more restrictive than STSs or IOSTSs. GAST basically implements a generic algorithm to enumerate the elements of an arbitrary algebraic data type. Such a type can be an input value, but also a whole path through the EFSM. Since the list of all elements of a recursive type is infinitely long, lazy evaluation is employed to generate only the fraction of this list that is actually needed. The elements are generated in increasing size, both the executed paths and the input values. GAST can be used to execute the generated tests on an SUT in an on-the-fly manner.

Overview. This paper is structured as follows. In Sect. 2 we briefly repeat notions from first order logic. The **ioco** test theory is summarised in Sect. 3. The framework of Symbolic Transition Systems is introduced in Sect. 4. We present an on-the-fly implementation for generating and executing test cases for Symbolic Transition Systems in Sect. 5. We finish with conclusions and future extensions in Sect. 6.

2   First Order Logic

We use basic concepts from first order logic as our framework for dealing with data. For a general introduction into logic we refer to [4]. From hereon we assume a first order structure as given, i.e.:

- A logical signature $\mathfrak{S} = (F,\ P)$ with
  - F is a set of *function symbols*. Each $f{\in}F$ has a corresponding arity $n{\in}\mathbb{N}$. If $n = 0$ we call f a *constant*.
  - P is a set of *predicate symbols*. Each $p{\in}P$ has a corresponding arity $n{>}0$.
- A model $\mathfrak{M} = (\mathfrak{U},\ (f_{\mathfrak{M}})_{f{\in}F},\ (p_{\mathfrak{M}})_{p{\in}P})$ with
  - $\mathfrak{U}$ being a nonempty set called *universe*.
  - For all $f{\in}F$ with arity n, $f_{\mathfrak{M}}$ is a function of type $\mathfrak{U}^n{\rightarrow}\mathfrak{U}$.
  - For every $p{\in}P$ with arity n we have $p_{\mathfrak{M}} \subseteq \mathfrak{U}^n$.

For simplicity, and without loss of generality we restrict to one-sorted signatures. Let $\mathfrak{X}$ be a set of *variables*. *Terms* over X, denoted $\mathfrak{T}(X)$, are built from function symbols F and variables $X \subseteq \mathfrak{X}$. We write $\mathsf{var}(t)$ to denote the set of variables appearing in a term t. Terms $t{\in}\mathfrak{T}(\emptyset)$ are called *ground terms*.

Example 1. Assume we have $X = \{x, y\}$. Let $\mathfrak{S} = (F,\ P)$ be given by $F = \{\mathtt{zero}, \mathtt{succ}, \mathtt{add}\}$ (with arities $0, 1$ and 2, resp.), and $P = \{\mathtt{leq}\}$ (with arity 2). An obvious model for this signature is the natural numbers with 0, *successor*, *addition* and the less-or-equal predicate; any other model that sticks to the given arities is fine too. Terms are, e.g. x, $\mathtt{succ}(x)$ and $\mathtt{add}(\mathtt{succ}(x), y)$. Ground terms are, e.g. $\mathtt{zero}$ and $\mathtt{add}(\mathtt{zero}, \mathtt{succ}(\mathtt{zero}))$.   □

A *term-mapping* is a function $\sigma{:}\mathfrak{X} \rightarrow \mathfrak{T}(\mathfrak{X})$. The term-mapping id, referred to as the *identity mapping*, is defined as $\mathsf{id}(x) = x$ for all $x{\in}\mathfrak{X}$. We use the following notation. For sets X, Y with $X \cup Y \subseteq \mathfrak{X}$, we write $\mathfrak{T}(Y)^X$ for the set of term-mappings that assign to each variable $x{\in}X$ a term $t{\in}\mathfrak{T}(Y)$, and to each variable $x \notin X$ the term x. Given a term-mapping $\sigma{\in}\mathfrak{T}(Y)^X$ we overload the var-notation as follows: $\mathsf{var}(\sigma) =_{def} \bigcup_{x{\in}X} \mathsf{var}(\sigma(x))$.

The set of free variables of a first order formula φ is denoted $\mathsf{free}(\varphi)$; the set of bound variables is denoted $\mathsf{bound}(\varphi)$. The set of first order formulas φ over $X \subseteq \mathfrak{X}$ is denoted $\mathfrak{F}(X)$; we have $\mathsf{free}(\varphi) \cup \mathsf{bound}(\varphi) \subseteq X$. A tautology is represented by $\top$. The *existential closure* of a formula φ, denoted $\bar{\exists}\varphi$, is defined as $\bar{\exists}\varphi =_{def} \exists x_1 \exists x_2 \ldots \exists x_n : \varphi$ with $\{x_1, \ldots, x_n\} = \mathsf{free}(\varphi)$.

Given a term-mapping σ and a formula φ, the *substitution* of $\sigma(x)$ for $x{\in}\mathsf{free}(\varphi)$ in φ is denoted $\varphi[\sigma]$. Substitutions are side-effect free, i.e. they do not add bound variables. This is achieved using α-renaming. The substitution of terms $\sigma(x)$ for variables $x{\in}\mathsf{var}(t)$, in a term t using a term-mapping σ, is denoted $t[\sigma]$.

Example 2. An example of a term mapping for $X = \{x, y\}$ is $\sigma = \{x \mapsto \mathtt{succ}(y), y \mapsto \mathtt{zero}\}{\in}\mathfrak{T}(X)^X$, with $\mathsf{var}(\sigma) = \{y\}$. The existential closure of the formula $\varphi = \forall y : \mathtt{leq}(x, y)$ with $\mathsf{bound}(\varphi) = \{y\}$ and $\mathsf{free}(\varphi) = \{x\}$ is $\bar{\exists}\varphi = \exists x \forall y : \mathtt{leq}(x, y)$. The substitution of σ in φ is not side-effect free, but can be achieved by renaming variable y to z, i.e. $\varphi[\sigma] = \forall z : \mathtt{leq}(\mathtt{succ}(y), z)$.   □

A *valuation* ϑ is a function $\vartheta{:}\mathfrak{X} \rightarrow \mathfrak{U}$. We denote the set of all valuations as $\mathfrak{U}^{\mathfrak{X}} =_{def} \{\vartheta{:}\mathfrak{X} \rightarrow \mathfrak{U} \mid \vartheta \text{ is a valuation of } \mathfrak{X}\}$. For a given $X \subseteq \mathfrak{X}$ we write $\vartheta{\in}\mathfrak{U}^X$ when only the values of the variables in X are of interest. For all the other variables $y{\in}\mathfrak{X} \setminus X$ we set $\vartheta(y) = *$, where $*$ is an arbitrary element of set $\mathfrak{U}$.

Having two valuations $\vartheta \in \mathfrak{U}^X$ and $\varsigma \in \mathfrak{U}^Y$ with $X \cap Y = \emptyset$, their union is defined as:

$$(\vartheta \cup \varsigma)(x) =_{def} \begin{cases} \vartheta(x) \text{ if } x \in X \\ \varsigma(x) \text{ if } x \in Y \\ * \quad \text{otherwise} \end{cases}$$

The *satisfaction* of a formula φ w.r.t. a given valuation ϑ is denoted $\vartheta \models \varphi$. When free$(\varphi) = \emptyset$ we write $\mathfrak{M} \models \psi$ because the satisfaction is independent of a concrete valuation.

The extension to evaluate whole terms based on a valuation ϑ is called a *term-evaluation* and denoted $\vartheta_{\mathsf{eval}} : \mathfrak{T}(\mathfrak{X}) \to \mathfrak{U}$. The evaluation of ground terms is denoted $\mathsf{eval} : \mathfrak{T}(\emptyset) \to \mathfrak{U}$.

To ease notation, we often treat a tuple $\langle x_1, \ldots, x_n \rangle \in A_1 \times \cdots \times A_n$ as the set $\{x_1, \ldots, x_n\}$. We denote the composition of functions $f : B \to C$ and $g : A \to B$ as $f \circ g$.

Example 3. Assuming the standard model for natural numbers as given in example 1, an example valuation is $\vartheta = \{x \mapsto 24, y \mapsto 7\} \in \mathfrak{U}^{\{x,y\}}$. For the formula φ of example 2, the valuation ϑ and the standard model for natural numbers we find $\vartheta \not\models \varphi$ and $\mathfrak{M} \models \overline{\exists} \varphi$ and we get $\vartheta_{\mathsf{eval}}(\mathsf{add}(x, \mathsf{succ}(y))) = 32$. □

Our example of a logical structure for natural numbers shows that many, even infinite ground terms may evaluate to the same value, e.g. the ground terms zero and add(zero, zero) both evaluate to 0. We assume we have a unique ground term representative for every value to facilitate the bidirectional translation.

3 Testing Labelled Transition Systems

We briefly review the **ioco**$_\mathcal{F}$ test theory on which this paper is based. For a more detailed overview, we refer to [8]. The semantical model we use to model reactive systems is based on *Labelled Transition Systems* (LTSs).

Definition 1. *A* Labelled Transition System *is a tuple* $\mathcal{L} = \langle S, s_0, \Sigma, \to \rangle$, *where*

- S *is a (possibly infinite) set of* states.
- $s_0 \in S$ *is the* initial state.
- Σ *is a (possibly infinite) set of* action labels. *The special action label* $\tau \notin \Sigma$ *denotes an* unobservable *action. In contrast, all other actions are* observable. *We write* Σ_τ *to denote the set* $\Sigma \cup \{\tau\}$.
- $\to \subseteq S \times \Sigma_\tau \times S$ *is the* transition relation. *When* $(s, \mu, s') \in \to$ *we write* $s \xrightarrow{\mu} s'$.

We often identify an LTS $\mathcal{L}$ *with its initial state* s_0.

Unobservable actions can be used to model events that cannot be seen by an observer of a system. The generalised transition relation $\Rightarrow \subseteq S \times \Sigma^* \times S$ captures this phenomenon: it abstracts from τ actions preceding, in-between and following a (possibly empty) sequence of observable actions. Given an LTS

Table 1. Deduction rules for generalised transitions

$$
s \stackrel{\epsilon}{\Longrightarrow} s
\qquad
\frac{s \stackrel{\sigma}{\Longrightarrow} s'' \quad s'' \stackrel{\tau}{\longrightarrow} s'}{s \stackrel{\sigma}{\Longrightarrow} s'}
\qquad
\frac{s \stackrel{\sigma}{\Longrightarrow} s'' \quad s'' \stackrel{\mu}{\longrightarrow} s' \quad \mu \neq \tau}{s \stackrel{\sigma\mu}{\Longrightarrow} s'}
$$

$\mathcal{L} = \langle S, s_0, \Sigma, \rightarrow \rangle$, this relation is defined by the deduction rules of Table 1. We define two operations on LTSs. Given an LTS $\mathcal{L} = \langle S, s_0, \Sigma, \rightarrow \rangle$ and a (possibly new) action μ. The *action prefix* $\mu; \mathcal{L}$ is defined as

$$
\mu; \mathcal{L} =_{def} \langle S \cup \{s\}, s, \Sigma \cup \{\mu\}, \rightarrow \cup \{s \stackrel{\mu}{\longrightarrow} s_0\} \rangle \tag{1}
$$

with $s \notin S$ being a fresh state. For a set of LTSs $\overline{\mathcal{L}} = \{\mathcal{L}_1, \ldots, \mathcal{L}_n\}$ with $n \geq 0$ of the form $\mathcal{L}_i = \langle S_i, s_{0i}, \Sigma_i, \rightarrow_i \rangle$, we define the *alternative composition* of all LTSs $\mathcal{L}_i$, denoted $\sum(\overline{\mathcal{L}})$, as follows:

$$
\sum(\overline{\mathcal{L}}) =_{def} \langle \bigcup_{i \leq n} S_i \cup \{s\}, s, \bigcup_{i \leq n} \Sigma_i, \bigcup_{i \leq n} (\rightarrow_i \cup \{s \stackrel{\mu}{\longrightarrow} s' \mid s_{0i} \stackrel{\mu}{\longrightarrow} s'\}) \rangle \tag{2}
$$

with $s \notin \bigcup_{i \leq n} S_i$ being a fresh state. The operator $\sum$ is associative and commutative. We sometimes write $\mathcal{L}_1 + \mathcal{L}_2$ instead of $\sum\{\mathcal{L}_1, \mathcal{L}_2\}$.

3.1   The Test Relation ioco$_\mathcal{F}$

We introduce the following shorthand notation. For a $\mu \in \Sigma_\tau$ we write $s \stackrel{\mu}{\longrightarrow}$ when there is a state s' such that $s \stackrel{\mu}{\longrightarrow} s'$, and, likewise, given a $\sigma \in \Sigma^*$ we write $s \stackrel{\sigma}{\Longrightarrow}$ when there is a state s' such that $s \stackrel{\sigma}{\Longrightarrow} s'$.

Definition 2. *Let* $\mathcal{L} = \langle S, s_0, \Sigma, \rightarrow \rangle$ *be an LTS and let* $s \in S$.

1. $init(s) =_{def} \{ \mu \in \Sigma_\tau \mid s \stackrel{\mu}{\longrightarrow} \}$.
2. $traces(s) =_{def} \{ \sigma \in \Sigma^* \mid s \stackrel{\sigma}{\Longrightarrow} \}$.
3. $\mathcal{L}$ *has* finite behaviour *if all* $\sigma \in traces(s_0)$ *satisfy* $|\sigma| < n$ *for some* $n \in \mathbb{N}$.
4. $\mathcal{L}$ *is* deterministic *if for all* $\sigma \in \Sigma^*$, $|\{s' \mid s_0 \stackrel{\sigma}{\Longrightarrow} s'\}| \leq 1$.

We assume that implementations of a reactive system can be given as an *input-output transition system* (IOTSs). An IOTS is an LTS in which the set of action labels Σ is partitioned in a set of *input actions* Σ_I and a set of *output actions* Σ_U, and for which it is assumed that all input actions are enabled in all states.

Definition 3. *Let* $\mathcal{L} = \langle S, s_0, \Sigma_I \cup \Sigma_U, \rightarrow \rangle$ *be an LTS. A state* $s \in S$ *is* quiescent, *denoted by* $\delta(s)$, *if* $\forall \mu \in \Sigma_U \cup \{\tau\}: s \not\stackrel{\mu}{\longrightarrow}$.

Let δ be a special action label, not part of any action label set. For a given set of action labels Σ, we abbreviate $\Sigma \cup \{\delta\}$ with Σ_δ. The suspension transitions $\Longrightarrow_\delta \subseteq S \times \Sigma_\delta^* \times S$ are given by the deduction rules of Table 2. The set of all *suspension traces* of $\mathcal{L}$ is denoted $Straces(\mathcal{L}) = \{\sigma \in \Sigma_\delta^* \mid \mathcal{L} \stackrel{\sigma}{\Longrightarrow}_\delta\}$.

Table 2. Deduction rules for suspension transitions

$$\frac{s \xRightarrow{\sigma} s'}{s \xRightarrow{\sigma}_\delta s'} \qquad \frac{\delta(s)}{s \xRightarrow{\delta}_\delta s} \qquad \frac{s \xRightarrow{\sigma}_\delta s'' \qquad s'' \xRightarrow{\upsilon}_\delta s'}{s \xRightarrow{\sigma\upsilon}_\delta s'}$$

Definition 4. *Let $\mathcal{L} = \langle S, s_0, \Sigma, \rightarrow \rangle$ be an LTS, let $s \in S$ be a state and let $\sigma \in \Sigma_\delta^*$ be a suspension trace. We define* s **after** $\sigma =_{def} \{\, s' \mid s \xRightarrow{\sigma}_\delta s' \,\}$. *We overload this notation as follows:* $\mathcal{C}$ **after** $\sigma =_{def} \bigcup_{s \in C} s$ **after** σ, *where* $C \subseteq S$.

The set of *observations* that can be made in a specific state s is given by the set of all output actions that are possible from that state. When no output action is possible the only observation that can be made is quiescence.

Definition 5. *Let $\mathcal{L} = \langle S, s_0, \Sigma_I \cup \Sigma_U, \rightarrow \rangle$ be an LTS and let $s \in S$ be a state. We define* $\mathbf{out}(s) =_{def} \{\delta\}$ *if $\delta(s)$ and otherwise* $\mathbf{out}(s) =_{def} \{\mu \in \Sigma_U \mid s \xrightarrow{\mu}\}$. *We overload this notation as follows:* $\mathbf{out}(\mathcal{C}) =_{def} \bigcup_{s \in C} \mathbf{out}(s)$, *where* $C \subseteq S$.

Next, we define the conformance relation $\mathbf{ioco}_\mathcal{F}$.

Definition 6. *Let $\mathcal{F} \subseteq Straces(\mathcal{L})$ be a subset of suspension traces of a speci-fication $\mathcal{L}$. When a (physical) implementation (given as an IOTS) $\mathcal{P}$ is $\mathbf{ioco}_\mathcal{F}$-conform to $\mathcal{L}$ we write $\mathcal{P} \mathbf{ioco}_\mathcal{F} \mathcal{L}$, where:*

$$\mathcal{P} \mathbf{ioco}_\mathcal{F} \mathcal{L} \text{ iff } \forall \sigma \in \mathcal{F} : \mathbf{out}(\mathcal{P} \text{ after } \sigma) \subseteq \mathbf{out}(\mathcal{L} \text{ after } \sigma) \qquad (3)$$

3.2   Testing for $\mathbf{ioco}_\mathcal{F}$

A *test case* is a special LTS, which is executed on a given SUT. It has a tree-like structure with leaves **pass** and **fail**. To formally differentiate between observed quiescence and specified quiescence, we use θ instead of δ in the test cases, representing observed quiescence.

Definition 7. *A test case is an LTS $t = \langle S, s_0, \Sigma_I \cup \Sigma_U \cup \{\theta\}, \rightarrow \rangle$, satisfying:*

- *t is deterministic and has finite behaviour.*
- *$\{\mathbf{pass}, \mathbf{fail}\} \subseteq S$ are terminal states satisfying $init(\mathbf{pass}) = init(\mathbf{fail}) = \emptyset$.*
- *for any state $s \in S \setminus \{\mathbf{pass}, \mathbf{fail}\}$ either $init(s) = \{\mu\}$ for some input $\mu \in \Sigma_I$ or $init(s) = \Sigma_U \cup \{\theta\}$.*

Test cases are executed simultaneously with implementations. While their inputs and outputs must be executed synchronously, quiescence is synchronised with the θ action of a test case and internal actions of the implementation are executed autonomously. Let $\mathcal{P} = \langle S, s_0, \Sigma_I \cup \Sigma_U, \rightarrow_\mathcal{P} \rangle$ be an IOTS and $t = \langle T, t_0, \Sigma_I \cup \Sigma_U \cup \{\theta\}, \rightarrow_t \rangle$ a test case. The simultaneous execution of t and $\mathcal{P}$ is defined by the LTS $t \| \mathcal{P} = \{T \times S, (t_0, s_0), \Sigma_I \cup \Sigma_U \cup \{\theta\}, \rightarrow \rangle$, where $\rightarrow$ is defined by the rules of Table 3. We say that an implementation $\mathcal{P}$ *passes a test suite T* (i.e. a set of test cases) iff for all its test cases, no test run leads to the verdict **fail**.

Table 3. Deduction rules for synchronous execution

$$\frac{\mathcal{P} \xrightarrow{\tau}_\mathcal{P} \mathcal{P}'}{t\|\,\mathcal{P} \xrightarrow{\tau} t\|\,\mathcal{P}'} \qquad \frac{t \xrightarrow{\mu}_t t' \quad \mathcal{P} \xrightarrow{\mu}_\mathcal{P} \mathcal{P}' \quad \mu{\in}\Sigma_I \cup \Sigma_U}{t\|\,\mathcal{P} \xrightarrow{\mu} t'\|\,\mathcal{P}'} \qquad \frac{t \xrightarrow{\theta}_t t' \quad \delta(\mathcal{P})}{t\|\,\mathcal{P} \xrightarrow{\theta} t'\|\,\mathcal{P}}$$

$$\mathcal{P} \textbf{ passes } T \text{ iff } \forall t{\in}T : \forall\sigma{\in}(\Sigma_I \cup \Sigma_U \cup \{\theta\})^* : \forall \mathcal{P}' : t\|\,\mathcal{P} \xRightarrow{\sigma\not\Rightarrow} \textbf{fail}\|\,\mathcal{P}' \quad (4)$$

In [8] an algorithm is presented which, given a specification LTS $\mathcal{L}$ and a set $\mathcal{F} \subseteq Straces(\mathcal{L})$, produces test cases for $\textbf{ioco}_\mathcal{F}$. We recapitulate the algorithm, expressed in a slightly simpler way.

Definition 8. *Let $\mathcal{L} = \langle S, s_0, \Sigma_I \cup \Sigma_U, \rightarrow\rangle$ be an LTS and let $\mathcal{F} \subseteq Straces(\mathcal{L})$. Let $C \subseteq S$ be a non-empty set of states, initially $C = \{s_0\}$. We use two special LTSs which contain the terminal states* **pass** *and* **fail**:

$$\textbf{pass} =_{def} \langle\{\textbf{pass}\}, \textbf{pass}, \emptyset, \emptyset\rangle$$
$$\textbf{fail} =_{def} \langle\{\textbf{fail}\}, \textbf{fail}, \emptyset, \emptyset\rangle$$

A test case t is obtained from C by a finite number of recursive applications of one of the following three nondeterministic choices:

- $t := \textbf{pass}$
  The single-state test case **pass** *is always a sound test case. It stops the recursion and terminates the test case.*
- $t := \mu \;;\; t'$
  where $\mu{\in}\Sigma_I$ and $C \textbf{ after } \mu \neq \emptyset$. We obtain t' by recursively applying the algorithm for $C' = C \textbf{ after } \mu$ and $\mathcal{F}' = \{\sigma{\in}\Sigma_\delta^* \mid \mu \cdot \sigma{\in}\mathcal{F}\}$.
- $t := \sum\{\mu; \textbf{fail} \mid \epsilon{\in}\mathcal{F} \text{ and } ((\mu{\in}\Sigma_U, \mu \notin \textbf{out}(C)) \text{ or } (\mu = \theta, \delta \notin \textbf{out}(C)))\}$

  $+ \sum\{\mu; \textbf{pass} \mid \epsilon \notin \mathcal{F} \text{ and } ((\mu{\in}\Sigma_U, \mu \notin \textbf{out}(C)) \text{ or } (\mu = \theta, \delta \notin \textbf{out}(C)))\}$

  $+ \sum\{\mu; t_\mu \mid \mu{\in}\Sigma_U, \; \mu{\in}\textbf{out}(C)\}$

  $+ \sum\{\theta; t_\theta \mid \delta{\in}\textbf{out}(C)\}$

  where t_μ and t_θ are obtained by recursively applying the algorithm for $C \textbf{ after } \mu$ with $\mathcal{F}' = \{\sigma{\in}\Sigma_\delta^* \mid \mu \cdot \sigma{\in}\mathcal{F}\}$, and $C \textbf{ after } \delta$ with $\mathcal{F}' = \{\sigma{\in}\Sigma_\delta^* \mid \delta \cdot \sigma{\in}\mathcal{F}\}$, respectively.

It is imperative that such an algorithm only produces test cases which are sound w.r.t. $\textbf{ioco}_\mathcal{F}$ and a given specification, i.e. an implementation which is $\textbf{ioco}_\mathcal{F}$-correct passes every test case generated by the algorithm. Furthermore we want completeness, i.e. for every implementation which is not $\textbf{ioco}_\mathcal{F}$-correct, the algorithm can in principle generate a test case which detects such a non-conformance. The following definition formalises these properties based on a given test suite:

Definition 9. *Let $\mathcal{L}$ be a specification LTS and let T be a test suite, then for an implementation relation* $\mathbf{ioco}_{\mathcal{F}}$*:*

T is sound and complete	$=_{\mathrm{def}}$	$\forall \mathcal{P} : \mathcal{P} \ \mathbf{ioco}_{\mathcal{F}} \ \mathcal{L} \Leftrightarrow \mathcal{P} \ \mathbf{passes} \ T$
T is sound	$=_{\mathrm{def}}$	$\forall \mathcal{P} : \mathcal{P} \ \mathbf{ioco}_{\mathcal{F}} \ \mathcal{L} \Rightarrow \mathcal{P} \ \mathbf{passes} \ T$
T is complete	$=_{\mathrm{def}}$	$\forall \mathcal{P} : \mathcal{P} \ \mathbf{ioco}_{\mathcal{F}} \ \mathcal{L} \Leftarrow \mathcal{P} \ \mathbf{passes} \ T$

Theorem 1 (Tretmans [8]). *Let $\mathcal{L}$ be an LTS and let $\mathcal{F} \subseteq Straces(\mathcal{L})$.*

1. *A test case obtained with the algorithm given in Def. 8 from $\mathcal{L}$ and $\mathcal{F}$ is sound for $\mathcal{L}$ w.r.t.* $\mathbf{ioco}_{\mathcal{F}}$*.*
2. *The set of all possible test cases that can be obtained with the algorithm in Def. 8 is complete.*

Remark that test cases obtained with the algorithm given in Def. 8 have finite behaviour. Nevertheless, this does not imply that they are finitely branching, i.e. a test case can specify for a possibly infinite set of outputs how to proceed next; this problem can be seen as a *state space explosion*. This makes the algorithm in general only feasible for LTSs with finite action alphabets at best.

4   Symbolic Transition Systems

While conceptually LTSs are nice, they lack the required level of abstraction for modelling complex systems. We next define the model of *Symbolic Transition Systems* (STSs). STSs extend on LTSs by incorporating an explicit notion of data and data-dependent control flow (such as guarded transitions), founded on first order logic. The STS model clearly reflects the LTS model, which is done to smoothly transfer LTS-based test theory concepts to an STS-based test theory. The model is kept as simple as possible to avoid unnecessary case distinctions in subsequent definitions and theorems.

Definition 10. *A* Symbolic Transition System *is a tuple* $\langle L, l_0, \mathcal{V}, \iota, \mathcal{I}, \Lambda, \rightarrow \rangle$*:*

- *L is a countable set of locations and $l_0 {\in} L$ is the initial location.*
- *$\mathcal{V}$ is a countable set of location variables.*
- *$\iota \in \mathfrak{T}(\emptyset)^{\mathcal{V}}$ is an initialisation of the location variables.*
- *$\mathcal{I}$ is a set of interaction variables, disjoint from $\mathcal{V}$.*
- *Λ is a finite set of gates. The unobservable gate is denoted τ ($\tau \notin \Lambda$); we write Λ_τ for $\Lambda \cup \{\tau\}$. The arity of a gate $\lambda {\in} \Lambda_\tau$, denoted $\mathsf{arity}(\lambda)$, is a natural number. The type of a gate $\lambda {\in} \Lambda_\tau$, denoted $\mathsf{type}(\lambda)$, is a tuple of length $\mathsf{arity}(\lambda)$ of distinct interaction variables. We fix $\mathsf{arity}(\tau) = 0$, i.e. the unobservable gate has no interaction variables.*
- *$\rightarrow \ \subseteq L \times \Lambda_\tau \times \mathfrak{F}(\mathcal{V} \cup \mathcal{I}) \times \mathfrak{T}(\mathcal{V} \cup \mathcal{I})^{\mathcal{V}} \times L$ is the switch relation. We write $l \xrightarrow{\lambda, \varphi, \rho} l'$ instead of $(l, \lambda, \varphi, \rho, l') {\in} \rightarrow$, where φ is referred to as the switch restriction (acting as a guard) and ρ as the update mapping. We require $\mathsf{free}(\varphi) \cup \mathsf{var}(\rho) \subseteq \mathcal{V} \cup \mathsf{type}(\lambda)^1.$*

---

[1] Note that, here, we treat a tuple of variables as a set of variables.

In line with LTSs and IOTSs, we partition a set of gates Λ in *input gates* Λ_I and *output gates* Λ_U. Moreover, for the remainder of the paper, we consider STSs to which the following restrictions apply:

1. All sequences of τ-switches have finite length. Thus, we also do not allow for (syntactic) τ-loops.
2. For each location $l \in L$, the set of outgoing switches $\{(l, \lambda, \varphi, \rho, l') \mid l \xrightarrow{\lambda, \varphi, \rho} l'\}$ is finite, i.e. we restrict to finitely symbolic branching STSs.

Example 4. The STS $\langle\{l_0, l_1, l_2, l_3\}, l_0, \{v\}, \{v \mapsto 0\}, \{i\}, \{\text{coin}, \text{tray}\}, \rightarrow\rangle$, is depicted in Fig. 2, where $\rightarrow$ is given by the directed edges linking the locations. It models a simple slot-machine, in which a player can insert a coin, and (non-deterministically) win the jackpot (modelled by passing v coins over interaction variable i of output gate tray) or lose his coin. After that, the slot machine behaves as initially, but with a different amount of coins in the jackpot.   □

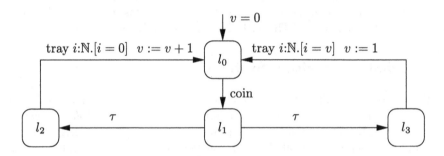

Fig. 2. An STS representing a simple slot-machine

We define the semantics of an STS by associating it to an LTS.

Definition 11. *Let* $\mathcal{S} = \langle L, l_0, \mathcal{V}, \iota, \mathcal{I}, \Lambda, \rightarrow\rangle$ *be an STS. The interpretation of* $\mathcal{S}$ *is given by the LTS* $[\![\mathcal{S}]\!] = \langle S, s_0, \Sigma, \rightarrow\rangle$, *where*

- $S = L \times \mathfrak{U}^{\mathcal{V}}$ *is the set of* states.
- $s_0 = (l_0, \text{eval} \circ \iota) \in S$ *is the initial* state.
- $\Sigma = \bigcup_{\lambda \in \Lambda_\tau}(\{\lambda\} \times \mathfrak{U}^{\text{arity}(\lambda)})$, *is the set of* actions.
  $\Sigma_I = \bigcup_{\lambda \in \Lambda_I}(\{\lambda\} \times \mathfrak{U}^{\text{arity}(\lambda)})$, *and, analogously,* $\Sigma_U = \bigcup_{\lambda \in \Lambda_U}(\{\lambda\} \times \mathfrak{U}^{\text{arity}(\lambda)})$.
- $\rightarrow \subseteq S \times \Sigma \times S$ *is the transition relation, defined by the rule of Table 4.*

In Sect. 3.1, the **ioco**$_\mathcal{F}$ relation was defined as a relation between an implementation, modelled as an IOTS, and a specification, given as an LTS. We lift this definition to the level of STSs by appealing to their semantics.

Definition 12. *Let* $\mathcal{S}$ *be an STS and* $\mathcal{P}$ *a physical system, modelled as an IOTS. Then* $\mathcal{P}$ **ioco**$_\mathcal{F}$ $\mathcal{S}$ *iff* $\mathcal{P}$ **ioco**$_\mathcal{F}$ $[\![\mathcal{S}]\!]$.

Table 4. Deduction rule for transitions

$$\frac{l \xrightarrow{\lambda,\varphi,\rho} l' \quad \mathsf{type}(\lambda) = \langle \nu_1, \ldots, \nu_n \rangle \quad \varsigma \in \mathfrak{U}^{\mathsf{type}(\lambda)} \quad \vartheta \cup \varsigma \models \varphi \quad \vartheta' = (\vartheta \cup \varsigma)_{\mathsf{eval}} \circ \rho}{(l, \vartheta) \xrightarrow{(\lambda, \langle \varsigma(\nu_1),\ldots,\varsigma(\nu_n) \rangle)} (l', \vartheta')}$$

5   On-the-Fly Testing

Lifting the **ioco**$_\mathcal{F}$ test theory to STSs by appealing to their semantics, as we did in the previous section, puts us in a position to reuse the standard algorithm of Sect. 3.2 for STSs. However, as we already remarked in that section, that algorithm suffers from a state space explosion. Note that also the computation of the LTS that is associated to an STS in general is of infinite size.

5.1   Symbolic Ingredients

Given an STS with a switch relation $\rightarrow$. We define a generalised switch relation $\Longrightarrow \subseteq L \times \Lambda_\tau \times \mathfrak{F}(\mathcal{V} \cup \mathcal{I}) \times \mathfrak{T}(\mathcal{V} \cup \mathcal{I})^\mathcal{V} \times L$ (see the deduction rules of Table 5). The intuition behind this relation is that it abstracts from the unobservable events that possibly precede and follow an observable event. It is subsequently used in the definition of a symbolic counterpart of the **after** relation of Sect. 3.1.

Table 5. Deduction rules for generalised switches

$$l \xRightarrow{\tau,\mathsf{T},\mathsf{id}} l \qquad \frac{l \xRightarrow{\tau,\varphi,\rho} l''' \quad l''' \xrightarrow{\lambda,\psi,\pi} l'' \quad l'' \xRightarrow{\tau,\chi,\varsigma} l' \quad \lambda \in \Lambda_\tau}{l \xRightarrow{\lambda, \varphi \wedge \psi[\rho] \wedge (\chi[\pi])[\rho], [\rho] \circ [\pi] \circ \varsigma} l'}$$

Definition 13. *Let* $\langle L, l_0, \mathcal{V}, \iota, \mathcal{I}, \Lambda, \rightarrow \rangle$ *be an STS.*

- *An* instantiated location *is a pair* (l, ϖ), *where* $l \in L$ *is a location and* ϖ *is a mapping of the set of location variables to ground terms, i.e.* $\varpi \in \mathfrak{T}(\emptyset)^\mathcal{V}$.
- *A* stimulus *(resp.* reaction*) is a pair* (λ, η), *where* $\lambda \in \Lambda_I$ *is an input gate (resp.* $\lambda \in \Lambda_U$ *is an output gate) and* $\eta \in \mathfrak{T}(\emptyset)^{\mathsf{type}(\lambda)}$ *is a mapping of the interaction variables of* λ *to ground terms.*

Input constraints represent the conditions for the input gates under which an instantiated location is specified to proceed.

Definition 14. *Let* (l, ϖ) *be an instantiated location. The* input constraints *for* (l, ϖ), *denoted* $\Omega(l, \varpi)$, *are defined as*

$$\Omega(l, \varpi) = \bigcup_{\lambda \in \Lambda_I} \{(\lambda, \bigvee \{\psi[\varpi] \mid l \xrightarrow{\lambda,\psi,\rho} l'\})\}$$

We generalise this to $\Omega(\mathcal{C}) = \bigcup_{(l,\varpi) \in \mathcal{C}} \Omega(l, \varpi)$.

The concept of quiescence (cf. Sect. 3.1) is lifted to the level of STSs.

Definition 15. *An instantiated location* (l, ϖ) *is quiescent, denoted* $\delta(l, \varpi)$, *iff:*

$$\forall \lambda \in \Lambda_U \cup \{\tau\} : \neg \left(\exists l' : l \xrightarrow{\lambda, \varphi, \rho} l' \text{ with } \mathfrak{M} \models \bar{\exists}(\varphi[\varpi]) \right) \tag{5}$$

By observing a reaction or providing a stimulus (λ, η) at an instantiated location (l, ϖ), location l is left and some location of a set of new locations (with updated location variables) can be reached. This set is given by the operator **after**$_s$:

$$(l, \varpi) \, \textbf{after}_s(\lambda, \eta) = \{(l', [\eta] \circ [\varpi] \circ \pi) \mid l \xrightarrow{\lambda, \psi, \pi} l' \text{ and } \mathfrak{M} \models (\psi[\varpi])[\eta]\} \tag{6}$$

For the special case where quiescence is observed, we define:

$$(l, \varpi) \, \textbf{after}_s \, \delta = \{(l', [\varpi] \circ \pi) \mid l \xrightarrow{\tau, \psi, \pi} l', \mathfrak{M} \models \psi[\varpi] \text{ and } \delta(l', [\varpi] \circ \pi)\} \tag{7}$$

We overload the operator **after**$_s$ to yield the set of instantiated locations that are reached when the stimulus or reaction is made from a given set of instantiated locations. Let $\mathcal{C} \subseteq L \times \mathfrak{T}(\emptyset)^\mathcal{V}$ and x be a stimulus or reaction, including quiescence. Then $\mathcal{C} \, \textbf{after}_s \, x = \bigcup_{(l, \varpi) \in \mathcal{C}} (l, \varpi) \, \textbf{after}_s \, x$.

5.2   Algorithm

To avoid the state space explosion problem, we combine test generation from STSs with an on-the-fly execution of the test cases. This means that the generation of the test case proceeds in lock-step with its execution, see also [1]. This has the advantage, that only the part of the state space is generated, which corresponds to the observations made while testing.

To implement the test generation for the **ioco**$_\mathcal{F}$ relation we assume that there is a function $\texttt{InF}: \Sigma_\delta^* \rightarrow \texttt{boolean}$ to decide whether the currently executed (suspension) trace is an element of $\mathcal{F}$, i.e. $\texttt{InF}(\sigma) = \texttt{true} \Leftrightarrow \sigma \in \mathcal{F}$. The algorithm keeps track of the executed trace σ and checks if $\texttt{InF}(\sigma)$ holds before giving verdicts. In the case of **ioco**$_{Straces(\mathcal{L})}$ (which is implemented in the test tool TORX [9]), $\texttt{InF}(\sigma) = \texttt{true}$ for all σ, and can therefore be omitted in the algorithm.

The algorithm we present next follows the same structure as the one in Sect. 3.2. It maintains a set of instantiated locations $\mathcal{C}$ which symbolically represents the set of states in which the SUT may currently be. This is in general not a singleton (due to possible non-determinism in system specifications), but it is always finite. This is because we restrict to STSs which are finitely branching, and which do not allow for infinite sequences of τ-switches. Furthermore, all these locations in $\mathcal{C}$ are instantiated due to an on-the-fly execution, i.e. the algorithm knows for every location the actual values of the location variables. We first present the algorithm, and subsequently discuss it.

Definition 16. *Given an STS* $\mathcal{S} = \langle L, l_0, \mathcal{V}, \iota, \mathcal{I}, \Lambda, \rightarrow \rangle$ *and an SUT. Let* $\mathcal{C}$ *be a non-empty set of instantiated locations and let* σ *be a suspension trace of* $[\![\mathcal{S}]\!]$. *Initially, we use* $\mathcal{C} = \{(l, \rho[\iota]) \mid l_0 \xrightarrow{\tau, \varphi, \rho} l, \text{ with } \mathfrak{M} \models \varphi[\iota]\}$ *and* $\sigma = \epsilon$. *The algorithm executes a finite number of applications of the following three nondeterministic choices:*

(1) **Stop testing**
    01. *Give the verdict* **pass**.
(2) **Give input to the SUT**
    02. *Compute $\Omega(\mathcal{C})$.*
    03. *Choose $(\lambda, \psi) \in \Omega(\mathcal{C})$ and a stimulus (λ, η), such that $\mathfrak{M} \models \psi[\eta]$.*
    04. *Send $w = \langle \mathsf{eval}(\eta(\nu_1)), \dots, \mathsf{eval}(\eta(\nu_n)) \rangle$ over λ, where $\langle \nu_1, \dots, \nu_n \rangle = \mathsf{type}(\lambda)$.*
    05. *Compute $\mathcal{C}' = \mathcal{C} \,\textbf{after}_s(\lambda, \eta)$.*
    06. *Repeat the algorithm with the set $\mathcal{C}'$ and trace $\sigma' = \sigma \cdot (\lambda, w)$.*
(3) **Observe output of the SUT**
    07. *If quiescence is observed then*
    08.   *Compute $\mathcal{C}' = \mathcal{C} \,\textbf{after}_s \delta$.*
    09.   *If $\mathcal{C}' \neq \emptyset$ then*
    10.   *Repeat the algorithm with set $\mathcal{C}'$ and trace $\sigma' = \sigma \cdot \delta$.*
    11.   *else*
    12.   *Give verdict* **fail** *when* $\mathrm{InF}(\sigma)$, *and* **pass** *otherwise.*
    13. *else*
    14.   *Receive $w = \langle w_1, \dots, w_n \rangle$ over λ.*
    15.   *Compute η, satisfying $\mathsf{eval}(\eta(\nu_i)) = w_i$ for all $\nu_i \in \mathsf{type}(\lambda)$.*
    16.   *Compute $\mathcal{C}' = \mathcal{C} \,\textbf{after}_s(\lambda, \eta)$.*
    17.   *If $\mathcal{C}' \neq \emptyset$ then*
    18.   *Repeat the algorithm with set $\mathcal{C}'$ and trace $\sigma' = \sigma \cdot (\lambda, w)$.*
    19.   *else*
    20.   *Give verdict* **fail** *when* $\mathrm{InF}(\sigma)$, *and* **pass** *otherwise.*

The above algorithm shares the base case *(1)* with the algorithm of Def. 8: it can terminate at any moment and give the verdict **pass**.

Differently from the algorithm of Def. 8, before sending an input to the SUT (in case *(2)*), first a set of input constraints for $\mathcal{C}$ is computed (line 02). This is a set of first order formulas specifying under which conditions certain data can be sent over one of the input gates. The input constraints in fact represent a subset of the possibly infinite set of inputs. The input constraint and the stimulus that are subsequently chosen in line 03 serve to identify an appropriate input w, which is sent over gate λ in line 04. The algorithm then proceeds with the calculation of a new set of instantiated locations (line 05), sets the new suspension trace, and continues with these new parameters, line 06.

When observing quiescence of the SUT (case *(3)*, line 07), we first check whether this is actually specified behaviour (lines 08 – 10) or not (lines 11 – 12). In the first case, the algorithm continues with the newly obtained set of instantiated locations and suspension trace. In the latter case, we assign the verdict **fail** when the executed trace was an element of $\mathcal{F}$, and **pass** otherwise.

If the SUT actually produces an output (case *(3)*, line 14), we receive a data value w over an output gate λ. To facilitate reasoning about this data value, we first find a corresponding mapping to ground terms η (line 15). Note that this η represents the *actual, concrete* values that are passed over the gate λ. Next, in line 16, the new set of instantiated locations found after observing reaction (λ, η), is computed. Note that since η represents the concrete values for the interaction variables, and due to the restrictions we pose on STSs, this new set of instantiated locations is finite. In line **17**, it is tested whether the observed output was allowed, and if so, testing is continued with the new set in line **18**. When the observed output is not allowed (line **19**), we assign the verdict **fail** or **pass**, dependent on whether the trace we executed thus far was part of $\mathcal{F}$. Note that the meaning of **pass** in lines **12** and **20** corresponds more to an **inconclusive** verdict (see also [7]). However, this verdict is currently not part of our test case definition.

Next we state the correctness and completeness of the algorithm above. That means that we have not lost any detection power compared to the (infeasible) algorithm of Sect. 3.2.

Theorem 2. *Let $\mathcal{S}$ be an STS and let $\mathcal{F} \subseteq Straces(\llbracket \mathcal{S} \rrbracket)$. Given an SUT assumed to behave like an IOTS $\mathcal{P}$ we have:*

1. *$\mathcal{P}\ \mathbf{ioco}_{\mathcal{F}}\ \mathcal{S} \Rightarrow$ every application of the algorithm given in Def. 16 on $\mathcal{S}, \mathcal{F}$ and the SUT results in **pass**.*
2. *$\neg(\mathcal{P}\ \mathbf{ioco}_{\mathcal{F}}\ \mathcal{S}) \Rightarrow$ there exists an application of the algorithm given in Def. 16 on $\mathcal{S}, \mathcal{F}$ and the SUT which potentially results in **fail**.*

The *potentially* in *2.* is because the SUT can behave non-deterministically: if the SUT chooses (non-deterministically) a non-erroneous path, the algorithm cannot observe the fault, of course.

5.3   Discussion

The decidability (and computability) of the first order formulas occurring in STSs is an issue of utmost importance when considering a computer implementation of the algorithm of Def. 16. Two entities, viz. the set of input constraints $\Omega(\mathcal{C})$ and partly the new sets of instantiated locations $\mathcal{C}\ \mathbf{after}_s(\lambda, \eta)$ can be computed purely on the basis of syntax. At some point, though, it is necessary to decide whether a (possibly existentially closed) formula has a solution. In general, this may not even be computable. While we did not address this issue in this paper, as it is orthogonal to the general idea behind the algorithm we presented, we did identify where decidability and computability are of concern. A way to proceed here is to use feasible subsets of first order logic, possibly assisted by (dedicated) theorem provers.

A second point of attention is the selection of appropriate stimuli to be passed on to the SUT (case *(2)* of the algorithm). While the question of decidability and computability is certainly important here, the strategy of filtering interesting stimuli out of a huge set of mainly uninteresting input stimuli satisfying some constraint in the set $\Omega(\mathcal{C})$ is equally challenging. This is where tools such as GAST may come into play. Such tools can automatically generate such stimuli based on given strategies. For instance, GAST uses generics to represent a data type; using a strategy which is similar to unfolding and traversing a tree-like structure, values of the data type are obtained. Other strategies are to employ the syntactical structure of a data type, or to use some uniformity hypothesis for generating and selecting interesting data values.

6 Conclusions

We have tackled the state space explosion problem that is often encountered in state-based test tools. This is achieved by lifting a test theory for Labelled Transition Systems (LTSs), called $\mathbf{ioco}_\mathcal{F}$, to Symbolic Transition Systems (STSs). Unlike in LTSs, data is treated symbolically in an STS. As a side-effect, system descriptions given as an STS are at a natural level of abstraction and in general more concise than their LTS counterparts. In fact, the semantics of STSs (which is given by a translation to LTSs) can yield LTSs of infinite size.

Due to this LTS semantics of the STS, the original $\mathbf{ioco}_\mathcal{F}$ test relation could be reused in our symbolic setting, including the classical test case generation algorithm for $\mathbf{ioco}_\mathcal{F}$. While in theory, this algorithm generates test cases that can be infinitely branching, in practice, this is effectively solved by an on-the-fly implementation of the algorithm working directly on STSs. This solution is only apparent on account of the orthogonal treatment of data and control in STSs.

Several issues remain open, such as the identification of feasible subsets of first order formulas and a running implementation of our algorithm.

References

1. A. Belinfante, J. Feenstra, R.G. de Vries, J. Tretmans, N. Goga, L. Feijs, S. Mauw, and L. Heerink. Formal test automation: A simple experiment. In G. Csopaki, S. Dibuz, and K. Tarnay, editors, 12th Int. Workshop on Testing of Communicating Systems, pages 179–196. Kluwer Academic Publishers, 1999.
2. A. Belinfante, L. Frantzen, and C. Schallhart. Tools for test case generation. In M. Broy, B. Jonsson, J.P. Katoen, M. Leucker, and A. Pretschner, editors, Model-based Testing of Reactive Systems - A Seminar Volume, LNCS. Springer Verlag, 2004. To appear.
3. K. Claessen and J. Hughes. Quickcheck: a lightweight tool for random testing of haskell programs. SIGPLAN Not., 35(9):268–279, 2000.
4. M.R.A. Huth and M. Ryan. Logic in computer science: modelling and reasoning about systems. Cambridge University Press, 2000.
5. P. Koopman, A. Alimarine, J. Tretmans, and R. Plasmeijer. Gast: Generic automated software testing. In Proceedings 14th International Workshop on the Implementation of Functional Languages, IFL 2002, Selected Papers, Madrid, Spain, September 16-18, 2002, Springer Verlag, LNCS 2670, pages 84–100, 2003.
6. P. Koopman and R. Plasmeijer. Testing reactive systems with GAST. In Proceedings Fourth symposium on Trends in Functional Programming, Edinburgh, Scotland, September 11-12, 2003., 2004.
7. V. Rusu, L. du Bousquet, and T. Jéron. An Approach to Symbolic Test Generation. In W. Grieskamp, T. Santen, and B. Stoddart, editors, Integrated Formal Methods – IFM 2000, volume 1945 of Lecture Notes in Computer Science, pages 338–357. Springer-Verlag, 2000.
8. J. Tretmans. Test generation with inputs, outputs and repetitive quiescence. Software—Concepts and Tools, 17(3):103–120, 1996.
9. J. Tretmans and E. Brinksma. TORX : Automated Model Based Testing. In A. Hartman and K. Dussa-Zieger, editors, First European Conference on Model-Driven Software Engineering. Imbuss, Möhrendorf, Germany, December 11-12 2003.

Symbolic Test Case Generation for Primitive Recursive Functions

Achim D. Brucker and Burkhart Wolff

Information Security, ETH Zürich, ETH Zentrum, CH-8092 Zürich, Switzerland
{brucker, bwolff}@inf.ethz.ch

Abstract. We present a method for the automatic generation of test cases for HOL formulae containing primitive recursive predicates. These test cases can be used for the animation of specifications as well as for black-box testing of external programs.

Our method is two-staged: first, the original formula is partitioned into test cases by transformation into a Horn-clause normal form (HCNF). Second, the test cases are analyzed for instances with constant terms satisfying the premises of the clauses. Particular emphasis is put on the control of test hypotheses and test hierarchies to avoid intractability.

We applied our method to several examples, including AVL-trees and the red-black tree implementation in the standard library from SML/NJ.

Keywords: symbolic test case generations, black box testing, theorem proving, Isabelle/HOL.

1 Introduction

Today, essentially two software validation techniques are used: *software verification* and *software testing*. Whereas verification is rarely used in "large-scale" software development, testing is widely used, but normally in an ad-hoc manner. Therefore, the attitude towards testing has been predominantly negative in the formal methods community, following what we call *Dijkstra's verdict* [11, p.6]:

> "Program testing can be used to show the presence of bugs, but never to show their absence!"

More recently, three research areas, albeit driven by different motivations, converge and result in a renewed interest in testing techniques:

- *Abstraction Techniques:* model-checking raised interest in techniques to abstract infinite models to finite ones. Provided that the abstraction has been proven sound, testing may be sufficient for establishing correctness [5, 9].
- *Systematic Testing:* the discussion over *test adequacy criteria* [21], i.e., criteria answering the question "when did we test enough to meet a given test hypothesis", led to more systematic approaches for *partitioning* the space of possible test data and the choice of representatives. New systematic testing methods and abstraction techniques can be found in [12, 13].

J. Grabowski and B. Nielsen (Eds.): FATES 2004, LNCS 3395, pp. 16–32, 2005.

- *Specification Animation:* constructing counter-examples has raised interest also in the theorem proving community, when combined with animations of evaluations, they may help to find modeling errors early and to increase the overall productivity [14].

The first two areas are motivated by the question "are we building the program right?", the latter is focused on the question "are we specifying the right program?". While the first area shows that Dijkstra's Verdict is no longer true under all circumstances, the latter area shows that it simply does not apply to important situations in practice. In particular, if a formal model of the environment of a software system (e.g., based on, amongst other things, the operating system, middleware or external libraries) must be reverse-engineered, testing — in the sense of "experimenting" — is without alternative (see [7]).

Following standard terminology [21], our approach is a *specification-based unit test.* A test procedure for such an approach can be divided into:

- *Test Case Generation:* for each operation, the pre/post-condition relation is divided into sub-relations. It assumes that all members of a sub-relation lead to a similar behavior of the implementation.
- *Test Data Selection:* for each test case (at least) one representative is chosen so that coverage of all test cases is achieved. From the resulting test data, test input data processable by the implementation is extracted.
- *Test Execution:* the implementation is run with the selected test input data in order to determine the test output data.
- *Test Result Verification:* the pair of input/output data is checked against the specification of the test case.

As an example for a specification-based unit-test approach, QuickCheck [8] has attracted interest in various research communities. QuickCheck performs random tests, potentially improved by hand-programmed test data generators, and provides a simple test execution and test result verification environment for programs written in Haskell.

However, it is well-known that random test can be ineffective in many cases;[1] in particular, if complex preconditions of programs like "the input tree must be balanced" or "the input must be a well-formed abstract syntax tree" rule out most of randomly generated data. In our approach, we will exploit the specification of pre- and postconditions of a program — the *test specification* — in a preprocessing step, the *test case generation.* Our implementation TestGen of a test case generator is built on top of the theorem prover Isabelle/HOL [17]. Isabelle is programmed to execute the underlying symbolic computations in an automatic, but logically safe way. Based on the resulting *test cases,* a random test based data selection procedure can be controlled in a problem-oriented way and achieve a significantly better test coverage. As a particular feature, the automated deduction-based process can log the test hypothesis underlying the test.

---

[1] Consider abs(x-2) >= 0 where abs from the Haskell Integer library computes the absolute value. Here it is very unlikely that QuickCheck finds the problem...

Provided that the test hypotheses are valid for the program and provided the program passes the test successfully, the program must guarantee correctness with respect to the test specification.

We proceed as follows: we will introduce our implementation built on top of the theorem prover Isabelle by a tiny, but classical example [12] (Sec. 2). This demonstration serves as a means to motivate concepts like *test specification*, *testing normal form*, *test cases*, *test statements*. In Sec. 3, we will discuss the test case generation in more detail. In Sec. 4, we will discuss a technique for controlling the *state explosion* by generating *abstract test cases*. Finally, we apply our technique to a number of non-trivial examples (Sec. 5) involving recursive data types and recursive predicates and functions over them.

2 Symbolic Test Case Generation: A Guided Tour

Our test case generator `TestGen` is integrated into the specification and theorem proving environment Isabelle/HOL. As a specification language, HOL offers data types, recursive function definitions and fairly rich libraries with theories of, e.g., arithmetics; it is often viewed as a "functional programming language with logical quantifiers". As a theorem proving environment, Isabelle is based on a relatively small proof engine (based on higher-order resolution) providing a *proof state* that can be transformed via elementary *tactics* into logically equivalent ones, until a final proof state is reached where a derived formula has the appropriate form.

Our running example for automatic test case generation is described as follows: given three integers representing the lengths of the sides of a triangle, a small algorithm has to check, whether these integers describe an equilateral, isosceles, scalene triangle, or no triangle at all. First we define an abstract data type describing the possible results in Isabelle/HOL:

datatype   Triangles := equilateral | scalene | isosceles | error

For clarity (and as an example for specification modularization) we define an auxiliary predicate deciding if the three lengths are describing a triangle:

constdefs *triangle*   :: $[\text{nat}, \text{nat}, \text{nat}] \rightarrow \text{bool}$
$$triangle\ x\ y\ z \equiv (0 < x) \wedge (0 < y) \wedge (0 < z) \wedge (z < x + y)$$
$$\wedge (x < y + z) \wedge (y < x + z)$$

Now we define the behavior of the triangle program by initializing the internal Isabelle proof state with the test specification *TS*:

$\text{prog}(x, y, z) = $ **if** *triangle* $x\ y\ z$ **then**
    if $x = y$ **then**
        if $y = z$ **then** equilateral **else** isosceles
    else if $y = z$ **then** isosceles
        else if $x = z$ **then** isosceles **else** scalene
else error

Note that the variable **prog** is used to label an arbitrary implementation as the current *program under test* that should fulfill the test specification.

In the following we show how our test package **TestGen** can be applied to the automatic test data generation problem for the triangle problem. Our method proceeds in the following steps:

1. By applying **gen_test_case_tac** we bring the proof state into *testing normal form* (TNF). In this example, we decided to generate symbolic test cases up to depth 0 (discussed later) and to unfold the *triangle* predicate by its definition before the process. This leads to a formula with 26 clauses, among them:

$$[\![0 < z; z < z + z]\!] \Longrightarrow \text{prog}(z, z, z) = \text{equilateral}$$

$$\begin{bmatrix} x \neq z; 0 < x; 0 < z; \\ z < x + z; x < z + z \end{bmatrix} \Longrightarrow \text{prog}(x, z, z) = \text{isosceles}$$

$$[\![y \neq z; z \neq y; \neg z < z + y]\!] \Longrightarrow \text{prog}(z, y, z) = \text{error}$$

We call each Horn-clause of the proof state a *symbolic test case*. As a result of **gen_test_case_tac**, we can extract the current proof state and get the *test theorem* which has the form $[\![A_1; \ldots; A_{26}]\!] \Longrightarrow TS$ where the A_i abbreviate the above test cases.

2. We compute the concrete *test statements* by instantiating variables by constant terms in the symbolic test cases for "**prog**" via a random test procedure (**genadd_test_data**). The latter operation selects the test cases from the test theorem and produces the test statements (excerpt):

$$\text{prog}(3, 3, 3) = \text{equilateral} \qquad\qquad \text{prog}(4, 6, 0) = \text{error}$$

A test statement can be compiled into a test program by simply mapping all operators to external code (where **prog** is the code for calling the program under test). This can be automated with Isabelle's code-generator. If such a compilation is possible for a formula A, i.e., if A only consists of constant symbols for which this map is defined, we call A *executable*. This definition essentially rules out unbounded logical quantifiers and more arcane HOL constructs like the Hilbert-operator.

In our triangle example, standard simplification was able to eliminate the assumptions of the (instantiated) test cases automatically. In general, assumptions in test statements (also called *constraints*) may remain. Provided that all test statements are executable, clauses with constraints can nevertheless be interpreted as an abstract test program. For its result, three cases may be distinguished: (i) if one of the clauses evaluates to false, the test is *invalid*, otherwise *valid*. A valid test may be (ii) a *successful test* if and only if the evaluation of all conclusions (including the call of **prog**) also evaluates to true; (iii) otherwise the test contains at least one *test failure*. Rephrased in this terminology, the ultimate goal of the test data selection is to construct successful tests, which means that *ground substitutions* (i.e. instantiations of variables with constant terms) must be found that make the remaining *constraints* valid.

Coming back to our example, there is a viable alternative for the process above: instead of unfolding *triangle* and trying to generate ground substitutions satisfying the constraints, one may keep *triangle* in the test theorem, treating it as a building block for new constraints. It turns out that a special test theorem and test data (like "*triangle*(3, 4, 5) = True") can be generated "once and for all" and inserted before the *test data selection* phase producing a "partial" grounding. It will turn out that the main state explosion is shifted from the test case generation to the test data selection phase, possibly at the cost of test adequacy. This technique to modularize test data generation will be discussed in Sec. 4 in more detail.

3   Concepts of Test Case Generation

As input of the test case generation phase, the *test specification*, one might expect a special format like $\text{pre}(x) \rightarrow \text{post } x \ (\text{prog}(x))$. However, this rules out trivial instances such as $3 < \text{prog}(x)$ or just $\text{prog}(x)$ (meaning that prog must evaluate to True for x). Therefore, we do not impose any other restriction on a specification other than the final test statements being executable, i.e., the result of the process can be compiled into a test program.

Processing this test specification, our method `gen_test_case_tac` can be separated into the following conceptual phases (in reality, these phases were performed in an interleaved way):

- *Tableaux Normal Form Computation:* via a tableaux calculus (see Tab. 1), the specification is transformed into Horn-clause normal form (HCNF).
- *Rewriting Normal Form Computation:* via the standard rewrite rules the current specification is simplified.
- *Testing Normal Form Computation:* by re-ordering of the clauses, the calls of the program under test are rearranged such that they only occur in the conclusion, where they must occur at least once.
- *Testing Normal Form Minimization:* redundancies, e.g., clauses subsumed by others, are eliminated.
- *Exploiting Regularity Hypothesis:* for free variables occurring in recurring argument positions of primitive recursive predicates, a suitable *data separation lemma* is generated and applied (leading to a test hypothesis *THYP*).
- *Exploiting Uniformity Hypothesis:* for all Horn-clauses not representing a test hypothesis, a uniformity hypothesis is generated and exploited.

After a brief introduction of concepts and use of Isabelle in our setting, we will follow the sequence of these phases and describe them in more detail in the subsequent sections. We will conclude with a discussion of coverage criteria.

3.1 Concepts and Use of Isabelle/HOL

Isabelle [17] is a generic theorem prover of the LCF prover family; as such, we use the possibility to build programs performing symbolic computations over formulae in a logically safe (conservative) way on top of the logical core engine: this is what TestGen technically is. Throughout this paper, we will use Isabelle/HOL, the instance for Church's higher-order logic. Isabelle/HOL offers support for data types, primitive and well-founded recursion, and powerful generic proof engines based on rewriting and tableaux provers.

Isabelle's proof engine is geared towards Horn-clauses (called "subgoals"): $A_1 \Longrightarrow \ldots \Longrightarrow A_n \Longrightarrow A_{n+1}$, written $[\![A_1; \ldots; A_n]\!] \Longrightarrow A_{n+1}$, is viewed as a rule of the form "from assumptions A_1 to A_n, infer conclusion A_{n+1}". A *proof state* in Isabelle contains an implicitly conjoint sequence of Horn-clauses $\phi_1, \ldots, \phi_n$ and a *goal* ϕ. Since a Horn-clause

$$[\![A_1; \ldots; A_n]\!] \Longrightarrow A_{n+1}$$

is logically equivalent to

$$\neg A_1 \vee \cdots \vee \neg A_n \vee A_{n+1},$$

a Horn-clause normal form (HCNF) can be viewed as a conjunctive normal form (CNF). Note, that in order to cope with quantifiers naturally occurring in specifications, we generalize the idea of a Horn-clause to Isabelle's format of a *subgoal*, where variables may be bound by a built-in meta-quantifier:

$$\bigwedge x_1, \ldots, x_m. \; [\![A_1; \ldots; A_n]\!] \Longrightarrow A_{n+1}$$

Subgoals and goals may be extracted from the proof state into theorems of the form $[\![\phi_1; \ldots; \phi_n]\!] \Longrightarrow \phi$; this mechanism is used to generate test theorems. The meta-quantifier $\bigwedge$ is used to capture the usual side-constraints "x must not occur free in the assumptions" for quantifier rules; meta-quantified variables can be considered as free variables. Further, Isabelle supports meta-variables (written $?x, ?y, \ldots$), which can be seen as "holes in a term" that can still be substituted. Meta-variables are instantiated by Isabelle's built-in higher-order unification.

3.2 Normal Form Computations

In this section, we describe the tableaux, rewriting and testing normal form computations in more detail. In Isabelle/HOL, the automated proof procedures for HOL formulae depend heavily on tableaux calculi [10] presented as (derived) natural deduction rules. The core tableaux calculus is shown in Tab. 1 in the Appendix. Note, that with the notable exception of the elimination rule for the universal quantifier (see Tab. 1(c)), any rule application leads to a logically equivalent proof state: therefore, all rules (except $\forall$ elimination) are called *safe*. When applied bottom up in backwards reasoning (which may introduce meta-variables explicitly marked in Tab. 1), the technique leads in a deterministic manner to a HCNF.

Horn-clauses can be normalized by a number of elementary logical rules (e.g., False $\implies P = $ True), the usual injectivity and distinctness rules for constructors implied by data types and computation rules resulting from recursive definitions. Both processes together bring an original specification into *Rewriting HCNF*.

However, these forms do not exclude clauses of the form:

$$[\neg(\textbf{prog } x = c); \neg(\textbf{prog } x = d)] \implies A_{n+1}$$

where **prog** is the program under test. Equivalently, this clause can be transformed into

$$[\neg(A_{n+1})] \implies \textbf{prog } x = c \lor \textbf{prog } x = d$$

We call this form of Horn-clauses *testing normal form* (TNF). More formally, a Horn-clause is in TNF for program under test F if and only if

- F does not occur in the constraints, and
- F does occur in the conclusion.

Note that not all specifications can be converted to TNF. For example, if the specification does not make a suitably strong constraint over program F, in particular if F does not occur in the specification. In such cases, `gen_test_case_tac` stops with an exception.

3.3   Minimizing TNF

A TNF computation as described so far may result in a proof state with redundancies. Redundancies in a proof state may result in superfluous test data and should therefore be eliminated. A proof state may have:

1. several occurrences of identical clauses
2. several occurrences of clauses with subsuming assumption lists; this can be eliminated by the transformation

$$\frac{[P; R] \implies A; \quad [P; Q; R] \implies A;}{[P; R] \implies A;}$$

3. and in particular, clauses that subsume each other after distribution of $\lor$; this can be eliminated by the transformation

$$\frac{[P; R] \implies A; \quad [\neg P; Q] \implies B; \quad [R; Q] \implies A \lor B;}{[P; R] \implies A; \quad [\neg P; Q] \implies B;}$$

The notation above refers to logical transformations on a subset of clauses within a proof state and not, as usual, on formulae within a clause. Since in backward proofs the proof state below is a refinement of the proof state above, the logical implication goes from bottom to top.

3.4   Exploiting Regularity Hypothesis for Recursive Predicates

In the following, we address the key problem of test case generation in our setting, i.e.; recursive predicates occurring in preconditions of a program. As an introductory example, we consider the membership predicate of an element in a list:

$$\textbf{primrec} \quad \begin{aligned} & x \ mem \ [] && = \text{False} \\ & x \ mem \ (y\#ys) && = \textbf{if} \ y = x \ \textbf{then} \ \text{True} \ \textbf{else} \ x \ mem \ ys \end{aligned} \tag{1}$$

which occurs as precondition in an (abstract) program specification:

$$x \ mem \ S \to \textbf{prog} \ x \ S$$

For the testing of recursive data structure, Gaudel suggested in [13] the introduction of a *regularity hypothesis* as one possible form of a test hypothesis, a kind of weak induction rule:

$$\frac{\begin{array}{c} [|x| < k] \\ \vdots \\ P \ x \end{array}}{P \ x}$$

This rule formalizes the hypothesis that provided a predicate P is true for all data x whose *size*, denoted by $|x|$, is less than a given depth k, it is always true. The original rule can be viewed as a meta-notation: In a rule for a concrete data-type, the premises $|x| < k$ can be expanded to a number of premises enumerating constructor terms.

For all variables in clauses that occur as (recurring) arguments of primitive recursive functions, we will use a testing hypothesis of this kind — called *data separation lemma* — in an exercise in poly-typic theorem proving [19] described in the following.

The Isabelle/HOL data type package generates definitions of poly-typic functions (like case-match and recursors) from data type definitions and derives a number of theorems over them (like induction, distinctness of constructors, etc.). In particular, for any data type, we can assume the size function and reduction rules allowing to compute $|[a, b, c]| = 3$, for example. Moreover, there is a standard *exhaustion-theorem*, which for lists has the form

$$[\![y = [] \Longrightarrow P; \bigwedge x \ xs. \ y = x\#xs \Longrightarrow P]\!] \Longrightarrow P$$

Now, since we can separate any data x belonging to a data type τ into:

$$x \in \{ z :: \tau. \ |z| < d \} \lor x \in \{ z :: \tau. \ d \le |z| \} \tag{2}$$

i.e., x is either in the set of data smaller d or in the remaining set. Note that both sets are infinite in general; the bound for the size produces "data test cases" and not just finite sets of data. Consequently, we can derive for each given type τ

and each d a destruction rule that enumerates the data of size $0, 1, \ldots, k - 1$. For lists x and $d = 2, 3$, it has the form:

$$x \in \{z :: \alpha \text{ list. } |z| < 2\} \to (x = []) \vee (\exists a.\ x = [a])$$
$$x \in \{z :: \alpha \text{ list. } |z| < 3\} \to (x = []) \vee (\exists a.\ x = [a]) \vee (\exists ab.\ x = [a, b]) \qquad (3)$$

Putting equation (2) together with the destruction rule (3), instead of the unsafe regularity hypothesis in the sense of Gaudel we automatically construct the safe data separation lemma, i.e. an exhaustion theorem of the form:

$$\frac{\begin{array}{c} [x = []] \\ \vdots \\ P(x) \end{array} \bigwedge a. \begin{array}{c} [x = [a]] \\ \vdots \\ P(x) \end{array} \bigwedge a\, b. \begin{array}{c} [x = [a, b]] \\ \vdots \\ P(x) \end{array} \quad THYP\big(3 \leq |x| \to P(x)\big)}{P(x)}$$

The purpose of this rule in backward proof is to split a statement over a program into several cases, each with an additional assumption that allows to "rewrite-away" the x appropriately. Here, the constant $THYP$ :: bool $\to$ bool (defined as the identity function) is used to label the test hypothesis in the proof state. Since we do not unfold it, formulae labeled by $THYP$ are protected from decomposition by the tableaux rules shown in Tab. 1.

The equalities introduced by this rule of depth $d = 3$ allow for the simplification of the primitive recursive predicate mem which leads to further decompositions during the TNF computation. Thus, for our test specification:

$$x \text{ mem } S \to \mathbf{prog}\ x\ S$$

executing **gen_test_case_tac** results in the following TNF:

1. $\mathbf{prog}\ x\ [x]$

2. $\bigwedge b.\ \mathbf{prog}\ x\ [x, b]$

3. $\bigwedge a.\ a \neq x \to \mathbf{prog}\ x\ [a, x]$

4. $THYP(3 \leq |S| \to x \text{ mem } S \to \mathbf{prog}\ x\ S)$

The simplification of the mem predicate along its defining rules (1) leads to nested "**if then else**" constructs. Their decomposition during HCNF computation results in the constraint that the lists fulfilling the precondition must have a particular structure. Even the simplest "generate-and-test"-method for test data selection will now produce adequate test statements, while it would have produced mostly test failures when applied directly to the original specification.

The handling of quantifiers ranging over data types can be done analogously: since $\forall x.\ P(x)$ is equivalent to $\forall x : UNIV.\ P(x)$ and since the universal set $UNIV = \{z :: \tau.\ |z| < d\} \cup \{z :: \tau.\ d \leq |z|\}$, the universal quantifier can be decomposed into a finite conjunction for the test cases smaller than d and a test hypothesis $THYP$ for the rest.

From the above example it follows that the general form of a test theorem is $[A_1; \ldots; A_n; THYP(H_1); \ldots; THYP(H_m)] \implies TS$. Here the A_i represent the test cases, the H_i the test hypothesis, and TS the testing specification.

3.5   Exploiting Uniformity Hypothesis

After introducing the uniformity hypothesis and computing a TNF (except for clauses containing *THYP*s), we use the clauses to construct another form of testing hypothesis, namely the *uniformity hypothesis* [13] (sometimes also called *partitioning hypothesis*) for each test case. This kind of hypothesis has the form:

$$THYP(\exists x_1, \ldots, x_n.\ P\ x_1, \ldots, x_n \rightarrow \forall x_1, \ldots, x_n.\ P\ x_1, \ldots, x_n)$$

This means that whenever there is a successful test for a test case, it is assumed that the program will behave correctly for *all* data of this test case.

Using a uniformity hypothesis for each (non-*THYP*) clause allows for the replacement of free variables by meta-variables; e.g., for the case of two free variables, we have the following transformation on proof states:

$$\frac{[\![A_1\ x\ y; \ldots; A_n\ x\ y]\!] \Longrightarrow A_{n+1}\ x\ y}{[\![A_1\ ?x\ ?y; \ldots; A_n\ ?x\ ?y]\!] \Longrightarrow A_{n+1}\ ?x\ ?y; \quad THYP((\exists xy.\ P\ x\ y) \rightarrow (\forall xy.\ P\ x\ y));}$$

where $P\ x\ y \equiv A_1\ x\ y \wedge \ldots \wedge A_n\ x\ y \rightarrow A_{n+1}\ x\ y$. This transformation is logically sound. Moreover, the construction introduces individual meta-variables into each clause for the ground instances to be substituted in the test data selection; this representation allows for partial instantiation of variable with constant terms and is also a prerequisite for structured test data selection as discussed in Sec.4.

3.6   Coverage Criteria: A Discussion

In their seminal work, Dick and Faivre [12] propose to transform the original specification into disjunctive normal form (DNF), followed by a case splitting phase converting the disjunctions $A \vee B$ into $A \wedge B$, $\neg A \wedge B$ and $A \wedge \neg B$ and further (logical and arithmetic) simplifications and minimizations on the disjunctions. The resulting cases are also called the *partitions of the specification* or the *(DNF) test cases*. The method suggests the following test adequacy criterion: a set of test data is *partition complete* if and only if for any test case there is a test data. Consequently, a program P is tested adequately to partition completeness with respect to a specification S if it passes a partition complete test data set.

Our notion of a *successful test*, see Sec. 2, is a HCNF based adequacy criterion. DNF and HCNF based adequacy result in the same partitioning in many practical cases, as in the triangle example, while having no clear-cut advantage in others. Since the DNF technique has the disadvantage of producing a double exponential blow-up (the case splitting phase alone can produce an exponential blow-up) while HCNF computation is simply exponential, and since HCNF-computation can be more directly and efficiently implemented in the Isabelle proof engine, we chose the latter.

HCNF adequacy subsumes another interesting adequacy criterion under certain conditions, namely *branch coverage* with respect to the specification. Branch coverage means that in any (mutual) recursive system of functions, all reachable branches, e.g., of the **if** P **then** A **else** B statements, were activated at least once. For a mutual recursive system consisting only of *primitive* recursive functions, (i.e., with each call the size of data will decrease exactly by one), it can be concluded that if the testing depth d is chosen larger than the size of the maximal strong component of the call graph of the recursive system, each function is unfolded at least once. Since the unfold results in conditionals that were translated to $(P \rightarrow A) \wedge (\neg P \rightarrow B)$, any branch will lead to a test case.

Thus, while `gen_test_case_tac` often produces reasonable results for arbitrarily recursive functions, we can assure only for primitive recursions that the underlying HCNF adequacy of our method subsumes branch coverage.

4   Structured Test Data Selection

The motivations to separate test data selection from test case generation are both conceptual and technical. Conceptually, test data selection is a process where we would also like to admit more heuristic techniques like random data generation or generate-and-test with the constraints; since test data selection yields sequences of ground theorems (no meta-variables, no type variables), this paves the way for highly efficient evaluation by compiled code more capable to cope with the unavoidable state explosion in the late stages. A purely technical motivation for this separation is Isabelle-related: within a test theorem, it is not possible to instantiate polymorphic type variables α in different ways when generating test statements, however, this flexibility may be desirable.

The generation of a multitude of ground test statements from one test theorem containing the test cases and the test hypothesis is essentially based on a random-procedure followed by a test of the satisfaction of the constraints (similar to QuickCheck). For each type, this default procedure may be overwritten in `TestGen`-specific generators that may be user defined; thus, the usual heuristics like trying $[0, 1, 2, maxint, maxint+1]$ can be easily implemented, or the counter-example generation integrated in Isabelle's arithmetic procedure can be plugged in (which, in our experience, is difficult to control in larger examples).

Now we will discuss the issue of structured test data generation. Similar to theorem proving, the question of "how many definitions should be unfolded" is crucial; exploiting suitable abstractions is the major weapon against complexity. In our first attempt to generate a test theorem for the triangle example (see Sec. 2), the auxiliary predicate *triangle* is unfolded in the test specification. This resulted in the aforementioned 26 cases. If we do not unfold it, the resulting test theorem has only 10 test cases, but contains "abstract constraints" such as:

$$[\![triangle\ z\ z\ z]\!] \Longrightarrow \mathbf{prog}(z, z, z) = \text{equilateral}$$
$$[\![\neg triangle\ z\ z\ z]\!] \Longrightarrow \mathbf{prog}(z, z, z) = \text{error}$$
$$[\![y \neq z; z \neq y; triangle\ z\ y\ z]\!] \Longrightarrow \mathbf{prog}(z, y, z) = \text{isosceles}$$

Thus, a substantial part of the proof state explosion can be postponed by treating *triangle* as a building block in the constraints or, in other words, by generating more *abstract* test cases.

Now, if we could generate an *local test theorem* for *triangle* as such, generate the *local* test data separately and resolve the resulting test statements for it into the test theorem for the global computation, the state explosion could be shifted to the test data selection. The trick can be done as follows: we define a trivially true proof goal for:

$$\mathbf{prog}(x, y, z) = triangle\ x\ y\ z \Longrightarrow \mathbf{prog}(x, y, z) = triangle\ x\ y\ z$$

unfold *triangle* and compute TNF(**prog**). When folding back *triangle* via the assumption we get the following local test cases:

$$\neg triangle\ 0\ y\ z \qquad\qquad \neg z < x + y \Longrightarrow \neg triangle\ x\ y\ z$$
$$\neg triangle\ x\ 0\ z \qquad\qquad \neg x < y + z \Longrightarrow \neg triangle\ x\ y\ z$$
$$\neg triangle\ x\ y\ 0 \qquad\qquad \neg y < x + z \Longrightarrow \neg triangle\ x\ y\ z$$
$$\left[\!\!\left[\begin{array}{c} 0 < x; 0 < y; 0 < z; \\ z < x + y; x < y + z; y < x + z \end{array} \right]\!\!\right] \Longrightarrow \quad triangle\ x\ y\ z$$

which can easily be converted into *abstract test statements* such as *triangle* 1 1 1. When resolving the latter in all combinations into the abstract global test theorem, instances for variables with randomly generated constants were made superfluous. Thus, the test statements of previously developed theories can be reused when building up larger units. Of course, when building up test data in a modular way, this comes at a price: since the local test statements do not have the same logical information available as their application context in a more global test theorem, the instantiation may result in unsatisfiable constraints. Nevertheless, since the criterion for success of a decomposition is clear — at the very end we want constraint-free test statements achieving a full coverage of the TNF— the implementor of a test has more flexibility here helping to deal with larger problems. In our example, there is no loss at all: test data for the local predicate is valid for the global goal, and by construction, the set of test statements is still complete for HCNF coverage.

5 Applications

We applied our method to specifications of two widely used variants of balanced binary search trees: AVL trees and red-black trees. These case studies were performed using Isabelle 2003 compiled with SML of New Jersey running on Linux with 512 MBytes of RAM, and an Intel 1.6 GHz P4 processor.

5.1 AVL Trees

In 1962 Adel'son-Vel'skiĭ and Landis [3] introduced a class of balanced binary search trees (called AVL trees) that guarantee that a tree with n internal nodes has height $O(\log n)$. Based on an AVL-theory from the Isabelle library we generated test cases for the following invariant: if an element y is in the tree after insertion of x in the tree t then either $x = y$ holds or y was already stored in t. Based on the depth 3, this *test specification* leads to an amazing 236 test cases which were computed in less than 30 seconds.

5.2   Red-Black Trees

A widely used variant of balanced search trees was presented by Bayer [4]. In this data structure, the balancing information is stored in one additional bit per node. This is called "color of a node" (which can either be red or black), hence the name *red-black trees*. A valid (balanced) red-black tree must fulfill the following two invariants:

- *Red Invariant:* each red node has a black parent.
- *Black Invariant:* each path from the root to an empty node has the same number of black nodes.

We aimed for testing a "real-world" implementation of red-black trees and decided to test the red-black trees provided in the standard library of SML of New Jersey (SML/NJ) [2]. There, red-black trees are used for implementing finite sets and maps which are intensively used throughout the SML/NJ compiler itself.

Our specification is based on the formalization [16] of the SML/NJ red-black trees (based on version 110.44 of SML/NJ). The specification starts with the basic data type declaration for binary trees:

datatype color $= R \mid B$
          α tree $= E \mid T$ color (α tree) (α item) (α tree)

In this example we have chosen not only to check if keys are stored or deleted correctly in the trees but also to check if the trees fulfill the balancing invariants. Therefore our specification has to formalize the red and black invariants. This is done by the following recursive predicates:

consts
  redinv :: (α item) tree $\Rightarrow$ bool
  blackinv:: (α item) tree $\Rightarrow$ bool

recdef *redinv* "measure ($\lambda t.$ (size t))"
  "*redinv* E $=$ True"
  "*redinv* (T B a y b) $= (redinv\ a \wedge redinv\ b)$"
  "*redinv* (T R (T R a x b) y c)$=$ False"
  "*redinv* (T R a x (T R b y c))$=$ False"
  "*redinv* (T R a x b) $= (redinv\ a \wedge redinv\ b)$"

recdef *blackinv* "measure ($\lambda t.$ (size t))"
  "*blackinv* E $=$ True"
  "*blackinv*(T color a y b) $= ((blackinv\ a) \wedge (blackinv\ b)$
                          $\wedge((max\_B\_height\ a) = (max\_B\_height\ b)))$"

We use the following test specification for checking if the delete operation fulfills these invariants:

$$(redinv\ t \wedge blackinv\ t) \rightarrow (redinv\ (delete\ x\ t) \wedge blackinv\ (delete\ x\ t))$$

In other words, for all trees the deletion operation maintains the red and black invariant. For testing purposes, we instantiated *item* with Integers. The test case generation takes less than two minutes and results in 348 test cases. Among them

delete 8 (*T B* (*T B* (*T R E* 2 *E*) 5 *E*) 6 (*T B E* 8 *E*))

$$= (T\ B\ (T\ B\ E\ 2\ E)\ 5\ (T\ B\ E\ 6\ E))$$

which describes that the deletion of the node 8 in the tree shown in Fig. 1(a) must result in the tree shown in Fig. 1(b). This test case revealed a major error in the standard library of SML/NJ. Using a simple SML test script one observes:

```
val input = T (B,T (B,T (R,E,2,E),5,E),6,T (B,E,8,E))
- val output = delete(input,8);
val output = T (B,E,2,T (B,T (R,E,5,E),6,E))
```

Obviously, the black invariant does not hold for output (see Fig. 1(c)).

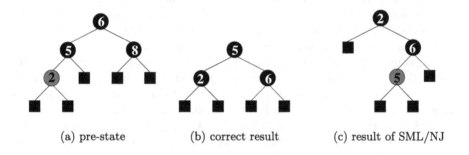

| (a) pre-state | (b) correct result | (c) result of SML/NJ |

Fig. 1. Test Data for Deleting a Node in a Red-Black Tree

This example shows that specification based testing can find efficiency bugs: combinations of insert and delete operations of the SML/NJ implementation easily lead to trees that degenerate to sorted lists. In our case, the revealed flaw has not been detected in the last 12 years, although red-black trees are widely used within the SML/NJ compiler itself. Fixing this bug will presumably lead to a perceptible performance gain of the SML/NJ compiler.

Based on our definitions, the bug could be reproduced by QCheck/SML [1], a QuickCheck-like random testing tool. Although this particular bug can even be found without using a hand-programmed test data generator, the QuickCheck method imposes to write one in general. Moreover, our method allows to conclude that certain coverage criteria are fulfilled and makes all underlying test hypotheses explicit. Further, our approach can profit from the underlying theories for data-types offering the potential for problem-specific case splits.[2]

---

[2] ... such as $[\![P(\texttt{minBound} :: \texttt{Int}); a \neq \texttt{minBound} \implies P(-a)]\!] \implies P(-a)$ which also produces the critical test case $x = \texttt{minBound} + 2$ for the mentioned problem `abs(x-2)>=0` after unfolding abs to `if x >= 0 then x else -x`.

6   Conclusion

We have presented the theory and implementation of a test case generator for unit tests. In contrast to [20] (which also provides a recent survey), which attempts to analyze imperative programs with non-trivial data-structures, our approach is focused on functional programs. Since imperative programs can be provided with a functional interface (by compiling a functional call to a statement sequence consisting of (i) initialization, (ii) executing constructors representing data types, (iii) calling the program under test, and (iv) checking the result), this is not a real limitation of our approach except if complex reference structures have to be analyzed. We demonstrated the practical feasibility of our approach by testing functions from the SML/NJ library, which revealed a major bug leading to inefficiency in basic data structures of the SML/NJ compiler.

In our opinion, test data generation is an activity that clearly needs *some* user interaction: as in model-checking, one has to experiment with the form of the specifications and basic parameters (depth of *data separation*, the level of abstraction, the decision which definitions should be unfold, etc.) in order to get a feasible test data set for the test of a "real program". Therefore, we believe such an activity is best supported by an integration into an *interactive* theorem proving environment such as Isabelle. Since TestGen is ca. 400 lines of SML code that is loaded into Isabelle, we still consider our approach fairly "lightweight". Nevertheless, TestGen is at present the only implementation of a test case generator that combines state-of-the-art deduction technology based on derived rules (formally proven inside Isabelle) with a powerful logic.

We believe that there is another line of criticism against Dijkstra's verdict. A successful test together with explicitly stated test hypotheses is not fundamentally different from program verification: all sorts of modeling assumptions were made, adding test hypothesis is just one more of them. The nature and trustworthiness of these assumptions may be different, but a clear-cut line between testing and verification does not exist.

6.1   Future Work

We see the following lines of extension of our work:

1. *Investigating the test hypothesis*: a new test hypothesis (like congruence hypothesis on data, for example) may dramatically improve the viability of the approach. Furthermore, it should be explored if the verification of the test hypothesis for a given abstract program offers new lines of automation.
2. *Better control of the process*: at the moment, our implementation can only be controlled by very globally applied parameters such as depth. The approach could be improved by generating the test hypothesis and the test data depending on the local context within the test theorems.
3. *Integration tests*: integrating/combining our framework into behavioral modeling leads to the generation of *test sequences* as in [15, 18].
4. *Generating test data for many-valued logics* such as HOL-OCL [6] should make our approach applicable to formal methods more accepted in industry.

References

[1] QCheck/SML. http://contrapunctus.net/league/haques/qcheck/.

[2] SML of New Jersey. http://www.smlnj.org/.

[3] G. M. Adel'son-Vel'skiĭ and E. M. Landis. An algorithm for the organization of information. *Soviet Mathematics Doklady*, 3:1259–1263, 1962.

[4] R. Bayer. Symmetric binary B-trees: Data structure and maintenance algorithms. *Acta Informatica*, 1(4):290–306, 1972.

[5] A. Biere, A. Cimatti, E. Clarke, O. Strichman, and Y. Zhu. *Bounded Model Checking*. Number 58 in Advances In Computers. 2003.

[6] A. D. Brucker and B. Wolff. A proposal for a formal OCL semantics in Isabelle/HOL. In C. Muñoz, S. Tahar, and V. Carreño, editors, *TPHOLs*, volume 2410 of *LNCS*, pages 99–114. Springer-Verlag, Hampton, VA, USA, 2002.

[7] A. D. Brucker and B. Wolff. A case study of a formalized security architecture. In T. Arts and W. Fokkink, editors, *FMICS'03*, volume 80 of *Electronic Notes in Theoretical Computer Science*, Roros, 2003. Elsevier Science Publishers.

[8] K. Claessen and J. Hughes. QuickCheck: a lightweight tool for random testing of Haskell programs. In *Proceedings of the fifth ACM SIGPLAN international conference on Functional programming*, pages 268–279. ACM Press, 2000.

[9] P. Cousot and R. Cousot. Abstract interpretation: a unified lattice model for static analysis of programs by construction or approximation of fixpoints. In *Proceedings of the 4th ACM SIGACT-SIGPLAN symposium on Principles of programming languages*, pages 238–252. ACM Press, 1977.

[10] M. D'Agostino, D. Gabbay, R. Hähnle, and J. Posegga, editors. *Handbook of Tableau Methods*. Kluwer, Dordrecht, 1996.

[11] O.-J. Dahl, E. W. Dijkstra, and C. A. R. Hoare. *Structured Programming*, volume 8 of *A.P.I.C. Studies in Data Processing*. Academic Press, London, 1972.

[12] J. Dick and A. Faivre. Automating the generation and sequencing of test cases from model-based specications. In J. Woodcock and P. Larsen, editors, *FME 93*, volume 670 of *LNCS*, pages 268–284. Springer-Verlag, 1993.

[13] M.-C. Gaudel. Testing can be formal, too. In P. D. Mosses, M. Nielsen, and M. I. Schwartzbach, editors, *TAPSOFT 95*, volume 915 of *LNCS*, pages 82–96. Springer-Verlag, Aarhus, Denmark, 1995.

[14] S. Hayashi. Towards the animation of proofs—testing proofs by examples. *Theoretical Computer Science*, 272(1–2):177–195, 2002.

[15] F. Huber, B. Schätz, A. Schmidt, and K. Spies. AutoFocus - a tool for distributed systems specification. In *FTRTFT 96*, volume 1135 of *LNCS*, pages 467–470. Springer-Verlag, 1996.

[16] A. Kimmig. Red-black trees of smlnj. Studienarbeit, Universität Freiburg, 2003.

[17] T. Nipkow, L. C. Paulson, and M. Wenzel. *Isabelle/HOL — A Proof Assistant for Higher-Order Logic*, volume 2283 of *LNCS*. Springer-Verlag, 2002.

[18] A. Pretschner. Classical search strategies for test case generation with constraint logic programming. In E. Brinksma and J. Tretmans, editors, *Proc. Formal approaches to testing of software*, pages 47–60. BRICS, 2001.

[19] K. Slind and J. Hurd. Applications of polytypism in theorem proving. In D. Basin and B. Wolff, editors, *TPHOLs*, volume 2758 of *LNCS*, pages 103–119. Springer-Verlag, Rome, Italy, 2003.

[20] W. Visser, C. S. Păsăreanu, and S. Khurshid. Test input generation with Java PathFinder. *SIGSOFT Softw. Eng. Notes*, 29(4):97–107, 2004.

[21] H. Zhu, P. A. Hall, and J. H. R. May. Software unit test coverage and adequacy. *ACM Computing Surveys*, 29(4):366–427, 1997.

A   Appendix

Table 1. The Standard Tableaux Calculus for HOL

$$\dfrac{P\ ?x}{\exists x.\ P\ x} \qquad\qquad \dfrac{\bigwedge x.\ P\ x}{\forall x.\ P\ x}$$

(a) Quantifier Introduction Rules

$$\dfrac{}{t=t} \quad \dfrac{}{\text{True}} \quad \dfrac{P \quad Q}{P \wedge Q} \quad \dfrac{\begin{array}{c}[\neg Q]\\ \vdots\\ P\end{array}\quad Q}{P \vee Q} \quad \dfrac{\begin{array}{c}[P]\\ \vdots\\ Q\end{array}}{P \to Q} \quad \dfrac{\begin{array}{c}[P]\\ \vdots\\ \text{False}\end{array}}{\neg P} \quad \dfrac{\begin{array}{c}[P]\\ \vdots\\ Q\end{array}\quad\begin{array}{c}[Q]\\ \vdots\\ P\end{array}}{P = Q}$$

(b) Safe Introduction Rules

$$\dfrac{\forall x.\ P\ x \qquad \begin{array}{c}[P\ ?x]\\ \vdots\\ R\end{array}}{R} \qquad\qquad \dfrac{\forall x.\ P\ x \qquad \begin{array}{c}[\forall x.\ P\ x;\ P\ ?x]\\ \vdots\\ R\end{array}}{R}$$

(c) Unsafe Elimination Rules

$$\dfrac{\text{False}}{P} \quad \dfrac{P \wedge Q \quad \begin{array}{c}[P\quad Q]\\ \vdots\\ R\end{array}}{R} \quad \dfrac{P \vee Q \quad \begin{array}{c}[P]\\ \vdots\\ R\end{array}\quad \begin{array}{c}[Q]\\ \vdots\\ R\end{array}}{R} \quad \dfrac{P \to Q \quad \begin{array}{c}[\neg P]\\ \vdots\\ R\end{array}\quad \begin{array}{c}[Q]\\ \vdots\\ R\end{array}}{R}$$

$$\dfrac{\exists x.\ P\ x \quad \bigwedge x.\ \begin{array}{c}[P\ x]\\ \vdots\\ Q\end{array}}{Q} \qquad \dfrac{P = Q \quad \begin{array}{c}[P\quad Q]\\ \vdots\\ R\end{array}\quad \begin{array}{c}[\neg P\quad \neg Q]\\ \vdots\\ R\end{array}}{R}$$

(d) Safe Elimination Rules

$$\textbf{if } P \textbf{ then } A \textbf{ else } B = (P \to A) \wedge (\neg P \to B)$$

(e) Rewrites

Preserving Contexts for Soft Conformance Relation

David de Frutos Escrig* and Carlos Gregorio Rodríguez**

Department of Sistemas Informáticos y Programación,
Universidad Complutense de Madrid
{defrutos, cgr}@sip.ucm.es

Abstract. This paper addresses the study of bisimulation based conformance relations in which input and output actions not presented in the specification are added to the implementation. A new definition, that we called *soft conformance*, is given. Then, we concentrate on the study of the conditions under which a context preserves the soft conformance relation of two agents. These conditions depend both on the specification and the implementation in the conformance relation and also on the context. Since the addition of extraneous actions to the implementation allows to define malicious contexts that would not preserve the conformance relation, such a characterisation of the family of contexts preserving each individual pair (implementation and specification) in the conformance relation is the best result that can be expected in this direction.

1 Introduction

Conformance relations have been introduced and studied since late eighties, providing a testing methodology for communicating systems. Conformance relations look for the adequate way to check when a concrete system should be considered a correct implementation of a given specification. The most popular conformance relations are based on traces and refusals [Hoa85], and probably that called conf [BSS86, Bri88] is the most widely spread and accepted.

First definitions on the subject were quite informal and tried to capture by means of some simple, but sometimes vague, conditions those *reasonable* requirements to get a correct implementation of a given specification. Fortunately, it was not too difficult to obtain formal definitions which captured the intuitive ideas supporting the original proposals, as the relation conf cited above.

The bad news were that although these formal definitions where rather simple and elegant they did not satisfy some also simple and clearly desirable properties, such as transitivity and substitutivity, and therefore they were far from being precongruencies.

In [Led91, Led92] an extensive and careful study of the subject can be found. There the relation conf-eq is introduced and proved to be the biggest equivalence relation contained in the nucleus $\text{conf} \cap \text{conf}^{-1}$ of the conformance relation, while $\text{conf}^* = \text{conf} \circ \text{conf}$ is proved to be its transitive closure.

---

* Partially supported by the MCyT project TERMAS TIC2003-07848-C02-01, JCCM project PAC-03-001 and MRTN-CT-2003-505121/TAROT.
** Partially supported by the MCyT project TERMAS TIC2003-07848-C02-01.

J. Grabowski and B. Nielsen (Eds.): FATES 2004, LNCS 3395, pp. 33–48, 2005.

Since traces and failures are strongly related with the semantic information given by testing formalisms [Hen88], several works have studied this relation. For instance, in [dFLN97] it was proved that conf* can be characterised by means of an special kind of testing mechanisms, the so called *friendly testing*, which is thoroughly studied in [dFLN98].

Together with the testing school, there are other approaches to define the equivalence between concurrent processes in process algebras. Equivalences based on *bisimulation* [Mil80, Mil89] are also widely used. It is well known that bisimulation equivalences are stronger than testing equivalences, but also much easier to decide, which seem to be two important reasons to prefer them to the others. Clearly, if it is possible to prove bisimilarity of two processes, then they would be also testing equivalent. But this strong power of bisimulation can also became a weakness, since there are not clear reasons to consider that two processes which are testing equivalent, but not bisimilar, should not be considered to be equivalent. Besides, weak bisimulation is not a congruence for languages such as CSP [Hoa85], where there exists an external choice operator (see [dFLN99]).

In [Ste94] a bisimulation based conformance, called *logical conformance*, is presented where classical bisimulation rules are relaxed and asymmetrical conditions related to the specification and the implementation are introduced. In [BS02] a new version of this conformance relation is given. In this relation it is allowed for the process describing the implementation system to execute both input and output new actions. Similar ideas have also been followed, in conformance relations defined by testing semantics, for instance [Bri88, dFLN97].

As it happens in the conformance relation based on testing semantics, the addition in [BS02] of new input and output actions to the implementation yields to a conformance relation that it is neither transitive nor preserved by most of the algebraic operators in CCS. To overcome these problems was the main goal of [BS02], and their authors concluded the paper by asserting that they have defined the *congruent weak conformance* induced by their *weak conformance* relation. Unfortunately, even if in that paper there are several interesting ideas, and some useful partial results, we have to present here some criticisms because there are several technical mistakes in that work, as we will show by means of some counterexamples later.

However, our main intended goal in this paper it is mainly to continue the research in conformance relations in which input and output actions not presented in the specification are added to the implementation, looking for the adequate way to get preservation results in order to make the conformance relation useful.

To be more concrete, what indeed is done in [BS02] is to find a collection of properties which have to be satisfied in order to preserve the presented conformance relation. Most of these conditions would restrict the containing context and not the relationship between the given implementation and the corresponding specification. Therefore, it is not possible to use those conditions to try to define a precongruence which would preserve the conformation relation.

Instead, what we propose is to characterise which are the contexts that would preserve each particular pair in the conformation relation. In fact, these contexts would be different for each pair in the relation, and therefore, out of some trivial cases, we cannot look for a family of contexts totally preserving the conformance relation. As a consequence, the weaker precongruence relation stronger than the conformance relation would be just the weak bisimulation equivalence, where we have no possibility to add any new action when implementing a given specification.

We address this goal in the next sections organised as follows: in Section 2 classic definition of agents and previously bisimulation based conformance relations are introduced, besides, definition of weak conformance [BS02] is discussed and some flaws of that relation are shown; in Section 3 we present our own definition of bisimulation like conformance relation, that we call *soft conformance*; Section 4 presents the results of the paper: we prove that the soft conformance relation can be preserved by contexts under some conditions related to a given pair of specification and implementation agents; finally, in Section 5 we present our conclusions.

2   Basic Definitions and Bisimulation Based Conformances

In this paper we will mainly use the operators from CCS [Mil80, Mil89], whose syntax and semantics we will briefly recall below.

We have a set of action names, called $\mathcal{A}$, from which we obtain the set of barred actions, $\overline{\mathcal{A}} = \{\overline{a} \mid a \in \mathcal{A}\}$. Following [BS02], we will assume that plain names represent input actions, while barred names would correspond to output actions. Finally, we have an internal action $\tau \notin \mathcal{A} \cup \overline{\mathcal{A}}$, and we define the alphabet $Act = \mathcal{A} \cup \overline{\mathcal{A}} \cup \{\tau\}$.

Definition 1 ([Mil89]). *Given a set of actions Act, as described above, the set of CCS agents is defined by the following BNF-expression:*

$$E ::= \mathbf{0} \mid \alpha.E \mid E + E \mid E|E \mid E[f] \mid E \backslash L$$

where $\alpha \in Act$, L denotes a finite subset of $\mathcal{A}$ and $f : \mathcal{A} \longrightarrow \mathcal{A}$ denotes a relabelling function.

The inactive agent, represented by **0**, is not capable of executing any action; prefix operator defines the execution of sequential actions; choice operator introduces into the language a choice between two alternative behaviours; parallel operator represents the parallel execution of two independent agents, but allowing the synchronisation between them by the execution of a pair of conjugated actions, a and $\overline{a}$, thus producing the internal action denoted by τ; relabelling operator, by means of a function $f : \mathcal{A} \longrightarrow \mathcal{A}$, produces a change in the name of the executed actions, by executing $f(a)$ instead of a and $\overline{f(a)}$ instead of $\overline{a}$; and finally the restriction of the actions in a set L would disallow the execution of actions in $L \cup \overline{L}$.

The operational semantics of CCS formalise the ideas above and can be found in [Mil80, Mil89]. From the operational semantics of processes we can construct the bisimulations and the definition of bisimulation equivalences. Semantic equivalences, and in particular weak bisimulation equivalence [Mil89], have been proposed as a way to formalise the implementation relations, but it seems too strong to use an equivalence relation to accomplish such a task, even if we can abstract away from internal details of the implementation, as allowed by the weak character of that equivalence relation. Instead, conformance relations allow the introduction of new actions in the implementation, when they do not interfere with the rest of the behaviour of the system. This idea has been developed in [Ste94], where the author proposed his *logic conformance* (see definition 2 below).

The classical notation on computation of agents is used: The ability of an agent P to perform some action $\alpha \in Act$ and to evolve into an agent Q is denoted by $P \xrightarrow{\alpha} Q$. Similarly, $P \xRightarrow{\alpha} Q$ is used to denote the ability of P to evolve into Q through the execution of α and any number of additional τ actions. Considering sequences of actions, $s \in Act^*$, the transition relations are naturally extended to get $\xrightarrow{s}$ and $\xRightarrow{s}$, which describe the evolution of an agent when executing a sequence of actions. For the empty sequence we have only the second of this transitions which in this case it is just denoted by $\Rightarrow$. The hat operator over a sequence of actions, $\hat{s}$, denotes its projection over the set of visible (input and output) actions, so that we have $\hat{s} \in (\mathcal{A} \cup \overline{\mathcal{A}})^*$.

Definition 2 ([Ste94]: Definition 30). *Implementation I logically conforms to specification S, written $I \succeq_l S$, iff $\forall \alpha \in Act, \forall \beta \in \overline{\mathcal{A}} \cup \{\tau\}$ and $\forall \gamma \in \mathcal{A}$:*

(1) Whenever $S \xrightarrow{\alpha} S'$ then $\exists I' : I \xRightarrow{\hat{\alpha}} I'$ and $I' \succeq_l S'$.

(2) Whenever $I \xrightarrow{\beta} I'$ then $\exists S' : S \xRightarrow{\hat{\beta}} S'$ and $I' \succeq_l S'$.

(3) Whenever $I \xrightarrow{\gamma} I'$ and $S \xRightarrow{\gamma}$ then $\exists S'$ such that $S \xRightarrow{\gamma} S'$ and $I' \succeq_l S'$.

If we compare this definition with that of plain weak bisimulation we find that the difference comes only from the third clause that allow the implementation to accept additional input actions which are not imposed by the specification.

In [BS02] this definition is considered too strong, and two reasons are argued: (1) an implementation must implement every specified output action, even when there is output concurrency, that is, when multiple output events are produced without interleaving with any input action, and the order of output events is unimportant; (2) it is not possible for the implementation to generate output signals not in the specification.

Then, in order to allow even more flexible implementations a new relation called *weak conformance* is introduced. To define it, they first introduce the *weak conformation* relations defined as follows:

Definition 3 ([BS02]: Definition 7). *A binary process relation $\mathcal{W}$ is a weak conformation if $\forall \alpha \in \mathcal{A}(S) \cup \{\tau\}$, $\forall \beta \in \overline{\mathcal{A}}(I) \cup \{\tau\}$, $\forall \gamma \in \mathcal{A}(S) : I \,\mathcal{W}\, S$ implies the following four laws:*

Law of Specified Input or Tau (LSIT). *If $S \xrightarrow{\alpha} S'$ then $\exists t \in (\mathcal{A}(S) \cup \overline{Extr}(I, S))^*$ such that*
(1) $I \xRightarrow{t} I'$ (2) $t \restriction \mathcal{A}(S) = \hat{\alpha}$ (3) $I' \,\mathcal{W}\, S'$

Law of Specified Output (LSO). *Let X be a maxoctset of S. $\exists s \in X$ and $\exists t \in \overline{\mathcal{A}}(I)^+$ such that*
(1) $S \xRightarrow{s} S'$ (2) $I \xRightarrow{t} I'$ (3) $t \restriction \overline{\mathcal{A}}(S) = s$ (4) $I' \,\mathcal{W}\, S'$

Law of Implemented Input (LII). *Whenever $I \xrightarrow{\gamma} I'$ and $S \xRightarrow{\gamma}$ then*
(1) $S \xRightarrow{\gamma} S'$ (2) $I' \,\mathcal{W}\, S'$

Law of Implemented Output or Tau (LIOT). *If $I \xrightarrow{\beta} I'$ and $\delta \equiv \beta \restriction \overline{\mathcal{A}}(S)$ then*
(1) $S \xRightarrow{\delta} S'$ (2) $I' \,\mathcal{W}\, S'$

Where $\mathcal{A}(P)$ and $\overline{\mathcal{A}}(P)$ define the input and output sorts of an agent P, respectively; the binary operator $\restriction$ applies to a sequence s of actions and a set of

actions A, $s \upharpoonright A$, projecting the actions in s over the set A. Besides, $Extr(I, S) = $
$\mathcal{A}(I) - \mathcal{A}(S)$ is called the extraneous input sort and $\overline{Extr}(I, S) = \overline{\mathcal{A}}(I) - \overline{\mathcal{A}}(S)$ is
called the extraneous output sort.

Definition 4 ([BS02]: Definition 9). *The* weak conformance *relation, written*
$\succeq_W$, *is the union of all the weak conformations.*

To formally define the condition capturing their intention of getting a more
flexible implementation of output concurrency, a rather complex concept of *maxoctset* (maximal output confluent transition set) is defined in [BS02] and used in
LSO rule. The concept of maxoctset tried to capture those maximal partial behaviours of a system which correspond to the parallel execution of several output
actions.

But to reduce the output concurrency in the implementation is not compatible with the goal of getting a precongruence from the conformance relation. Let
us consider the specification $S = a.(\overline{b}|\overline{c})$. To Reduce the output concurrency im-
plies not to force any implementation of S to implement all the specified output
sequences, but just some of them. So, $I = a.\overline{b}.\overline{c}$ would be an adequate implementation of S. But then, we cannot expect this conformance relation to be a
precongruence: if we take the agent $C = c.b$ and put it in parallel with the specifi-
cation S and the implementation I, then we have that the agent $S|C$ can execute
the trace $t = ab\overline{b}$, because after executing a action in S, C and S can synchronise
and arrive to a state in which they can interleave the actions b and $\overline{b}$. On the
contrary, $I|C$ cannot execute such a trace. All this is illustrated in figure 1.

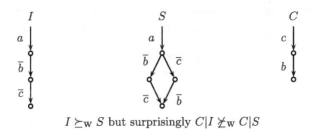

$I \succeq_W S$ but surprisingly $C|I \not\succeq_W C|S$

Fig. 1. Not implementation of output concurrency do not allow $\succeq_W$ to be a congruence

But even if we would not mind this lack of substitutivity, using the definition of
maxoctset in [BS02] in order to allow the reduction of output concurrency yields
to undesirable implementations. Maxoctsets are maximal traces which correspond
to a locally confluent behaviour. A trace t corresponds to a locally confluent
behaviour if $P \overset{t}{\Longrightarrow}$ and for each s that is a permutation of t with $P \overset{s}{\Longrightarrow}$, if we
have $P \overset{t}{\Longrightarrow} P'$ and $P \overset{s}{\Longrightarrow} P''$, P' and P'' are weak bisimulation equivalent. The
authors of [BS02] where too generous allowing that not any permutation of s
would be a trace of P. Let us consider the agents in figure 2. If we take $S = \overline{a}.\overline{b}.\overline{c}$,
we have that the trace $\overline{a}\overline{b}\overline{c}$ would be a maxoctset of S. But this would be also the
case for a specification such as $S' = \overline{a}.\overline{b}.\overline{c} + \overline{a}.\overline{b}.d + \overline{b}.\overline{a}.e$ that has added behaviour.
It is clear that the trace $\overline{a}\overline{b}$ is not a locally confluent behaviour of S', but under

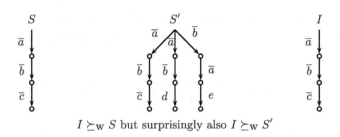

$I \succeq_{\mathrm{w}} S$ but surprisingly also $I \succeq_{\mathrm{w}} S'$

Fig. 2. Maxoctset definition yields to improper implementations

the definition in [BS02] the trace $\bar{a}\bar{b}\bar{c}$ would still be a locally confluent behaviour of S' and then a maxoctset of it. As a consequence the behaviours of S' after the execution of the traces $\bar{a}\bar{b}$ and $\bar{b}\bar{a}$ would not be considered when checking the weak conformance of any implementation. Then, $I = \bar{a}.\bar{b}.\bar{c}$, where neither d nor e can be executed, would be considered to be an admissible implementation of S', which does not seem reasonable at all.

Finally, to conclude with the comments on [BS02], we show one more flaw on the definition of the weak conformance relation arising from the way rule LII is asserted (definition 3). Transitivity of $\succeq_{\mathrm{w}}$ is not guaranteed just by imposing that an implementation would not execute any extraneous output action in the beginning.

Let us consider the agents in figure 3: $Q = a.\bar{v}.b.c$ is an implementation of $R = a.b.c$, because rule LSIT allows the introduction of output actions, provided that they do not appear in the specification. Rule LII also allows to introduce new input actions into the implementation, but it is too generous since it is just imposed that these actions could not be executed by the initial state of the specification. So, agent $P = a.(\bar{v}.b.c + b)$ is an implementation of Q. But the added choice executing the action b makes P not to be an implementation of R, thus spoiling transitivity of the conformance relation.

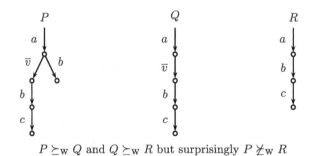

$P \succeq_{\mathrm{w}} Q$ and $Q \succeq_{\mathrm{w}} R$ but surprisingly $P \not\succeq_{\mathrm{w}} R$

Fig. 3. $\succeq_{\mathrm{w}}$ relation is not transitive

3   Soft Conformance Relation

In this section we present a new variant of conformance relations, that we call *soft conformations*. The union of all soft conformation relations define the *soft conformance*, denoted by $\succeq_s$. This new notion gathers the desired conditions discussed above, namely the capability of the implementation to introduce new input and output actions in its behaviour.

In order to give the definition of soft conformations some new notation has to be introduced. As usual $\longrightarrow$ and $\Longrightarrow$ relations denote the capability of an agent to evolve through a single action or an action preceded and followed by any number of τ actions, respectively. Besides, we introduce the new transition relation $\Longmapsto$ that gathers the idea that once a specification is fixed, the extraneous output actions in the implementations play the same role as τ actions. That is, given the specification S and the implementation I, $I \overset{\alpha}{\Longmapsto}_s I'$ indicates that I evolves to I' after executing the action α preceded and followed by any number of transitions executing either τ actions or output actions $\overline{b} \in \overline{Extr}(I, S)$. For the sake of simplicity, if S is clear from the context where the $\Longmapsto$ relation is used, we will avoid the subscript S, writing just $I \overset{\alpha}{\Longmapsto} I'$.

In order to define soft conformations relations, the sort of an agent, that is, the set of actions that it could possibly execute, has to be introduced:

Definition 5. *The set of executable actions of an agent E, denoted by $Exec(E)$, is inductively defined as follows:*

- $Exec(\mathbf{0}) = \emptyset$
- $Exec(\alpha.E) = \{\alpha\} \cup Exec(E)$
- $Exec(E_1 + E_2) = Exec(E_1|E_2) = Exec(E_1) \cup Exec(E_2)$
- $Exec(E[f]) = f(Exec(E))$
- $Exec(E\backslash L) = Exec(E) - L$

Definition 6. *Binary process relation $\mathcal{V}$ is a soft conformation if $\forall \alpha \in Act$, $\forall a \in \mathcal{A}(S)$, $\forall \beta \in \overline{\mathcal{A}}(I) \cup \{\tau\} : I \mathcal{V} S$ implies that $Exec(S) \subseteq Exec(I)$ and the following laws are satisfied:*

Law of Specified Behaviour (LSB)

   If $S \overset{\alpha}{\longrightarrow} S'$ then $\exists I' : I \overset{\hat{\alpha}}{\Longmapsto} I'$ and $I' \mathcal{V} S'$.

Law of Implemented Input (LII)

   If $I \overset{a}{\longrightarrow} I'$ and $a \in Exec(S)$ then $\exists S' : S \overset{a}{\Longrightarrow} S'$ and $I' \mathcal{V} S'$.

Law of Implemented Output or Tau (LIOT)

   If $I \overset{\beta}{\longrightarrow} I'$ and $\beta \in Exec(S)$ then $\exists S' : S \overset{\beta}{\Longrightarrow} S'$ and $I' \mathcal{V} S'$.

   If $I \overset{\beta}{\longrightarrow} I'$ and $\beta \notin Exec(S)$ then $\exists S' : S \Longrightarrow S'$ and $I' \mathcal{V} S'$.

Therefore the differences between our soft conformations and the weak conformations in definition 3 are that we have drop out the considerations about output concurrency and then the two laws of specified input and output have became a single law; besides in LII rule we only allow the additional execution by the implementation of extraneous input actions.

Proposition 1. *Let $\mathcal{V}$ and $\mathcal{V}'$ be soft conformation relations, then*

(1) The identity relation is a soft conformation relation.
(2) The composition $\mathcal{V} \mathcal{V}'$ is a soft conformation relation.
(3) The union $\mathcal{V} \cup \mathcal{V}'$ is a soft conformation relation.

Definition 7. *The implementation I is said to softly conform to the specification S, denoted by $I \succeq_s S$, if there exists some soft conformation relation $\mathcal{V}$ with $I \mathcal{V} S$. That is, the soft conformance relation, denoted by $\succeq_s$, is the union of all the soft conformation relations.*

4   Contexts That Preserve Soft Conformance

In this section we address the main goal of our paper: given a specification S and an a soft conformance implementation of it, $I \succeq_S S$, to determine the properties that a context $C(X)$ should verify in order to get $C(I) \succeq_S C(S)$. We will start by formalising the concept of context. In order to get a simpler presentation, we will first just consider contexts with a single hole.

Definition 8. *Given a set of actions Act, the set of contexts is defined by the following BNF-expression:*

$$C ::= \mathbf{0} \mid X \mid \alpha.C \mid E + C \mid C + E \mid E|C \mid C|E \mid C[f] \mid C \backslash L$$

where X represents a single (hole) variable, E represents CCS agents (definition 1), $\alpha \in Act$, L denotes a finite subset of $\mathcal{A}$ and $f : \mathcal{A} \longrightarrow \mathcal{A}$ denotes a relabelling function.

The operational semantics of contexts is defined in the same way as agents, since there is no rule for the hole X.

To define the conditions that contexts have to satisfy in order to preserve the soft conformance relation we need to use a collection of auxiliary functions and predicates that we will define below. All of them are defined by structural induction.

Definition 9. *The following functions are defined over both contexts and agents:*

***Exec*()** *computes the set of executable actions of a context.*

$$\begin{aligned}
Exec(X) &= Exec(\mathbf{0}) &&= \emptyset \\
Exec(\alpha.C) &= \{\alpha\} \cup Exec(C) \\
Exec(E + C) &= Exec(C + E) = Exec(E|C) = Exec(C|E) = Exec(C) \cup Exec(E) \\
Exec(C[f]) &= f(Exec(C)) \\
Exec(C \backslash L) &= Exec(C) - L
\end{aligned}$$

***Init*()** *computes the set of initials actions that a context can execute.*

$$\begin{aligned}
Init(X) &= Init(\mathbf{0}) &&= \emptyset \\
Init(\alpha.C) &= \{\alpha\} \\
Init(E + C) &= Init(C + E) = Init(C) \cup Init(E) \\
Init(E|C) &= Init(C|E) = Init(C) \cup Init(E) \cup \{\tau | \text{ if } \exists \alpha \in Init(E), \bar{\alpha} \in Init(C)\} \\
Init(C[f]) &= f(Init(C)) \\
Init(C \backslash L) &= Init(C) - L
\end{aligned}$$

***Guar*()** *defines a boolean function that indicates whether a context has its hole guarded by an action.*

$$\begin{aligned}
Guar(X) &= false \\
Guar(\mathbf{0}) &= true \\
Guar(\alpha.C) &= true \\
Guar(E + C) &= Guar(C + E) = Guar(E|C) = Guar(C|E) = \\
Guar(C[f]) &= Guar(C \backslash L) = Guar(C)
\end{aligned}$$

***Choice-app*()** *defines a boolean function that indicates if a choice operator applies directly on the hole of a context.*

$$
\begin{aligned}
Choice\text{-}app(X) &= Choice\text{-}app(\mathbf{0}) &&= false \\
Choice\text{-}app(\alpha.C) &= Choice\text{-}app(C) \\
Choice\text{-}app(E + C) &= Choice\text{-}app(C + E) &&= Choice\text{-}app(C) \vee \neg Guar(C) \\
Choice\text{-}app(E|C) &= Choice\text{-}app(C|E) &&= Choice\text{-}app(C[f]) &&= \\
&\ \ Choice\text{-}app(C\backslash L) &&= Choice\text{-}app(C)
\end{aligned}
$$

***Exec-par*()** *defines the set of actions that can be executed in parallel with the hole and the context.*

$$
\begin{aligned}
Exec\text{-}par(X) &= Exec\text{-}par(\mathbf{0}) &&= \emptyset \\
Exec\text{-}par(\alpha.C) &= Exec\text{-}par(C) \\
Exec\text{-}par(E + C) &= Exec\text{-}par(C + E) &&= Exec\text{-}par(C) \cup Exec\text{-}par(E) \\
Exec\text{-}par(E|C) &= Exec\text{-}par(C|E) &&= Init(C|E) \\
Exec\text{-}par(C[f]) &= f(Exec\text{-}par(C)) \\
Exec\text{-}par(C\backslash L) &= Exec\text{-}par(C) - L
\end{aligned}
$$

***Rest*()** *defines the set of restricted actions over the hole in the context.*

$$
\begin{aligned}
Rest(X) &= Rest(\mathbf{0}) &&= \emptyset \\
Rest(\alpha.C) &= Rest(C) \\
Rest(E + C) &= Rest(C + E) = Rest(E|C) = Rest(C|E) = Rest(C) \\
Rest(C[f]) &= f(Rest(C)) \\
Rest(C\backslash L) &= Rest(C) \cup L
\end{aligned}
$$

***Renamed*()** *defines the set of actions that are either renamed or renamed to over the hole in the context.*

$$
\begin{aligned}
Renamed(X) &= Renamed(\mathbf{0}) &&= \emptyset \\
Renamed(\alpha.C) &= Renamed(C) \\
Renamed(E + C) &= Renamed(C + E) = Renamed(E|C) = \\
&\ \ Renamed(C|E) \quad = Renamed(C) \\
Renamed(C[f]) &= Renamed(C) \cup \{a \mid f(a) \neq a \vee \exists b \neq a : f(b) = a\} \\
Renamed(C\backslash L) &= Renamed(C) - L
\end{aligned}
$$

From the previous functions, we define the following ones:

$\overline{\textbf{\textit{Init}}}$**()** *defines the initial output or τ actions that a context can execute.*

$$
\overline{Init}(C) = Init(C) \cap (\overline{A} \cup \{\tau\})
$$

$\overline{\textbf{\textit{Init-extr}}}$**()** *defines the initial output extraneous actions of I with respect to S.*

$$
\overline{Init\text{-}extr}(I, S) = \overline{Init}(I) \cap (\overline{Extr}(I, S) \cup \{\tau\})
$$

***IOExtr*(,)** *defines the union of extraneous input and output actions.*

$$
IOExtr(I, S) = Extr(I, S) \cup \overline{Extr}(I, S)
$$

Exec-par() *defines the* complementary *set of actions with respect to the set* Exec-par().

$$\overline{Exec\text{-}par(C)} = \{\overline{\alpha} \mid \alpha \in Exec\text{-}par(C)\}$$

where $\overline{\overline{\alpha}} = \alpha$ *and* $\overline{\tau} = \tau$.

The following proposition explains which is the relation between the syntactically defined functions and predicates introduced in definition 9 and the semantic behaviour of the involved elements.

Proposition 2. *The functions declared in definition 9 verify the following characteristic properties:*

1. *For any action* α *in any trace* s *such that* $C \xLongrightarrow{s}$ *it holds that* $\alpha \in Exec(C)$.
2. *For any action* $\beta \in \overline{Extr(I,S)} \cup \{\tau\}$ *such that* $C \xrightarrow{\beta}$ *then* $\beta \in \overline{Init\text{-}extr(I,S)}$.
3. *If there exists some computation* $C(X) \xLongrightarrow{s} C'(X)$ *such that* $C'(\omega.\omega') \xrightarrow{\omega} C''(\omega')$ *with* $C' \neq C''$ *then* Choice-app(C) *is true.*
4. *If there exists some computation* $C(X) \xLongrightarrow{s} C'(X)$ *such that* $C'(X) \xrightarrow{\overline{\alpha}} C''(X)$ *and* $C'(\alpha.\omega) \xrightarrow{\tau} C''(\omega)$, *by the synchronisation of the first transition with the execution of action* α *in the hole, then* $\overline{\alpha} \in Exec\text{-}par(C)$.
5. *If there exists some computation* $C(X) \xLongrightarrow{s} C'(X)$ *such that* $C'(\omega.\omega') \xrightarrow{\omega} C''(\omega')$ *but* $C'(\alpha.\omega') \xnrightarrow{\alpha}$, *then* $\alpha \in Rest(C)$.
6. *If* $a \notin Renamed(C(X)) \wedge \overline{a} \notin Renamed(C(X))$ *and there exists some computation* $C(X) \xLongrightarrow{s} C'(X)$ *such that* $C'(a.\omega') \xrightarrow{\alpha} C''(\omega')$ *then* $a = \alpha$.

Where ω *and* ω' *denote* fresh *actions that are not in* $Exec(C) \cup Exec(I)$.

We can now give the conditions that determine when a context preserve the soft conformance relation that holds between two agents.

Definition 10. *Given two agents* I *and* S, $I \succeq_s S$, *and a context* C, *it is said that* C *is a* preserving context *with respect to the pair* (I,S) *if the following five conditions are fulfilled:*

i. $IOExtr(I,S) \cap Exec(C) = \emptyset$
ii. $\neg Choice\text{-}app(C) \vee (\overline{Init\text{-}extr}(I,S) = \emptyset)$
iii. $IOExtr(I,S) \cap \overline{Exec\text{-}par(C)} = \emptyset$
iv. $\overline{Extr}(I,S) \cap Rest(C) = \emptyset$
v. $Renamed(C) \cap IOExtr(I,S) = \emptyset$

Next proposition tie together some properties that will be useful when proving the main result of our paper: the preservation theorem.

Proposition 3. *If* C *is a preserving context with respect to the pair* (I,S), *where the* X *appears, then the following properties are satisfied:*

1. $IOExtr(C(I),C(S)) = IOExtr(I,S)$
2. *If* $C(X) \xLongrightarrow{\alpha} C'(X)$, *then* C' *is also a preserving context with respect to the pair* (I,S).
3. *If* $C(\omega.\omega') \xrightarrow{\omega} C'(\omega')$ *then for any* $P \xLongrightarrow{s} P'$ *with* $s = \alpha_1 \ldots \alpha_n$, *and* $\forall i \; \alpha_i \notin Renamed(C)$ *and* $\alpha_i \notin Rest(C)$ *we have also* $C(P) \xLongrightarrow{s} C'(P')$.

4. If $I \stackrel{\hat{\alpha}}{\Longrightarrow} I'$ and $C(\omega.\omega') \stackrel{\omega}{\longrightarrow} C'(\omega')$ and $C(S) \stackrel{\alpha}{\longrightarrow} C'(S')$ then $C(I) \stackrel{\hat{\alpha}}{\Longrightarrow} C'(I')$ and C' is a preserving context with respect to (I', S').

5. If $S \stackrel{\beta}{\longrightarrow} S'$ and $C(X) \stackrel{\overline{\beta}}{\longrightarrow} C'(X)$ and it is possible to get a synchronisation step $C(S) \stackrel{\tau}{\longrightarrow} C'(S')$, then $C(I) \stackrel{\tau}{\longrightarrow} C'(I')$ and C' is a preserving context with respect to (I', S').

Proof. Let us prove the previous statements:

1. By a simple structural induction over the form of the contexts.
2. If C' is such a derived context from C then:

$$
\begin{aligned}
Exec(C') &\subseteq Exec(C) \\
Choice\text{-}app(C') &\Rightarrow Choice\text{-}app(C) \\
Exec\text{-}par(C') &\subseteq Exec\text{-}par(C) \\
Rest(C') &= Rest(C) \\
Renamed(C') &= Renamed(C)
\end{aligned}
$$

and therefore C' verify the conditions $(i)\ldots(v)$ with respect to (I, S).
3. By structured induction over the form of C:

   - $C = a.C''$. This cannot be the case, since then $C(\omega.\omega') \stackrel{\omega}{\not\longrightarrow}$
   - $C = Q + C''$. If $C(\omega.\omega') \stackrel{\omega}{\longrightarrow} C'(\omega')$ then we should have $C''(\omega.\omega') \stackrel{\omega}{\longrightarrow} C'(\omega')$, and by induction hypothesis $C''(P) \stackrel{s}{\Longrightarrow} C'(P')$ and therefore $C(P) \stackrel{s}{\Longrightarrow} C'(P')$.
   - $C = Q|C''$. If $C(\omega.\omega') \stackrel{\omega}{\longrightarrow} C'(\omega')$ we have $C' = Q|C'''$ with $C''(\omega.\omega') \stackrel{\omega}{\longrightarrow} C'''(\omega')$. Then we have $C''(P) \stackrel{s}{\Longrightarrow} C'''(P')$ and $C(P) \stackrel{s}{\Longrightarrow} Q|C'''(P') = C'(P')$.
   - $C = C''[f]$. If $C(\omega.\omega') \stackrel{\omega}{\longrightarrow} C'(\omega')$ we have also $C''(\omega.\omega') \stackrel{\omega}{\longrightarrow} C'''(\omega')$ with $C' = C'''[f]$. Then we have $C''(P) \stackrel{s}{\Longrightarrow} C'''(P')$ and since f does not rename any action in s we have also $C(P) \stackrel{s}{\Longrightarrow} C'(P')$.
   - $C = C''\backslash L$. If $C(\omega.\omega') \stackrel{\omega}{\longrightarrow} C'(\omega')$ we have also $C''(\omega.\omega') \stackrel{\omega}{\longrightarrow} C'''(\omega')$ with $C' = C'''\backslash L$. Then we have $C''(P) \stackrel{s}{\Longrightarrow} C'''(P')$ and since the actions in s are not in $Rest(C)$ in particular the are not in L, and therefore $C(P) \stackrel{s}{\Longrightarrow} C'(P')$.

4. Let us consider the sequence of visible actions s which corresponds to the computation $I \stackrel{\hat{\alpha}}{\Longrightarrow}{}_{I'}$, then since $C(S) \stackrel{\alpha}{\longrightarrow} C'(S')$ and the rest of the actions in s are also in $IOExtr(I, S)$, by proposition 3(1), $C(I) \stackrel{\hat{\alpha}}{\Longrightarrow} C'(I')$.
   The proof that C' is a preserving context with respect to (I', S') is similar to that of proposition 3(2) considering that $Choice\text{-}app(C')$ is always false. This statement can be proved by structural induction as before.
5. Similar to the previous one.

$\square$

Theorem 1 (Preservation theorem). *If $I \succeq_s S$ and C is a preserving context of the pair (I, S) then $C(I) \succeq_s C(S)$.*

Proof. We have to prove that there exists a soft conformation relation $\mathcal{V}$ containing the pair $\langle C(I), C(S) \rangle$. We define

$$\mathcal{V} = \{\langle C(I), C(S) \rangle \mid I \succeq_s S \text{ and } C \text{ is a preserving context w.r.t. } (I, S)\}$$

and we will check that $\mathcal{V}$ verifies the laws in definition 6.

LSB. *Let us suppose that* $C(S) \xrightarrow{\alpha} T$. *There are three different possibilities:*

1. $T = C'(S)$ *and* $C(X) \xrightarrow{\alpha} C'(X)$, *then* $C(I) \xrightarrow{\alpha} C'(I)$ *and, by proposition 3,* C' *is a preserving context with respect to* (I, S) *and therefore* $C'(I)$ *and* $C'(S)$ *are in the conformation relation* $\mathcal{V}$.

2. $S \xrightarrow{\alpha} S'$ *and* $C(S) \xrightarrow{\alpha} C'(S')$, *where the context* C' *is derived from* C *by means of the execution of an action of its hole. From* $I \succeq_s S$ *we know that* $I \overset{\hat{\alpha}}{\Longrightarrow}_s I'$ *and* $I' \succeq_s S'$ *and then, by proposition 3(4)* $C(I) \overset{\hat{\alpha}}{\Longrightarrow} C(I')$ *and* C' *is a preserving context with respect to* (I', S') *and therefore* $C'(I') \mathcal{V} C'(S')$.

3. *Finally, if* $\alpha = \tau$ *and there exists some* β *such that* $S \xrightarrow{\beta} S'$, *and* $C(X) \xrightarrow{\overline{\beta}} C'(X)$ *and there is a synchronisation step of these two complementary actions which produces* $C(S) \xrightarrow{\tau} C'(S')$. *Then,* $I \overset{\beta}{\Longrightarrow} I'$ *and* $I' \succeq_s S'$, *considering proposition 3(5), we have* $C(I) \xrightarrow{\tau} C'(I')$, *and combining the arguments in the two previous cases we get that* C' *is a preserving context with respect to* (I', S'), *and therefore* $C'(I') \mathcal{V} C'(S')$.

LII. *Let us suppose that* $C(I) \xrightarrow{a} T$ *and* $a \in Exec(C(S))$, *then two cases should be considered:*

1. $C(X) \xrightarrow{a} C'(X)$ *and* $T = C'(I)$ *then, by proposition 3(2),* C' *is a preserving context with respect to* (I, S) *and therefore* $C'(I) \mathcal{V} C'(S)$.

2. $I \xrightarrow{a'} I'$ *and* $C(I) \xrightarrow{a} C'(I')$ *where the context* C' *is derived from* C *by means of the execution of an action of its hole, and* $a \in Renamed(C)$. *By definition 10(i),* $a' \in Exec(S)$, *by proposition 2(1),* $a' \in Exec(I)$ *and if it were the case that* $a' \notin Exec(S)$ *then* $a' \in Extr(I, S)$ *and by using conditions (i), (iv) and (v) of definition 10, we would conclude that* $a \in Extr(C(I), C(S))$ *and then* $a \notin Exec(C(S))$ *against the hypothesis.*

   Then, since $I \succeq_s S$ *we have that* $S \overset{a'}{\Longrightarrow} S'$ *with* $I' \succeq_s S'$ *and, reasoning as in LSB rule, we get that* $C(S) \overset{a}{\Longrightarrow} C'(S')$ *with* C' *a preserving context with respect to* (I', S'), *so that* $C'(I') \mathcal{V} C'(S')$.

LIOT. *We consider two cases:*

1. $C(I) \xrightarrow{\overline{a}} T$ *with* $\overline{a} \in Exec(C(S))$. *Once again we consider two cases:*

   (a) $C(X) \xrightarrow{\overline{a}} C'(X)$ *and* $T = C'(I)$, *then by proposition 3(2),* C' *is a preserving context with respect to* (I, S) *and therefore* $C'(I) \mathcal{V} C'(S)$.

   (b) $I \xrightarrow{\overline{a'}} I'$ *and* $C(I) \xrightarrow{\overline{a}} C'(I')$ *for* C' *derived from* C *by means of the execution of an action in its hole, and* $a \in Renamed(C)$. *Then, we have that* $S \overset{\overline{a'}}{\Longrightarrow} S'$ *with* $I' \succeq_s S'$ *and therefore, as in the previous case, we conclude that* $C'(I') \mathcal{V} C'(S')$.

2. $C(I) \xrightarrow{\beta} T$ *were* $\beta = \tau$ *or* $\beta = \overline{a} \notin Exec(C(I))$. *Now there are three possible cases:*

(a) $C(X) \xrightarrow{\beta} C'(X)$ and $T = C'(I)$, as in the corresponding case above, C' is a preserving context with respect to (I, S) and as a consequence $C'(I) \mathcal{V} C'(S)$.

(b) $I \xrightarrow{\beta'} I'$ and $C(I) \xrightarrow{\beta} C'(I')$ with $\beta \in Renamed(C)$. Due to condition (ii) in definition 10 this case is only possible if $C' = C$. Then, by proposition 2(2), the hole X in C cannot be under a choice operator and so $S \xRightarrow{\beta'} S'$ and $C(S) \xRightarrow{\beta} C(S')$, with C preserving (I', S'), and therefore $C(I') \mathcal{V} C(S')$.

(c) $\beta = \tau$ and there exists some γ' such that $I \xrightarrow{\gamma} I'$, and $C(X) \xrightarrow{\bar{\gamma}} C'(X)$ after a renaming of γ' into γ and there is a synchronisation step of these two actions which produces $C(I) \xrightarrow{\tau} C'(I)$. Then $\gamma' \in Exec(S)$ because C verifies condition (iii) in definition 10, and we can proceed either as in the previous case (1) of the LIOT rule, or as for the law LII to conclude that $S \xRightarrow{\gamma'} S'$ and $C(S) \xRightarrow{\gamma} C'(S')$ where C' is a preserving context with respect to the pair (I', S'), thus concluding that $C'(I') \mathcal{V} C'(S')$.

□

In definition 8, contexts with a single hole were defined and the preservation theorem proves that preserving contexts (definition 10) allow the substitutivity of agents that are in soft conformation getting a new pair of agents in soft conformation. We next generalised the results to contexts with a finite set of variable names.

Definition 11. *Let us consider a (finite) set of* hole variables $\mathcal{X} = \{\mathcal{X}_1, \ldots, \mathcal{X}_k\}$. *We define* generalised contexts *exactly as simple contexts (definition 8) but changing the unique symbol X by a representative element of the set $\mathcal{X}$, and replacing all the metavariables C in that definition by that corresponding to a generalised context $\mathcal{C}$.*

We do not want to have contexts with repeated appearances of the same hole, therefore, we forbid such possibility and concentrate on what we call *valid generalised contexts*.

Definition 12. *The following function and predicate are defined over generalised contexts:*

Holes() *computes the set of hole variables of a generalised context.*

$$Holes(\mathcal{X}_i) = \{\mathcal{X}_i\}$$
$$Holes(\alpha.\mathcal{C}) = Holes(\mathcal{C}[f]) \;\; = Holes(\mathcal{C} \backslash L) \qquad = Holes(\mathcal{C})$$
$$Holes(\mathcal{C}_1 + \mathcal{C}_2) = Holes(\mathcal{C}_1 | \mathcal{C}_2) = Holes(\mathcal{C}_1) \cup Holes(\mathcal{C}_2)$$

Valid() *indicates if a generalised context has no hole names repeated.*

$$Valid(\mathcal{X}_i) = true$$
$$Valid(\alpha.\mathcal{C}) = Valid(\mathcal{C}[f]) \;\; = Valid(\mathcal{C} \backslash L) = Valid(\mathcal{C})$$
$$Valid(\mathcal{C}_1 + \mathcal{C}_2) = Valid(\mathcal{C}_1 | \mathcal{C}_2) =$$
$$Valid(\mathcal{C}_1) \wedge Valid(\mathcal{C}_2) \wedge (Holes(\mathcal{C}_1) \cap Holes(\mathcal{C}_2) = \emptyset)$$

Par-holes() *a binary function that applies on valid generalised contexts, that is* $Valid(\mathcal{C}) = true$ *and* $\mathcal{X}_i \in \mathcal{X}$, *and computes the set of hole names that are in the context* $\mathcal{C}$ *in parallel with the given hole name* X_i.

$$Par\text{-}holes(\mathcal{X}_j, \mathcal{X}_i) = \emptyset$$
$$Par\text{-}holes(\alpha.\mathcal{C}, \mathcal{X}_i) = Par\text{-}holes(\mathcal{C}[f], \mathcal{X}_i) = Par\text{-}holes(\mathcal{C}\backslash L, \mathcal{X}_i) =$$
$$Par\text{-}holes(\mathcal{C}, \mathcal{X}_i)$$
$$Par\text{-}holes(\mathcal{C}_1 + \mathcal{C}_2, \mathcal{X}_i) = Par\text{-}holes(\mathcal{C}_1, \mathcal{X}_i) \cup Par\text{-}holes(\mathcal{C}_2, \mathcal{X}_i)$$
$$Par\text{-}holes(\mathcal{C}_1|\mathcal{C}_2, \mathcal{X}_i) = \begin{cases} Par\text{-}holes(\mathcal{C}_1, \mathcal{X}_i) \cup Holes(\mathcal{C}_2) & \text{if } X_i \in Holes(\mathcal{C}_1) \\ Par\text{-}holes(\mathcal{C}_2, \mathcal{X}_i) \cup Holes(\mathcal{C}_1) & \text{if } X_i \in Holes(\mathcal{C}_2) \\ \emptyset & \text{if } \mathcal{X}_j \notin Holes(\mathcal{C}_1) \cup Holes(\mathcal{C}_2) \end{cases}$$

Definition 13. *Given a set of hole variables* $\mathcal{X} = \{\mathcal{X}_1, \ldots, \mathcal{X}_k\}$ *and a family of pairs of agents* $\mathcal{F} = \{(I_i, S_i)\}_{i \in 1..k}$ *and a valid generalised context* $\mathcal{C}$, *we say that it is a* preserving generalised context *with respect to the family* $\mathcal{F}$ *if, besides the conditions in definition 10, for each pair* (I_i, S_i) *with* $\mathcal{X}_i \in Holes(\mathcal{C})$ *we have also*

vi. *For each* i, j *with* $\mathcal{X}_i \in Holes(\mathcal{C})$

$$IOExtr(I_i, S_i) \cap Exec(S_j) = \emptyset$$

vii. *For each* $\mathcal{X}_i \in Holes(\mathcal{C})$ *and* $\mathcal{X}_j \in Par\text{-}holes(\mathcal{C}, \mathcal{X}_i)$

$$IOExtr(I_i, S_i) \cap \overline{Exec(I_j)} = \emptyset$$

Theorem 2. *If* $\mathcal{C}$ *is a preserving generalised context with respect to a family* $\mathcal{F} = \{(I_i, S_i)\}_{i \in 1..k}$ *and for each* $i \in 1..k$ *we have that* $I_i \succeq_s S_i$ *then* $\mathcal{C}(\overline{I}) \succeq_s \mathcal{C}(\overline{S})$ *where, as usual,* $\mathcal{C}(\overline{E})$ *denotes the substitution of the hole variables* $\mathcal{X}_i$ *in* $\mathcal{C}$ *by the corresponding agent* E_i.

5   Conclusions and Future Work

Conformance relations define when a communicating system should be considered a correct implementation of a given specification. In this paper we have studied the conditions under which a context preserves a bisimulation based conformance. It is clear that as soon as we allow extraneous actions in an admissible implementation then there exists a malicious context that would not preserve that conformance relation, and then the only preorder stronger than it being a precongruence would be weak bisimulation, that does not allow the introduction of any extraneous actions with respect to the given specification.

Therefore such a characterisation of the family of contexts preserving each individual pair in the conformance relation is the best result that we can expect in this direction.

In order to get a clearer exposition, and simpler proofs, we have not considered either recursive agents or contexts containing recursive components (without hole variables involved), but it would not be difficult to extend our results to cover also these recursive sceneries. Instead, we think it would be more complicated to extend the results to cover the case in which it is the recursive construction itself that we want to preserve the conformance relation. In such a case, it is necessary to decide how the conformance relation should be extended to the case in which we have higher order agents where the free variables are introduced to be instantiated by first order agents. This question is far from being simple, as studied in detail in [Ren00].

In [BdFMM00] it is shown that tile bisimulation, where weak bisimulation is extended to contextualized processes in a very algebraic way, is not always a congruence, and it is also discussed under which conditions it is possible to get the preservation of that relation. We are interested on a more thorough study of the relations between our paper and this mentioned work.

Besides, [dFLN99] studied several notions of global bisimulation, where weak bisimulation is relaxed by allowing more flexible moves when playing the bisimulation game. Again, there were problems when trying to get a congruence, and therefore it would be also interesting to compare that work with the results and ideas in the current paper.

Also into the testing based conformances, the problem of getting precongruences should be more intensively studied, as appointed in [Led91, dFLN97]. The relations between testing based and bisimulation based conformances deserves, in our opinion, a deeper study, not only in the [Abr87] style, where the testing semantics is presented as a bisimulation semantics, but also on the opposite way, as in [dFLN99], where bisimulation semantics are presented as testing semantics.

References

[Abr87]   Samson Abramsky. Observational equivalence as a testing equivalence. *Theoretical Computer Science*, 53(3):225–241, 1987.

[BdFMM00]   Roberto Bruni, David de Frutos-Escrig, Narciso Martí-Oliet, and Ugo Montanari. Bisimilarity congruences for open terms and term graphs via tile logic. In *CONCUR*, volume 1877 of *Lecture Notes in Computer Science*, pages 259–274. Springer, 2000.

[Bri88]   E. Brinksma. A theory for the derivation of tests. In *Protocol Specification, Testing and Verification VIII*, pages 63–74. North Holland, 1988.

[BS02]   Ronald W. Brower and Kenneth S. Stevens. Congruent weak conformance, a partial order among processes. In *Formal Techniques for Networked and Distributed Systems-FORTE 2002*, volume 2529 of *Lecture Notes in Computer Science*, pages 34–49. Springer, 2002.

[BSS86]   E. Brinksma, G. Scollo, and C. Steenbergen. LOTOS specifications, their implementations and their tests. In *Protocol Specification, Testing and Verification VI*, pages 349–360. North Holland, 1986.

[dFLN97]   D. de Frutos-Escrig, L.F. Llana-Díaz, and M. Núñez. Friendly testing as a conformance relation. In *Formal Description Techniques and Protocol Specification, Testing, and Verification FORTE X/ PSTV XVII*, pages 283–298. Chapman & Hall, 1997.

[dFLN98]   D. de Frutos-Escrig, L.F. Llana-Díaz, and M. Núñez. An invitation to friendly testing. *Journal of Computer Science and Technology*, 13(6):531–545, 1998.

[dFLN99]   David de Frutos-Escrig, Natalia López, and Manuel Núñez. Global timed bisimulation: An introduction. In *Formal Methods for Protocol Engineering and Distributed Systems, FORTE XII / PSTV XIX*, pages 401–416. Kluwer Academic Publishers, 1999.

[Hen88]   Matthew Hennessy. *Algebraic Theory of Processes*. MIT Press, 1988.

[Hoa85]   C.A.R. Hoare. *Communicating Sequential Processes*. Prentice Hall, 1985.

[Led91]   G. Leduc. Conformance relation, associated equivalence, and minimum canonical tester in LOTOS. In *Protocol Specification, Testing and Verification XI*, pages 249–264. North Holland, 1991.

[Led92]   G. Leduc. A framework based on implementation relations for implementing LOTOS specifications. *Computer Networks and ISDN Systems*, 25(1):23–41, 1992.

[Mil80]   Robin Milner. *A Calculus of Communicating Systems*. LNCS 92. Springer, 1980.

[Mil89]   Robin Milner. *Communication and Concurrency*. Prentice Hall, 1989.

[Ren00]   Arend Rensink. Bisimilarity of open terms. *Information and Computation*, 156(1–2):345–385, 2000.

[Ste94]   Kenneth S. Stevens. *Practical Verification and Synthesis of Low Latency Asynchronous Systems*. PhD thesis, University of Calgary, 1994.

Testing of Symbolic-Probabilistic Systems*

Natalia López, Manuel Núñez, and Ismael Rodríguez

Dept. Sistemas Informáticos y Programación,
Facultad de Informática,
Universidad Complutense de Madrid,
E-28040 Madrid, Spain
{natalia, mn, isrodrig}@sip.ucm.es

Abstract. In this paper we consider the testing of systems where probabilistic information is not given by means of fixed values but as sets of probabilities. We will use an extension of finite state machine where choices among transitions labeled by the same input are probabilistically resolved. We will introduce our notion of test and we will define how tests are applied to the implementation under test (IUT). We will also present an implementation relation to assess the conformance, *up to* a level of confidence, of an implementation to a specification. In order to define this relation we will take finite *samples* of executions of the implementation and compare them with the probabilistic constraints imposed by the specification. Finally, we will give an algorithm for deriving sound and complete test suites with respect to this implementation relation.

1 Introduction

Formal methods try to keep a balanced trade-off between expressivity of the considered language and complexity of the underlying semantic framework. In the beginning they mainly concentrated on the functional behavior of systems, that is, on what a system could/should do. In this regard, and considering specification formalism, we may mention the (original) notions of process algebras, Petri nets, and Moore/Mealy machines among others. Once the roots were well consolidated other considerations were taken into account. The next step was to deal with quantitative information such as the *time* underlying the performance of the system or the *probabilities* resolving the choices that a system may undertake. These characteristics gave raise to new models where time and/or probabilities were included (for example, [20, 16, 12, 10, 1, 4, 13] among many others).

Usually, probabilistic extensions incorporate probabilistic information by using fixed values, that is, we may have conditions such as "the probability of such an event to happen is $\frac{1}{3}$." In this paper we will consider the testing of

---
* Work supported by the Spanish MCyT project *MASTER* (TIC2003-07848-C02-01), the Junta de Castilla-La Mancha project *DISMEF* (PAC-03-001), and the Marie Curie project *TAROT* (MRTN-CT-2003-505121).

J. Grabowski and B. Nielsen (Eds.): FATES 2004, LNCS 3395, pp. 49–63, 2005.

systems presenting a more relaxed kind of probabilistic constraints. For example, we may deal with expressions such as "the probability of such an event to happen belongs to the interval $[\frac{1}{3}, \frac{2}{3})$." In fact, there are situations where it is rather difficult to be precise when specifying a probability. A very good example is the specification of *faulty channels* (e.g. the classical ABP [2]). Usually, these protocols contain information such as "the probability of losing the message is equal to 0.05." However, in most situations it would be more appropriate to say "the probability of losing the message is smaller that 0.05."

In order to specify probabilistic systems dealing with this kind of probabilities, that we call *symbolic probabilities*, we will consider the probabilistic extension of finite state machines recently introduced in [14]. Our probabilistic systems will be defined by using transitions such as $s \xrightarrow{i/o}_{\bar{p}} s'$. Intuitively, such a transition indicates that if the machine is in a state s and receives an input i then it will produce an output o and it will change its state to s'. Besides, the probability with which the previous sequence of events is performed belongs to the range given by $\bar{p}$. Let us remark that probabilistic information will not be the same for specifications and implementations. In the former case we might allow the specifier to use symbolic probabilities. In contrast, implementations will have fixed probabilities governing their behavior. For example, we may specify a *not-very-unfair coin* as a coin such that the probability of obtaining tails belongs to the interval $[0.4, 0.6]$ (and the same for faces). Given a *real* coin (i.e. an implementation) the probability p_t of obtaining tails (resp. p_f for faces) will be a fixed number (possibly unknown, but fixed). If $p_t, p_f \in [0.4, 0.6]$ then we will consider that the implementation conforms to the specification.

An important issue when dealing with probabilities consists in fixing how different actions/transitions are related according to the probabilistic information. In this paper we consider a variant of the *reactive* interpretation of probabilities (see for example [12]). Intuitively, a reactive interpretation imposes a probabilistic relation among transitions labeled by the same action, but without quantifying choices between different actions. Our probabilistic finite state machines express probabilistic relations between transitions outgoing from a given state and having the same input action (while the output action may vary). For example, let us suppose that the unique transitions from a state s are

$$t_1 = s \xrightarrow{i_1/o_1}_{\bar{p}_1} s_1 \qquad t_2 = s \xrightarrow{i_1/o_2}_{\bar{p}_2} s_2 \qquad t_3 = s \xrightarrow{i_1/o_3}_{\bar{p}_3} s_2$$
$$t_4 = s \xrightarrow{i_2/o_1}_{\bar{p}_4} s_3 \qquad t_5 = s \xrightarrow{i_2/o_3}_{\bar{p}_5} s_1$$

If the environment (in our case, if the test) offers the input action i_1 then the choice between t_1, t_2, and t_3 will be resolved according to some probabilities fulfilling the conditions $\bar{p}_1$, $\bar{p}_2$, and $\bar{p}_3$. All we know about these values is that they fulfill the imposed restrictions, that they are non-negative, and that the sum of them equals 1. Something similar happens for the transitions t_4 and t_5. However, there does not exist any probabilistic relation between transitions labeled with different input actions (e.g. t_1 and t_4).

We follow a black-box testing approach (see e.g. [15, 3]), that is, if we apply an input to an IUT then we will observe an output and we may continue the testing procedure according to this result. However, we will not be able to *see* the probabilities that the IUT has assigned to each of the choices. Thus, even though implementations will behave according to fixed probabilities we will not be able to *read* their values. In order to compute the probabilities associated with each choice of the implementation we will apply the same test several times and analyze the obtained responses. The set of tests used to check the suitability of an implementation will be constructed from the given specification. By collecting the observations and comparing them with the symbolic probabilities of the specification, we will be able to assess the validity of the IUT. This comparison will be performed by using *hypothesis contrasts*. Hypothesis contrasts allow to (probabilistically) decide whether an observed sample follows the pattern given by a random variable. For example, even if we do not know the exact probabilities governing a *coin under test*, if we toss the coin 1000 times and we get 502 faces and 498 tails then we can infer, with a big probability, that the coin conforms with the specification of *not-very-unfair coin*.

There is already significant work on testing preorders and equivalences for probabilistic processes [6, 26, 18, 22, 7, 5, 17]. However, most of these proposals follow the *de Nicola and Hennessy's style* [9, 11], that is, the interaction between tests and processes is given by their concurrent execution, synchronizing on a set of actions. For example, we may say that two processes are *equivalent* if for any test T, out of a set of tests $\mathcal{T}$, the application of T to each of the processes returns an *equivalent* result. These frameworks are not very related to ours since our main task is to determine whether an implementation conforms to a specification. Even though some of the aforementioned preorders can be used for this purpose, our approach is more based on *pushing buttons*: The test applies an input to the IUT and we check whether the returned output is expected by the specification. Moreover, none of these papers use the kind of *statistical testing* that we use: Apply the same test several times and extract conclusions about the probabilities governing the implementation. In this sense, the work closest to this paper is reported in [23, 19]. In fact, we take the statistical machinery from [19], where a testing framework to deal with systems presenting time information given by stochastic time is introduced. In [23] the authors present a testing scenario for a notion of probabilistic automata. In order to replicate the same experiment several times they introduce a *reset* button. Since this button is the only way to influence the behavior of the IUT, they can capture only trace-like semantics. Actually, their equivalence coincides with a certain notion of trace distribution equivalence. Finally, it is worth to mention that all of the previous approaches use fixed probabilities. In contrast, our testing framework is developed on top of the symbolic probabilities framework introduced in [14].

The rest of the paper is organized as follows. In Section 2 we review our notion of probabilistic finite state machine. In Section 3 we present the notion of test and define how they are applied to implementations. In Section 4 we introduce an implementation relation based on samples. Hypothesis contrasts are used to assess whether the behavior of an implementation corresponds, *up to* a certain confidence, to the probabilistic behavior defined in the specification. In Section 5 we present an algorithm to derive sound and complete test suites. In Section 6 we present our conclusions and lines for future work. In the appendix we give some basic statistical concepts that are (abstractly) used along the paper.

2   Probabilistic Finite State Machines

As we have mentioned, probabilistic information is included in our probabilistic state machines by using certain constraints on the considered probabilities. By taking into account the inherent nature of probabilities, we consider that a *symbolic probability* is any non-empty (open or closed) interval contained in $(0, 1]$.

Definition 1. We define the set of *symbolic probabilities*, denoted by simbP, as the following set of intervals

$$\text{simbP} = \left\{ \$p_1, p_2 \& \left| \begin{array}{l} p_1, p_2 \in [0,1] \ \wedge \ p_1 \leq p_2 \ \wedge \ \$ \in \{ (, [\} \ \wedge \ \& \in \{),] \} \wedge \\ 0 \notin \$p_1, p_2 \& \ \wedge \ \$p_1, p_2 \& \neq \emptyset \end{array} \right. \right\}$$

If we have a symbolic probability as $[p, p]$, with $0 < p \leq 1$, we simply write p.

Let $\bar{p}_1, \ldots, \bar{p}_n \in \text{simbP}$ be symbolic probabilities such that for any $1 \leq i \leq n$ we have $\bar{p}_i = \$_i p_i, q_i \&_i$, with $\$_i \in \{ (, [\}$ and $\&_i \in \{),] \}$. We define the *product* of $\bar{p}_1, \ldots, \bar{p}_n$, denoted by $\prod \bar{p}_i$, (respectively the *addition* of $\bar{p}_1, \ldots, \bar{p}_n$, denoted by $\sum \bar{p}_i$) as the symbolic probability $\$ \prod p_i, \prod q_i \&$ (respectively $\$ \sum p_i, \sum q_i \&$). The limits of the interval are defined in both cases as:

$$\$ = \begin{cases} (& \text{if } \exists 1 \leq i \leq n : \$_i = (\\ [& \text{otherwise} \end{cases} \qquad \& = \begin{cases}) & \text{if } \exists 1 \leq i \leq n : \&_i =) \\ ] & \text{otherwise} \end{cases}$$

□

We do not allow transitions with probability 0 because, in addition to probabilities, we would have to deal with priorities. This fact strongly complicates the model (in [8] different approaches for introducing priorities are reviewed).

Definition 2. A *Probabilistic Finite State Machine*, in short PFSM, is a tuple $M = (S, I, O, \delta, s_0)$ where S is the set of states, I and O denote the sets of input and output actions, respectively, $\delta \subseteq S \times I \times O \times \text{simbP} \times S$ is the set of transitions, and s_0 is the initial state. Each transition belonging to δ is a tuple $(s, i, o, \bar{p}, s')$ where $s, s' \in S$ are the initial and final states, $i \in I$ is an input action, $o \in O$ is an output action, and $\bar{p} \in \text{simbP}$ is the symbolic probability associated with the transition. We will usually denote transitions as $(s, i, o, \bar{p}, s')$ by $s \xrightarrow{i/o}_{\bar{p}} s'$. Besides, we consider that for any $s \in S$, $i \in I$, and the set $\alpha_{s,i} = \{ t \mid \exists o \in O, \bar{p} \in \text{simbP}, s' \in S : t = (s, i, o, \bar{p}, s') \in \delta \}$ the following two conditions hold:

- If $| \alpha_{s,i} | > 1$ then for any $s \xrightarrow{i/o}_{\bar{p}} s' \in \alpha_{s,i}$ we have that $1 \notin \bar{p}$.
- $1 \in \sum \{ \bar{p} \mid \exists o \in O, s' \in S : s \xrightarrow{i/o}_{\bar{p}} s' \in \alpha_{s,i} \}$.

□

Let us comment the restrictions introduced at the end of the previous definition. The first constraint indicates that a symbolic probability such as $\overline{p} = \$p, 1]$ can appear in a transition $s \xrightarrow{i/o}_{\overline{p}} s' \in \delta$ only if it is the unique transition for s and i. Let us note that if there would exist two different transitions $s \xrightarrow{i/o}_{\overline{p}} s', s \xrightarrow{i/o'}_{\overline{p}'} s'' \in \delta$ and the probability of one of them (say $\overline{p}$) included 1, then the probability associated to the other transition ($\overline{p}'$) could be 0, which is forbidden. Regarding the second condition, since the *real* probabilities for each state $s \in S$ and for each input $i \in I$ should add up to 1, we require that 1 is within the lower and upper bounds of the associated symbolic probabilities.

Next we define some additional conditions that we will sometimes impose on our finite state machines.

Definition 3. Let $M = (S, I, O, \delta, s_0)$ be a PFSM. We say that M is *input-enabled* if for any $s \in S$ and $i \in I$ there exist $s' \in S$, $o \in O$, and $\overline{p} \in$ simbP such that $(s, i, o, \overline{p}, s') \in \delta$. We say that M is *deterministically observable* if for any $s \in S$, $i \in I$, and $o \in O$ there do not exist two different transitions $(s, i, o, \overline{p}_1, s_1), (s, i, o, \overline{p}_2, s_2) \in \delta$. $\square$

The notion of deterministically observable is different from the more restricted notion of deterministic finite state machine. In particular, we allow transitions from the same state labeled by the same input action, as long as the outputs are different. During the rest of the paper we will consider that specifications and implementations are given by deterministically observable PFSMs. Moreover, we will assume that PFSMs representing implementations are input-enabled. The idea is that an implementation should not be able to refuse an input provided by a test.

In the next definition we introduce the notion of (probabilistic) trace. The probability of a trace will be obtained by multiplying the probabilities of all transitions involved in the trace.

Definition 4. Let $M = (S, I, O, \delta, s_0)$ be a PFSM. We write the *generalized* transition $s \xRightarrow{(i_1/o_1, \ldots, i_n/o_n)}_{\overline{p}} s'$ if there exist $s_1, \ldots, s_{n-1} \in S, \overline{p}_1, \ldots, \overline{p}_n \in$ simbP such that $s \xrightarrow{i_1/o_1}_{\overline{p}_1} s_1 \xrightarrow{i_2/o_2}_{\overline{p}_2} s_2 \cdots s_{n-1} \xrightarrow{i_n/o_n}_{\overline{p}_n} s'$ and $\overline{p} = \prod \overline{p}_i$.

We say that $\rho = (i_1/o_1, \ldots, i_n/o_n)$ is a *non-probabilistic trace*, or simply a *trace*, of M if there exist $s' \in S$ and $\overline{p} \in$ simbP such that $s_0 \xRightarrow{\rho}_{\overline{p}} s'$.

Let $\rho = (i_1/o_1, \ldots, i_n/o_n)$ and $\overline{p} \in$ simbP. We say that $\overline{\rho} = (\rho, \overline{p})$ is a *probabilistic trace* of M if there exists $s' \in S$ such that $s_0 \xRightarrow{\rho}_{\overline{p}} s'$.

We denote by $\texttt{Traces}(M)$ and $\texttt{pTraces}(M)$ the sets of non-probabilistic and probabilistic traces of M, respectively. $\square$

We conclude this section by introducing notations related to hypothesis contrasts (an operational definition of these concepts will be given in the appendix of this paper). We call *event* any reaction we can detect from a system or environment. A *sample* contains information about the number of times we have detected each event along a set of observations. Besides, we associate a random variable with each set of events. Its purpose is to provide the theoretical (*a priori*) probability of each event in the set. In our framework, these random variables will be inferred from the PFSMs denoting the (ideal) probabilistic behavior of systems, while the samples will be collected by interacting with the implementation under test. We will consider a variant of random variables allowing to deal with *symbolic* probabilities, as our PFSMs do.

Definition 5. Let $A = \{a_1, \ldots, a_n\}$ be a set of *events*. A *sample* of A is a set $J = \{(a_1, m_1), \ldots, (a_n, m_n)\}$ where for any $1 \leq i \leq n$ we have that m_i represents the number of times that we have observed the event α_i.

We say that a function $\xi : A \rightarrow \texttt{simbP}$ is a *symbolic random variable* for the set of events A if $1 \in \sum_{a \in A} \xi(a)$. We denote the set of symbolic random variables for the set of events A by $\mathcal{RV}(A)$. We denote the set of symbolic random variables for any set of events by $\mathcal{RV}$.

Given the symbolic random variable ξ and the sample J we denote the *confidence* of ξ on J by $\gamma(\xi, J)$.   □

We assume that $\gamma(\xi, J)$ takes values in the interval $[0, 1]$. Intuitively, bigger values of $\gamma(\xi, J)$ denote that the observed sample J is more likely to be produced by the symbolic random variable ξ. There exist several hypothesis contrasts to compute these confidence levels. In the appendix of this paper we show one of them to indicate how the notion of confidence may be formally defined.

In the next definition we particularize the previous notions in the context of our framework. Given a sequence of inputs we consider the sequence of input/outputs that the system can return. Hence, the set of events are those sequences of outputs that could be produced in response. The random variable to denote the theoretical probability of each event is computed by considering the symbolic probability of the corresponding trace in the specification.

Definition 6. Let $M = (S, I, O, \delta, s_0)$ be a PFSM and $\pi = (i_1, \ldots, i_n)$ be a sequence of inputs. The *set of trace events* associated to M with respect to π, denoted by $\texttt{TraceEvents}(M, \pi)$, is defined as

$$\texttt{TraceEvents}(M, \pi) = \big\{(o_1, \ldots, o_n) \,\big|\, (i_1/o_1, \ldots, i_n/o_n) \in \texttt{Traces}(M)\big\}$$

The *symbolic random variable* associated to the sequence π, denoted by ξ_M^π, is defined in such a way that for any $(o_1, \ldots, o_n) \in \texttt{TraceEvents}(M, \pi)$ we have $\xi_M^\pi(o_1, \ldots, o_n) = \overline{p}$, being $((i_1/o_1, \ldots, i_n/o_n), \overline{p}) \in \texttt{pTraces}(M)$.   □

3   Testing Probabilistic Systems

In this section we introduce the notion of test and we present how they are applied to implementations. In our context, to test an IUT consists in applying a sequence of inputs to the IUT. Once an output is received we check whether it is an expected one or not. In the former case, either a pass signal is emitted (indicating successful termination) or the testing process continues by applying another input. In the latter case, a fail signal is produced, the testing process stops, and we conclude that the implementation does not conform to the specification. The methodology to *guess* the probabilities associated with each bundle associated with an input action in the implementation consists in applying several times the same test.

If we are testing an IUT with input and output sets I and O, respectively, tests are deterministic acyclic I/O labeled transition systems (i.e. trees) with a strict alternation between an input action and the whole set of output actions. A branch labeled by an output action can be followed by a leaf or by another input action. Moreover, leaves of the tree represent either *successful* or *failure* states. In addition, successful states will have a symbolic random variable associated with them. This random variable will denote the *probabilistic constraint* imposed in the test for the trace leading to that state. Basically, a hypothesis contrast will compare the samples collected for that event with the probabilistic constraint imposed by the test.

Definition 7. A *test* is a tuple $T = (S, I, O, \delta, s_0, S_I, S_O, S_F, S_P, \zeta)$ where S is the set of states, I and O, with $I \cap O = \emptyset$, are the sets of input and output actions, respectively, $\delta \subseteq S \times I \cup O \times S$ is the transition relation, $s_0 \in S$ is the initial state, and the sets $S_I, S_O, S_F, S_P \subseteq S$ are a partition of S. The transition relation and the sets of states fulfill the following conditions:

- S_I is the set of *input* states. We have that $s_0 \in S_I$. For any input state $s \in S_I$ there exists a unique outgoing transition $(s, i, s') \in \delta$. For this transition we have that $i \in I$ and $s' \in S_O$.
- S_O is the set of *output* states. For any output state $s \in S_O$ we have that for any $o \in O$ there exists a unique state $s' \in S$ such that $(s, o, s') \in \delta$; in each case, $s' \notin S_O$. Moreover, there do not exist $i \in I$ and $s' \in S$ such that $(s, i, s') \in \delta$.
- S_F and S_P are the sets of *fail* and *pass* states, respectively. We say that these states are *terminal*. That is, for any state $s \in S_F \cup S_P$ we have that there do not exist $a \in I \cup O$ and $s' \in S$ such that $(s, a, s') \in \delta$.

Finally, $\zeta : S_P \longrightarrow \mathcal{RV}$ is a function associating passing states with (symbolic) random variables.

We say that the test T is *valid* if the graph induced by T is a tree with root at its initial state s_0. □

Next we define the set of traces that a test can perform. These traces are sequences of input/output actions reaching terminal states. Depending on the final state we will classify them as either *successful* or *failure* traces.

Definition 8. Let $\rho = (i_1/o_1, \ldots, i_r/o_r)$ be a sequence of input/output actions, $T = (S, I, O, \delta, s_0, S_I, S_O, S_F, S_P, \zeta)$ be a test, and $s \in S$. We say that ρ is a *trace of T reaching s*, denoted by $T \stackrel{\rho}{\Longrightarrow} s$, if $s \in S_F \cup S_P$ and there exist states $s_{12}, s_{21}, s_{22}, \ldots s_{r1}, s_{r2} \in S$ such that $\{(s_0, i_1, s_{12}), (s_{r2}, o_r, s)\} \subseteq \delta$, and for any $2 \leq j \leq r$ we have $(s_{j1}, i_j, s_{j2}) \in \delta$ and $(s_{(j-1)2}, o_{j-1}, s_{j1}) \in \delta$. □

The next definition presents some auxiliary predicates that we will use during the rest of the paper. While the first two notions are easy to understand, the last one needs some additional explanation. Given a trace ρ and a set H of pairs (trace, natural number), $\mathtt{IPrefix}(H, \rho)$ is another set of pairs including all traces such that its sequence of input actions matches that of ρ. The number attached to each trace corresponds with the number of traces belonging to H *beginning* with that trace. Given a sample of executions from an implementation, we will use this function to compute the number of times that the implementation has performed each sequence of outputs in response to some sequence of inputs. Let us note that if we observe that the sequence of outputs $(o_1, \ldots, o_n)$ has been produced in response to the sequence of inputs $(i_1, \ldots, i_n)$ then, for any $j \leq n$, we know that the sequence of outputs $(o_1, \ldots, o_j)$ has been produced in response to $(i_1, \ldots, i_j)$. Hence, the observation of a trace is useful to compute the number of instances of its prefixes.

Definition 9. Let $\sigma = (u_1, \ldots, u_n)$ and $\sigma' = (u'_1, \ldots, u'_m)$ be two sequences. We say that σ is *a prefix of* σ', denoted by $\mathtt{Prefix}(\sigma, \sigma')$, if $n < m$ and for any $1 \leq i \leq n$ we have $u_i = u'_i$.

Let $\rho = (i_1/o_1, \ldots, i_m/o_m)$ be a sequence of input/output actions. We define the *input actions of the sequence* ρ, denoted by $\mathtt{inputs}(\rho)$, as the sequence $(i_1, \ldots, i_m)$, and the *output actions of the sequence* ρ, denoted by $\mathtt{outputs}(\rho)$, as the sequence $(o_1, \ldots, o_m)$.

Let $H = \{(\rho_1, r_1), \ldots, (\rho_m, r_m)\}$ be a set of pairs (trace, natural number) and $\rho = (i_1/o_1, \ldots, i_n/o_n)$ be a trace. The *set of input prefixes* of ρ in H, denoted by $\mathtt{IPrefix}(H, \rho)$, is defined as

$$\mathtt{IPrefix}(H, \rho) = \left\{ (\rho', r') \;\middle|\; \begin{array}{l} \mathtt{inputs}(\rho) = \mathtt{inputs}(\rho') \wedge r' > 0 \wedge \\ r' = \sum\!\{\!| r'' \mid (\rho'', r'') \in H \wedge \mathtt{Prefix}(\rho', \rho'') |\!\} \end{array} \right\}$$

$\square$

In the previous definition the delimiters $\{\!|$ and $|\!\}$ are used to denote multisets. Next we present the notions that we will use to denote that a given event has been detected in an IUT. We will also compute the sequences of actions that the implementation performs when a test is applied.

Definition 10. Let $\mathcal{I} = (S, I, O, \delta, s_0)$ be a PFSM representing an IUT. We say that $(i_1/o_1, \ldots, i_n/o_n)$ is an *execution* of $\mathcal{I}$ if the sequence $(i_1/o_1, \ldots, i_n/o_n)$ can be performed by $\mathcal{I}$.

Let $\rho_1, \ldots, \rho_n$ be executions of $\mathcal{I}$ and $r_1, \ldots, r_n \in \mathbf{N}$. We say that the set $H = \{(\rho_1, r_1), \ldots, (\rho_n, r_n)\}$ is an *execution sample* of $\mathcal{I}$.

Let $T = (S', I, O, \delta', s'_0, S_I, S_O, S_F, S_P, \zeta)$ be a valid test. We say that $H = \{(\rho_1, r_1), \ldots, (\rho_n, r_n)\}$ is an *execution sample of* $\mathcal{I}$ *under a test* T if H is an execution sample and for any $(\rho, r) \in H$ we have that $T \stackrel{\rho}{\Longrightarrow} s$, with $s \in S'$.

Let $\Omega = \{T_1, \ldots, T_n\}$ be a test suite and $H_1, \ldots, H_n$ be execution samples of $\mathcal{I}$ under T_i. We say that $H = \{(\rho_1, r_1), \ldots, (\rho_n, r_n)\}$ is an *execution sample of* $\mathcal{I}$ *under* Ω if for any $(\rho, r) \in H$ we have $r = \sum\!\{\!| r' \mid 1 \leq i \leq n \wedge (\rho, r') \in H_i |\!\}$. $\square$

In the definition of execution sample under a test we have that each number r, with $(\rho, r) \in H$, denotes the number of times we have observed the execution ρ in $\mathcal{I}$ under the (repeated) application of T.

Now we present the conditions required to *pass* a test. Passing a test consists in fulfilling two different constraints. First, we require that the test never reaches a failure state as a result of its interaction with the implementation. This condition concerns what is *possible*. Second, we require that the random variables attached to successful states conform to the samples collected during the (repeated) application of the test to the IUT. This condition concerns what is *probable*. We will consider that the set of executions analyzed to pass a test does not only include those executions obtained by applying that test, but also the executions obtained by applying other tests. Let us remark that the very same traces that are available in a test could be part of other tests as well. Let us also note that the validity of any hypothesis contrast improves with the number of samples. Hence, it would not be efficient to apply each hypothesis contrast to the *limited* collection of samples obtained by a single test. On the contrary, samples collected by different tests will be shared so that our statistical information grows and the hypothesis contrast procedure improves. Let us note that this testing methodology is opposite to usual techniques where the application of each test is independent from other tests.

Definition 11. Let $H = \{(\rho_1, r_1), \ldots, (\rho_n, r_n)\}$ be an execution sample of $\mathcal{I}$ under the test suite $\Omega = \{T_1, \ldots, T_n\}$ and let $0 \le \alpha \le 1$. Let us consider $T \in \Omega$. We say that the implementation $\mathcal{I}$ $(\alpha, H)-passes$ the test T if for any trace $\rho \in \mathtt{Traces}(\mathcal{I})$, with $T \overset{\rho}{\Longrightarrow} s$, we have that $s \notin S_F$ and if $s \in S_P$ then $\gamma(\zeta(s), R) > \alpha$, where

$$R = \{(\mathtt{outputs}(\rho'), r) \mid (\rho', r) \in \mathtt{IPrefix}(H, \rho)\}$$

We say that $\mathcal{I}$ $(\alpha, H)-passes$ the test suite Ω if $\mathcal{I}$ $(\alpha, H)-passes$ T_i, for any $1 \le i \le n$. $\qquad\square$

4   Implementation Relation Based on Samples

In this section we introduce an implementation relation that take into account the practical limitations to collect probabilistic information from an implementation. This relation allows us to claim the accurateness of the probabilistic behavior of an implementation with respect to a specification *up to* a given confidence level. Given a set of execution samples, we will apply a hypothesis contrast to check whether the probabilistic choices taken by the implementation follow the patterns given by the specification.

Our implementation relation follows the classical pattern of formal conformance relations defined in systems distinguishing between inputs and outputs (see e.g. [24, 25]). That is, an IUT conforms to a specification $\mathcal{S}$ if for any possible evolution of $\mathcal{S}$ the outputs that the IUT may perform after a given input are a subset of those for the specification. Let us remark that this constraint could be rewritten in probabilistic terms: The confidence we have on the fact that the implementation will not perform forbidden behaviors is 1 (i.e. *complete*). However, since no hypothesis contrast can provide full confidence, it is preferable to keep the constraints over actions separated from the probabilistic constraints and deal with them in the classic way, that is, an implementation is incorrect with respect to forbidden behavior if such a behavior is detected. Let us remind that the reverse is not true: We cannot claim that the implementation is correct even if no forbidden behavior is detected after a finite number of interactions with it.

Definition 12. Let S and $\mathcal{I}$ be PFSMs. We say that $\mathcal{I}$ *non-probabilistically conforms* to S, denoted by $\mathcal{I} \operatorname{conf} S$, if for any $\rho = (i_1/o_1, \ldots, i_n/o_n) \in \mathtt{Traces}(S)$, with $n \geq 1$, we have

$$\rho' = (i_1/o_1, \ldots, i_{n-1}/o_{n-1}, i_n/o'_n) \in \mathtt{Traces}(\mathcal{I}) \text{ implies } \rho' \in \mathtt{Traces}(S)$$

□

Let us note that the relation $\mathtt{conf}$ does not coincide with trace inclusion. For example, an implementation may be able to perform a trace $(i_1/o_1, \ldots, i_n/o_n)$ that the specification is not as long as the corresponding (sub-)sequence of inputs $(i_1, \ldots, i_n)$ cannot be performed by the specification. Regarding probabilistic constraints, we put together all the observations of the implementation. Then, the set of samples corresponding to each trace of the specification will be composed by taking all the observations such that the trace is a *prefix* of them. By doing so we will be able to compare the number of times the implementation has performed the chosen trace with the number of times the implementation has performed any other behavior. We will use hypothesis contrasts to decide whether the probabilistic choices of the implementation conform to the probabilistic constraints imposed by the specification. In particular, a hypothesis contrast will be applied to each sequence of inputs considered by the specification. This contrast will check whether the different sequences of outputs associated with these inputs are distributed according to the probability distribution of the random variable associated with that sequence of inputs in the specification.

Definition 13. Let S be a specification and $\mathcal{I}$ be an IUT. Let H be an execution sample and let $0 \leq \alpha \leq 1$. We say that $\mathcal{I}$ $(\alpha, H)-$*probabilistically conforms to* S, denoted by $\mathcal{I} \operatorname{confp}^{(\alpha, H)} S$, if $\mathcal{I} \operatorname{conf} S$ and for any $\rho \in \mathtt{Traces}(S)$ we have $\gamma(\xi_S^\pi, R) > \alpha$, where $\pi = \mathtt{inputs}(\rho)$ and

$$R = \{(\mathtt{outputs}(\rho'), r) \mid (\rho', r) \in \mathtt{IPrefix}(H, \rho)\}$$

□

In the previous relation ξ_S^π denotes the symbolic random variable associated with the sequence of input actions π for the PFSM S (see Definition 6). Besides, each trace observed in the implementation will add one instance to the accounting of its prefixes. We could consider an alternative procedure where traces are independently accounted and each observed trace does not affect the number of instances of other traces being prefix of it. However, as we already pointed out, this method would lose valuable information that might negatively affect the quality of the hypothesis contrasts.

5   Test Derivation

In this section we provide an algorithm to derive tests from specifications. In addition, we will show that the derived test suite is *complete* up to a given confidence α with respect to the conformance relation presented in Definition 13. As usually, the idea consists in traversing the specification to get all the possible traces in the adequate way. Thus, each test is generated so that it *focuses* on chasing a concrete trace of the specification. Besides, test cases contain probabilistic constraints so that they can detect faulty probabilistic behaviors in the IUT. First, we give some auxiliary functions.

Definition 14. Let $M = (S, I, O, \delta, s_0)$ be a PFSM. We define the set of possible outputs in state s after input i as $\text{out}(s, i) = \{o \,|\, \exists s' : (s, i, o, \overline{p}, s') \in \delta\}$. For any transition $(s, i, o, \overline{p}, s') \in \delta$ we write $\text{after}(s, i, o) = s'$.   □

Let us remark that, due to the assumption that PFSMs are deterministically observable, $\text{after}(s, i, o)$ is uniquely determined.

Our derivation algorithm is presented in Figure 1. By considering the possible choices we get a set of tests extracted from the specification M. We denote this set of tests by $\text{tests}(M)$. In this algorithm, the set of pending states S_{aux} keeps track of the states of the test whose definition has not been *finished* yet. A tuple $(s^M, s^T, \pi) \in S_{aux}$ indicates that the current state in the traversal of the specification is s^M, that the description of the state s^T of the test is not concluded yet, and that the sequence of inputs traversed from s_0 to s^T is π. The set S_{aux} initially contains a tuple with the initial states (of both specification and test) and an empty sequence. For each tuple in S_{aux} we may choose one possibility. It is important to remark that the second possibility is applied at most to one of the possible tuples (see side condition imposing that S_{aux} is a singleton). Thus, our derived tests are valid as introduced in Definition 7.

The first possibility simply indicates that the state of the test becomes a successful state. In this case, we attach a symbolic random variable to this state. This random variable must encode the probability distribution, according to the specification, for all possible traces having the sequence of inputs π.

The second possibility takes an input and generates a transition in the test labeled by this input. Then, the whole sets of outputs is considered. If the output is not expected by the specification then a transition leading to a failure state is created (see 2.(e) in Figure 1). This could be simulated by a single branch in the test, labeled by `else`, leading to a failure state (in the algorithm we suppose that *all* the possible outputs appear in the test). For the rest of outputs we create a transition with the corresponding output and add the appropriate tuple to the set S_{aux} (see 2.(f) in Figure 1).

Input: $M = (S, I, O, \delta, s_0)$.
Output: $T = (S', I, O, \delta', s'_0, S_I, S_O, S_F, S_P, \zeta)$.

Initialization:

- $S' := \{s'_0\}, \delta' := S_I := S_O := S_F := S_P := \emptyset$.
- $S_{aux} := \{(s_0, s'_0, (\ ))\}$.

Inductive Cases: Apply one of the following two possibilities until $S_{aux} = \emptyset$.

1. If $(s^M, s^T, \pi) \in S_{aux}$ then perform the following steps:
   (a) $S_{aux} := S_{aux} - \{(s^M, s^T, \pi)\}$.
   (b) $S_P := S_P \cup \{s^T\}$.
   (c) $\zeta(s^T) := \xi^\pi_M$.
2. If $S_{aux} = \{(s^M, s^T, \pi)\}$ is a singleton and there exists $i \in I$ such that
   $\text{out}(s^M, i) \neq \emptyset$ then perform the following steps:
   (a) $S_{aux} := \emptyset$.
   (b) Choose i such that $\text{out}(s^M, i) \neq \emptyset$.
   (c) Create a fresh state $s' \notin S'$ and perform $S' := S' \cup \{s'\}$.
   (d) $S_I := S_I \cup \{s^T\}$; $S_O := S_O \cup \{s'\}$; $\delta' := \delta' \cup \{(s^T, i, s')\}$.
   (e) For each $o \notin \text{out}(s^M, i)$ do
       - Create a fresh state $s'' \notin S'$ and perform $S' := S' \cup \{s''\}$.
       - $S_F := S_F \cup \{s''\}$; $\delta' := \delta' \cup \{(s', o, s'')\}$.
   (f) For each $o \in \text{out}(s^M, i)$ do
       - Create a fresh state $s'' \notin S'$ and perform $S' := S' \cup \{s''\}$.
       - $\delta' := \delta' \cup \{(s', o, s'')\}$.
       - $s^M_1 := \text{after}(s^M, i, o)$.
       - Let $(s^M, i, o, \bar{p}, s^M_1) \in \delta$. $S_{aux} := S_{aux} \cup \{(s^M_1, s'', \pi \circ i)\}$.

Fig. 1. Test Derivation Algorithm

Let us remark that our derivation algorithm returns only finite test cases. We consider that tests are constructed by running the algorithm a finite number of times. Thus, the definition of a test finishes by considering a step where the second inductive case is not applied.

The next results states that for a specification $\mathcal{S}$, the test suite $\text{tests}(\mathcal{S})$ can be used to distinguish those (and only those) implementations conforming with respect to confp. We cannot properly say that the test suite is complete since both passing tests and the considered implementation relation have a probabilistic component. So, we may say *completeness* up to a certain confidence level. The proof of the *non-probabilistic* part of the result is strongly based on that for ioco [24]. The proof of the *probabilistic* component follows the scheme introduced for the relation confs [19] (a complete proof can be found in [21]).

Proposition 1. Let $\mathcal{I}$ and $\mathcal{S}$ be PFSMs. For any $0 \leq \alpha \leq 1$ and execution sample H we have $\mathcal{I} \ \text{confp}^{(\alpha, H)} \ \mathcal{S}$ iff $\mathcal{I} \ (\alpha, H)-passes \ \text{tests}(\mathcal{S})$. $\qquad\square$

6   Conclusions and Future Work

We have presented a testing methodology to check whether an implementation properly follows the behavior described by a given specification. The particularity of our framework is that specifications can explicitly express the desired *propensity* of each option in each non-deterministic choice of the system. This propensity is denoted in terms of probabilities. Moreover, in order to improve the expressivity of specifications, symbolic probabilities are introduced. These features increase the complexity of the testing methodology, as it is impossible to infer the actual probabilities associated with implementations from a set of interaction samples. In order to cope with this problem, hypothesis contrasts are used.

Even though we have used a specific model to represent systems, we think that our ideas and methodology can be applied to other formalisms. For example, it would be rather easy to introduce our symbolic probabilities in a framework of probabilistic automata as the ones used in [22, 23]. We also plan to study the integration of our framework within that presented in [19], where a testing methodology for stochastic timed processes is introduced. In this line we are already implementing a tool to apply both the testing framework presented in this paper and the one given in [19].

Acknowledgments. We would like to thank the anonymous reviewers of this paper for the careful reading and interesting suggestions.

References

1. J.C.M. Baeten and C.A. Middelburg. *Process algebra with timing*. EATCS Monograph. Springer, 2002.
2. K.A. Bartlett, R.A. Scantlebury, and P.T. Wilkinson. A note on reliable full-duplex transmission over half-duplex links. *Communications of the ACM*, 12(5):260–261, 1969.
3. B. Beizer. *Black Box Testing*. John Wiley and Sons, 1995.
4. M. Bravetti and A. Aldini. Discrete time generative-reactive probabilistic processes with different advancing speeds. *Theoretical Computer Science*, 290(1):355–406, 2003.
5. D. Cazorla, F. Cuartero, V. Valero, F.L. Pelayo, and J.J. Pardo. Algebraic theory of probabilistic and non-deterministic processes. *Journal of Logic and Algebraic Programming*, 55(1–2):57–103, 2003.
6. I. Christoff. Testing equivalences and fully abstract models for probabilistic processes. In *CONCUR'90, LNCS 458*, pages 126–140. Springer, 1990.
7. R. Cleaveland, Z. Dayar, S.A. Smolka, and S. Yuen. Testing preorders for probabilistic processes. *Information and Computation*, 154(2):93–148, 1999.
8. R. Cleaveland, G. Lüttgen, and V. Natarajan. Priority in process algebra. In J.A. Bergstra, A. Ponse, and S.A. Smolka, editors, *Handbook of process algebra*, chapter 12. North Holland, 2001.
9. R. de Nicola and M.C.B. Hennessy. Testing equivalences for processes. *Theoretical Computer Science*, 34:83–133, 1984.

10. R. van Glabbeek, S.A. Smolka, and B. Steffen. Reactive, generative and stratified models of probabilistic processes. *Information and Computation*, 121(1):59–80, 1995.
11. M. Hennessy. *Algebraic Theory of Processes*. MIT Press, 1988.
12. K. Larsen and A. Skou. Bisimulation through probabilistic testing. *Information and Computation*, 94(1):1–28, 1991.
13. N. López and M. Núñez. An overview of probabilistic process algebras and their equivalences. In *Validation of Stochastic Systems, LNCS 2925*, pages 89–123. Springer, 2004.
14. N. López, M. Núñez, and I. Rodríguez. Formal specification of symbolic-probabilistic systems. In *European Performance Engineering Workshop (EPEW'04), LNCS 3236*. Springer, 2004. In press.
15. G.J. Myers. *The Art of Software Testing*. John Wiley and Sons, 1979.
16. X. Nicollin and J. Sifakis. An overview and synthesis on timed process algebras. In *Computer Aided Verification'91, LNCS 575*, pages 376–398. Springer, 1991.
17. M. Núñez. Algebraic theory of probabilistic processes. *Journal of Logic and Algebraic Programming*, 56(1–2):117–177, 2003.
18. M. Núñez and D. de Frutos. Testing semantics for probabilistic LOTOS. In *Formal Description Techniques VIII*, pages 365–380. Chapman & Hall, 1995.
19. M. Núñez and I. Rodríguez. Towards testing stochastic timed systems. In *FORTE 2003, LNCS 2767*, pages 335–350. Springer, 2003.
20. G.M. Reed and A.W. Roscoe. A timed model for communicating sequential processes. *Theoretical Computer Science*, 58:249–261, 1988.
21. I. Rodríguez. *Especificación de sistemas concurrentes usando conceptos de teoría económica: Sintaxis, semántica, aplicaciones y extensiones del lenguaje formal PAMR*. PhD thesis, Universidad Complutense de Madrid, 2004.
22. R. Segala. Testing probabilistic automata. In *CONCUR'96, LNCS 1119*, pages 299–314. Springer, 1996.
23. M. Stoelinga and F. Vaandrager. A testing scenario for probabilistic automata. In *ICALP 2003, LNCS 2719*, pages 464–477. Springer, 2003.
24. J. Tretmans. Test generation with inputs, outputs and repetitive quiescence. *Software – Concepts and Tools*, 17(3):103–120, 1996.
25. J. Tretmans. Testing concurrent systems: A formal approach. In *CONCUR'99, LNCS 1664*, pages 46–65. Springer, 1999.
26. W. Yi and K.G. Larsen. Testing probabilistic and nondeterministic processes. In *Protocol Specification, Testing and Verification XII*, pages 47–61. North Holland, 1992.

Appendix. Statistics Background: Hypothesis Contrasts

In this appendix we introduce one of the standard ways to measure the confidence that a random variable has on a sample. In order to do so we will present a methodology to perform *hypothesis contrasts*. Intuitively, a sample will be *rejected* if the probability of observing that sample from a given random variable is low. We will present *Pearson's χ^2 contrast*. This contrast can be applied both to continuous and discrete random variables. The mechanism is the following. Once we have collected a sample of size n we perform the following steps:

- We split the sample into k classes covering all the possible range of values. We denote by O_i the *observed frequency* in class i (i.e. the number of elements belonging to the class i).

- We calculate, according to the proposed random variable, the probability p_i of each class i. We denote by E_i the *expected frequency* of class i, that is, $E_i = n \cdot p_i$.
- We calculate the *discrepancy* between observed and expected frequencies as $X^2 = \sum_{i=1}^{n} \frac{(O_i - E_i)^2}{E_i}$. When the model is correct, this discrepancy is approximately distributed as a random variable χ^2.
- The number of freedom degrees of χ^2 is $k - 1$.
- We will *accept* that the sample follows the proposed random variable if the probability to obtain a discrepancy greater than or equal to the detected discrepancy is high enough, that is, if $X^2 < \chi_\alpha^2(k-1)$ for some α high enough. Actually, as such margin to accept the sample decreases as α increases, we can obtain a measure of the validity of the sample as $\max\{\alpha | X^2 \le \chi_\alpha^2(k-1)\}$.

According to the previous steps, we can now give an operative definition of the function γ which has been presented before in Definition 5. Since we will use hypothesis contrasts to compare samples with *symbolic* random variables but the previous procedure refers to *standard* random variables, we must be carefull when applying the previous ideas in our framework. Let us note that symbolic random variables encapsulate a set of standard random variables. For instance, let us consider the set of events $\mathcal{A} = \{a, b\}$ and the symbolic random variable $\xi : \mathcal{A} \to \text{simbP}$ with $\xi(a) = \xi(b) = (\frac{1}{4}, \frac{3}{4})$. Then, a possible standard random variable fitting into ξ is $\xi' : \mathcal{A} \to (0, 1]$ with $\xi'(a) = \frac{1}{3}$ and $\xi'(b) = \frac{2}{3}$. Another possibility is $\xi'' : \mathcal{A} \to (0, 1]$ with $\xi''(a) = \xi''(b) = \frac{1}{2}$. Since ξ embraces both possibilities, assessing the confidence of ξ on a sample should consider both of them. Actually, we will consider that the sample is adequate for ξ if it would be so for some standard random variable fitting into ξ. In this line, an *instance* of a symbolic random variable is a (standard) random variable where each probability fits into the margins of the symbolic random variable for the corresponding class. Besides, these probabilities must add up to 1. In order to compute the confidence of a symbolic random variable on a sample we consider the instance of it that returns the highest confidence on that sample.

Definition 15. Let $\mathcal{A} = \{a_1, \ldots, a_k\}$ be a set of events, $\xi : \mathcal{A} \to \text{simbP}$ be a symbolic random variable, $\xi' : \mathcal{A} \to (0, 1]$ be a random variable, and J be a sample of $\mathcal{A}$. We say that the random variable ξ' is an *instance* of ξ, denoted by $\text{Instance}(\xi', \xi)$, if for any $a \in \mathcal{A}$ we have $\xi'(a) \in \xi(a)$ and $\sum_{a \in \mathcal{A}} \xi'(a) = 1$.

For any random variable $\xi' : \mathcal{A} \to (0, 1]$ let X^2 denote the discrepancy level of J on ξ' calculated as explained above by splitting the sampling space into the set of events $\mathcal{A}$. Let $\xi : \mathcal{A} \to \text{simbP}$ denote a symbolic random variable. We define the confidence of ξ on J, denoted by $\gamma(\xi, J)$, as follows:

$$\gamma(\xi, J) = \max \left\{ \alpha \, \middle| \, \begin{array}{l} \exists\, \xi' : \text{Instance}(\xi', \xi) \wedge \\ \alpha = \max\{\alpha' \mid X^2 \le \chi_{\alpha'}^2(k-1)\} \end{array} \right\}$$

$\square$

A Test Generation Framework for *quiescent* Real-Time Systems

Laura Brandán Briones and Ed Brinksma

Faculty of Computer Science, University of Twente,
P.O.Box 217, 7500AE Enschede,
The Netherlands. Fax - (31 53)-489-3247
{brandanl, brinksma}@cs.utwente.nl

Abstract. We present an extension of Tretmans' theory and algorithm for test generation for input-output transition systems to real-time systems. Our treatment is based on an operational interpretation of the notion of *quiescence* in the context of real-time behaviour. This gives rise to a family of implementation relations parameterized by observation durations for *quiescence*. We define a nondeterministic (parameterized) test generation algorithm that generates test cases that are sound with respect to the corresponding implementation relation. Also, the test generation is exhaustive in the sense that for each non-conforming implementation a test case can be generated that detects the non-conformance.

1 Introduction

Although testing has always been the most important technique for the validation of software systems it has only become a topic of serious academic research in the past decade or so. In this period research on the use of formal methods for model-driven test generation and execution of functional test cases has led to a number of promising methods and tools for systematic black-box testing of systems, e.g. [1, 13, 9, 10]. Most of these approaches are limited to the qualitative behaviour of systems, and exclude quantitative aspects such as real-time properties. The explosive growth of embedded software, however, has also caused a growing need to extend existing testing theories to the testing of real-time reactive systems. In this paper we present an extension of Tretmans' **ioco** theory for test generation [12] for input-output transition systems that includes real-time behaviour.

A central concept in the non-timed theory is the notion of *quiescence*, which characterizes systems states that will not produce any output response without the provision of a new input stimulus. By treating *quiescence* as a special sort of system output the notion of behavioural trace can be generalized to include observations of *quiescence*. In turn, this leads to an implementation relation that defines unambiguously if implemented behaviour conforms to a given specification model, viz. if after all specified generalized traces of the implementation all possible generalized outputs are allowed according to the specification. Or,

J. Grabowski and B. Nielsen (Eds.): FATES 2004, LNCS 3395, pp. 64–78, 2005.

more informally, if all outputs and *quiescence* are correctly predicted by the specification.

In practice, the above implementation criterion means that implementations can be more deterministic than their specifications. Although it is good engineering practice to not introduce unnecessary nondeterminism in reactive systems, it is often unavoidable in the context of testing, and it should therefore be part of a sensible testing theory. The reason for this is twofold:

- although the implementation under test may be deterministic, it can often only be tested through a testing environment that includes operating system features, communication media, etc. that typically introduce nondeterminism into the observed behaviour;
- an implementation under test often consists of concurrent components in an asynchronous parallel composition. The loss of information about the relative progress of components results in nondeterministic properties of their integrated behaviour.

Our proposed extension of the **ioco** theory to real-time systems is based on an operational interpretation of the notion of *quiescence*. This gives rise to a family of implementation relations parameterized by observation durations for *quiescence*. We define a nondeterministic (parameterized) test generation algorithm that generates test cases that are sound with respect to the corresponding implementation relation. This means that if an implementation fails any of the generated tests, it must be non-conforming. The algorithm is also exhaustive in the sense that for every non-conforming implementation a test case can be generated that will detect its non-conformance.

The rest of this paper is organized as follows. Section 2 introduces the model of timed input-output transition systems and our conformance relation. Section 3 presents the real-time test generation algorithm. Section 4 illustrates the theory with an example in the setting of timed automata. Section 5 compares our achievements to related work. Finally, section 6 presents the conclusions and future work.

2   Implementation Relations for Real-Time *quiescence*

2.1   Timed Input-Output Transition Systems

In this section we introduce the concept of Timed Labelled Transition Systems, their properties and notation, and then specialize them to obtain the model of Timed Input-Output Transition Systems. After that, we proceed to obtain a conformance relation between a specification and an implementation, defined as timed input-output transition systems, analogous to the **ioco** relation for the untimed case.

For details of the underlying theory (the implementation relation **ioco**) we refer to [12]. To save space we omitted the proof of lemmas and theorems in this paper, but they can be found in the full version [15].

We distinguish three types of actions: *time-passage actions*, *visible labelled actions* and the special *internal action* τ. All except the time-passage actions are thought of as occurring instantaneously, i.e. without consuming time. To specify time, a dense time domain is used, viz. the nonnegative reals ($\mathbb{R}^+$); no lower *a priori* bounds are imposed on the delays between events.

Definition 1. *A timed labelled transition system (TLTS) is a 4-tuple* $\langle S, s_0, Act_{\tau\varepsilon}, \rightarrow \rangle$, *where*

- *S is a non-empty set of states*
- *$s_0 \in S$ is the initial state*
- *$Act_{\tau\varepsilon} \overset{def}{=} Act \cup \{\tau\} \cup \mathcal{D}$ are the actions Act including the internal action τ and time-passage actions; where $\mathcal{D}$ is $\{\varepsilon(d) \mid d \in \mathbb{R}^+\}$*
- $\rightarrow \subseteq (S \times Act_{\tau\varepsilon} \times S)$ *is the transition relation with the following consistency constraints:*
  - **Time Determinism** *whenever* $s \xrightarrow{\varepsilon(d)} s'$ *and* $s \xrightarrow{\varepsilon(d)} s''$ *then* $s' = s''$
  - **Time Additivity** $\forall\, s, s'' \in S \land \forall\, d_1, d_2 \geq 0 : (\exists\, s' \in S : s \xrightarrow{\varepsilon(d_1)} s' \xrightarrow{\varepsilon(d_2)} s'')$ *iff* $s \xrightarrow{\varepsilon(d_1+d_2)} s''$
  - **Null Delay** $\forall\, s, s' \in S : s \xrightarrow{\varepsilon(0)} s'$ *iff* $s = s'$.

The labels in Act_ε $(Act_\varepsilon \overset{def}{=} Act \cup \mathcal{D})$ represent the observable actions of a system, i.e. labelled actions and passage of time; the special label τ represents an unobservable internal action. A transition $(s, \mu, s') \in \rightarrow$ is denoted as $s \xrightarrow{\mu} s'$. A *computation* is a finite or infinite sequence of transitions:

$$s_0 \xrightarrow{\mu_1} s_1 \xrightarrow{\mu_2} s_2 \xrightarrow{\mu_3} \cdots \xrightarrow{\mu_{n-1}} s_{n-1} \xrightarrow{\mu_n} s_n (\rightarrow \cdots)$$

A *timed trace* captures the observable aspects of a computation; it is the sequence of observable actions. The set of all *finite* sequences of actions over Act_ε is denoted by Act_ε^*, while ϵ denotes the empty sequence. If $\sigma_1, \sigma_2 \in Act_\varepsilon^*$ then $\sigma_1 \cdot \sigma_2$ is the concatenation of σ_1 and σ_2.

We denote the class of all timed labelled transition systems over Act by $TLTS(Act)$. Some additional notations and properties are introduced in the next definitions.

Definition 2. *Let* $p = \langle S, s_0, Act_{\tau\varepsilon}, \rightarrow \rangle$ *be a TLTS(Act) with* $s, s', s_i \in S; d, d',$ $e \in \mathbb{R}^+; \mu_i \in Act_{\tau\varepsilon}; \beta \in Act; \alpha_i \in Act_\varepsilon; \alpha \in Act_\varepsilon^*$, *then*

$s \xrightarrow{\mu_1 \cdots \mu_n} s' \overset{def}{=} \exists s_0, \ldots, s_n : s = s_0 \xrightarrow{\mu_1} s_1 \xrightarrow{\mu_2} \cdots \xrightarrow{\mu_n} s_n = s'$		$s \xrightarrow{\mu_1 \cdots \mu_n} \overset{def}{=} \nexists s' : s \xrightarrow{\mu_1 \cdots \mu_n} s'$	
$s \xrightarrow{\mu_1 \cdots \mu_n} s' \overset{def}{=} \exists s' : s \xrightarrow{\mu_1 \cdots \mu_n} s'$			
$s \overset{\varepsilon}{\Rightarrow} s' \overset{def}{=} s = s'$ or $s \xrightarrow{\tau \cdots \tau} s'$		$s \overset{\beta}{\Rightarrow} s' \overset{def}{=} \exists s_1, s_2 : s \overset{\varepsilon}{\Rightarrow} s_1 \xrightarrow{\beta} s_2 \overset{\varepsilon}{\Rightarrow} s'$	
$s \overset{\varepsilon(d)}{\Rightarrow} s' \overset{def}{=} (\exists s_1, s_2 : s \overset{\varepsilon}{\Rightarrow} s_1 \xrightarrow{\varepsilon(d)} s_2 \overset{\varepsilon}{\Rightarrow} s')$ or		$s \overset{\alpha_1 \cdots \alpha_n}{\Longrightarrow} s' \overset{def}{=} \exists s_0 \ldots s_n$	
$(\exists s_1, d', e : d' + e = d : s \overset{\varepsilon(d')}{\Rightarrow} s_1 \overset{\varepsilon(e)}{\Rightarrow} s')$		$: s = s_0 \overset{\alpha_1}{\Rightarrow} s_1 \overset{\alpha_2}{\Rightarrow} \cdots \overset{\alpha_n}{\Rightarrow} s_n = s'$	
$s \overset{\alpha}{\Rightarrow} \overset{def}{=} \exists s' : s \overset{\alpha}{\Rightarrow} s'$		$s \overset{\alpha}{\not\Rightarrow} \overset{def}{=} \nexists s' : s \overset{\alpha}{\Rightarrow} s'$.	

We do not always distinguish between a timed labelled transition system and its initial state: if $p = \langle S, s_0, Act_{\tau\varepsilon}, \rightarrow \rangle$ we will often identify the process p with its initial state s_0, e.g. we write $p \overset{\alpha}{\Rightarrow}$ instead of $s_0 \overset{\alpha}{\Rightarrow}$.

Definition 3.

- $ttraces(p) \overset{def}{=} \{\sigma \in Act_\varepsilon^* \mid p \overset{\sigma}{\Rightarrow} \}$
- $init(p) \overset{def}{=} \{\mu \in Act_{\tau\varepsilon} \mid p \xrightarrow{\mu} \}$

- $der(p) \overset{def}{=} \{p' \mid \exists\, \sigma \in Act_\varepsilon^* : p \overset{\sigma}{\Rightarrow} p'\}$
- p **after** $\sigma \overset{def}{=} \{p' \mid p \overset{\sigma}{\Rightarrow} p'\}$
- P **after** $\sigma \overset{def}{=} \underset{p \in P}{\bigcup}\ (p\ \textbf{after}\ \sigma)$, where P is a set of states
- p is deterministic *if* $\forall\, \sigma \in Act_\varepsilon^* : (p\ \textbf{after}\ \sigma)$ *has at most one element.*
  If $\sigma \in ttraces(p)$, *then* $(p\ \textbf{after}\ \sigma)$ *is overloaded to denote this element.*

In the context of timed systems there are some further important properties.

Definition 4. *Let* $p = \langle S, s_0, Act_{\tau\varepsilon}, \rightarrow \rangle$ *be a TLTS(Act), then*
*p is **time divergent**: if for all $s \in S$ there exists an infinite computation σ from*
s with infinite cumulative delay:
$$\forall\, s \in S : \exists\, \sigma \in Act_{\tau\varepsilon}^\omega : \sigma = \mu_1 \cdot \mu_2 \cdot \mu_3 \cdots : s \overset{\sigma}{\rightarrow}\ \wedge\ \Sigma\{d_i \mid \mu_i = \varepsilon(d_i)\} = \infty$$
*p has **Zeno behaviour**: if there exists a state $s \in S$ and an infinite computation*
from s with infinitely many non-delay actions and finite cumulative delay:
$$\exists\, s \in S : \exists\, \sigma \in Act_{\tau\varepsilon}^\omega : \sigma = \mu_1 \cdot \mu_2 \cdot \mu_3 \cdots : s \overset{\sigma}{\rightarrow}\ \wedge\ \mid \{i \mid \mu_i \neq \varepsilon(d_i)\} \mid = \infty$$
$$\wedge\ \Sigma\{d_i \mid \mu_i = \varepsilon(d_i)\} < \infty.$$

We assume that for all $p \in TLTS$ we are working with, p is time divergent, and does not have Zeno behaviour.

We now introduce timed input-output transition systems (*TIOTS*) to model timed systems for which the set of actions can be partitioned into *output actions* and *input actions*. To do this properly, we formalize the notion of *input enabling*: if an input action is initiated by the environment, the system is always prepared to participate in such an interaction: all the inputs can always be accepted without letting time pass. Also, we want to exclude the possibility that the flow of time in a system can be blocked because the environment does not provide certain input actions, i.e. there must be no *forced inputs*.

Definition 5. *A timed input-output transition system (TIOTS) is a timed labelled transition system* $\langle S, s_0, Act_{\tau\varepsilon}, \rightarrow \rangle$ *with Act partitioned into* input actions, *Act_I, and* output actions, *Act_U, $(Act_I \cup Act_U = Act, Act_I \cap Act_U = \emptyset)$, that has the properties of*
weak input enabling: $\forall\, s \in S : \forall\, \mu \in Act_I : s \overset{\mu}{\Rightarrow}$
no forced inputs: *iff for all $s \in S$ there exists an infinite computation σ from s containing no input actions and with infinite cumulative delay:* $\forall\, s \in S : \exists\, \sigma \in$
$(Act_U \cup \{\tau\} \cup \mathcal{D})^\omega : \sigma = \mu_1 \cdot \mu_2 \cdots : s \overset{\sigma}{\rightarrow}\ \wedge\ \Sigma\{d_i \mid \mu_i = \varepsilon(d_i)\} = \infty$
   The class of timed input-output transition systems with input actions in Act_I and output actions in Act_U is denoted by $TIOTS(Act_I, Act_U) \subseteq TLTS(Act_I \cup Act_U)$.

We follow the convention that input actions are identified by names followed by a *?*-symbol, and output actions by names followed by a *!*-symbol.

A timed trace σ is a sequence of actions and delays, e.g. $\sigma = a? \cdot \varepsilon(d_1) \cdot \varepsilon(d_2) \cdot b!$. Obviously, it would be more natural to avoid consecutive delays, as in $\sigma = a? \cdot \varepsilon(d_1 + d_2) \cdot b!$. Such traces could alternatively be written as sequences of actions with relative time stamps, viz. $\sigma = a?(0) \cdot b!(d_1 + d_2)$. This idea motivates the definition of *normalized timed traces*.

Definition 6. *Let $\sigma \in Act_\varepsilon^*$, then*

- σ *is a* normalized timed trace *iff $\sigma \in (\mathcal{D}\cdot Act)^*$*
- $nttraces(p) = \{\sigma \in (\mathcal{D}\cdot Act)^* \mid p \overset{\sigma}{\Rightarrow}\}$
- *for normalized timed traces $\sigma = \varepsilon(d_0)\cdot a_0\cdot\varepsilon(d_1)\cdot a_1 \cdots \varepsilon(d_n)\cdot a_n$ we also write $\widehat{\sigma} = a_0(d_0)\cdot a_1(d_1) \cdots a_n(d_n)$.*

If a timed trace begins with an action it can always be converted to a *normalized timed trace* by combining delays, or adding zero delays $\varepsilon(0)$ in the appropriate places. But if a timed trace ends with a delay, such as $\sigma = \varepsilon(d_0)\cdot a\cdot\varepsilon(d_1)\cdot b\cdot\varepsilon(d_2)$ then is not possible to interpret it as a *normalized timed trace*. The next lemma shows, however, that in the presence of input enabledness *normalized timed traces* preserve the information of timed traces.

Lemma 7. *Let p_1, $p_2 \in TIOTS(Act_I, Act_U)$, then*
$$ttraces(p_1) \subseteq ttraces(p_2) \ \text{iff} \ nttraces(p_1) \subseteq nttraces(p_2).$$

From now on we will not distinguish between a timed trace σ and its normalization $\widehat{\sigma}$ if it exist.

Similarly to Tretmans' work, we proceed to introduce the notion of *quiescence* in the timed setting. In the presence of time we define a *quiescent* state as one where the system is unable to produce an output immediately or in the future without receiving further input stimuli.

Definition 8. *Let $p \in TIOTS(Act_I, Act_U)$. A state s of p is* quiescent, *denoted by $\delta(s)$, iff $\forall \mu \in Act_U : \forall d \in \mathbb{R}^+ : s \overset{\mu(d)}{\not\to}$.*

As before in the untimed case, we can start out by representing *quiescence* as a special action δ ($\delta \notin Act \cup \{\tau\}$)[1], and extending the timed transition relation of a *TIOTS* p to include self-loop transitions $s \overset{\delta}{\to} s$ iff s is a *quiescent* state. Moreover, let $\Delta(p)$ denote the extended timed transition system of p that is obtained in this way.

2.2   Timed Implementation Relations

The extension of the timed transition relation allows us to define the following relation over *TIOTS*.

Definition 9. *Let p and $q \in TIOTS(Act_I, Act_U)$, then*
$$q \sqsubseteq_{tiorf} p \ \text{iff} \ nttraces(\Delta(q)) \subseteq nttraces(\Delta(p)).$$

For specifications $p \in TIOTS$ the *quiescent* states can, in principle, be identified by analyzing the timed transition system, i.e. we can assume that $\Delta(p)$ is

---

[1] In [12] the action symbol θ is used for the observation of *quiescence*. We prefer to use δ for both *quiescence* and its observation, in line with the philosophy that identical actions synchronize.

at our disposal. For implementations q, however, we only can detect *quiescence* by waiting for outputs. But we cannot wait forever, and therefore need to choose a maximal duration M. This motivates the following parameterized version of $\sqsubseteq_{tiorf}$, where σ can only appear after M time-units.

Definition 10. *Let p and $q \in TIOTS$, then $q \sqsubseteq^M_{tiorf} p$ iff $\Delta_M(q) \subseteq \Delta_M(p)$*

where $\Delta_M(r) \stackrel{def}{=} nttraces(\Delta(r)) \cap (\mathcal{D} \cdot Act \cup \varepsilon(M) \cdot \delta)^*$.

The above definition takes only into account observations of *quiescence* that are made after a minimal delay of M time units. Naturally this definition implies a pre-order.

Lemma 11. *If $M_1 < M_2$, then if $q \sqsubseteq^{M_1}_{tiorf} p$ then $q \sqsubseteq^{M_2}_{tiorf} p$.*

This is not without consequences: in contrast to the untimed case, time delays can change the system state, which has interesting consequences, as shown in the quirky coffee machine of Figure 1, inspired by [21].

Example 12. Figure 1 shows two quirky coffee machines with time. Suppose both graphs are saturated with input action transitions in each state by adding self-loops for all input transitions that are not explicitly given. For simplicity, in the figure, we use m? for money, b? for bang, c?, c! for coffee, and t?, t! for tea. We suppose that each action resets the clock x and that $k < M$ (we used the representation of timed automata). Here after introducing *money?* we can switch between the coffee and tea modes. If we order *coffee?* and *bang?* fast enough we always will have coffee in the right-hand machine and some times in the left-hand machine, but if we *bang?* after waiting for the *quiescence* we will not notice the difference between machines. It follows from the one that cannot switch modes. This is a consequence of the fact that observing *quiescence* takes time.

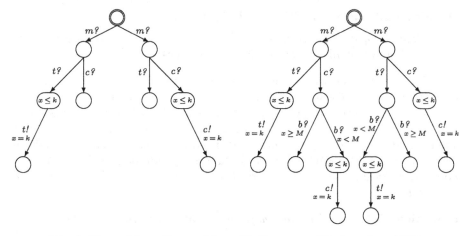

Fig. 1. The quirky coffee machine with time, a modified version of [21]

The output set of a given state of a system in $TIOTS(Act_I, Act_U)$ consists of the time stamped output actions that are allowed from that state (abstracting from τ-actions), including δ-actions after a delay of M time-units.

Definition 13. *Let p be a state of an (extended) timed transition system in $TIOTS(Act_I, Act_U)$,*

then $out_M(p) = \{\mu(d) \mid \mu \in Act_U \wedge p \overset{\mu(d)}{\Rightarrow} \} \cup \{\delta(M) \mid p \overset{\delta(M)}{\Rightarrow} \}$
and for P a set of states, then $out_M(P) = \underset{p \in P}{\cup} out_M(p)$.

Lemma 14. *Let p and $q \in TIOTS(Act_I, Act_U)$, then*

$$q \sqsubseteq_{tiorf}^M p \ iff$$
$$\forall \, \sigma \in (\mathcal{D} \cdot Act \cup \varepsilon(M) \cdot \delta)^* : out_M(\Delta(q) \textbf{ after } \sigma) \subseteq out_M(\Delta(p) \textbf{ after } \sigma).$$

Finally, we are in position to define the relation we use to test real time systems: **tioco**$_M$. For p and $q \in TIOTS(Act_I, Act_U)$, q will be **tioco**$_M$ to p if the set of outputs of q *after every normalized timed trace σ of p* including observations $\delta(M)$, is a subset of the outputs of p after the same timed trace σ.

Definition 15. *Let p and $q \in TIOTS(Act_I, Act_U)$, then*

$$q \sqsubseteq_{tioco}^M p \ iff \ \forall \, \sigma \in \Delta_M(p) : out_M(\Delta(q) \textbf{ after } \sigma) \subseteq out_M(\Delta(p) \textbf{ after } \sigma)$$

we also write $\sqsubseteq_{tioco}^M$ as **tioco**$_M$.

2.3 An Operational Model

To obtain an effective theory of *quiescence* in a timed setting we need more than stipulating that observing *quiescence* takes time. Since with physical implementations we can only observe absence of outputs over finite time intervals we must stipulate when such observations will be interpreted as *quiescence*.

Definition 16. *Let q be a TIOTS and $M \in \mathbb{R}^+$, then*

- *a state s of q is M-quiescent iff $\forall \, s' \in (s \textbf{ after } \varepsilon(M)) : s'$ is quiescent*
- *q is M-quiescent iff all states s of q are M-quiescent.*

In line with the above development we now want to formalize how *normalized timed traces* of *TIOTSs* may be enriched directly with δ-actions. Whenever the *normalized timed trace* allows an action with a delay of more than M time-units this creates a possibility to observe *quiescence*. For example, if $M = 4$ and $\sigma = a?(2) \cdot b?(5) \cdot c!(3)$ is an observed timed trace then it is also possible to observe $\sigma' = a?(2) \delta(4) \cdot b?(1) \cdot c!(3)$. We formalize the addition of δ-observations to *normalized timed traces* as a formal relation δ_M between (extended) *normalized timed traces*.

Definition 17. *Let σ, σ' be normal form of $\sigma, \sigma' \in (\mathcal{D} \cdot (Act \cup \delta))^*$, then*

- $\sigma \, \delta_M \, \sigma'$ *iff* $\exists \, \sigma_1, \sigma_2 : \exists \, \mu : \exists \, d \geq M : \sigma = \sigma_1 \mu(d) \sigma_2 \wedge \sigma' = \sigma_1 \delta(M) \mu(d-M) \sigma_2$

- let Σ *be a set of normalized timed traces, then* $\delta_M(\Sigma) = pref\left(\bigcup_{\sigma \in \Sigma} \{\sigma' | \sigma\ \delta_M^*\ \sigma'\}\right)$
  where pref(S) is interpreted as the prefix-closure of a set of traces S and δ_M^*
  is the reflexive transitive closure of the relation δ_M.

If δ-actions are introduced in *normalized timed traces* on the basis observations of delays of (at least) M time units, we must check for consistency, i.e. we must have the property expressed in the following lemma.

Lemma 18. *Let* $q \in TIOTS(Act_I, Act_U)$ *be* M-quiescent, *then*
$$\not\exists\ \sigma \in \delta_M(nttraces(q)) : \exists\ \mu \in Act_U : \sigma = \sigma' \cdot \delta(M) \cdot \mu(d).$$

Corollary 19. *Let* $q \in TIOTS$ *be* M-quiescent, *then* $\delta_M(nttraces(q)) = \Delta_M(q)$.

This corollary means that if an implementation q can be assumed to be M-*quiescent* we may use the set of enriched observations $\delta_M(nttraces(q))$ to obtain $\Delta_M(q)$, whose definition is based on the unobservable timed transition system $\Delta(q)$. This will be the basis for our test derivation algorithm.

3   A Real-Time Test Generation Framework

In this section we define the concept of real-time test cases, the nature of their execution, and the evaluation of their success or failure.

Definition 20.   • *A test case* t *is a TLTS* $\langle S, s_0, Act_\varepsilon \cup \{\delta\}, \rightarrow \rangle$ *such that*
- t *is deterministic and has* bounded behaviour, *i.e.* $\exists\ N > 0 : \forall\ \sigma$:
  $\sigma = \mu_1.\mu_2.\mu_3 \ldots : |\{i \mid \mu_i \neq \varepsilon(d_i)\}| < \infty$ *and* $\Sigma\{d_i \mid \mu_i = \varepsilon(d_i)\} < N$
- S *contains the terminal states* **pass** *and* **fail**, *with* init(**pass**) = init(**fail**) = $\emptyset$
- *for any state* $t' \in S$ *of the test case with* $t' \neq$ **pass**, **fail**, $\exists\ d > 0$ *with* init(t' **after** $\varepsilon(d')$) = $Act_U \cup \{\varepsilon(e) \mid e = d - d'\}$ *for all* $d' < d$, init(t' **after** $\varepsilon(d)$) = μ *with* $\mu \in Act_I$ *or* $\mu = \delta$
- t *does not have* τ-*transitions*
  The class of test cases over Act_I *and* Act_U *is denoted as* $TT\mathcal{EST}(Act_I, Act_U)$ *but we represent it similarly as a timed automata, only for simplifying the notation*
- *A test suite* **T** *is a set of test cases:* $\mathbf{T} \subseteq TT\mathcal{EST}(Act_I, Act_U)$.

A test run of an implementation with a test case is modelled by the synchronous parallel execution of the test case with the implementation under test. This run continues until no more interactions are possible, i.e. until a deadlock occurs.

Definition 21. *Let* $t \in TT\mathcal{EST}(Act_I, Act_U)$ *and* $imp \in TIOTS(Act_I, Act_U)$ M-quiescent, *then*

- *Running a test case t with an implementation imp is modelled by the parallel operator $|| : TTEST(Act_I, Act_U) \times TIOTS(Act_I, Act_U) \to TIOTS(Act_I, Act_U)$ which is defined by the following inference rules:*

$$imp \xrightarrow{\tau} imp' \qquad\qquad \vdash \quad t||imp \xrightarrow{\tau} t||imp'$$
$$t \xrightarrow{\delta} t' \qquad\qquad\qquad \vdash \quad t||imp \xrightarrow{\delta} t'||imp$$
$$t \xrightarrow{\mu} t', imp \xrightarrow{\mu} imp', \mu \in Act \quad \vdash \quad t||imp \xrightarrow{\mu} t'||imp'$$
$$t \xrightarrow{\varepsilon(d)} t', imp \xrightarrow{\varepsilon(d)} imp' \qquad \vdash \quad t||imp \xrightarrow{\varepsilon(d)} t'||imp'$$

- *A test run of t with imp, is a $\sigma \in \Delta_M$ of $t||imp$ leading to a terminal state of t : σ is a test run of t and*

$$imp \stackrel{def}{=} \exists\, imp' : (t||imp \stackrel{\sigma}{\Rightarrow} \mathbf{pass}||imp') \ or\ (t||imp \stackrel{\sigma}{\Rightarrow} \mathbf{fail}||imp')$$

- *An implementation imp **passes** test case t, if all their test runs lead to the* **pass** *state of t:*

$$imp\ \mathbf{passes}\ t \stackrel{def}{=} \forall\, \sigma \in \Delta_M : \forall\, imp' : t||imp \stackrel{\sigma}{\not\Rightarrow} \mathbf{fail}||imp'$$

- *An implementation imp **passes** a test suite $\mathbf{T}$, if it **passes** all test cases in $\mathbf{T}$:*

$$imp\ \mathbf{passes}\ \mathbf{T} \stackrel{def}{=} \forall\, t \in \mathbf{T} : imp\ \mathbf{passes}\ t$$

If imp does not pass the test suite, it fails if:

$$imp\ \mathbf{fails}\ \mathbf{T} \stackrel{def}{=} \exists\, t \in \mathbf{T} : imp\ \mathbf{passes}\ t.$$

Since an implementation can behave nondeterministically, different test runs of the same test case with the same implementation may lead to different terminal states and hence to different verdicts. An implementation **passes** a test case if an only if all possible test runs lead to the verdict **pass**.

3.1 Nondeterministic Test Case Construction

For the description of test cases we use, as we already did before, a process-algebraic behaviour notation with a syntax inspired by LOTOS [8]:

$$B \stackrel{def}{=} a; B \mid B + B \mid \Sigma\, \mathcal{B}$$

where $a \in Act_\varepsilon$, $\mathcal{B}$ is a countable set of behaviour expressions, and the axioms and the inference rules are:

$$a \in Act \qquad\qquad\qquad \vdash\ a; B \xrightarrow{a} B'$$
$$a = \varepsilon(d), d' < d \qquad\qquad \vdash\ a; B \xrightarrow{\varepsilon(d')} \varepsilon(d - d'); B'$$
$$a = \varepsilon(d) \qquad\qquad\qquad \vdash\ a; B \xrightarrow{\varepsilon(d)} B'$$
$$B_1 \xrightarrow{\mu} B_1', \mu \in Act_\varepsilon \qquad \vdash\ B_1 + B_2 \xrightarrow{\mu} B_1'$$
$$B_2 \xrightarrow{\mu} B_2', \mu \in Act_\varepsilon \qquad \vdash\ B_1 + B_2 \xrightarrow{\mu} B_2'$$
$$B \xrightarrow{\mu} B', B \in \mathcal{B}, \mu \in Act_\varepsilon\ \vdash\ \Sigma\, \mathcal{B} \xrightarrow{\mu} B'$$

Moreover, we use $\mu(d)$ as syntactic sugar for $\varepsilon(d); \mu$.

Test case generation procedure. We define a procedure to generate test cases from a given specification timed transition system. Similar to [12] test cases result from the nondeterministic, recursive application of three test generation steps, corresponding to: (1) termination, (2) generation of an input, and (3) observation of output (including *quiescence*). It should be noted that the construction steps involve (negations of) predicates of the form $o(d) \in out_M(S)$, which on the general level of timed input-output transition systems are undecidable. The procedure given here, therefore, should be seen as a meta-algorithm that can be used to generate tests effectively for subclasses of *TIOTS* for which these predicates are decidable, such as timed automata [16, 14].

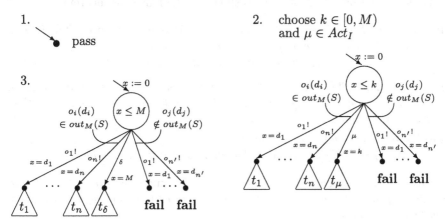

1. *termination*
   $t := \mathbf{pass}$
   The single state test case **pass** is always a sound test case. It stops the recursion in the algorithm, and thus terminates the test case.

2. *inputs*
   $$t := \quad \Sigma\{o_i(d_i); t_i \mid o_i \in Act_U \wedge o_i(d_i) \in out_M(S)\}$$
   $$+ \mu(k); t_\mu$$
   $$+ \Sigma\{o_j(d_j); \mathbf{fail} \mid o_j \in Act_U \wedge o_j(d_j) \notin out_M(S)\}$$
   where x is a clock, k is a timed variable and t_i and t_μ are obtained by recursively applying the algorithm for $(S \text{ after } o_i(d_i))$ and $(S \text{ after } \mu(k))$, respectively.
   Test case t is waiting for k time-units an treating to make and input (μ). If an output arrives from the implementation it checks; if it is an invalid response, i.e. $o_j(d_j) \notin out_M(S)$ then the test case terminates in **fail**; if it is a valid response after the timed pass then the test case continues recursively. If the time pass then the test makes the input (μ) and continues recursively.

3. *waiting for outputs*
   $$t := \quad \Sigma\{o_i(d_i); t_i \mid o_i \in Act_U \wedge o_i(d_i) \in out_M(S)\}$$
   $$+ \Sigma\{\delta(M); t_\delta \mid \delta \in out_M(S \text{ after } \varepsilon(M))\}$$
   $$+ \Sigma\{\delta(M); \mathbf{fail} \mid \delta \notin out_M(S \text{ after } \varepsilon(M))\}$$
   $$+ \Sigma\{o_j(d_j); \mathbf{fail} \mid o_j \in Act_U \wedge o_j(d_j) \notin out_M(S)\}$$
   where x is a clock and t_i and t_δ are obtained by recursively applying the algorithm for $(S \text{ after } o_i(d_i))$ and $(S \text{ after } \varepsilon(M))$, respectively.

Test case t is waiting for M time-units if an output arrive from the implementation it checks; if it is an invalid response, i.e. $o_j(d_j) \notin out_M(S)$ then the test case terminates in **fail**; if it is a valid response after the timed pass then the test case continues recursively. The observation of *quiescence* δ is treated separately, using the constant M given by the M-*quiescent* property.

Soundness. The test generation procedure presented is sound with respect to the **tioco**$_M$ relation. This property is shown in the following theorem.

Theorem 22. *Let* $spec \in TIOTS$, *then for all* M-quiescent $imp \in TIOTS$ *and all test cases* t *obtained from spec by the above procedure:*
$$imp \ \textbf{tioco}_M \ spec \Rightarrow imp \ \textbf{passes} \ t.$$

Exhaustiveness. The test generation procedure is also exhaustive in the sense that for each non-conforming implementation a test case can be generated that detects the non-conformance.

Definition 23. *Let* $p \in TIOTS$, *then*
$\sigma \in \Delta_M(p)$ *is* $\delta(M)$-*saturated iff for all* σ' *with* $\sigma \ \delta_M \ \sigma'$ *we have* $\sigma = \sigma'$.

Theorem 24. *Let* $spec \in TIOTS$, *then for all* M-quiescent $imp \in TIOTS$ *with* $imp \ \textbf{ti\not{o}co}_M \ spec$, *there exists a test case* t *generated from spec by the procedure such that:* $imp \ \textbf{pa\not{s}ses} \ t$.

The exhaustiveness of our test generation procedure as proven in [15] is less useful than the corresponding result in the untimed case. There, it implies that the test generation algorithm, if repeatedly executed in a fair non-terminating manner, will generate all test cases in the limit, and therefore, in the limit, achieve full coverage with respect to **ioco** and the given specification *spec*.

Here, the number of potential test cases is uncountable because of the underlying continuous model of time, and no countable repetition of test generations suffices. It is possible, however, to obtain a version of the stronger form of exhaustiveness for real-time test generation as well by considering equivalence classes of (minimal) error traces. It can be shown that reasonable assumptions of our test generation procedure will hit each such equivalence class in the limit. This result will be reported in detail in a forthcoming publication.

4   Example

In the setting of timed automata, deciding the predicate $o_i(d_i) \in out_M(S)$ amounts to reachability analysis. For the simpler version of **tioco** based on timed trace inclusion (i.e. excluding *quiescence*) this has already been implemented in the tool environment IF [16], the UPPAAL-based testing tool TUPPAAL, and a real-time extension of TORX. We present an example of our test case generation based on a timed automaton model of a coffee machine, similar to the previous one, but with infinite behaviour due to cycles.

Example 25. Figure 2 shows two quirky coffee machines with time. The first one is a specification and the second one is a wrong implementation. To the

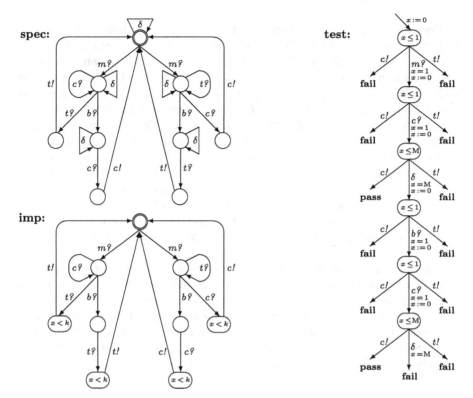

Fig. 2. A specification of a quirky coffee machine with time, an implementation with $M = k$, and a test case derived from the specification

right, there is a test case derived by the algorithm that can detect the error in the implementation. We suppose both machines are saturated with all input actions in each state. In the specification we show the δ-transitions, while in the implementation we detect them using $M = k$. We assume that $k > 1$.

The problem appears because:

out(*spec* **after** $m?(1) \cdot c?(1) \cdot \delta(k) \cdot b?(1) \cdot c?(1)) = \{c![0, \infty)\}$

and out(*imp* **after** $m?(1) \cdot c?(1) \cdot \delta(k) \cdot b?(1) \cdot c?(1)) = \{\delta(k)\}$

where we use the notation $c![0, \infty)$ to denote that the output $c!$ can be at any time between 0 and ∞.

5   Related Work

As already indicated before this work is closely related to work carried out by Krichen et al. in [16], and closely related work by Larsen et al. [14], who deal with a *quiescence*-free interpretation of timed **ioco** based on timed trace inclusion for timed automata. Our work shows how such results may be extended to deal with *quiescence*, and provides a general framework at the level of timed transition systems.

Previous attempts of extending testing with time include older work by Nielsen et al. in [2], for testing a subclass of timed automata called event-recording automata (ERA). The technique is based on the symbolic analysis of timed automata inspired by the UPPAAL model-checker, but lacks a suitable notion of implementation relation. Springintveld et al. in [11] present an exhaustive testing method for deterministic timed automata with dense time, using the notion of a grid automaton that represents each clock region with a finite set of clock valuations. Although being exact, the grid method is impractical because it generates "an astronomically large number of test sequences" [11]. Cardell-Oliver presents a method for networks of deterministic timed automata extended with integer data variables [17], where only a part of the system is visibly using test views, so that a test is never exhaustive.

Several authors have tried to obtain good specification coverage for their test methods by adapting transition-tour methods from classical FSM-based testing [7, 22].

Clarke and Lee [3] use the algebra of communicating shared resources (ACSR) on a discrete time base. ACSR allows non-deterministic specifications, the use of internal events and priorities. For testing, only boundary points of the time domain are selected. Cleaveland et al. propose a testing method for probabilistic processes on a discrete model of time [18] that bears a close resemblance to the classical testing theory of Hennessy and De Nicola [19]. Mandrioli et al. use temporal logic with arithmetic on a discrete time base [5].

6   Conclusion and Future Work

In this paper we have presented an extension of Tretmans' **ioco** theory and algorithm for test generation for input-output transition systems to real-time systems. Our treatment is based on an operational interpretation of the notion of *quiescence* that gives rise to a family of implementation relations parameterized by observation durations M for *quiescence*. These relations detect differences in behaviour after the execution of suspension traces provided that the observations of *quiescence* all take longer than the stipulated duration M, but may not detect differences in refusal behaviour that require shorter observations of *quiescence*.

It is shown how this theory may be used to test real-time implementations under the assumption that the absence of system interaction with its environment for M time units implies *quiescence*. We have defined a nondeterministic (M-parameterized) test generation framework that generates test cases that are sound with respect to the corresponding implementation relation **tioco**$_M$. The test generation is also exhaustive in the sense that for each non-conforming implementation a test case can be generated that can detect the non-conformance.

The framework can be effectively instantiated for subclasses of timed input-output transition systems for which $out_M(\Delta(spec)$ **after** $\sigma)$ is computable, as is the case for timed automata. Using standard symbolic state space representation in the form of difference bounded matrices [4], a real-time version of TORX for timed automata models is being implemented.

The work presented here can be extended in a number of ways. As already indicated, it is possible to show a stronger exhaustiveness result for the test generation procedure based on an appropriate notion of equivalence of error traces. The generation procedure will hit each such class in the limit, provided that the error class in not negligible, i.e. it must have positive measure in some appropriate sense.

Another extension is to relax the requirement that there must be a uniform observation deadline M for *quiescence*. Obvious alternatives that we are studying are:

- the observation parameter $M(\sigma)$ is a function of the behaviour (trace) σ observed so far. This would allows us to model sequential phases of *quiescence*, i.e. slow vs. quick response times;
- the observation parameter $M(C_i)$ is a function of the communication channel C_i on which output is being observed. This would allows us to model different kinds of response times for different communication channels with the system under test, and would correspond to a real-time extension of the **mioco** implementation relation of [6].

Our real-time theory inherits its focus on control aspects of system behaviour from the existing **ioco** theory. Ultimately, it will be important to combine this testing theory with methods for testing the static data aspects of systems. It will be interesting to see to what extent the symbolic representation of data types can be combined with symbolic representations of time.

In a more general vein, one can say that the development of a real-time testing theory forces us to confront modelling issues with respect to physical aspects of time and implementation. From a physical point of view, for example, it is questionable whether negligible behaviour can be implemented. This has also implications for specification formalisms that can be used to specify such behaviour, e.g. timed automata can define negligible behaviour by using guards that force behaviour to go through specific points in time, such as $x = 3$. It would seem that realistic specifications and/or implementation relations allow for tolerances in the evaluation of clock conditions. This would then introduce a third source of non-determinism in the testing theory of real-time systems. At any rate, a more systematic study of the formal aspects of tolerance and robustness is definitely needed.

References

1. A.BELINFANTE, J.FEENSTRA, R.DEVRIES, J.TRETMANS, N.GOGA, L.FEIJS, S.MAUW, AND L.HEERINK. Formal test automation: A simple experiment. In *Int. Workshop on Testing of Communicating Systems 12* (1999), Kluwer, pp. 179–196.
2. B.NIELSEN, AND A.SKOU. *Automated Test Generation from Timed Automata.* TACAS 2001: 343-357, 2001.
3. D.CLARKE, AND I.LEE. Automatic test generation for the analysis of a real-time system: Case study. In *IEEE Real Time Technology and Applications Symp.* (1997), pp. 112–124.
4. D.DILL. Timing assumptions and verification of finite-state concurrent systems. In *Proceedings of the int. workshop on Automatic verification methods for finite state systems* (1990), Springer-Verlag NY, Inc., pp. 197–212.

5. D.MANDRIOLI, S.MORASCA, AND A.MORZENTI. Generating test cases for real-time systems from logic specifications. *TOCS 13*, 4 (1995), 365–398.
6. E.BRINKSMA, L.HEERINK, AND J.TRETMANS. Factorized test generation for multi input/output transition systems. In *Int. Workshop on Testing of Communicating Systems 11* (1998), Kluwer, pp. 67–82.
7. EN-NOUAARYA, R.DSSOULI, AND F.KHENDEK. Timed test cases generation based on state characterization technique. In *19th IEEE Real-Time Systems Symp.* (1998), pp. 220–229.
8. ISO8807. *Information processing systems, Open Systems Interconnection, LOTOS, A formal description technique based on the temporal ordering of observational behaviour*. Int. Organization for Standardization, 1989.
9. J-C.FERNANDEZ, C.JARD, T.JERON, AND C.VIHO. Using on-the-fly verification techniques for the generation of test suites. In *Copmuter Aided Verification CAV'96. LNCS 1102, Springer-Verlan* (1996), R.Alur and T.A.Hezinger.
10. J-C.FERNANDEZ, C.JARD, T.JERON, AND C.VIHO. An experiment in automatic generation of test suites for protocols with verification technology. In *Sience of Computer Programming - Special Issue on COST247, Verification and Validation Methods for Formal Descriptions, 29(1-2)* (1997), pp. 123–146.
11. J.SPRINGINTVELD, F.VAANDRAGER, AND P.D'ARGENIO. Testing timed automata. *Theoretical Computer Science 254*, 1–2 (2001), 225–257.
12. J.TRETMANS. Test generation with inputs, outputs and repetitive quiescence. In *Software-Concepts and Tools, 17(3)* (1996), Also: Technical Report N0. 96-26, Center for Telematics and Information Technology, University of Twente, The Netherlands, pp. 103–120.
13. J.TRETMANS, AND E.BRINKSMA. Torx: Automated model-based testing. In *First European Conference on Model-Driven Software Engineering, Nuremberg* (2003), A.Hartmann and K.Dussa-Ziegler.
14. K.LARSEN, M.MIKUCIONIS, AND B.NIELSEN. Real-time system testing on-the-fly. In *The 15th Nordic Workshop on Programming Theory (NWPT)* (2003), K.Sere, M.Walden, and A.Karlsson, Eds. Extended abstract.
15. L.BRANDÁN-BRIONES, AND E.BRINKSMA. A test generation framework for quiescent real-time systems. http://fmt.cs.utwente.nl/research/testing/files/BBB04.ps.gz.
16. M.KRICHEN, AND S.TRIPAKIS. Black-box conformance testing for real-time systems. In *SPIN 2004* (2004), Springer-Verlag Heidelberg, pp. 109–126.
17. R.CARDELL-OLIVER. Conformance test experiments for distributed real-time systems. In *Proceedings of the int. symp. on Software testing and analysis* (2002), ACM Press, pp. 159–163.
18. R.CLEAVELAND, I.LEE, P.LEWIS, AND S.SMOLKA. A theory of testing for soft real-time processes, 1996.
19. R.DENICOLA, AND M.HENNESSY. Testing equivalences for processes. In *ICALP83* (1983), vol. 154.
20. R.J.VANGLABBEEK. The linear time-branching time spectrum ii (the semantics of sequential systems with silent moves). In *CONCUR'93. LNCS 715* (1993), E.Best, pp. 66–81.
21. R.LANGERAK. A testing theory for lotos using deadlock detection. In *Proceedings of the IFIP WG 6.1 Ninth int. Symp. on Protocol Spec., Testing, and Verification* (1990), IFIP, pp. 87–98.
22. T.HIGASHINO, A.NAKATA, K.TANIGUCHI, AND R.CAVALLI. Generating test cases for a timed i/o automaton model. In *IWTCS 1999* (1999), pp. 197–214.

Online Testing of Real-Time Systems Using UPPAAL

Kim G. Larsen, Marius Mikucionis, and Brian Nielsen

Department of Computer Science, Aalborg University,
Fredrik Bajers Vej 7B, 9220 Aalborg Øst, Denmark
{kgl, marius, bnielsen}@cs.auc.dk

Abstract. We present T-UPPAAL — a new tool for online black-box testing of real-time embedded systems from non-deterministic timed automata specifications. We describe a sound and complete randomized online testing algorithm and how to implement it using symbolic state representation and manipulation techniques. We propose the notion of relativized timed input/output conformance as the formal implementation relation. A novelty of this relation and our testing algorithm is that they explicitly take environment assumptions into account, generate, execute and verify the result online using the UPPAAL on-the-fly model-checking tool engine. A medium size case study shows promising results in terms of error detection capability and computation performance.

1 Introduction

The goal of testing is to gain confidence in a physical computer based system by means of executing it. More than one third of typical project resources is spent on testing embedded and real-time systems, but still it remains ad-hoc, based on heuristics, and error-prone. Therefore systematic, theoretically well-founded and effective automated real-time testing techniques is of great practical value.

Model Based Testing. Testing conceptually consists of three activities: test case *generation*, test case *execution* and *verdict assignment*. Using model based testing, a behavioral model can be interpreted as a specification that defines the required and allowed observable (real-time) behavior of the implementation. It can therefore be used for generation of sound and (theoretically) complete test suites.

An embedded system interacts closely with its environment which typically consists of the controlled physical equipment (the plant) accessible via sensors and actuators, other computer based systems or digital devices accessible via communication networks using dedicated protocols, and human users. A major development task is to ensure that an embedded system works correctly in its real operating environment. Due to lack of resources it is not feasible to validate the system for all possible environments. Also it is not necessary if the environments are known to a large extent. However, the requirements and the assumptions of the environment should be clear and explicit.

We denote the system being developed IUT, and its real operating environment RealENV. These communicate by exchanging *input* and *output* signals (seen from the perspective of IUT). Using a model-based development approach, the environment assumptions and system requirements are captured through abstract behavioral models

J. Grabowski and B. Nielsen (Eds.): FATES 2004, LNCS 3395, pp. 79–94, 2005.

denoted $\mathcal{E}$ and $\mathcal{S}$ respectively, communicating on abstract signals $i \in A_{in}$ and $o \in A_{out}$ corresponding (via a suitable abstraction) to the real *input* and *output*, see Fig. 1(a).

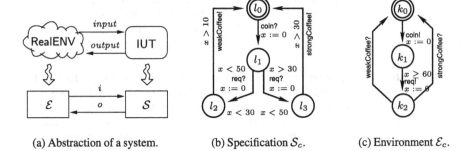

(a) Abstraction of a system.   (b) Specification $\mathcal{S}_c$.   (c) Environment $\mathcal{E}_c$.

Fig. 1. Embedded system and example models

Modeling the environment explicitly and separately and taking this into account during test generation has several advantages: 1) the test generation tool can synthesize only relevant and realistic scenarios for the given type of environment, which in turn reduces the number of required tests and improves the quality of the test suite; 2) the engineer can guide the test generator to specific situations of interest; 3) a separate environment model eases the system testing under different assumptions and use patterns.

The goal of relativized conformance testing is to check whether the behavior of the IUT is correct (conforming) to its specification $\mathcal{S}$ when operating under assumptions $\mathcal{E}$ about the environment. We propose relativized timed input/output conformance relation between model and IUT which coincides with timed trace inclusion taking the environment behavior into account.

Online Testing. Test cases can be generated from the model offline where the complete test scenarios and verdicts are computed apriori and before execution. Another approach is *online (on-the-fly) testing* that combines test generation and execution: only a single test primitive is generated from the model at a time which is then immediately executed on the IUT. Then the produced output by the IUT as well as its time of occurrence are checked against the specification, a new test primitive is produced and so forth until it is decided to end the test, or an error is detected. An observed test run is a trace consisting of an alternating sequence of (input or output) actions and time delays.

There are several advantages of online testing: 1) testing may potentially continue for a long time (hours or even days), and therefore long, intricate, and stressful test cases may be executed; 2) the state-space-explosion problem experienced by many offline test generation tools is reduced because only a limited part of the state-space needs to be stored at any point in time; 3) online test generators often allow more expressive specification languages, especially wrt. allowed non-determinism in real-time models.

Related Work. Model based test generation for real-time specifications has been investigated by others (see e.g., [6,9,11,13,14,18,20,21,25,26,28]), but remain relatively immature.

A solid and widespread implementation relation used in model based conformance testing of untimed systems is the input/output conformance relation by Tretmans [30]. Informally, input/output conformance requires for all specification traces that the implementation never produces an output not allowed by the specification, and that it never refuses to produce an output (stays quiescent) when the specification requires one.

As also noted in [18, 20] a timed input/output conformance relation can be obtained (assuming input enabledness) as timed trace inclusion between the implementation and its specification. Our work further extends this to a *relativized* conformance relation taking environment assumptions explicitly into account. In [30] the specification is permitted to be non-input enabled (thus making the conformance relation non-transitive in general) in order to capture environmental constraints. However, this requires explicit rewriting of the specification when different environments are to be used. Following the seminal work [19] our approach is based on an separate model of the environment. In particular, once conformance has been established under a particular environment, we can automatically conclude conformance under more restricted environments. Also, when the IUT is to be used in different environments, it suffices to test it under the most liberal environment assumptions. Furthermore, relativized conformance is transitive.

Model based *offline testing* is often based on a model coverage criterion like in [13, 15], on a test purpose as e.g. [17, 18], or a fault-model as [11, 14]. When specifications allow non-determinism, the generated test cases cannot be a sequence, but take the form of *behavior trees* adaptive to implementation controlled actions, e.g different outputs or timing. Therefore, most offline algorithms explicitly determinize the specification [10, 17, 25]. However, for expressive formalisms like timed automata this approach is infeasible because in general they cannot be determinized [2] and their unobservable actions cannot always (and when they can it may be very costly) be removed [32]. Much work on timed test generation from timed automata therefore restrict the amount and type of allowed non-determinism: [11, 13, 28] completely disallow non-determinism, [18, 25] restrict the use of clocks, guards or clock resets. However, in many cases it is important to allow non-determinism, because 1) specifications often contain a parallel composition of component-models, 2) it allows the implementor some freedom, and 3) the tester is usually concerned with abstract requirements rather than concrete details. In particular for real-time systems it may be crucial to specify timing uncertainty, e.g. an output is expected between 2 and 5 time units from now, but not exactly when. Timed automata model this by a non-determinism between delay and output transition.

In contrast, online testing is automatically adaptive and only implicitly determinizes the specification, and only partially up to the concrete trace observed so far. The (untimed) online testing algorithm proposed by Tretmans et. al. in [4, 34] continually computes the set of states that the specification can possibly occupy after the observations made so far. Online testing from Promela [34] and LOTOS specifications for untimed systems have been implemented in the TORX [33] tool, and practical application to real case studies show promising results [4, 31, 33]. However, TORX provides no support for real-time. Our work generalizes the TORX approach to timed systems and to the handling of the explicit environment assumptions. We allow a quite generous (non-deterministic) timed automata language. In addition, we compute the state-set symbolically to track the (potentially dense) timed state space.

Online testing from unrestricted non-deterministic timed automata using symbolic state-set computation [27] was first published by Krichen and Tripakis [20]. We implement a similar approach by extending the UPPAAL model-checker resulting in an integrated and mature testing and verification tool. Our work (originating from [7, 22, 24]; an abstract appeared in [23]) is different from [20] in that 1) the exact timed automata language variant is different and includes separable environment models, 2) we propose a relativized version of timed input/output conformance, 3) our algorithm (presented in much greater detail) generates tests relevant only for the specified environment, and 4) is shown to be sound and complete under certain assumptions, and finally 5) we provide experimental evidence of the feasibility of the technique.

Contributions. In this paper we describe a tool for online testing of real-time systems. Our main contributions are the notion of *relativized timed input/output conformance* and an implementation based on UPPAAL of a *symbolic algorithm* that performs online testing based on a (possibly densely timed and potentially non-deterministic) timed automata model of the IUT and its assumed environment. We prove under a certain testing hypothesis that our algorithm is sound and (in a precise probabilistic sense) complete. Furthermore, we apply T-UPPAAL to a medium sized case that demonstrates good error detection potential and very encouraging performance.

2   Test Specification

This section formally presents our semantic framework, and introduces TIOTS, timed automata, and our relativized input/output conformance relation.

2.1   Timed I/O Transition Systems

We assume a given set of actions A partitioned into two disjoint sets of output actions A_{out} and input actions A_{in}. In addition we assume that there is a distinguished unobservable action $\tau \notin A$. We denote by A_τ the set $A \cup \{\tau\}$.

Definition 1. *A timed I/O transition system (TIOTS) S is a tuple $(S, s_o, A_{in}, A_{out}, \rightarrow)$, where S is a set of states, $s_0 \in S$, and $\rightarrow \subseteq S \times (A_\tau \cup \mathbb{R}_{\geq 0}) \times S$ is a transition relation satisfying the usual constraints of time determinism (if $s \xrightarrow{d} s'$ and $s \xrightarrow{d} s''$ then $s' = s''$) and time additivity (if $s \xrightarrow{d_1} s'$ and $s' \xrightarrow{d_2} s''$ then $s \xrightarrow{d_1+d_2} s''$), $d \in \mathbb{R}_{\geq 0}$, where $\mathbb{R}_{\geq 0}$ denotes non-negative real numbers.*

Notation for TIOTS. Let $a, a_{1...n} \in A$, $\alpha \in A_\tau \cup \mathbb{R}_{\geq 0}$, and $d, d_{1...n} \in \mathbb{R}_{\geq 0}$. We write $s \xrightarrow{\alpha}$ iff $s \xrightarrow{\alpha} s'$ for some s'. We use $\Rightarrow$ to denote the τ-abstracted transition relation such that $s \xrightarrow{a} s'$ iff $s \xrightarrow{\tau}{}^* \xrightarrow{a} \xrightarrow{\tau}{}^* s'$, and $s \xrightarrow{d} s'$ iff $s \xrightarrow{\tau}{}^* \xrightarrow{d_1} \xrightarrow{\tau}{}^* \xrightarrow{d_2} \xrightarrow{\tau}{}^* \cdots \xrightarrow{\tau}{}^* \xrightarrow{d_n} \xrightarrow{\tau}{}^* s'$ where $d = d_1 + d_2 + \cdots d_n$. We extend $\Rightarrow$ to sequences in the usual manner.

We assume that the TIOTS S is strongly *input enabled* and *non-blocking*. S is strongly input enabled iff $s \xrightarrow{i}$ for all states s and for all input actions i. S is non-blocking iff for any state s and any $t \in \mathbb{R}_{\geq 0}$ there is a timed output trace $\sigma =$

$d_1 o_1 \ldots o_n d_{n+1}$ such that $s \overset{\sigma}{\Rightarrow}$ and $\sum_i d_i \geq t$. Thus $\mathcal{S}$ will not block time in any input enabled environment.

To model potential implementations it is usefull to define the properties of *isolated outputs* and *determinism*. We say that $\mathcal{S}$ has isolated outputs if whenever $s \overset{o}{\rightarrow}$ for some output action o, then $s \overset{\tau}{\nrightarrow}$ and $s \overset{d}{\nrightarrow}$ for all $d > 0$ and whenever $s \overset{o'}{\rightarrow}$ then $o' = o$. Finally, $\mathcal{S}$ is deterministic if for all delays or actions α and all states s, whenever $s \overset{\alpha}{\rightarrow} s'$ and $s \overset{\alpha}{\rightarrow} s''$ then $s' = s''$.

An observable *timed trace* $\sigma \in (A \cup \mathbb{R}_{\geq 0})^*$ is of the form $\sigma = d_1 a_1 d_2 \ldots a_k d_{k+1}$. We define the observable timed traces $\mathsf{TTr}(s)$ of a state s as:

$$\mathsf{TTr}(s) = \{\sigma \in (A \cup \mathbb{R}_{\geq 0})^* \mid s \overset{\sigma}{\Rightarrow}\} \tag{1}$$

For a state s (and subset $S' \subseteq S$) and a timed trace σ, s After σ is the set of states that can be reached after σ:

$$s \text{ After } \sigma = \{s' \mid s \overset{\sigma}{\Rightarrow} s'\}, \quad S' \text{ After } \sigma = \bigcup_{s \in S'} s \text{ After } \sigma \tag{2}$$

The set $\mathsf{Out}(s)$ of observable outputs or delays from states $s \in S' \subseteq S$ is defined as:

$$\mathsf{Out}(s) = \{a \in A_{out} \cup \mathbb{R}_{\geq 0} \mid s \overset{a}{\Rightarrow}\}, \quad \mathsf{Out}(S') = \bigcup_{s \in S'} \mathsf{Out}(s), \tag{3}$$

Timed automata [2] is an expressive and popular formalism for modelling real-time systems. Let X be a set of $\mathbb{R}_{\geq 0}$-valued variables called *clocks*. Let $\mathcal{G}(X)$ denote the set of *guards* on clocks being conjunctions of constraints of the form $x \bowtie c$, and let $\mathcal{U}(X)$ denote the set of *updates* of clocks corresponding to sequences of statements of the form $x := c$, where $x \in X$, $c \in \mathbb{N}$, and $\bowtie \in \{\leq, <, =, >, \geq\}$. A *timed automaton* over (A, X) is a tuple (L, ℓ_0, I, E), where L is a set of locations, $\ell_0 \in L$ is an initial location, $I : L \rightarrow \mathcal{G}(X)$ assigns invariants to locations, and E is a set of edges such that $E \subseteq L \times \mathcal{G}(X) \times A_\tau \times \mathcal{U}(X) \times L$. We write $\ell \xrightarrow{g, \alpha, u} \ell'$ iff $(\ell, g, \alpha, u, \ell') \in E$.

The semantics of a timed automaton is defined in terms of a TIOTS over states of the form $s = (\ell, \bar{v})$, where ℓ is a location and $\bar{v} \in \mathbb{R}_{\geq 0}^X$ is a clock valuation satisfying the invariant of ℓ. Intuitively, there are two kinds of transitions: discrete and delaying. In delaying transitions, $(\ell, \bar{v}) \overset{d}{\rightarrow} (\ell, \bar{v} + d)$, the values of all clocks of the automaton are incremented by the amount of the delay, d. Discrete transitions $(\ell, \bar{v}) \overset{\alpha}{\rightarrow} (\ell', \bar{v}')$ correspond to execution of edges $(\ell, g, \alpha, u, \ell')$ for which the guard g is satisfied by $\bar{v}$. The target state's $\bar{v}'$ is obtained by applying updates u and the invariants on ℓ' on $\bar{v}$.

Figure 1(b) shows a timed automaton specifying the requirements to a coffee machine. It has a facility that allows the user, after paying, to indicate his eagerness to get coffee by pushing a request button on the machine forcing it to output coffee. However, allowing insufficient brewing time results in a weak coffee. Waiting less than 30 time units definitely results in weak coffee, and waiting more than 50 definitely in strong coffee. Between 30 and 50 time units the choice is non-deterministic, meaning that the IUT/implementor may decide what to produce. After the request, it takes the machine an additional (non-deterministic) 10 to 30 (30 to 50) time units to produce weak coffee (strong coffee). The timed automaton in Fig. 1(c) models a potential (nice) user of the machine that pays before requesting coffee and wants strong coffee thus requesting only after 60 time units.

TIOTS Composition. Let $S = (S, s_0, A_{in}, A_{out}, \rightarrow)$ be an input enabled, non-blocking TIOTS. An *environment* $\mathcal{E}$ for S is itself an input enabled, non-blocking, TIOTS $\mathcal{E} = (E, e_0, A_{out}, A_{in}, \rightarrow)$. Here E is the set of environment states and the set of input (output) actions of $\mathcal{E}$ is identical to the output (input) actions of S. The parallel composition of S and $\mathcal{E}$ forms a *closed system* $S \parallel \mathcal{E}$ whose observable behavior is defined by the TIOTS $(S \times E, (s_0, e_0), A_{in}, A_{out}, \rightarrow)$ where $\rightarrow$ is defined as

$$\frac{s \xrightarrow{a} s' \quad e \xrightarrow{a} e'}{(s, e) \xrightarrow{a} (s', e')} \quad \frac{s \xrightarrow{\tau} s'}{(s, e) \xrightarrow{\tau} (s', e)} \quad \frac{e \xrightarrow{\tau} e'}{(s, e) \xrightarrow{\tau} (s, e')} \quad \frac{s \xrightarrow{d} s' \quad e \xrightarrow{d} e'}{(s, e) \xrightarrow{d} (s', e')} \quad (4)$$

The timed automata S_c and $\mathcal{E}_c$ respectively shown in Fig. 1(b) and 1(c) can be composed in parallel on actions $A_{in} = \{\text{req, coin}\}$ and $A_{out} = \{\text{weakCoffee, strongCoffee}\}$ forming a closed network (to avoid cluttering the figures we have not made them explicitly input enabled; for the unspecified inputs there is an undrawn self looping edge that merely consumes the input without changing the location).

2.2 Relativized Timed Conformance

In this section we define our notion of conformance between TIOTSs. Our notion derives from the input/output conformance relation (ioco) of Tretmans and de Vries [30,34] by taking time and environment constraints into account. Under assumptions of input enabledness our relativized timed conformance relation coincides with relativized timed trace inclusion. Like ioco, this relation ensures that the implementation has only the behavior allowed by the specification. In particular, 1) it is not allowed to produce an output at a time when one is not allowed by the specification, 2) it is not allowed to omit producing an output when one is required by the specification. Thus, timed trace inclusion offers the notion of time-bounded quiescence [8] that—in contrast to ioco's conceptual eternal quiescence—can be observed in a real-time system.

Definition 2. *Given an environment $e \in E$ the e-relativized timed input/output conformance relation* rtioco_e *between system states $s, t \in S$ is defined as:*

$$s \text{ rtioco}_e t \quad \text{iff} \quad \forall \sigma \in \text{TTr}(e). \text{Out}((s, e) \text{ After } \sigma) \subseteq \text{Out}((t, e) \text{ After } \sigma)$$

Whenever $s \text{ rtioco}_e t$ we will say that s is a correct implementation (or refinement) of the specification t under the environmental constraints expressed by e. Under the assumption of input-enabledness of both S and $\mathcal{E}$ we may characterize relativized conformance in terms of trace-inclusion as follows:

Lemma 1. *Let S and $\mathcal{E}$ be input-enabled with states $s, t \in S$ and $e \in E$ resp., then*

$$s \text{ rtioco}_e t \quad \text{iff} \quad \text{TTr}(s) \cap \text{TTr}(e) \subseteq \text{TTr}(t) \cap \text{TTr}(e)$$

Thus if $s \text{ rtioco}_e t$ does not hold then there exists a trace σ of e such that $s \overset{\sigma}{\Rightarrow}$ but $t \overset{\sigma}{\not\Rightarrow}$. Given the notion of relativized conformance it is natural to consider the preorder on environments based on their discriminating power, i.e. for environments e and f:

$$e \sqsubseteq f \quad \text{iff} \quad \text{rtioco}_f \subseteq \text{rtioco}_e \quad (5)$$

(to be read f is more discriminating than e). It follows from the definition of rtioco that $e \sqsubseteq f$ iff $\text{TTr}(e) \subseteq \text{TTr}(f)$. In particular there is a most (least) discriminating input enabled and non-blocking environment U (O) given by $\text{TTr}(U) = (A \cup$

$\mathbb{R}_{\geq 0}^{*}\ \left(\mathsf{TTr}(O) = (A_{out} \cup \mathbb{R}_{\geq 0})^{*}\right)$. The corresponding conformance relation rtioco$_U$ (rtioco$_O$) specializes to simple timed trace inclusion (timed output trace inclusion) between system states. Figures 2(a) and 2(b) show the most-discriminating and the least-discriminating environments.

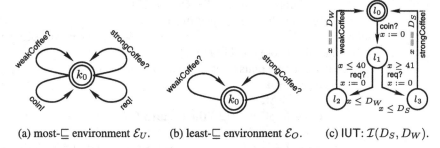

(a) most-$\sqsubseteq$ environment $\mathcal{E}_U$. (b) least-$\sqsubseteq$ environment $\mathcal{E}_O$. (c) IUT: $\mathcal{I}(D_S, D_W)$.

Fig. 2. Implementation of coffee machine

Examples. The specification machine $\mathcal{S}_c$ and environment $\mathcal{E}_c$ were described in Section 2.1. The (deterministic) implementation $\mathcal{I}(D_S, D_W)$ in Fig. 2(c) produces weak coffee (strong coffee) after less than 40 time units (more than 41 time units) and an additional brewing time of D_S (resp. D_W) time units. Observe that any trace of the implementation $\mathcal{I}(40, 20)$ (in any environment) can be matched by the specification; hence $\mathcal{I}(40, 20)$ rtioco$_{\mathcal{E}_U}$ S. Thus also $\mathcal{I}(40, 20)$ rtioco$_{\mathcal{E}_c}$ $\mathcal{S}_c$. In contrast $\mathcal{I}(70, 5)$ rti$\cancel{o}$co$_{\mathcal{E}_U}$ $\mathcal{S}_c$, but $\mathcal{I}(40, 5)$ rtioco$_{\mathcal{E}_c}$ $\mathcal{S}_c$ because $\mathcal{E}_c$ never requests weak coffee.

3 Test Generation and Execution

We present the main algorithm, its soundness, completeness and implementation.

3.1 The Main Algorithm

The input to Alg. 1 is two TIOTSs $\mathcal{S} \parallel \mathcal{E}$ respectively modelling the IUT and environment. It maintains the current reachable state set $\mathcal{Z} \subseteq S \times E$ that the test specification can possibly occupy after the timed trace observed so far. Knowing this, state estimate allows it to choose appropriate test primitives and to validate IUT outputs.

The tester can perform three basic actions: either send an input (enabled environment output) to the IUT, wait for an output for some time, or reset the IUT and restart. If the tester observes an output or a time delay it checks whether this is legal according to the state set. The state set is updated whenever an input is offered, an output or a delay is observed $\beta \in A \cup \mathbb{R}_{\geq 0}$: $\mathcal{Z}$ After $\beta = \{(s', e') \mid (s, e) \in \mathcal{Z}.(s, e) \overset{\beta}{\Rightarrow} (s', e')\}$. Illegal occurrence or absence of an output is detected if the state set becomes empty which is the result if the observed trace is not in the specification. The functions used in Alg. 1 are defined as: EnvOutput$(\mathcal{Z}) = \{a \in A_{in} \mid \exists(s, e) \in \mathcal{Z}.e \overset{a}{\rightarrow}\}$, ImpOutput$(\mathcal{Z}) = \{a \in A_{out} \mid \exists(s, e) \in \mathcal{Z}.s \overset{a}{\rightarrow}\}$, and Delays$(\mathcal{Z}) = \{d \mid \exists(s, e) \in \mathcal{Z}.e \overset{d}{\Rightarrow}\}$. Note that EnvOutput is empty if the environment has no outputs to offer. Similarly, Delays cannot pick at random from the entire domain of real-numbers if the environment must

---

Alg. 1 Test generation and execution: $TestGenExe(S, \mathcal{E}, \mathsf{IUT}, T)$. $\mathcal{Z} := \{(s_0, e_0)\}$.

    while $\mathcal{Z} \neq \emptyset \wedge \sharp iterations \leq T$ **do** switch(*action, delay, restart*) randomly:

        action: `// offer an input`

            if $\mathsf{EnvOutput}(\mathcal{Z}) \neq \emptyset$

                randomly choose $i \in \mathsf{EnvOutput}(\mathcal{Z})$

                send i to IUT, $\mathcal{Z} := \mathcal{Z}$ After i

        delay: `// wait for an output`

            randomly choose $d \in \mathsf{Delays}(\mathcal{Z})$

            sleep for d time units or wake up on output o at $d' \leq d$

            if o occurs **then**

                $\mathcal{Z} := \mathcal{Z}$ After d'

                if $o \notin \mathsf{ImpOutput}(\mathcal{Z})$ **then return** *fail*

                else $\mathcal{Z} := \mathcal{Z}$ After o

            else $\mathcal{Z} := \mathcal{Z}$ After d `// no output within d delay`

        restart: $\mathcal{Z} := \{(s_0, e_0)\}$, **reset** IUT `//reset and restart`

    if $\mathcal{Z} = \emptyset$ **then return** *fail* **else return** *pass*

---

produce an input to the IUT model before a certain moment in time. We use the efficient reachability algorithm implementation [3] to compute the operator After. It operates on bounded symbolic states, checks for inclusions and thus always terminates even if the model contains τ action loops.

3.2 Soundness and Completeness

Alg. 1 constitutes a randomized algorithm for providing stimuli to (in terms of input and delays) and observing resulting reactions from (in terms of output) a given IUT. Assuming the behavior of the IUT is a non-blocking, input enabled, deterministic TIOTS with isolated outputs the reaction to any given timed input trace $\sigma = d_1 i_1 \ldots d_k i_k d_{i+1}$ is completely deterministic. More precisely, given the stimuli σ there is a unique $\rho \in \mathsf{TTr}(\mathsf{IUT})$ such that $\rho \uparrow A_{in} = \sigma$, where $\rho \uparrow A_{in}$ is the natural projection of the timed trace ρ to the set of input actions.

Under a certain (theoretically necessary) testing hypothesis about the behavior of IUT and given that the TIOTSs S and $\mathcal{E}$ satisfy certain assumptions, the randomization used in Alg. 1 may be chosen such that the algorithm is both complete and sound in the sense that it (eventually with probability one) gives the verdict "fail" in all cases of non-conformance and the verdict "pass" in cases of conformance. The hypothesis and assumptions are based on the results on digitization techniques in [29][1] which allow the dense-time trace inclusion problem between two sets of timed traces to be reduced to discrete time. In particular it suffices to choose unit delays in Alg. 1 (assuming that the models and IUT share the same magnitude of a time unit).

Theorem 1. *Assume that the behavior of* IUT *may be modelled[2] as an input enabled, non-blocking, deterministic TIOTS with isolated outputs,* $\mathsf{TTr}(\mathsf{IUT})$ *and* $\mathsf{TTr}(\mathcal{E})$ *are*

---

[1] We refer the reader to [29] for the precise definition of digitization and inverse digitization.

[2] The assumption that the IUT can be modelled by a formal object in a given class is commonly referred to as the *test hypothesis*. Only its existence is assumed, not a known instance.

closed under digitization *and that* $\mathsf{TTr}(\mathcal{S})$ *is* closed under inverse digitization. *Then Alg. 1 with only unit delays is sound and complete in the following senses:*

1. *Whenever* $TestGenExe(\mathcal{S}, \mathcal{E}, \mathsf{IUT}, T) = fail$ *then* IUT rtịóco$_\mathcal{E}$ $\mathcal{S}$.
2. *Whenever* IUT rtịóco$_\mathcal{E}$ $\mathcal{S}$ *then* $\mathsf{Prob}\big(TestGenExe(\mathcal{S}, \mathcal{E}, \mathsf{IUT}, T) = fail\big) \xrightarrow{T \to \infty} 1$
   where T is the maximum number of iterations of the while-loop before exiting.

Proof. (Sketch) Soundness follows from an easy induction on $|\rho|$ that when starting each iteration of the while-loop the timed trace ρ observed since the last restart satisfies $\rho \in \mathsf{TTr}(\mathsf{IUT})$, $\rho \in \mathsf{TTr}(\mathcal{E})$ and $\rho \in \mathsf{TTr}(\mathcal{S})$ and that any chosen extension $\rho\alpha$ still lies in $\mathsf{TTr}(\mathsf{IUT}) \cap \mathsf{TTr}(\mathcal{E})$.

As for completeness assume that the IUT does not conform to $\mathcal{S}$ relative to $\mathcal{E}$. Then $\mathsf{TTr}(\mathsf{IUT}) \cap \mathsf{TTr}(\mathcal{E}) \not\subseteq \mathsf{TTr}(\mathcal{S})$. However due to the assumed properties of closure with respect to digitization respectively inverse digitization this failing timed trace inclusion is equivalent to the existence of a timed trace $\rho = d_1 a_1 d_2 a_2 \ldots d_k a_k d_{k+1}$ with all delays being integral such that $\rho \in \mathsf{TTr}(\mathsf{IUT}) \cap \mathsf{TTr}(\mathcal{E})$ but $\rho \notin \mathsf{TTr}(\mathcal{S})$. Now let $\sigma = \rho \uparrow A_{in}$; that is σ is the input-delay stimuli allowed by $\mathcal{E}$ which when given to IUT will result in the timed trace ρ. Now assume that the random choice of input action, unit delay and restart is made using a fixed discrete and finite probability distribution (with p being the smallest probability used) it is clear that:

$$\mathsf{Prob}(\sigma \text{ is generated between two given consecutive restarts}) \geq p^{K+D}$$

where K respectively D is the number of input actions respectively accumulated delay in σ. Now let $\epsilon = p^{K+D}$ it follows that

$$\mathsf{Prob}(\sigma \text{ is generated before k'th restart}) \geq 1 - (1 - \epsilon)^{k-1}$$

Obviously there will in general be several input stimuli that will reveal the lack of conformance. Hence the above probability just provides a lower bound for Alg. 1 yielding the verdict "fail" before the k'th restart. Obviously, as $T \to \infty$ also the number of restarts diverges and hence we see that $\mathsf{Prob}(\sigma \text{ is generated}) = 1$.   □

From [16, 29] it follows that the closure properties required in Theorem 1 are satisfied if the behavior of IUT and $\mathcal{E}$ are TIOTSs induced by closed timed automata (i.e. where all guards and invariants are non-strict) and $\mathcal{S}$ is a TIOTS induced by an open timed automaton (i.e. with guards and invariants being strict). In practice these requirements are not restrictive, e.g. for strict guards one can always scale the clock constants to obtain arbitrary high precision.

3.3   Symbolic State-Set Computation

We now discuss the concrete realization of Alg. 1. We use (well established) symbolic constraint solving techniques to represent sets of clock valuations compactly. A zone over a set of clocks X is a conjunction of clock in-equations of the form $x_i - x_j \prec c_{i,j}$, $x_i \prec c_{iu}$, and $c_{il} \prec x_i$, where $\prec \in \{<, \leq\}$, $c_{i,j}, c_{il}, c_{iu}$ are integer constants including $\pm\infty$, and $x_i, x_j \in X$. A *symbolic state* is a pair $\langle \bar{\ell}, Z \rangle$ consisting of a vector $\bar{\ell}$ of locations for each parallel automaton and the zone Z. Z denotes a set of clock valuations, i.e., a symbolic state represents a set of concrete states: $\langle \bar{\ell}, Z \rangle = \{(\bar{\ell}, \bar{v}) \mid \bar{v} \in Z\}$.

Henceforth $\mathcal{Z} = \{\langle \bar{\ell}_1, Z_1 \rangle \ldots \langle \bar{\ell}_n, Z_n \rangle\}$ denotes the set of concrete states represented by the union of the symbolic states of $\mathcal{Z}$.

We use the following operations on zones: conjunction $Z \wedge Z'$, future $Z^\uparrow = \{\bar{v} + d \mid \bar{v} \in Z, d \in \mathbb{R}_{\geq 0}\}$, clock x assignment to c value $Z_{x:=c} = \{\bar{v}[c/x] \mid \bar{v} \in Z\}$, Z_r the (successive) assignment of all clock assignments in r, containment check $Z \subseteq Z'$, and check for emptiness $Z = \emptyset$. The symbolic transition relation $\rightarrowtail$ between symbolic states denotes the possibility of taking a transition from a (concrete) state in the source symbolic state to one in the destination. It is computed as follows:

$$\langle \bar{\ell}, Z \rangle \xrightarrow{\gamma} \langle \bar{\ell}', (Z \wedge g)_r \wedge I(\bar{\ell}') \rangle \text{ if } \bar{\ell} \xrightarrow{g, \gamma, r} \bar{\ell}' \text{ where } \gamma \in A_\tau \qquad (6)$$

The required symbolic algorithms are similar to those used for model checking [1,3] except that only states up to a certain time limit need to be computed. This is most easily accomplished by introducing an auxiliary clock t that is set to zero whenever an observable action occurs.

Alg. 2 computes $\mathsf{Closure}_{\delta\tau}(\mathcal{Z}, d)$ that collects the reachable symbolic states within a delay of d: $\mathsf{Closure}_{\delta\tau}(\mathcal{Z}, d) = \bigcup_{0 \leq \delta \leq d} \{\langle \bar{\ell}', Z' \rangle \mid \langle \bar{\ell}, Z \rangle \in \mathcal{Z}, \langle \bar{\ell}, Z \rangle \xRightarrow{\delta} \langle \bar{\ell}', Z' \rangle\}$. The predicate $\mathsf{Contains}(\mathcal{Z}, \langle \bar{\ell}, Z \rangle)$ tests whether a symbolic state is covered by some symbolic state in $\mathcal{Z}$.

Alg. 2 $\mathsf{Closure}_{\delta\tau}(\mathcal{Z}, d)$. $passed := \emptyset$, $waits := \mathcal{Z}$

    while $waits \neq \emptyset$ **do**
        $waits := waits \setminus \{\langle \bar{\ell}, Z \rangle\}$ `// pick a symbolic state`
        $Z := Z^\uparrow \wedge (t \leq d) \wedge I(\bar{\ell})$ `// limited delay`
        $passed := passed \cup \{\langle \bar{\ell}, Z \rangle\}$
        for each symbolic transition $\langle \bar{\ell}, Z \rangle \xrightarrow{\tau} \langle \bar{\ell}', Z' \rangle$
            if not $\mathsf{Contains}(passed, \langle \bar{\ell}', Z' \rangle)$ **then** $waits := waits \cup \{\langle \bar{\ell}', Z' \rangle\}$
    return $passed$.

The function $\mathsf{Closure}_\tau(\mathcal{Z}) = \mathsf{Closure}_{\delta\tau}(\mathcal{Z}, 0)$ collects the reachable symbolic state set after all possible internal transitions in zero delay can be computed similarly. Given these functions, the algorithms for computing $\mathcal{Z}$ After d and $\mathcal{Z}$ After a become trivial:

$$\mathcal{Z} \text{ After } a = \mathsf{Closure}_\tau\left(\{\langle \bar{\ell}', Z' \rangle \mid \langle \bar{\ell}, Z \rangle \in \mathsf{Closure}_\tau(\mathcal{Z}), \langle \bar{\ell}, Z \rangle \xrightarrow{a} \langle \bar{\ell}', Z' \rangle\}\right) \quad (7)$$

$$\mathcal{Z} \text{ After } d = \left\{\langle \bar{\ell}, Z' \rangle \mid \langle \bar{l}, Z \rangle \in \mathsf{Closure}_{\delta\tau}(\mathcal{Z}, d), Z' = (Z \wedge (t == d))_{t:=0}\right\} \quad (8)$$

3.4 Choice of Delays

The environment model restricts the possible actions that can be chosen by the tester. It bounds the delays before an input must be given or output expected, and limits the possible inputs. In particular it is important to choose delays not exceeding the time bound within which the environment is required to offer an input (invariant conditions may force inputs). Thus $\mathsf{Delays}(\mathcal{Z})$ must not contain delays exceeding forced inputs.

To cheaply compute a safe delay given a symbolic state-set $\mathcal{Z}$ we propose the following technique: pick a random symbolic state $\langle \bar{\ell}, Z \rangle \in \mathcal{Z}$, compute its timed future as $Z' = (Z_{t:=0})^\uparrow \wedge I(\bar{\ell})$, and pick randomly $d \in [0, \max_t(Z'))$, where $\max_t(Z)$ extracts the maximum value of the auxiliary clock t in Z. Note that this will not compute the exact longest possible delay because it does not follow internal transitions (i.e the conjuncted invariant I may force an internal transition rather than an observable input). When the chosen delay has been performed, the state-set will be updated for the next iteration of the algorithm. Computing the exact delays is possible but would involve computing the more expensive $\mathsf{Closure}_{\delta\tau}(\mathcal{Z}, \infty)$.

Furthermore, it is desirable to compute time intervals where inputs are enabled for two reasons: 1) to optimize the algorithm avoiding too many superfluous attempts to offer inputs (condition $\mathsf{EnvOutput}(\mathcal{Z}) \neq \emptyset$ in Alg. 1), and 2) to guide the algorithm to cover the structure (transitions and locations) of the specification [25]. This optimization can be performed using the presented techniques, but we omit the details due to space limitations.

4 Experiments

We implemented our algorithm by extending the mature Uppaal model-checker tool to the testing tool T-Uppaal. Besides a graphical timed automata editor, Uppaal provides an efficient implementation of the basic symbolic operations. Unlike Uppaal, T-Uppaal does not store the reached state space, but only the current symbolic state set. We allow the full Uppaal timed automata language, including non-deterministic (action and timing) specifications and discrete variables. The IUT is connected to T-Uppaal via an adapter component translating abstract I/O actions into their real representation, and sends (receives) them to (from) the IUT.

This section presents the results of the first set of experiments using our implementation. The purpose is to indicate the feasibility of our technique in terms of applicability, error detection, and performance in terms of state-set size and computation time.

4.1 Test Specification

We slightly changed and adopted a simple railway control system specification from [35]. A rail-road intersection controller monitors trains on a set of tracks with a shared segment, e.g. a train-station. Its main objective is to ensure that only one train occupies the shared segment at a time, and to grant access in arrival order. We assume 4 tracks, and for simplicity 1 train per track at a time. Trains on track i signal the controller when they approach and leave the station using signals $appr_i$ and $leave_i$ respectively. When train i approaches an occupied segment the controller is required to issue a $stop_i$ within $5mtu$ (model time units), and issue go_i within $5mtu$ after the segment becomes free.

The environment assumption model consists of 4 concurrent timed automata each modeling the assumed behavior of a train. The model for train 1 is shown in Fig. 3(a); the remaining trains are identical except for the train-id. The model of the IUT requirements consists of 4 concurrent train control automata (Fig. 3(b)) tracking the position of each potential train, and one queue automaton tracking their arrival order (Fig. 3(c):

list is an array of integers, and i is an index into the array). We use UPPAAL syntax to illustrate timed automata. Initial locations are marked using a double circle. Edges are by convention labeled by the triple: guard, action, and assignment in that order. The internal τ-action is indicated by an absent action label. Committed locations are indicated by a location with an encircled "C". A committed location must be left immediately as the next transition taken by the system. Finally, bold-faced clock conditions placed under locations are location invariants.

The complete test specification is a reasonably large and nontrivial first experiment: it consists of 9 concurrent timed automata, 8 clocks, and a FIFO queue data structure.

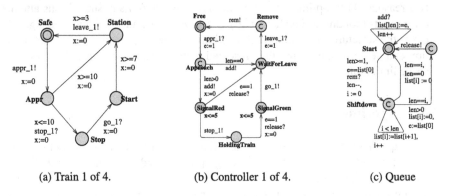

(a) Train 1 of 4.   (b) Controller 1 of 4.   (c) Queue

Fig. 3. Test specification for train controller: (a) as environment, (b) and (c) as implementation

4.2 Implementation Under Test

The IUT is implemented as an approximately 100 line C++ program following the basic structure of the specification. It uses POSIX Threads, locks and condition variables for multi-threading and synchronization. It consists of one thread per train, and queue data structure whose access is guarded by mutual exclusion and condition variables. In the experiment, the IUT runs in the same address space as the T-UPPAAL tool, and input/output actions are communicated to and from the driver/adapter via two single place bounded buffers. In addition we have created a number of erroneous mutations based on the *assumed* correct implementation (**M0**):

M1: The stop$_3$ signal is issued $1mtu$ too late.
M2: The controller issues stop$_1$ instead of stop$_3$.
M3: The controller never issues stop$_3$.
M4: The controller uses a bounded queue up to 3 trains, where the 4th train overwrites the 3rd.
M5: The controller uses LIFO queue instead of FIFO.
M6: The controller ignores appr$_3$, if a train arrives before $2mtu$ after entering the location Free.

4.3 Error Detection Capability

The experiments are run on an 8-processor workstation: T-UPPAAL runs on one CPU whereas the IUT may run on one or more of the remaining. T-UPPAAL itself does not require these extreme amount of resources, and it runs well on a standard PC, but a multiprocessor allows T-UPPAAL and the IUT to run in parallel as they would normally do in a black-box system level test.

To allow for faster and more experiments and reduce potential problems with real-time clock synchronization, we used a simulated clock progressing when both T-UPPAAL and the IUT need to let time pass. Each mutant is tested 1100 times each with an upper time limit of $100000mtu$. All runs of **M1-6** mutants failed and all runs of **M0** passed with timeout for testing. The minimum, maximum, and average running time and number of used input actions are summarized on the left side of Table 1.

The results show that all erroneous mutants are killed surprisingly quickly using less than 100 input actions and less than $2100mtu$. In contrast the assumed correct implementation **M0** was not killed and was subjected to at least 3500 inputs stimuli and survived for more than 300 times longer than other mutants in average. In conclusion, the results indicate that online real-time testing may be a highly effective technique.

Table 1. Error detection and performance measures

Mu-tant	Error detection capability						State-set size				Execution time, μs			
	Input actions			Duration, *mtu*			After(delay)		After(action)		After(delay)		After(action)	
	Min	Avg	Max	Min	Avg	Max	Avg	Max	Avg	Max	Avg	Max	Avg	Max
M1	2	4.8	16	0	68.8	318	2.3	18	2.7	28	1113	3128	141	787
M2	2	4.6	13	1	66.4	389	2.3	22	2.8	30	1118	3311	147	791
M3	2	4.7	14	0	66.4	398	2.2	22	2.7	30	1112	3392	141	834
M4	6	8.5	18	28	165.0	532	2.8	24	3.1	48	1113	3469	125	936
M5	4	5.6	12	14	89.8	364	2.8	24	3.3	48	1131	3222	146	919
M6	2	14.1	92	0	299.6	2077	2.7	27	2.9	36	1098	3531	110	861
M0	3565	3751.4	3966	10^5	10^5	10^5	2.7	31	2.9	46	1085	3591	101	950

4.4 Performance

Based on the same setup from Section 4.3 we instrumented T-UPPAAL to record the number of symbolic states, and the amount of CPU time used to compute the next state-set after a delay and an observable action. The right side of Table 1 summarizes the results. The state-set size is only 2-3 in average, but it varies a lot, up to 48 states. In average, the state-set sizes reached after performing a delay appear larger than after an action. In average it costs only $1.1ms$ to compute the successor state-set after a delay, and less than $0.2ms$ after an action. Thus it seems feasible to generate tests from much larger specifications, obviously depending on the scale of time units.

In conclusion, the performance of our technique looks very promising and appears to be fast enough for many real-time systems. Obviously, more experiments on varying size and complexity models are needed to find the firm limitations of the technique.

5 Conclusions and Future Work

We have presented the T-UPPAAL tool and approach to testing of embedded systems using real-time online testing from non-deterministic timed automata specifications.

Based on an experiment with a non-trivial specification we conclude that our notion of relativized input/output conformance and our sound and complete randomized online testing algorithm appear correct and feasible. We further conclude that our algorithm is implementable, and T-UPPAAL tool implementation shows encouraging results both in terms of error detection capability and performance of the symbolic state-set computation algorithm. However, further work and real-life applications are needed to evaluate the algorithm and the tool in detail.

Besides practical application, we plan to improve the tool in several directions. For instance, to estimate model coverage (e.g. like in [5]) of the trace and use it to guide the random choices made by the algorithm and investigate their impact on the error detection capability. For large case studies, we also need advanced test data generation support like in [12]. We also plan to include observation uncertainty into our algorithm (i.e., outputs and given stimuli classified in an interval of time rather than a time instance), to improve clock synchronization between T-UPPAAL and the implementation, and a value passing mechanism to make tool easier to adapt.

Acknowledgments. We would like to thank anonymous reviewer for a valuable insight to our relativized timed input/output conformance relation.

References

1. T. Henzinger and X. Nicollin and J. Sifakis and S. Yovine. Symbolic model checking for real-time systems. *Information and Computation*, 111(2):193–244, June 1994.
2. R. Alur and D.L. Dill. A Theory of Timed Automata. *Theoretical Computer Science*, 126(2):183–235, April 1994.
3. G. Behrmann, J. Bengtsson, A. David, K.G. Larsen, P. Pettersson, and W. Yi. Uppaal implementation secrets. In *Formal Techniques in Real-Time and Fault-Tolerant Systems: 7th International Symposium, FTRTFT 2002*, pages 3–22, September 2002.
4. A. Belinfante, J. Feenstra, R.G. de Vries, J. Tretmans, N. Goga, L. Feijs, S. Mauw, and L. Heerink. Formal test automation: A simple experiment. In 12th *Int. Workshop on Testing of Communicating Systems*, pages 179–196, 1999.
5. Johan Blom, Anders Hessel, Bengt Jonsson, and Paul Pettersson. Specifying and generating test cases using observer automata. In *Formal Approaches to Testing of Software*, Linz, Austria, September 21 2004. Lecture Notes in Computer Science.
6. V. Braberman, M. Felder, and M. Marré. Testing Timing Behaviors of Real Time Software. In *Quality Week 1997. San Francisco, USA.*, pages 143–155, April-May 1997 1997.
7. E. Brinksma, K.G. Larsen, B. Nielsen, and J. Tretmans. Systematic Testing of Realtime Embedded Software Systems (STRESS), March 2002. Research proposal submitted and accepted by the Dutch Research Council.
8. Laura Brandán Briones and Ed Brinksma. A test generation framework for quiescent real-time systems. In *Formal Approaches to Testing of Software*, Linz, Austria, September 21 2004. Lecture Notes in Computer Science.
9. R. Cardell-Oliver. Conformance Testing of Real-Time Systems with Timed Automata. *Formal Aspects of Computing*, 12(5):350–371, 2000.
10. R. Cleaveland and M. Hennessy. Testing Equivalence as a Bisimulation Equivalence. *Formal Aspects of Computing*, 5:1–20, 1993.

11. A. En-Nouaary, R. Dssouli, F. Khendek, and A. Elqortobi. Timed Test Cases Generation Based on State Characterization Technique. In *19th IEEE Real-Time Systems Symposium (RTSS'98)*, pages 220–229, December 2–4 1998.

12. Lars Frantzen, Jan Tretmans, and Tim Willemse. Test generation based on symbolic specifications. In *Formal Approaches to Testing of Software*, Linz, Austria, September 21 2004. Lecture Notes in Computer Science.

13. A. Hessel, K.G. Larsen, B. Nielsen, P. Pettersson, and A. Skou. Time-Optimal Test Cases for Real-Time Systems. In *3rd International Workshop on Formal approaches to Testing of Software (FATES 2003)*, Montréal, Québec, Canada, October 2003.

14. T. Higashino, A. Nakata, K. Taniguchi, and A R. Cavalli. Generating test cases for a timed i/o automaton model. In *IFIP Int'l Work. Test. Communicat. Syst.*, pages 197–214, 1999.

15. H.S. Hong, I. Lee, O. Sokolsky, and H. Ural. A temporal logic based theory of test coverage and generation. In *Proceedings of the 8th International Conference on Tools and Algorithms for the Construction and Analysis of Systems*, pages 327–341. Springer-Verlag, 2002.

16. J. Ouaknine and J. Worrell. Revisiting digitization, robustness, and decidability for timed automata. In *18th IEEE Symposium on Logic in Computer Science (LICS 2003) Ottawa, Canada*, pages 198–207. IEEE Computer Society, june 2003.

17. T. Jéron and P. Morel. Test generation derived from model-checking. In N. Halbwachs and D. Peled, editors, *CAV'99, Trento, Italy*, volume 1633 of *LNCS*, pages 108–122. Springer-Verlag, July 1999.

18. A. Khoumsi, T. Jéron, and H. Marchand. Test cases generation for nondeterministic real-time systems. In *3rd International Workshop on Formal Approaches to Testing of Software (FATES'03). LNCS 2931*, Montreal, Canada, 2003.

19. K.G. Larsen. A Context Dependent Equivalence Between Processes. *Theoretical Computer Science*, 49:185–215, 1987.

20. M. Krichen and S. Tripakis. Black-box Conformance Testing for Real-Time Systems. In *Model Checking Software: 11th International SPIN Workshop*, volume LNCS 2989. Springer, April 2004.

21. D. Mandrioli, S. Morasca, and A. Morzenti. Generating Test Cases for Real-Time Systems from Logic Specifications. *ACM Transactions on Computer Systems*, 13(4):365–398, 1995.

22. M. Mikucionis, K.G. Larsen, and B. Nielsen. Online on-the-fly testing of real-time systems. Technical Report RS-03-49, Basic Research In Computer Science (BRICS), December 2003.

23. M. Mikucionis, B. Nielsen, and K.G. Larsen. Real-time system testing on-the-fly. In *the 15th Nordic Workshop on Programming Theory*, number 34 in B, pages 36–38, Turku, Finland, October 29–31 2003. Åbo Akademi, Department of Computer Science, Finland. Abstracts.

24. M. Mikucionis and E. Sasnauskaite. On-the-fly testing using UPPAAL. Master's thesis, Department of Computer Science, Aalborg University, Denmark, June 2003.

25. B. Nielsen and A. Skou. Automated Test Generation from Timed Automata. In *Tools and Algorithms for the Construction and Analysis of Systems*, pages 343–357, April 2001.

26. J. Peleska, P. Amthor, S. Dick, O. Meyer, M. Siegel, and C. Zahlten. Testing Reactive Real-Time Systems. In *Material for the School – 5th International School and Symposium on Formal Techniques in Real-Time and Fault-Tolerant Systems (FTRTFT'98)*, 1998. Lyngby, Denmark.

27. S. Tripakis. Fault Diagnosis for Timed Automata. In *Formal Techniques in Real-Time and Fault Tolerant Systems (FTRTFT'02)*, volume LNCS 2469. Springer, 2002.

28. J. Springintveld, F. Vaandrager, and P.R. D'Argenio. Testing Timed Automata. *Theoretical Computer Science*, 254(1-2):225–257, March 2001.

29. T.A. Henzinger and Z. Manna and A. Pnueli. What good are digital clocks? In Werner Kuich, editor, *Automata, Languages and Programming, 19th International Colloquium, ICALP92, Vienna, Austria*, volume 623 of *LNCS*, pages 545–558. Springer, july 1992.

30. J. Tretmans. Testing concurrent systems: A formal approach. In J.C.M Baeten and S. Mauw, editors, *CONCUR'99 – 10th Int. Conference on Concurrency Theory*, volume 1664 of *Lecture Notes in Computer Science*, pages 46–65. Springer-Verlag, 1999.

31. J. Tretmans and A. Belinfante. Automatic testing with formal methods. In *EuroSTAR'99: 7th European Int. Conference on Software Testing, Analysis & Review*, Barcelona, Spain, November 8–12, 1999. EuroStar Conferences, Galway, Ireland.

32. V. Diekert, P. Gastin, A. Petit. Removing epsilon-Transitions in Timed Automata. In *14th Annual Symposium on Theoretical Aspects of Computer Science, STACS 1997*, pages 583–594, Lübeck, Germany, February 1997. LNCS, Vol. 1200, Springer.

33. R. de Vries, J. Tretmans, A. Belinfante, J. Feenstra, L. Feijs, S. Mauw, N. Goga, L. Heerink, and A. de Heer. Côte de resyste in PROGRESS. In STW Technology Foundation, editor, PROGRESS 2000 – *Workshop on Embedded Systems*, pages 141–148, Utrecht, The Netherlands, October 2000.

34. R.G. de Vries and J. Tretmans. On-the-fly conformance testing using SPIN. *Software Tools for Technology Transfer*, 2(4):382–393, March 2000.

35. Wang Yi, Paul Pettersson, and Mats Daniels. Automatic Verification of Real-Time Communicating Systems By Constraint-Solving. In Dieter Hogrefe and Stefan Leue, editors, *Proc. of the 7th Int. Conf. on Formal Description Techniques*, pages 223–238. North–Holland, 1994.

Testing Deadlock-Freeness in Real-Time Systems: A Formal Approach

Behzad Bordbar[1] and Kozo Okano[2]

[1] University of Birmingham
B.Bordbar@cs.bham.ac.uk
[2] Osaka University
okano@ist.osaka-u.ac.jp

Abstract. A *Time Action Lock* is a state of a Real-time system at which neither time can progress nor an action can occur. Time Action Locks are often seen as signs of errors in the model or inconsistencies in the specification. As a result, finding out and resolving Time Action Locks is a major task for the designers of Real-time systems. Verification is one of the methods of discovering deadlocks. However, due to state explosion, the verification of deadlock freeness is computationally expensive. The aim of this paper is to present a computationally cheap testing method for Timed Automata models and pointing out any source of *possible* Time Action Locks to the designer.

We have implemented the approach presented in the paper, which is based on the geometry of Timed Automata, via a Testing Tool called TALC (Time Action Lock Checker). TALC, which is used in the conjunction with the model checker UPPAAL, tests the UPPAAL model and provides feedback to the designer. We have illustrated our method by applying TALC to a model of a simple communication protocol.

Keywords: Testing, Real-time System, Deadlock, Timed Automata, Rational Presburger Sentences, Communication Protocol.

1   Introduction

In a general term, a deadlock is a state at which a system is unable to progress any further. Various types of deadlock in Real-time systems are studied in the literature [16, 8, 7, 27, 28]. In particular, a *Time Lock* [27] is a state at which time is prevented from passing beyond a certain point, and *Time Action Lock* [8] is a Time Lock state at which no action can occur. As a result, a Time Action Lock, is a state at which neither time can progress nor an action can occur.

In this paper, we shall deal with Real-time systems, which are modelled via Timed Automata [1]. Such systems can be verified with the help of model checkers such as UPPAAL [2, 6], which uses a variant of Timed Automata model of [1]. UPPAAL has been successfully applied to the verification of Real-time systems [5, 15, 20, 9, 2].

The process of verification of a property σ starts by creating a UPPAAL Timed Automata model of the Real-time system. Before conducting the verification of the property σ, we often check the model for the existence of deadlocks. This is to ensure the

J. Grabowski and B. Nielsen (Eds.): FATES 2004, LNCS 3395, pp. 95–109, 2005.
© Springer-Verlag Berlin Heidelberg 2005

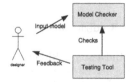

Fig. 1. Combining Testing tool and Model Checker

integrity of the design; as the existence of a deadlock is often interpreted as either an error in the model or a sign of inconsistencies in the specification. As a result, when a model checker informs us of the existence of a deadlock, we scrutinise the model to discover the cause of the deadlock. However, due to state explosion, the verification of deadlock freeness is computationally expensive. The aim of this paper is to present a method of testing of the Timed Automata models to point out any source of *possible* Time Action Locks to the designer. This is to help avoiding the verification of the model for deadlock-freeness, which is computationally expensive. Our approach can be implemented via a *Testing Tool*, which works in parallel with a model checker as depicted in Fig. 1. The *designer* creates a model of the system in the *Model Checker*. The Testing Tool *checks* the model for Time Action Locks and provides feedback to the designer. The feedback provided to the designer is either, *"the system is deadlock free"* or *"there is a possibility of deadlocks."* In the case that the system is declared deadlock free by the Testing Tool, there is no need to use the Model Checker to ensure the system is deadlock free, and the designer can focus on the verification of σ. If the Testing tool declares that there is a possibility of deadlocks, sources of the deadlock are pointed out, which can help the designer in scrutinising the model for finding any possible flaw in the model or inconsistencies in the specification.

The approach presented in this paper is based on the geometry of the Timed Automata. In a Timed Automaton, the progress of time is subject to a set of constraints, which form convex regions [27] in the n-dimensional Eucleadian space $\mathbb{R}^n$. As a result, for every location of a Timed Automaton, various types of constraint such as *invariants* and *guards* correspond to regions in $\mathbb{R}^n$. The idea behind our approach is to identify subsets of such regions that might cause a Time Action Lock and test them.

Based on our approach, we have developed a Testing Tool called *Time Action Lock Checker* (TALC). TALC, which works in conjunction with UPPAAL, tests the Timed Automata via Rational Presburger Sentences and is available for download at http://www.cs.bham.ac.uk/~bxb/TALC.html.

The paper is organised as follows. We shall start by a brief introduction on the Timed Automata. Section 3 follows with a brief review of the background material on Presburger Arithmetic. Section 4 reviews definitions of various types of Time Lock. Section 5 sketches our geometric approach for detecting Time Action Lock. Results related to the implementation via Rational Presburger Sentences are discussed in section 6. Section 7 explains the Testing Tool TALC and applies the method to the testing of a simple communication protocol for the existence of a Time Action Lock. The paper finishes with a conclusion section.

2   Timed Automata

In this section, we shall review a variation of Timed Automata model proposed by Alur and Dill [1], which is used in UPPAAL [2, 6, 21], a tool for the verification of behavioural properties of Real-time systems.

Consider $\mathcal{X} = \{x_1, \ldots, x_n\}$ a set of clock variables with values in $\mathbb{R}_+$, the set of non-negative real numbers. Suppose that $c_1(\mathcal{X})$ is the set of all constraints created from conjunctions of atomic formals of the form $x_i \sim q$, where $x_i \in \mathcal{X}$, $\sim \in \{\leq, \geq, <, >, =\}$ and $q \in \mathbb{Q}_+$, the set of non-negative Rational numbers. Also, assume that $c_2(\mathcal{X})$ is the set of all constraints created from the conjunction of atomic formula's of the form $x_i \sim q$ and $x_i - x_j \sim q$, where x_i, c and $\sim$ are as above and for $i \neq j$, $x_j \in \mathcal{X}$. The set of all possible constraints is defined by $c(\mathcal{X}) = c_1(\mathcal{X}) \cup c_2(\mathcal{X})$. We shall refer to $x_i \sim q$ and $x_i - x_j \sim q$, as *atomic* constraints.[1]

A *valuation* (*variable assignment*) is a map $v : \mathcal{X} \to \mathbb{R}_+$, which assigns to each clock a non-negative Real-number. For a valuation v, a delay $d \in \mathbb{R}_+$, which is denoted by $v + d$, is defined as $(v + d)(x) = v(x) + d$, if $x \in \mathcal{X}$. In other words, all clocks operate with the same speed. Let $V(A)$ denote the set of all valuations.

The value of clock can be *reset*. A reset statement is of the form $x := e$, where $x \in \mathcal{X}$. In the current version of UPPAAL, e must be an integer. A set of reset statements is called a *reset-set* or *reset* if each variable is assigned at most once. The result of applying a reset r to a valuation v is denoted by the valuation $r(v)$. If a variable x is such that no assignment of r changes its value then $v(x) = r(v)(x)$. Let R denotes the set of all resets.

A *Timed Automaton* A is a 6-tuple $(L, l_0, T, I, \mathcal{X}, init, A)$ such that

- $L = \{l_0, \ldots, l_N\}$ is a finite set of *locations* and $l_0 \in L$ is a designated location called the *initial location*. Assume that $init(l_0) \in c(\mathcal{X})$ assigns to the initial location an *initial region*.
- $\mathcal{X}$ and A are finite sets of clock variables and actions, respectively.
- $T \subset L \times A \times c(\mathcal{X}) \times R \times L$ is the set of transition relation. An element of T is of the form of (l_i, a, g, r, l_j), where $l_i, l_j \in L$ and $a \in A$ is an action, $g \in c(\mathcal{X})$ is called a *guard*, and $r \in R$ is a set of reset statements. We sometimes write $l_i \xrightarrow{a,g,r} l_j$ to depict that A evolves from a location l_i to a new location l_j, if the guard g is evaluated *true*, the action a is performed and clocks and data variables are reset according to r. In this case, we shall refer to $e = (a, g, r)$ as the edge connecting l_i and l_j. We shall also write $\text{Action}(e)$, $\text{guard}(e)$ and $\text{reset}(e)$ to denote a, g, and r, respectively.
- $I : L \to c(\mathcal{X})$ is a function that assigns to each location an *invariant*. Intuitively, a Timed Automata can stay in a location while its invariants are satisfied. The default invariant for a location is *true* $(x \geq 0)$.

Notation 1. *For a location $l \in L$, we shall write $°l$ to denote the set of all edges $e = (a, g, r)$ ending in l. Similarly, $l°$ denotes the set of all edges starting from l.*

---

[1] The Timed Automata model of UPPAAL contains both clock variables, as defined above, and *data variables*, which have integer values. In order to simplify our model, we shall only be dealing with clock variables. Also, the current version of TALC only implements the clock variables.

The semantics of Timed Automata can be interpreted over transition systems, *i.e.* triple $(S, s_0, \Rightarrow)$, where

- $S \subset L \times V$ is the set of *states*, i.e. each state is a pair (l, v), where l is a location and v is a valuation
- $s_0 \in S$ is an *initial state*, and
- $\Rightarrow \subset S \times (A \cup \mathbb{R}_+) \times S$ is a *transition relation*, where A is the set of *all* actions.

A transitions can be either a *discrete transitions*, e.g. (s_1, a, s_2), where $a \in A$ or a *time transitions*, e.g. (s_1, d, s_2), where $d \in \mathbb{R}_+$ and denotes the passage of d time units. Transitions are written: $s_1 \stackrel{a}{\Rightarrow} s_2$ and $s_1 \stackrel{d}{\Rightarrow} s_2$, respectively, and are defined according of the following inference rules:

$$\frac{l_1 \stackrel{a,g,r}{\longrightarrow} l_2, g(v)}{(l_1, v) \stackrel{e}{\Rightarrow} (l_2, r(v))} \qquad \frac{\forall d' \leq d \;\; I(l)(v + d')}{(l, v) \stackrel{d}{\Rightarrow} (l, v + d)}$$

To model concurrency and synchronisation between Timed Automaton, CCS [22] style parallel composition operators are introduced, which synchronise over half actions. We refer the interested reader to [2] for further details of the UPPAAL model of Timed Automata.

Assume that A is a Timed Automaton. A *run* σ of A is a finite/infinite sequence of transitions of the form $s_0 \stackrel{\lambda_1}{\Rightarrow} s_1 \stackrel{\lambda_2}{\Rightarrow} s_2 \cdots$ where s_0 is the initial state and $\lambda_i \in A \cup \mathbb{R}_+$, where A is the set of actions. For further information on network of Timed Automata and UPPAAL see [6, 21].

3   Rational Presburger Sentences

Assume that F denotes the set of all linear inequalities on integer variables and integer constants. A *Presburger Sentence* is a closed first-order logical statements on F. The phrase *closed* means that, there is no free variable in a Presburger Sentence. For example, $\forall x \exists y (3x+7 \leq y \lor y \geq 0)$ is a Presburger Sentence. Satisfiability of Presburger Sentence is decidable [19].

A *Rational Presburger Sentence* (RPS) is similar to the conventional Presburger Sentences, except that constants are rational numbers and variables range over rational (or real) numbers. As a result, the syntax of RPS is as follow:

fact ::=x | ax | b, where x is a rational-valued variable and a and b are integer (or rational) constants
exp ::= fact | fact $+$ exp | fact $-$ exp
lterm :: $=$ exp $=$ exp | exp $>$ exp | exp $<$ exp
lexp ::= lterm | $\neg$lexp | lexp $\land$ lterm
RPS ::=$\forall x$ lexp, where x is any free variable in lexp.

Note that, for RPS F and G, $\exists x F$ can be defined as $\neg \forall x \neg F$ and $F \lor G$ as $\neg(\neg F \land \neg G)$. Also $f \geq g$ and $f \leq g$ are defined $f > g \lor f = g$ and $f < g \lor f = g$, respectively. The decision problem for RPS is decidable [13, 24]. Moreover, the computational times for deciding the satisfiability for RPS is less than that of Presburger Sentences. RPS and original Presburger Sentences have been successfully applied to the verification of logical designs and network design protocols [10, 14, 3, 25, 4]. Tools [23, 24] are available for the verification of RPS and Presburger sentences.

4 Deadlock in Timed Automata

Deadlocks, which have often been seen as error situations in concurrent and distributed systems, are classically interpreted as states at which the system will never be able to perform an *action*. In a Timed Automaton, a deadlock can *also* be created by preventing the passing of timed beyond a certain point, i.e. the elapse of time causes a violation of at least one of the constraints of the system. This situation, which is referred to as a *Timelock*, is often created as a result of fault in the specification of guards or invariant in the model. Finding out and resolving Timelocks is a major problem for the analysis and design of time critical systems.

Various interpretations of deadlock are extensively studied in the literature [8, 7, 27, 16, 28]. There are two different forms of Timelock [8], *Zeno Timelock* and *Time Action Lock*. Zeno Timelock is the case that infinite number of actions are performed in a finite period of time. This paper is about Time Action Lock, which is defined as follows in [8].
Time-Action-Lock A *Time-Action-Lock* (TAL) is a state at which time can *only* progress for a finite amount $0 < d < \infty$ of time but no action can occur.

A special case of the above definition is the situation at which, there is a reachable state at which neither time can progress nor an action can occur [8].

Example 1. Fig. 2 depicts two Timed Automata with TAL at the location l_0. The Left Hand Side Timed Automata has a TAL at the state $(l_0, 10)$, as neither time can progress, because of the violation of the invariant $x \le 10$, nor an action can occur, because of the violation of the guard $8 \le x < 9$. In both Timed Automata the reachable state $(l_0, 9)$ is also a TAL, as time can pass $d = 1$ unit and no action can occur. However, $(l_0, 10)$ is not a TAL state of the Right Hand Side Timed Automaton, as it is not a reachable state.

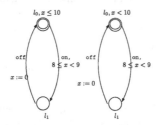

Fig. 2. Timed Automata with Time-Action-Lock

5 A Geometric Approach to the Detection of Time-Action-Locks

A valuation is a function assigning real values to clocks $\mathcal{X} = \{x_1, \dots, x_n\}$. As a result, we can identify a valuation $v : \mathcal{X} \to \mathbb{R}_+$ as a vector $\alpha = (\alpha_1, \dots, \alpha_n)$, where for each

$1 \leq i \leq n$, $\alpha_i = v(x_i)$. Hence, for each constraint $c \in \mathbf{c}(\mathcal{X})$ there is a subset of $\mathbb{R}^n_+$ of all points that satisfy c. We shall refer to such subset of $\mathbb{R}^n_+$ as the *corresponding region* of c and denote it with $\underline{c}$. *For the rest of this section assume that* $c \in \mathbf{c}(\mathcal{X})$ *and* $\underline{c}$ *denotes the corresponding region.*

Definition 1. *Assume that $n \geq 1$. For $x \in \mathbb{R}^n_+$, we shall write $\Gamma(x, \underline{c}) = \sup\{t \geq 0 \mid x + t \times \mathbf{1} \in \underline{c}\}$,[2] where $\mathbf{1} = (1, \ldots, 1) \in \mathbb{R}^n_+$. If there is a t such that $x + t \times \mathbf{1} \in \underline{c}$ and $\Gamma(x, \underline{c}) < \infty$, we shall write Fringe $(x, \underline{c}) = x + \Gamma(x, \underline{c}) \times \mathbf{1}$ and call it the Fringe of x with respect to $\underline{c}$. If $\Gamma(x, \underline{c}) = \infty$, we shall write $Fringe(x, \underline{c}) = \{\infty\}$. If there is no t such that $x + t \times \mathbf{1} \in \underline{c}$ then $\Gamma(x, \underline{c}) = -\infty$, and Fringe $(x, \underline{c}) = \{-\infty\}$.*

Example 2. Suppose that $n = 2$. Assume that a region c is specified by the conjunction of $x_1 \leq 1$, $x_2 \leq 2$, $x_1 \geq 0$ and $x_2 \geq 0.5$. Let $x = (0.5, 1)$, it can be seen in Fig. 3 that $\Gamma(x, \underline{c}) = 0.5$ and $Fringe(x, \underline{c}) = (1, 1.5)$.

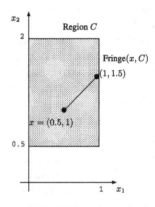

Fig. 3. Example 2

If we assume that the region $\underline{c}$ denotes the invariant of a location l of a Timed Automata A. For a reachable state (l, x), we have $x \in \underline{c}$, where $c = g(l)$, where $\underline{c}$ denotes the corresponding region. In this case, $\Gamma(x, \underline{c})$ is the maximum amount of time that can expire while the location remains in l.

Definition 2. *If $c_1, c_2 \in \mathbf{c}(\mathcal{X})$ and $\underline{c_1} \subset \underline{c_2}$, then define $Fringe(\underline{c_1}, c_2) = \cup_{x \in \underline{c_1}} Fringe(x, c_2)$.*

Assume that $c \in \mathbf{c}(\mathcal{X})$, then $\underline{c} \subset \mathbb{R}^n_+$ denotes the corresponding region. Assume that $\overline{c}$ denotes the Topological Closure of $\underline{c}$ [11]. The reader, who is not familiar with the notion of Topological Closure, can use the following instead of the definition of the Topological Closure.

---

[2] sup stands for *Supremum*. For each $A \subset \mathbb{R}$, sup A is the least upper bound of A. For example, $\sup[0, 1] = \sup[0, 1) = 1$. Each nonempty bounded subset of $\mathbb{R}$ has a supremum and the supremum of a nonempty unbounded subset of $\mathbb{R}$ is ∞. The supremum of empty set is defined as $-\infty$.

Lemma 1. *Suppose that $c_1 \in C(\mathcal{X})$ and c_2 is created from c_1 by replacing all $<$ ($>$) with $\leq$ ($\geq$), respectively. Then $\underline{c_2}$ is the Topological Closure of $\underline{c_1}$, i.e. $\underline{c_2} = \overline{(\underline{c_1})} = \overline{\underline{c_1}}$.*

Proof. By induction on the number of atomic constraints in c_1 and considering that the Topological Closure of the union of finite sets is the union of the Topological Closure.

The next theorem, in a layman language, states that a Timed Automaton is Time-Action-Lock free, if the fringe of the invariants of each location with respect to the guards of incoming transitions are covered by the Topological Closure of the guard of the outgoing transitions.

Theorem 1. *Assume that A is a Timed Automaton. A is Time-Action-Lock free if for each location l of A,*

$$Fringe(A_l, B_l) \subset \overline{C_l}, \tag{1}$$

where

- $A_l = \mathsf{init}(l)$, *if l is the initial location;*
- *if l is not an initial location or l is the initial [3] location with $^\circ l \neq \emptyset$, then $A_l = \bigcup_{e \in {}^\circ l} A_{l,e}$, in which $A_{l,e} = \mathsf{guard}(e) \cap \mathsf{inv}(l) \cap \mathsf{reset}(e)$, where $\mathsf{reset}(e)$ is the area of $\mathbb{R}_+^n$ corresponding the reset set of e, i.e. $\{x \in \mathbb{R}_+^n \mid x_i = 0 \text{ for } x_i \in \mathsf{reset}(e)\}$;*
- $B_l = \mathsf{inv}(l)$ *is the region corresponding to the invariant of l;*
- $C_l = \bigcup_{e \in l^\circ} C_{l,e}$, *where $C_{l,e} = \mathsf{guard}(e) \cap \mathsf{inv}(l)$;*
- $\overline{C_l}$ *denotes the Topological Closure of C_l.*

Proof. Assume that for all locations l the equation 1 is satisfied, but A has a Time-Action-Lock. As a result, there is Time-Action-Lock state (l, x). We shall prove that the above assumption results in a contradiction. Without any loss of generality, we can assume that $x \in A_l$. This is because, there is a reachable state (l, z), where $z \in A_l$, such that by elapse of $0 < d < \infty$ unit of time ends in (l, x) and we can state the proof for (l, z). [To see this, assume that $\sigma = s_0 \overset{\lambda_1}{\Rightarrow} \cdots \overset{\lambda_n}{\Rightarrow} s_n = (l, x)$ is a run of A starting at an initial state and ending in (l, x). Suppose that there exists an action transition in the set $\{\lambda_1, \ldots, \lambda_n\}$, and assume that s_i is the last state before s_n at which an action transition occurs. Then, there is an edge $e \in {}^\circ l$ such that λ_i is the action of e. After $\lambda_{i+1} + \ldots + \lambda_n$ unit of time, the state (l, x) is reached. If there is no action transition in $\{\lambda_1, \ldots, \lambda_n\}$, simply let (l, z) to be the initial state s_0 and the time elapse of $d = \sum \lambda_i$ ends in the state (l, x). So let us assume that $x \in A_l$.]

By the definition of Time-Action-Lock at the state (l, x) time can elapse *only* $0 \leq d < \infty$ units and no action can occur. As a result $\gamma = \sup\{t \mid x + t \times 1 \in B_l\} < \infty$ exists. Let $y = x + \gamma \times 1 =$ Fringe(x, B_l). By equation (1) $y \in \overline{C_l}$. As a result, there are two cases; either y is and *interior* point or a boundary point. **case 1:** $y \in C_l$, By the definition of C_l, there exists $e \in l^\circ$ such that $y \in \mathsf{guard}(e) \cap \mathsf{inv}(l)$. Hence at state (l, x) time can elapse γ units to the new state (l, y) and then e can occur. This contradicts

---

[3] If $^\circ l \neq \emptyset$ the initial location is studied twice, once with $A_l = \mathsf{init}(l)$ and the second time like any other location.

with (l, x) is a Time-Action-Lock state. **case 2:** $y \in \overline{C_l} \backslash C_l$, *i.e.*, y is in the Topological boundary of C_l. By the definition of the Topological boundary, each neighbourhood of y contains a point of C_l. Consider a point which also belongs to the line joining x to y. Then there is $0 < t < \gamma$ such that $x + t \times 1 \in C_l$. Hence, there is $e \in l^{\circ}$ such that $x + t \times 1 \in \text{guard}(e) \cap \text{inv}(l)$. This is a contradiction with (l, x) is a Time-Action-Lock as at state (l, x), time can pass t units to the new state $(l, x + t \times 1)$ and then e occurs. As a result, in both cases, assuming that A has a TAL, results in a contradiction. ///

Notice that the condition presented in the lemma is a necessary condition. In other words, if Equation (1) satisfies the Timed Automaton has no Time-Action-Lock. We argue that violation of equation 1, which *may* result in a Time-Action-Lock, is a sign of bad design. Based on this idea, we have developed a tool that carries a static analysis of the Timed Automata and points out to the designer any potential Time-Action-Lock. We shall explain our approach with the help of an example.

Example 3. Consider the Timed Automaton of Fig. 4, which models a switch on/off system. Fig. 5 depicts $A_{l1} = \text{guard}(e1) \cap \text{inv}(l1) \cap \text{reset}(e1) = \{x \in \mathbb{R}_+^2 \mid x_2 = 0, 0 \leq x_1 \leq 2\}$, $B_{l1} = \text{inv}(l1) = \{x \in \mathbb{R}_+^2 \mid x_2 \leq 1\}$ and $C_{l1} = \text{guard}(e2) \cap \text{inv}(l1) = \{x \in \mathbb{R}_+^2 \mid x_2 \leq 1 \text{ and } 2 \leq x_1\}$.

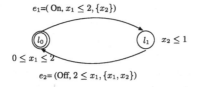

Fig. 4. A Timed Automata with Time Action Lock

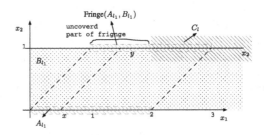

Fig. 5. Part of the Fringe is not covered

The next section presents a method of calculating the *Fringe*. Here, as depicted in Fig. 5, a direct use of the definition 1 shows that Fringe $(A_{l_1}, B_{l_1}) = \{x \in \mathbb{R}_+^2 \mid x_2 = 1, 2 \leq x_1 \leq 3\}$. It can clearly be seen that the part of Fringe (A_{l1}, B_{l1}) lying on $x_2 = 1$ with $x_1 < 2$ is not covered. The Fig. 5 demonstrates the idea behind the above Theorem. Clearly, at any state (l_1, x), where $x = (x_1, x_2)$ and $0 \leq x_1 \leq 1$ and $x_2 = 0$, if the time elapses by 1 unit, the state (l, y) is reached. At this point neither time can pass, since

$\text{inv}(l_1)$ gets violated, nor an action can occur, since no guard of an outgoing transition is satisfied. We can argue that the case presented in the above examples a clear case of wrong specification. In other words, there is a clear inconsistence in the specification that must be corrected. The contrary position, as explained in [8], is that such "error situations in behavioural techniques should have a behavioural/operational intuition that is justifiable in term of real world behaviour." This paper does not address the above hotly debated views. Our aim is to present a computationally cheap method of discovering such situations and pointing them to the designer.

Remark: The method presented in this paper deals *only* with a single Timed Automaton. As Bowman [8] points out, a Time Action Lock can *also* be created from unsuitable parallel composition. We are currently working on extending our method to cover *networks of Timed Automata*, i.e. parallel composition of Timed Automata. The current implementation of TALC, checks a *network of Timed Automata* only by studying each individual Timed Automaton component.

6   Applying Rational Presburger Sentences to Detect TAL

In this section, we shall present a method of detecting potential Time-Action-Lock (TAL) using Theorem 1. Considering equation 1 of Theorem 1, the aim is to present a technique to verify statements of the form $\text{Fringe}(\underline{c_1}, \underline{c_2}) \subset \underline{c_3}$, where c_1, c_2 and $c_3 \in c(\mathcal{X})$ and $\underline{c_1} \subset \underline{c_2}$. We shall verify such statements via Presburger sentences. However, first we shall present a set of results which facilitate the translation to suitable Rational Presburger Sentences, with minimal amount of computation.

Proposition 1. *For each $c \in \mathbf{c}(\mathcal{X})$ the corresponding $\underline{c}$ region is a convex set. Moreover, if $c \in \mathbf{c}_1(\mathcal{X})$, then $\underline{c}$ is a rectangular region, i.e. a Cartesian product of intervals.*

Proof. The convexity of the region is proved in [27]. The second part is by induction on the number of atomic formulas in c.

Notation 2. *Assume that $\underline{c}$ is a rectangular region of the form $I_1 \times \cdots \times I_n$, where each I_i is a (non-negative) real line interval. Then by Top Corner, we mean the point $(\alpha_1, \ldots, \alpha_n)$, where each α_i is the end point of I_i. Notice, in case of an unbounded interval, $\alpha_i = \infty$. Also, define the Bottom Corner to be the point $(\beta_1, \ldots, \beta_n)$, where each β_i is the starting point of the interval I_i.*

Calculating the Fringe for a rectangular region is straight forward.

Lemma 2. *If $c \in \mathbf{c}_1(\mathcal{X})$, i.e. $\underline{c}$ is a rectangular region, and $(\alpha_1, \ldots, \alpha_n)$ denotes the Top Corner point of the rectangular region $\underline{c}$, then for each point $x = (x_1, \ldots, x_n) \in \underline{c}$,*

- *$\Gamma(x, \underline{c}) = \min\{\alpha_i - x_i \mid 1 \leq i \leq n\}$ and*
- *$Fringe(x, \underline{c}) = x + \min\{\alpha_i - x_i \mid 1 \leq i \leq n\} \times \mathbf{1}$.*

Proof. If for each i, $\alpha_i = +\infty$, then $\Gamma(x, \underline{c}) = \infty$ and there is nothing to prove. Assume that for at least one co-ordinate t, $\alpha_t < \infty$. Since α_i is the end point of the interval coordinate of $\underline{c}$, $x + t \times \mathbf{1} \in \underline{c}$, if and only if for each coordinate i, $x_i + t \sim \alpha_i$, where $\sim \in \{\leq, <\}$. As a result, $\Gamma(x, \underline{c}) = \sup\{t \mid t \sim \alpha_i - x_i \text{ for } 1 \leq i \leq n\}$, which is the same as $\min\{\alpha_i - x_i \mid 1 \leq i \leq n\}$.

It might seem that, the above lemma, which provide an elegant way of computing the Fringe is only applicable to the rectangular regions. However, the following lemma shows that to calculate the Fringe, we only need to discard conditions of the form $x_i - x_j \sim q$ and focus on the rectangular regions.

Lemma 3. *If $\underline{c}$ is a non-empty region created from a constraint in $c \in \mathbf{c_2}(\mathcal{X})$. Let $c' \in \mathbf{c}(\mathcal{X})$ is a constraint created from modifying c by cancelling all atomic formulas of the form $x_i - x_j \sim q$. Also, assume that $\underline{c}'$ is the region (rectangular region) corresponding to c'. Then, $\underline{c} \subset \underline{c}'$ and for $x \in \underline{c}$ Fringe$(x, \underline{c})$ =Fringe$(x, \underline{c}')$.*

Proof. Since c' is created from the relaxing conditions of c, we have $\underline{c} \subset \underline{c}'$. For each $x \in \underline{c}$, we shall prove that $\sup\{t \mid x + t \times \mathbf{1} \in \underline{c}\} = \sup\{t \mid x + t \times \mathbf{1} \in \underline{c}'\}$. To see this, let LS denotes the left hand side supremum and RS denotes the right hand side supremum. Since $\underline{c} \subset \underline{c}'$, we get $LS \leq RS$. If the two are not equal by the definition of the supremum, there is a t such that $x + t \times \mathbf{1} \notin \underline{c}$ and $x + t \times \mathbf{1} \in \underline{c}'$. This can only happen because there is a condition of the form of $x_i - x_j \sim q$ that the vector $x + t \times \mathbf{1}$, does not satisfy i.e. the inequality $(x_i - t) - (x_j - t) \sim q$ is not satisfied. But, this is impossible, as $(x_i - t) - (x_j - t) = x_i - x_j$ and $x_i - x_j \sim q$.

In other words, to calculate the Fringe, we can ignore constraints of the form of $x_i - x_j \sim q$ and focus on the rectangular regions. The following result identifies a less complex set that embodies the Fringe of a point.

Lemma 4. *If $\underline{c}$ is a non-empty region created from a constraint in $c \in \mathbf{c_1}(\mathcal{X})$ and $\alpha = (\alpha_1, \ldots, \alpha_n)$ is the Top Corner of $\underline{c}$. For $x \in \underline{c}$, Fringe$(x, \underline{c}) \subset \mathcal{F}(c)$, where if $\alpha = (\infty, \ldots, \infty)$ then $\mathcal{F}(c) = \{\infty\}$, otherwise, $\mathcal{F}(c) = \cup_{\alpha_i \neq \infty}\{x \in \mathbb{R}^n_+ \mid x_i = \alpha_i\}$.*

Proof. Fringe$(x, \underline{c}) = x + \min\{\alpha_i - x_i \mid 1 \leq i \leq n\} \times \mathbf{1}$. Assume that $\min\{\alpha_i - x_i \mid 1 \leq i \leq n\} = \alpha_j - x_j$. If $\alpha_j - x_j = \infty$, then for each i, $\alpha_i = \infty$. As a result, Fringe$(x, \underline{c}) = \{\infty\}$. If $\alpha_j - x_j < \infty$, then x_j, the j-th coordinate of the Fringe$(x, \underline{c})$, is $\alpha_j = x_j + (\alpha_j - x_j)$. ///

Assume that $c \in \mathbf{c}(\mathcal{X})$ and $x \in \underline{c}$. In a layman language, Fringe $(x, \underline{c})$ is the final point that an imaginary person can arrive at, if he/she starts from the point x and moves on a line in the direction of the vector $\mathbf{1} = (1, \ldots, 1)$, while his/her trajectory of movement avoids violating c. In a similar way, moving in the direction of $(-1, \ldots, -1)$ can be considered.

Definition 3. *Assume that $c \in \mathbf{c}(\mathcal{X})$ and $x \in \underline{c}$, we shall write [4] $\Delta(x, \underline{c}) = \sup\{t \geq 0 \mid x - t \times \mathbf{1} \in \underline{c}$, where $\mathbf{1} = (1, \ldots, 1)$. Let us write AntiFringe$(x, \underline{c}) = x - \Delta(x, \underline{c}) \times \mathbf{1}$. Moreover, if $c_1 \in \mathbf{c}(\mathcal{X})$ and $\underline{c_1} \subset \underline{c}$ then define AntiFringe$(\underline{c_1}, \underline{c}) = \cup_{x \in \underline{c_1}}$AntiFringe$(x, \underline{c})$.*

The following result, which is also depicted in Fig. 6 explains that to calculate the Fringe, we can use the AntiFringe.

---

[4] Notice, the supremum always exists.

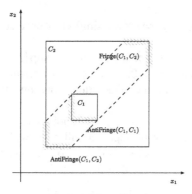

Fig. 6. Fringe(C_1, C_2) = Fringe(AntiFringe$(C_1, C_2), C_2$)

Lemma 5. *Assume that $c_1 \subset c_2$ are both in* $\mathbf{c}(\mathcal{X})$ *then*

$$Fringe(\underline{c_1}, \underline{c_2}) = Fringe(AntiFringe(\underline{c_1}, \underline{c_1}), \underline{c_2}).$$

Proof. The proof is straight forward and omitted.

The following lemma is the equivalent of Lemma 4 for AntiFringe.

Lemma 6. *Assume that $c \in \mathbf{c}(\mathcal{X})$ and $\beta = (\beta_1, \ldots, \beta_n)$ is the Bottom corner point of the region created by discarding all atomic formulae of the from $x_i - x_j \sim q$. Then AntiFringe$(\underline{c}, \underline{c}) = \bigcup_{i=1}^{n} P_i(c)$ where for $1 \leq i \leq n$, $P_i(c)$ is created from c by*

1. *replacing $x_i > q$ or $x_i \geq q$ with $x_i = \beta_i$, and*
2. *for $j \neq i$ replacing any $x_j > q$ with $x_j \geq q$.*

Proof. Assume that $z \in$ AntiFringe $(\underline{c}, \underline{c})$, then there is $y \in \underline{c}$ such that $z = y - \Delta(y, \underline{c}) \times 1$. Using a similar discussion to Lemma 2, we can prove that AntiFringe $(y, \underline{c}) = y - \min\{y_i - \beta_i \mid 1 \leq i \leq n\}$. Hence, if $\min\{y_i - \beta_i \mid 1 \leq i \leq n\} = y_r - \beta_r$, we show that $z \in \underline{P_r(c)}$. There are four types of atomic formulae in $\underline{P_r(c)}$.

1. Atomic formulae of c of the form $x_i > q$ or $x_i \geq q$, which are replaced with $x_i = \beta_i$.
2. For $j \neq i$, atomic formulae of the form $x_j > q$, which are replaced with $x_j \geq q$.
3. For $1 \leq j \leq n$, atomic formulae of c of the form $x_j < q$ or $x_j \leq q$.
4. For $1 \leq j, i \leq n$ and $i \neq j$, atomic formulae of c of the form $x_j - x_i \sim q$.

We shall prove that z satisfies formulas which are created from the above atomic formulas. Clearly, z satisfies formulae of type 1 above, since $z_r = y_r - \Delta(y, \underline{c}) = y_r - (y_r + \beta_r) = \beta_r$.

By the definition of $\Delta(y, \underline{c})$ there is an increasing sequence $\{t_k\}$ such that $\lim_k t_k = \Delta(y, \underline{c})$. Hence $z_k = y - t_k \times 1 \rightarrow y - \Delta(y, \underline{c}) = z$ and for each k, $y - t_k \times 1 \in \underline{c}$. Using this sequence, we can show that z satisfies atomic formulae of type 2–4. For example, if c has an atomic formula of the form $x_j \geq q$ for $j \neq i$ then since $y - t_k \times 1 \in c$, $y_i - t_k > q$. As a result $z_i \geq q$.

The other two conditions can be proved similarly. Conversely, assume that $z \in P_r(\underline{c})$. There are two cases.

Case 1: $z \in \underline{c}$. In this case, we claim $\Delta(z, \underline{c}) = \sup\{t \geq 0 \mid z - t\mathbf{1} \in \underline{c}\} = 0$. Otherwise $\Delta(z, \underline{c}) > 0$. Then $\exists t > 0, z - t\mathbf{1} \in \underline{c}$. As a result, $z_r - t = \beta_r$. Since $z \in \underline{c}$, $z_r = \beta_r$. Hence, $t = 0$, which is a contradiction. Consequently, $z =$ AntiFringe$(z, \underline{c}) \in$ AntiFringe$(\underline{c}, \underline{c})$.

Case 2: $z \notin \underline{c}$. In this case, since $z \in \overline{(\underline{c})}$, the topological closure. Notice, Topological closure, by Lemma 1 is created by replacing all $>, <$ with $\geq, \leq$, respectively. Now, using the definition of closure, there is a point y on the half line $\{y + t \times \mathbf{1} \mid t > 0\}$ which also belongs to $\underline{c}$, then $z =$ AntiFringe$(y, \underline{c})$. ///

The next result presents a method of detecting the TAL via Presburger Sentences.

Theorem 2. *Assume that $c_1, c_2 \in \mathbf{c}(\mathcal{X})$ and $\underline{c_1} \subset \underline{c_2}$. Let c_3 denote disjunction of finite number of elements of $\mathbf{c}(\mathcal{X})$. Then the following is valid.*

$$Fringe(\underline{c_1}, c_2) \subset \underline{c_3}. \tag{2}$$

if and only if for each $1 \leq i \leq n$

$$\forall x \in \underline{P_i(c_1)}((\exists t \geq 0 \; x + t\mathbf{1} \in \mathcal{F}(c_2')) \Rightarrow x + t\mathbf{1} \in \underline{c_3}.) \tag{3}$$

where $P_i(c_1)$ is defined in the Lemma 6, c_2' is the rectangular region created from c by cancelling atomic formulae of the form $x_i - x_j \sim q$ and $\mathcal{F}(c_2')$ is defined in Lemma 4.

Proof. Direct result of applying Lemma 2, 3, 4 and Lemma 6.

The equation (3) above is an RPS. $P_i(c_1), \mathcal{F}(c_2')$ and c_3 are first order logic formulae on the atomic formulae $x_i \sim q$ and $x_i - y_i \sim q$, where q is a rational number. Moreover, the formula is closed, as variables $x_1, \ldots, x_n$ and t are in the scope of $\forall x$ and $\exists t$.

7   Time Action Lock Checker (TALC)

We have developed a tool called *Time Action Lock Checker* (TALC), which works in conjunction with UPPAAL version 3.2.X and runs under Linux. Fig. 7 depicts the architecture of TALC, which consists of the following five components [26]:

- Model Checker UPPAAL, which saves network of Timed Automata models as eXtensible Markup Language (XML)[12] files.

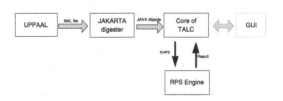

Fig. 7. The Architecture of TALC

- **Jakarta Digester** [18] transfers XML files to Java objects which captures the information regarding the network of Timed Automata in Java.
- **Core of TALC** implements the theory described in previous section and uses Java objects created by the above component to create a set of Rational Presburger Sentences, which are used to evaluate Time Action Lock freeness of the system, see Theorem 2.
- **RPS Engine** is a component software based on [24] that evaluates Rational Presburger Sentences. It can be invoked by the **Core of TALC** and receives Rational Presburger Sentences create by **Core of TALC** in form of *queries*, evaluates the correctness of the Rational Presburger Sentences and returns the *results* of the evaluation.
- TALC includes a user interface component (GUI) which enables the user to interact with the system.

The next example applies the TALC to the verification of a simplified media Synchronisation Protocol motivated by an example studied in [17].

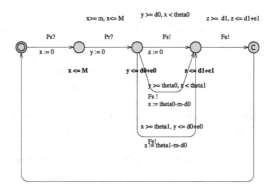

Fig. 8. Synchronised Protocol Module

Example: Fig. 8 depicts a Timed Automata model of Synchronisation Protocol Module (SPM), used in a video streaming system for reducing the jitter caused by the network delay. The Timed Automaton includes signals *Ps* and *Pr*, corresponding to *sending* and *receiving* of packets, respectively. The outputs of SPM are signals *Fs* and *Fe*, which mark *starting* and *ending* of the *frame* display, respectively.

There is a clock x, which resets when a packet is sent *i.e.*, *Ps?*. For the signal *Pr* to receive, there is a delay with a value in $[m, M]$, where m and M are constant rational numbers. On the arrival of *Pr* another clock y resets. At this stage packets are decoded into frames. Decoding requires a delay in $[d_0, d_0 + e_0]$, where d_0 and e_0 are constant rational numbers. According to the time of the sending of a packet, measured by x, and the time of arrival of that packet, measured by y, there are three possible scenarios. Each scenario compares the value of x and y with constants θ_0 and θ_1 and assigns the value of a new clock z, which will be used to determine the time of termination of the display of frames marked by the output signal *Fe*. Using TALC, we can test the above Timed Automaton and infer that the system is deadlock free.

8   Conclusion

This paper presents a geometric method for the detection of Time Action Lock in Timed Automata, the paper makes use of the geometry of $\mathbb{R}^n$ to identify the part of the specification that may result in Time Action Lock. The emphasis is on testing and identifying possible sources of defects in the design by studying various regions representing guards and invariants of the Timed Automata. In particular, the method is based on the study of subsets of such regions known as Fringes. Evaluating various first order closed formulae are carried out via a Real Presburger Sentences solver. The method is implemented in a tool called TALC and is successfully applied to the verification of a simple communication protocol.

References

1. R. Alur and D.L. Dill: *A Theory for Timed Automata*, In Theoretical Computer Science **125**, pp.183–235, 1994.
2. T. Amnell, G. Behrmann, J. Bengtsson, P. R. D'Argenio, A. David, A. Fehnker, T. Hune, B. Jeannet, K. G. Larsen, O. Möller, P. Pettersson, C. Weise and W. Yi: *UPPAAL—Now, Next and Future* In proceedings of Modelling and Verification of Parallel Processes (MOVEP2k), LNCS **2067**, pp.100–125, 2001.
3. T. Amon, G. Borriello, T. Hu and J. Liu *Symbolic Timing Verification of Timing Diagrams Using Presburger Formulas* 34th ACM/IEEE Design Automation Conference (DAC), June 1997.
4. C. W. Barett, D. L. Dill, and J. R. Levitt: *Validity Checking for Combinations of Theories with Equality,* LNCS **818**, pp.187–201, 1996.
5. J. Bengtsson, W. O. D. Griffioen, K.J. Kristoffersen, K. G. Larsen, F. Larsson, P. Pettersson and W. Yi: *Verification of an Audio Protocol with Bus Collision Using UPPAAL,* In Proceedings of the 8th International Conference on Computer-Aided Verification, LNCS **1102**, pp.244–256, 1996.
6. J. Bengtsson, K. G. Larsen, F. Larsson, P. Pettersson and W. Yi: *UPPAAL, a Tool suite for automatic verification of Real-time systems* In Proceedings of Workshop on Hybrid Systems III: Verification and Control, LNCS **1066** pp.232–243, 1995.
7. S. Bornot and J. Sifakis *On the composition of hybrid systems* In Hybrid systems: computation and Control, LNCS **1386**, pp.49–63, 1998.
8. H. Bowman *Time and action lock freedom properties of timed automata*, In M. Kim, B. Chin, S. Kang, and D. Lee, editors, Formal Techniques for Networked and Distributed Systems, pp.119–134. Kluwer Academic Publishers, 2001.
9. H. Bowman, G. Faconti, and M. Massink: *Specification and verification of media constraints using UPPAAL*, In Proceedings of Design, Specification and Verification of Interactive Systems '98, Markopoulos and P. Johnos, editors, pp.261–277 Springer, 1998.
10. T. Bultan, R. Gerber, W. Pugh *Symbolic Model Checking of Infinite State Programs Using Presburger Arithmetic* Proceedings of the 9th International Conference on Computer Aided Verification (CAV '97), Orna Grumberg, ed., LNCS **1254**, pp.400–411, 1997.

11. N. Bourbaki: *Elements of Mathematics —General Topology—*, chapters 1-4, Springer-Verlag 1980.
12. *eXtensible Markup Language*(XML), http://www.w3.org/XML/.
13. J. Ferrante and C. Rackoff: *A Deicision Procedure for the first Order Theory of Real Addition with order,* SIAM Journal of Computation **4**, pp.69–76, 1975.
14. A. Finkel and J. Leroux *How to compose Presburger-accelerations: Applications to broadcast protocols* In Proc. 22nd Conf. Found. of Software Technology and Theor. Comp. Sci. (FST and TCS 2002), Kanpur, India LNCS **2556**, pp.145–156, 2002.
15. K. Havelund, A. Skou, K. G. Larsen and K. Lund: *Formal Modelling and Analysis of an Audio/Video Protocol: An Industrial Case Study Using UPPAAL* In Proceedings of the 18th IEEE Real-Time Systems Symposium, pp.2–13, 1997.
16. T. A. Henzinger *Sooner is Safer Than Later*, Inf. Process. Lett. 43(3) pp. 135-141, 1992.
17. T. Higashino, A. Nakata, K. Taniguchi, A. R. Cavalli: *Generating Test Cases for a Timed I/O Automaton Model*, Proceedings of the Twelfth IFIP Workshop on Testing of Communicating Systems (IWTCS'99), pp.197–214, 1999.
18. Apache Jakarta Project, Common digester, (jakarta.apache.org/commons/digester/)
19. G. Kreisel and J. Krivine *Elements of Mathematical Logic; Model Theory* North-Holland Publishing Company, 1967.
20. H. Lönn and P. Pettersson: *Formal Verification of a TDMA Protocol Start-Up Mechanism*, In Proceedings of 1997 IEEE Pacific Rim International Symposium on Fault-Tolerant Systems, pp.235–242, 1997.
21. K. G. Larsen, Paul Pettersson and W. Yi: *UPPAAL in a Nutshell*, In Springer International Journal of Software Tools for Technology Transfer **1(1+2)** 1997.
22. R. Milner, *Communication and concurrency*, Prentice Hall, Upper Saddle River, NJ, 1989.
23. *The Omega Project,* http://www.cs.umd.edu/projects/omega/
24. N. Shibata, K. Okano, T. Higashino and K. Taniguchi: *A decision algorithm for prenex normal form rational Presburger sentences based on combinatorial geometry,* Proceedings of the 2nd International Conf. on Discrete Mathematics and Theoretical Computer Science and the 5th Australasian Theory Symposium (DMTCS'99+CATS'99), pp.344–359 1999.
25. T. R. Shiple, J. H. Kukula, and R. K. Ranjan: *A Comparison of Presburger Engines for EFSM Reachability,* LNCS **1427**, p.280, 1998.
26. D. Gruntz, S. Murer and C. Szyperski *Component Software - Beyond Object-Oriented Programming*, Second Edition, Addison-Wesley, 2002
27. S. Tripakis, *Verifying Progress in Timed Systems*, In ARTS'99,Formal Method for Real-Time and Probabilistic Systems Bamberg, LNCS **1601**, 1999.
28. F. Wang, G. Hwang and F. Yu *TCTL Inevitability Analysis of Dense-Time Systems* LNCS **2759**, pp. 176–187, 2003.

Using Model Checking for Reducing the Cost of Test Generation

Hyoung Seok Hong[1] and Hasan Ural[2]

[1] Concordia Institute for Information Systems Engineering,
Concordia University
hshong@ciise.concordia.ca
[2] School of Information Technology and Engineering,
University of Ottawa
ural@site.uottawa.ca

Abstract. This paper presents a method for reducing the cost of test generation. A spanning set for a coverage criterion is a set of entities such that exercising every entity in the spanning set guarantees exercising every entity defined by the coverage criterion. The central notion used in constructing a minimum spanning set is subsumption relation. An entity subsumes another entity if exercising the former guarantees exercising the latter. We develop a method for finding subsumption relations which can be uniformly applied to a family of control flow and data flow oriented coverage criteria by reducing the problem of determining whether an entity subsumes another entity to the model checking problem of the linear temporal logic LTL.

1 Introduction

In structural testing, we are given a coverage criterion defining a set of entities in the structure of a program and we generate a test suite satisfying the coverage criterion. A test suite is a set of test sequences and is said to satisfy a coverage criterion if for every entity defined by the coverage criterion, there is a test sequence in the test suite exercising the entity. There are a number of coverage criteria for structural testing and most of them are based on the information of control flow and data flow. We refer the interested readers to [20, 7, 17] for surveys of coverage criteria in software testing, protocol conformance testing, and hardware testing, respectively. Control flow oriented coverage criteria call for exercising single entities such as statements and branches. Data flow oriented coverage criteria call for exercising associations between definitions and uses of variables such as definition-use pairs[16], definition-use chains of fixed length[15], definition-use chains between inputs and outputs[18, 19], and ordered definition contexts[11].

For a program and a coverage criterion, the *optimal test generation problem* consists of generating a test suite satisfying the coverage criterion with a minimum number of test sequences. In [9, 10], the authors show that the complexity

J. Grabowski and B. Nielsen (Eds.): FATES 2004, LNCS 3395, pp. 110–124, 2005.

of this problem is NP-hard. Hence approaches for reducing the cost of test generation should be heuristic. In the software testing literature, several approaches have been proposed[1, 3, 4, 5, 6, 8, 13, 14]. The main idea of these approaches is to construct a subset of entities for a coverage criterion such that exercising every entity in the subset guarantees exercising every entity defined by the coverage criterion. That is, if a test suite covers every entity in the subset, the test suite satisfies the coverage criterion. Following the terminology of [13, 14], we call the subset a *spanning set* for the coverage criterion. A minimum spanning set allows one to significantly reduce the cost of test generation by focusing only the entities in the spanning set. For example, experiments in [1] show that for all-statements and all-branches coverage criteria, the entities of minimum spanning sets are around 30% of the original entities.

The central notion used in constructing a minimum spanning set is *subsumption* relation. An entity subsumes another entity if exercising the former guarantees exercising the latter. Once we have a test sequence exercising an entity, all the entities subsumed by the entity can be safely ignored. In [1, 3, 4, 5, 6, 8, 13, 14], a number of methods have been proposed for finding subsumption relations. All of them, however, investigate only simple coverage criteria such as all-statements and all-branches coverage criteria [1, 3, 4, 5, 6, 14] and all-uses coverage criterion[8, 13, 14] and cannot be generalized to more complicated data flow oriented coverage criteria.

In this paper, we develop a method for finding subsumption relations which can be uniformly applied to various coverage criteria ranging from all-statements and all-branches coverage criteria to data flow oriented coverage criteria proposed by Rapps and Weyuker[16], Ntafos[15], Ural *et al.*[18, 19], and Laski and Korel[11]. For each coverage criterion, we reduce the problem of determining whether an entity subsumes another entity to the model checking problem of the linear temporal logic LTL[12] in a succinct and rigorous way. We associate an LTL formula with every entity defined by a coverage criterion. Each formula has the following property: a path is a test sequence exercising the entity if and only if the path satisfies the formula. As a direct consequence of this property, we have that an entity e subsumes another entity e' if and only if every path satisfies $\psi \rightarrow \psi'$, where ψ and ψ' are the LTL formulas associated with e and e', respectively.

In addition to being applicable to various coverage criteria, our method has two other distinguishing features. First, the method is language independent in that the temporal logic formulas employed in the method can be applied to various kinds of programming languages and requirements specification languages. Since all the details about algorithms and implementations for finding subsumption relations are hidden in model checkers, it is not necessary to build a dedicated tool for each language. Second, the method enables one to reduce the cost of test generation for large and complex software whose size is limited by the capabilities of current model checkers. More importantly, we can enjoy the continuing and rapid advances in the model checking literature.

The remainder of the paper is organized as follows. Section 2 recalls the basics of LTL and flow graph, which are the logic and model employed in our method, respectively. Section 3 defines spanning sets and describes how to construct a minimum spanning set. Section 4 reduces the problem of finding subsumption relations to the problem of LTL model checking, which is the main result of the paper. Finally, Section 5 concludes the paper with a discussion of future work.

2   Preliminaries

Formulas of LTL are built from a set AP of atomic propositions, the standard boolean operators, and the temporal operators $\mathbf{X}$ (next time) and $\mathbf{U}$ (until) according to the following grammar: $\psi := p \mid \neg\psi \mid \psi \wedge \psi \mid \mathbf{X}\psi \mid \psi\mathbf{U}\psi$ where $p \in AP$. We also use the temporal operators $\mathbf{F}$ (eventually) and $\mathbf{G}$ (always) defined by $\mathbf{F}\psi \equiv true\mathbf{U}\psi$ and $\mathbf{G}\psi \equiv \neg\mathbf{F}\neg\psi$.

A Kripke structure is a tuple $M = (Q, q_{init}, L, R)$ where Q is a finite set of states, $q_{init} \in Q$ is the initial state, $L: Q \rightarrow 2^{AP}$ is the function that labels each state with atomic propositions, and $R \subseteq Q \times Q$ is the transition relation which is total, i.e., for every state q, there exists a state q' such that $(q, q') \in R$. A path of a Kripke structure is an infinite sequence $\pi = q_0q_1...$ of states such that for every $i \geq 0$, $(q_i, q_{i+1}) \in R$. For a position i, $\pi(i)$ is the i-th element of a path π and π^i is the suffix $q_iq_{i+1}...$ of π.

For a path π and an LTL formula ψ, we write $\pi \models \psi$ to denote that π satisfies ψ. The satisfaction relation $\models$ is defined inductively as follows:

- $\pi \models p$ iff $p \in L(\pi(0))$.
- $\pi \models \neg\psi$ iff $\pi \not\models \psi$.
- $\pi \models \psi_1 \wedge \psi_2$ iff $\pi \models \psi_1$ and $\pi \models \psi_2$.
- $\pi \models \mathbf{X}\psi$ iff $\pi^1 \models \psi$.
- $\pi \models \psi_1\mathbf{U}\psi_2$ iff there exists $i \geq 0$ such that $\pi^i \models \psi_2$ and $\pi^j \models \psi_1$ for every $0 \leq j < i$.

For a Kripke structure M and an LTL formula ψ, we write $M \models \psi$ if for every path π such that $\pi(0) = q_{init}$, $\pi \models \psi$. The model checking problem of LTL is to decide if for given M and ψ, it holds that $M \models \psi$.

A *flow graph* of a program module is a directed graph $G = (V, v_s, v_f, A)$ where V is a finite set of vertices, $v_s \in V$ is the start vertex, $v_f \in V$ is the final vertex, and $A \subseteq V \times V$ is a finite set of arcs. The start vertex v_s and final vertex v_f represent the single entry and single exit point of a program module, respectively. A vertex represents a simple statement (such as assignment, input, and output) or the condition of a conditional or repetitive statement. An arc represents possible flow of control between statements. A finite path $v_1...v_n$ of a flow graph is *complete* if $v_1 = v_s$ and $v_n = v_f$. A *test sequence* is a complete path and a *test suite* is a finite set of test sequences. Figure 1 shows a flow graph where v_1 is the start vertex and v_6 is the final vertex. There are two test sequences $v_1v_2v_3v_4v_5v_6$ and $v_1v_2v_3v_5v_6$ in Figure 1.

Each variable occurrence in a program module is classified as a definition or use. A variable x is *defined* at a vertex v, denoted by $d(x,v)$, if v represents

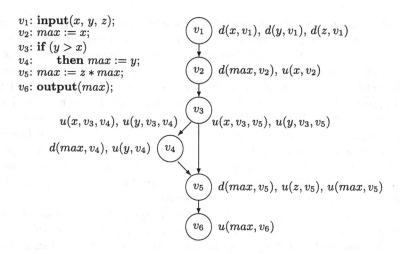

Fig. 1. An example of flow graphs

a statement assigning a value to x. A variable x is *computation-used* (c-used) at a vertex v, denoted by $u(x, v)$, if v represents a statement referencing x. A variable x is *predicate-used* (p-used) at an arc (v, v'), denoted by $u(x, v, v')$, if v represents the condition of a conditional or repetitive statement referencing x. A *use* is either a c-use or p-use.

We view a flow graph as a Kripke structure. The Kripke structure corresponding to a flow graph $G = (V, v_s, v_f, A)$ is $(V, v_s, L, A \cup \{(v_f, v_f)\})$ where $L(v) = \{v\}$ for every vertex $v \in V$. The tuple (v_f, v_f) is necessary to guarantee that the transition relation be total. We will not distinguish between flow graphs and their Kripke structures because of their simple correspondence. In addition, we will identify a test sequence $v_s...v_f$ with the infinite path $v_s...v_f v_f v_f...$.

3   Spanning Sets

We adopt the following terminology introduced in [13, 14]. For a flow graph G and a coverage criterion C, $E(G, C)$ is the set of entities of G required to be exercised by C. A subset of $E(G, C)$ is a *spanning set* if exercising every entity in the subset guarantees exercising every entity in $E(G, C)$. A *minimum spanning set* is a spanning set S such that $|S| \leq |S'|$ for every spanning set S'. It is easy to see that a test suite exercises every entity in a spanning set if and only if the test suite satisfies the coverage criterion. For example, for the flow graph shown in Figure 1 and all-statements coverage criterion, we observe that $E(G, C)$ is $\{v_1, v_2, v_3, v_4, v_5, v_6\}$ and $\{v_4\}$ is a spanning set for $E(G, C)$. Indeed, $\{v_4\}$ is a minimum spanning set. Consider a test suite $\{v_1 v_2 v_3 v_4 v_5 v_6\}$. Since the test suite exercises v_4, it also exercises all the statements $v_1, v_2, v_3, v_4, v_5, v_6$.

The central notion used in constructing a minimum spanning set is *subsumption relation*. An entity subsumes another entity if a test sequence exercising the former also exercises the latter. Once we have a test sequence exercising an entity, we do not need to generate test sequences exercising the entities subsumed by the entity. In addition, if an entity is not subsumed by any other entities, a test sequence exercising the entity should be generated. In the next section, we will show how to find subsumption relations for various coverage criteria.

We construct a minimum spanning set using two graphs called *subsumption graph* and *reduced subsumption graph*[13, 14]. For a flow graph G and a coverage criterion C, the subsumption graph is $(E(G, C), SR)$ where SR is the subsumption relation between the entities in $E(G, C)$. Note that the subsumption relation SR is not a partial order and hence subsumption graphs may have strongly connected components. A reduced subsumption graph is a directed acyclic graph obtained by collapsing each strongly connected component of a subsumption graph into one vertex. Let $v_1, ..., v_n$ be the vertices of the reduced subsumption graph that have no incoming arcs, that is, the vertices that are not subsumed by any other vertices. Let $V_1, ..., V_n$ be the strongly connected components corresponding to $v_1, ..., v_n$, respectively. A minimum spanning set is $\{v'_1, ..., v'_n\}$ such that $v'_i \in V_i$ for every $1 \le i \le n$.

4   Subsumption Relations

This section addresses the problem of finding subsumption relations. Figure 2 shows an algorithm for finding subsumption graph in a generic fashion without being specific about any coverage criteria. For a flow graph G and a coverage criterion C, we first construct the set $E(G, C)$ of entities (Line 2) and in turn the set PE of pairs of entities (Line 3). For every pair (e, e') in PE, we determine whether e subsumes e' by model-checking the LTL formula $\text{ltl}(e) \rightarrow \text{ltl}(e')$ against the flow graph G, where $\text{ltl}(e)$ and $\text{ltl}(e')$ are the LTL formulas associated with e and e', respectively (Line 5). Theorem 1 proves the correctness of the algorithm.

INPUT: a flow graph G and a coverage criteron C
OUTPUT: the subsumption graph $(E(G, C), SR)$

1: $SR := \emptyset$;
2: construct the set $E(G, C)$ of entities of G required by C;
3: $PE := \{(e, e') \mid e, e' \in E(G, C), e \neq e'\}$;
4: **for** every pair (e, e') in PE **do**
5:     model check $\text{ltl}(e) \rightarrow \text{ltl}(e')$ against G;
6:       **if** $G \models \text{ltl}(e) \rightarrow \text{ltl}(e')$ **then** $SR := SR \cup \{(e, e')\}$;
7: **return** $(E(G, C), SR)$;

Fig. 2. An algorithm for finding a subsumption graph

Theorem 1. Assume that the LTL formula ltl(e) has the the following property: a path π is a test sequence exercising e if and only if $\pi \models$ ltl(e). Then we have that e subsumes e' if and only if $G \models$ ltl(e) $\rightarrow$ ltl(e').

Proof. e subsumes e' if and only if for every path π, π is a test sequence exercising e implies π is a test sequence exercising e' if and only if for every path π, $\pi \models$ ltl(e) $\rightarrow \pi \models$ ltl(e') if and only if for every path π, $\pi \models$ ltl(e) $\rightarrow$ ltl(e') if and only if $G \models$ ltl(e) $\rightarrow$ ltl(e'). □

In the above algorithm, the total number of model checking performed is $O(|E(G,C)|^2)$ both in the best case and worst case. Note that the subsumption graph $(E(G,C), SR)$ is used to identify all possible minimum spanning sets. If we are only interested in one minimum spanning set rather than all possible ones, we can significantly reduce the total number of model checking to $O(|E(G,C)|)$ in the best case using the new algorithm shown in Figure 3. It is not hard to see that the result of the new algorithm is a spanning forest of the subsumption graph $(E(G,C), SR)$. Moreover, the root nodes of the spanning forest comprise a minimum spanning set.

INPUT: a flow graph G and a coverage criteron C
OUTPUT: a spanning forest $(E(G,C), SF)$ for the subsumption graph $(E(G,C), SR)$

```
 1: SF := ∅;
 2: construct the set E(G, C); let E(G, C) = {e₁, ..., eₙ};
 3: for i := 1 to n do L[i] := eᵢ; marked[i] := false;
 4: for i := 1 to n do
 5:     if marked[i] = false then
 6:         for j := 1 to n, j ≠ i do
 7:             if marked[j] = false then
 8:                 model check ltl(L[i]) → ltl(L[j]) against G;
 9:                 if G ⊨ ltl(L[i]) → ltl(L[j]) then
10:                     SF := SF ∪ {(L[i], L[j])};
11:                     marked[j] := true;
12: return (E(G, C), SF);
```

Fig. 3. An algorithm for finding a spanning forest of the subsumption graph

In the following sections, for each coverage criterion, for each entity e in $E(G,C)$, we will define the LTL formula ltl(e) and show its property that a path π is a test sequence exercising e if and only if $\pi \models$ ltl(e).

4.1   Statements and Branches

All-Statements Coverage Criterion. We say that a test sequence π exercises a vertex v if there is $i \geq 0$ such that $\pi(i) = v$. A test suite Π satisfies *all-statements coverage criterion* if every vertex of a flow graph is exercised by a test sequence in Π. For a vertex v, we associate an LTL formula defined by

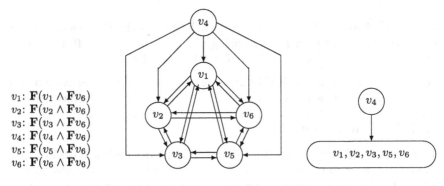

v_1: $\mathbf{F}(v_1 \wedge \mathbf{F}v_6)$
v_2: $\mathbf{F}(v_2 \wedge \mathbf{F}v_6)$
v_3: $\mathbf{F}(v_3 \wedge \mathbf{F}v_6)$
v_4: $\mathbf{F}(v_4 \wedge \mathbf{F}v_6)$
v_5: $\mathbf{F}(v_5 \wedge \mathbf{F}v_6)$
v_6: $\mathbf{F}(v_6 \wedge \mathbf{F}v_6)$

(a) LTL formulas   (b) subsumption graph   (c) reduced subsumption graph

Fig. 4. All-statements coverage criterion for Figure 1

$$\mathrm{ltl}(v) = \mathbf{F}(v \wedge \mathbf{F}v_f)$$

with the property that a path π is a test sequence exercising a vertex v if and only if there are $0 \leq i \leq j$ such that $\pi(i) \models v$ and $\pi(j) \models v_f$ if and only if $\pi \models \mathbf{F}(v \wedge \mathbf{F}v_f)$. Figure 4.(a) shows the vertices and their LTL formulas for the flow graph in Figure 1. By model-checking the formula $\mathrm{ltl}(v) \to \mathrm{ltl}(v')$ for every pair (v, v') of vertices, we obtain the subsumption graph shown in Figure 4.(b). We then collapse the strongly connected component $\{v_1, v_2, v_3, v_5, v_6\}$ into one vertex and obtain the reduced subsumption graph shown in Figure 4.(c). Finally we find a minimum spanning set $\{v_4\}$.

All-Branches Coverage Criterion. We say that a test sequence π exercises an arc (v, v') if there is $i \geq 0$ such that $\pi(i) = v$ and $\pi(i+1) = v'$. A test suite Π satisfies *all-branches coverage criterion* if every arc of a flow graph is exercised by a test sequence in Π. For an arc (v, v'), we associate an LTL formula defined by

$$\mathrm{ltl}(v, v') = \mathbf{F}(v \wedge \mathbf{X}(v' \wedge \mathbf{F}v_f))$$

with the property that a path π is a test sequence exercising an arc (v, v') if and only if there are $0 \leq i < j$ such that $\pi(i) \models v$, $\pi(i+1) \models v'$, $\pi(j) \models v_f$ if and only if $\pi \models \mathbf{F}(v \wedge \mathbf{X}(v' \wedge \mathbf{F}v_f))$. Figure 5 shows the arcs, their LTL formulas, and reduced subsumption graph for the flow graph in Figure 1. We have two minimum spanning sets $\{(v_3, v_4), (v_3, v_5)\}$ and $\{(v_4, v_5), (v_3, v_5)\}$.

4.2   Definition-Use Pairs

Rapps and Weyuker[16] propose a family of data flow oriented coverage criteria that require certain pairs between definitions and uses of the same variable be exercised. Let x be a variable, v be a vertex, and w be a vertex v' or arc (v', v'').

 - A finite path $v, v_1, ..., v_n, w$ is a *definition-clear* path from v to w with respect to x if x is not defined at v_i for every $1 \leq i \leq n$.

(v_1, v_2): $\mathbf{F}(v_1 \wedge \mathbf{X}(v_2 \wedge \mathbf{F}v_6))$
(v_2, v_3): $\mathbf{F}(v_2 \wedge \mathbf{X}(v_3 \wedge \mathbf{F}v_6))$
(v_3, v_4): $\mathbf{F}(v_3 \wedge \mathbf{X}(v_4 \wedge \mathbf{F}v_6))$
(v_3, v_5): $\mathbf{F}(v_3 \wedge \mathbf{X}(v_5 \wedge \mathbf{F}v_6))$
(v_4, v_5): $\mathbf{F}(v_4 \wedge \mathbf{X}(v_5 \wedge \mathbf{F}v_6))$
(v_5, v_6): $\mathbf{F}(v_5 \wedge \mathbf{X}(v_6 \wedge \mathbf{F}v_6))$

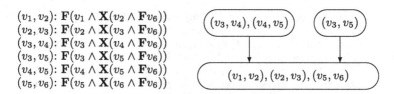

Fig. 5. All-branches coverage criterion for Figure 1

- For a definition $d(x, v)$ and use $u(x, w)$ of the same variable x, $d(x, v)$ *reaches* $u(x, w)$ if there is a definition-clear path from v to w with respect to x. If w is a vertex, the pair $(d(x, v), u(x, w))$ is called *definition-cuse pair* (dcu-pair). Otherwise, the pair is called *definition-puse pair* (dpu-pair).
- A *definition-use pair* (du-pair) is either a dcu-pair or dpu-pair.

In Figure 1, we observe that $(d(max, v_2), u(max, v_5))$ is a du-pair whose definition-clear path is $v_2 v_3 v_5$, while $(d(max, v_2), u(max, v_6))$ is not because there is no definition-clear path from v_2 to v_6 with respect to max.

Identifying du-Pairs. We note that the set of du-pairs of a flow graph can be identified using the conventional data flow analysis algorithm for the reaching-definition problem[2]. Recently, in [9,10], the authors show that the set of du-pairs can also be identified using CTL model checking.

All-Uses Coverage Criterion. We say that a test sequence π exercises a du-pair $(d(x, v), u(x, w))$ if π is of the form $\pi_1 \cdot \pi_2 \cdot \pi_3$, where π_2 is a definition-clear path from v to w with respect to x. A test suite Π satisfies *all-uses coverage criterion* if every du-pair $(d(x, v), u(x, w))$ of a flow graph is exercised by a test sequence in Π. Let $def(x)$ be the disjunction of all vertices at which x is defined. For example, in Figure 1, $def(x) ::= v_1$, $def(y) ::= v_1$, $def(z) ::= v_1$, $def(max)$ $::= v_2 \vee v_4 \vee v_5$. For a du-pair $(d(x, v), u(x, w))$, we associate an LTL formula defined by

- if the pair is a dcu-pair, i.e., w is a vertex v',
    $\text{ltl}(d(x, v), u(x, v')) = \mathbf{F}(v \wedge \mathbf{X}[\neg def(x)\mathbf{U}(v' \wedge \mathbf{F}v_f)])$
- if the pair is a dpu-pair, i.e., w is an arc (v', v''),
    $\text{ltl}(d(x, v), u(x, v', v'')) = \mathbf{F}(v \wedge \mathbf{X}[\neg def(x)\mathbf{U}(v' \wedge \mathbf{X}(v'' \wedge \mathbf{F}v_f))])$

with the property that a path π is a test sequence exercising a dcu-pair $(d(x, v), u(x, v'))$ if and only if there are $0 \leq i < j \leq k$ such that $\pi(i) \models v$, $\pi(l) \models \neg def(x)$ for $i < l < j$, $\pi(j) \models v'$, and $\pi(k) \models v_f$ if and only if $\pi \models \mathbf{F}(v \wedge \mathbf{X}[\neg def(x)\mathbf{U}(v' \wedge \mathbf{F}v_f)])$. The same property also holds for dpu-pairs. Figure 6 shows the du-pairs, their LTL formulas, and the reduced subsumption graph for the flow graph in Figure 1.

All-Defs Coverage Criterion. For a definition $d(x, v)$, define $DUPAIR$ $(d(x, v))$ as the set of du-pairs whose definition is $d(x, v)$. We say that a test sequence π exercises a definition $d(x, v)$ if π exercises a du-pair in $DUPAIR(d(x, v))$.

$(d(x, v_1), u(x, v_2))$: $\mathbf{F}(v_1 \wedge \mathbf{X}[\neg def(x)\mathbf{U}(v_2 \wedge \mathbf{F}v_6)])$
$(d(x, v_1), u(x, v_3, v_4))$: $\mathbf{F}(v_1 \wedge \mathbf{X}[\neg def(x)\mathbf{U}(v_3 \wedge \mathbf{X}(v_4 \wedge \mathbf{F}v_6))])$
$(d(x, v_1), u(x, v_3, v_5)))$: $\mathbf{F}(v_1 \wedge \mathbf{X}[\neg def(x)\mathbf{U}(v_3 \wedge \mathbf{X}(v_5 \wedge \mathbf{F}v_6))])$
$(d(y, v_1), u(y, v_4))$: $\mathbf{F}(v_1 \wedge \mathbf{X}[\neg def(y)\mathbf{U}(v_4 \wedge \mathbf{F}v_6)])$
$(d(y, v_1), u(y, v_3, v_4))$: $\mathbf{F}(v_1 \wedge \mathbf{X}[\neg def(y)\mathbf{U}(v_3 \wedge \mathbf{X}(v_4 \wedge \mathbf{F}v_6))])$
$(d(y, v_1), u(y, v_3, v_5))$: $\mathbf{F}(v_1 \wedge \mathbf{X}[\neg def(y)\mathbf{U}(v_3 \wedge \mathbf{X}(v_5 \wedge \mathbf{F}v_6))])$
$(d(z, v_1), u(z, v_5))$: $\mathbf{F}(v_1 \wedge \mathbf{X}[\neg def(z)\mathbf{U}(v_5 \wedge \mathbf{F}v_6)])$
$(d(max, v_2), u(max, v_5))$: $\mathbf{F}(v_2 \wedge \mathbf{X}[\neg def(max)\mathbf{U}(v_5 \wedge \mathbf{F}v_6)])$
$(d(max, v_4), u(max, v_5))$: $\mathbf{F}(v_4 \wedge \mathbf{X}[\neg def(max)\mathbf{U}(v_5 \wedge \mathbf{F}v_6)])$
$(d(max, v_5), u(max, v_6))$: $\mathbf{F}(v_5 \wedge \mathbf{X}[\neg def(max)\mathbf{U}(v_6 \wedge \mathbf{F}v_6)])$

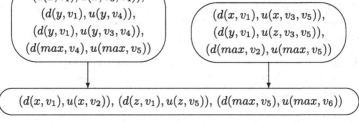

Fig. 6. All-uses coverage criterion for Figure 1

A test suite Π satisfies *all-defs coverage criterion* if every definition $d(x, v)$ of a flow graph is exercised by a test sequence in Π. For a definition $d(x, v)$, we associate an LTL formula defined by

$$\text{ltl}(d(x, v)) = \bigvee_{(d(x,v),u(x,w)) \in DUPAIR(d(x,v))} \text{ltl}(d(x, v), u(x, w))$$

with the property that a path π is a test sequence exercising $d(x, v)$ if and only if π exercises a du-pair in $DUPAIR(d(x, v))$ if and only if $\pi \models \text{ltl}(d(x, v))$. Figure 7 shows the definitions, their LTL formulas, and the reduced subsumption graph for the flow graph in Figure 1.

4.3   Required k-Tuples

Ntafos[15] emphasizes interactions between different variables. Such interactions are captured in terms of sequences of du-pairs.

- A sequence $[d(x_1, v_1), u(x_1, w_1), \ldots d(x_n, v_n), u(x_n, w_n)]$ of du-pairs is a *data flow chain* (df-chain)[18] if for every $1 \le i < n$, $w_i = v_{i+1}$, that is, $u(x_i, w_i)$ and $d(x_i, v_{i+1})$ occur at the same vertex and hence the definition $d(x_i, v_{i+1})$ is given in terms of $u(x_i, w_i)$. Note that $u(x_i, w_i)$, $1 \le i < n$, is a c-use and the final use $u(x_n, w_n)$ may be either a c-use or p-use.
- A df-chain consisting of $k - 1$ du-pairs, $k \ge 2$, is a *k-definition/reference interaction* (k-dr interaction) in the terminology of [15].

$d(x, v_1)$: $\mathrm{ltl}(d(x, v_1), u(x, v_2)) \lor \mathrm{ltl}(d(x, v_1), u(x, v_3, v_4)) \lor \mathrm{ltl}(d(x, v_1), u(x, v_3, v_5))$
$d(y, v_1)$: $\mathrm{ltl}(d(y, v_1), u(y, v_4)) \lor \mathrm{ltl}(d(y, v_1), u(y, v_3, v_4)) \lor \mathrm{ltl}(d(y, v_1), u(y, v_3, v_5))$
$d(z, v_1)$: $\mathrm{ltl}(d(z, v_1), u(z, v_5))$
$d(max, v_2)$: $\mathrm{ltl}(d(max, v_2), u(max, v_5))$
$d(max, v_4)$: $\mathrm{ltl}(d(max, v_4), u(max, v_5))$
$d(max, v_5)$: $\mathrm{ltl}(d(max, v_5), u(max, v_6))$

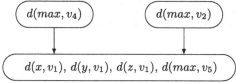

Fig. 7. All-defs coverage criterion for Figure 1

– A path $v_1\pi_1 w_1...v_n\pi_n w_n$ is an *interaction path* of a df-chain if for every $1 \leq i \leq n$, $v_i\pi_i w_i$ is a definition-clear path from v_i to w_i with respect to x_i.

In Figure 1, we observe that $[d(x, v_1), u(x, v_2)]$ is a 2-dr interaction that has $v_1 v_2$ as its interaction path and $[d(x, v_1), u(x, v_2), d(max, v_2), u(max, v_5)]$ is a 3-dr interaction that has $v_1 v_2 v_3 v_5$ as its interaction path.

Identifying k-dr Interactions. Let $\kappa = [d(x_1, v_1), u(x_1, w_1), ... d(x_{k-1}, v_{k-1}), u(x_{k-1}, w_{k-1})]$. By definition, κ is a k-dr interaction if and only if $(d(x_1, v_1), u(x_1, w_1))$ is a du-pair, $w_1 = v_2$, and $[d(x_2, v_2), u(x_2, w_2), ... d(x_{k-1}, v_{k-1}), u(x_{k-1}, w_{k-1})]$ is a $(k-1)$-dr interaction. This leads to a recursive algorithm for identifying the set of k-dr interactions.

Required k-Tuples Coverage Criterion. We say that a test sequence π exercises a k-dr interaction κ if π is of the form $\pi_1 \cdot \pi_2 \cdot \pi_3$, where π_2 is an interaction path of κ. A test suite Π satisfies *required k-tuples coverage criterion* if every k-dr interaction of a flow graph is exercised by a test sequence in Π. For a k-dr interaction κ, $k \geq 2$, we associate an LTL formula inductively defined by

– $\mathrm{ltl}(\kappa) = \mathbf{F}ltl(\kappa)$,
– if κ is $[d(x, v), u(x, v')] \cdot \kappa'$, then $ltl(\kappa) = (v \land \mathbf{X}[\neg def(x)\mathbf{U}ltl(\kappa')])$,
– if κ is $[d(x, v), u(x, v')]$, then $ltl(\kappa) = (v \land \mathbf{X}[\neg def(x)\mathbf{U}(v' \land \mathbf{F}v_f)])$,
– if κ is $[d(x, v), u(x, v', v'')]$, then $ltl(\kappa) = (v \land \mathbf{X}[\neg def(x)\mathbf{U}(v' \land \mathbf{X}(v'' \land \mathbf{F}v_f))])$.

By induction on the number of du-pairs in κ, it can be shown that a path π is a test sequence exercising a k-dr interaction κ if and only if $\pi \models \mathrm{ltl}(\kappa)$. Figure 8 shows the 3-dr interactions, their LTL formulas, and the reduced subsumption graph for the flow graph in Figure 1.

4.4   IO-df-Chains

Ural *et al.*[18, 19] also emphasize interactions between different variables. While required k-tuples coverage criterion considers df-chains consisting of a fixed number of du-pairs, all-IO-df-chains coverage criterion in [18, 19] considers df-chains

$[d(x, v_1), u(x, v_2), d(max, v_2), u(max, v_5)]$:
  $\mathbf{F}(v_1 \wedge \mathbf{X}[\neg def(x)\mathbf{U}(v_2 \wedge \mathbf{X}[\neg def(max)\mathbf{U}(v_5 \wedge \mathbf{F}v_6)])])$
$[d(y, v_1), u(y, v_4), d(max, v_4), u(max, v_5)]$:
  $\mathbf{F}(v_1 \wedge \mathbf{X}[\neg def(y)\mathbf{U}(v_4 \wedge \mathbf{X}[\neg def(max)\mathbf{U}(v_5 \wedge \mathbf{F}v_6)])])$
$[d(z, v_1), u(z, v_5), d(max, v_5), u(max, v_6)]$:
  $\mathbf{F}(v_1 \wedge \mathbf{X}[\neg def(z)\mathbf{U}(v_5 \wedge \mathbf{X}[\neg def(max)\mathbf{U}(v_6 \wedge \mathbf{F}v_6)])])$
$[d(max, v_2), u(max, v_5), d(max, v_5), u(max, v_6)]$:
  $\mathbf{F}(v_2 \wedge \mathbf{X}[\neg def(max)\mathbf{U}(v_5 \wedge \mathbf{X}[\neg def(max)\mathbf{U}(v_6 \wedge \mathbf{F}v_6)])])$
$[d(max, v_4), u(max, v_5), d(max, v_5), u(max, v_6)]$:
  $\mathbf{F}(v_4 \wedge \mathbf{X}[\neg def(max)\mathbf{U}(v_5 \wedge \mathbf{X}[\neg def(max)\mathbf{U}(v_6 \wedge \mathbf{F}v_6)])])$

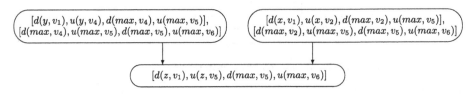

Fig. 8. 3-dr interaction coverage criterion for Figure 1

consisting of an arbitrary (but finite) number of du-pairs which start with inputs and end with outputs. In this paper, we define an *input* as a definition occurring at an input statement and *output* as a use occurring at an output statement. The rationale here is to capture the functionality of a module in terms of the interactions with its environment by identifying the effects of inputs accepted from the environment on outputs offered to the environment. Let $d(x, v)$ be a definition and $u(x', w)$ be a use.

- $d(x, v)$ *affects* $u(x', w)$ if either $x = x'$ and $(d(x, v), u(x', w))$ is a du-pair or there is a use $u(x, v')$ such that $(d(x, v), u(x, v'))$ is a du-pair and there is a definition $d(x'', v')$, given in terms of $u(x, v')$, that affects $u(x', w)$.
- $(d(x, v), u(x', w))$ is an *affect-pair* if $d(x, v)$ affects $u(x', w)$. By definition, $(d(x, v), u(x', w))$ is an affect-pair if and only if there is a df-chain $[d(x_1, v_1), u(x_1, w_1), \ldots d(x_n, v_n), u(x_n, w_n)]$ such that $d(x_1, v_1) = d(x, v)$ and $u(x_n, w_n) = u(x', w)$.

Among the particular affect-pairs of interest are those starting with inputs and ending with outputs, which we call *io-pairs*. In Figure 1, there are three inputs $d(x, v_1)$, $d(y, v_1)$, $d(z, v_1)$ and one output $u(max, v_6)$. Consider the input $d(x, v_1)$ and output $u(max, v_6)$. We observe that $d(x, v_1)$ affects $u(max, v_6)$ through the df-chain $[d(x, v_1), u(x, v_2),\ d(max, v_2), u(max, v_5),\ d(max, v_5), u(max, v_6)]$.

Identifying Simple df-Chains. For a definition $d(x, v)$ and use $u(x', w)$, we use $CHAIN(d(x, v), u(x', w))$ to denote the set of df-chains $\kappa = [d(x_1, v_1), u(x_1, w_1), \ldots d(x_n, v_n), u(x_n, w_n)]$ such that $d(x_1, v_1) = d(x, v)$ and $u(x_n, w_n) = u(x', w)$. In general, there may be multiple occurrences of the same du-pair in

κ thereby causing the possibility of an infinite number of df-chains in $CHAIN$ $(d(x, v), u(x', w))$. In order to put an upper bound on the size of $CHAIN(d(x, v), u(x', w))$, we consider its subset $SCHAIN(d(x, v), u(x', w))$ consisting of *simple* df-chains that are allowed to have at most one occurrence of each du-pair. By definition, κ is a simple df-chain in $SCHAIN(d(x, v), u(x', w))$ if and only if $d(x_1, v_1) = d(x, v)$, $u(x_n, w_n) = u(x', w)$, $(d(x_1, v_1), u(x_1, w_1))$ is a du-pair, and $[d(x_2, v_2), u(x_2, w_2), ... d(x_n, v_n), u(x_n, w_n)]$ is a simple df-chain that does not contain the first du-pair $(d(x_1, v_1), u(x_1, w_1))$. This leads to a recursive algorithm for identifying the set of simple df-chains.

All-IO-df-Chains Coverage Criterion. A test suite Π satisfies *all-IO-df-chains coverage criterion* if for every io-pair (i, o), every simple df-chain in $SCHAIN(i, o)$ is covered by a test sequence in Π. For a simple df-chain κ in $SCHAIN(i, o)$, we associate the LTL formula $\mathsf{ltl}(\kappa)$. For example, in Figure 1, there are three io-pairs $(d(x, v_1), u(max, v_6))$, $(d(y, v_1), u(max, v_6))$, and $(d(z, v_1), u(max, v_6))$. Figure 9 shows the simple chains for the io-pairs, their LTL formulas, and the reduced subsumption graph.

$[d(x, v_1), u(x, v_2), d(max, v_2), u(max, v_5), d(max, v_5), u(max, v_6)]$:
$\qquad \mathbf{F}(v_1 \wedge \mathbf{X}[\neg def(x)\mathbf{U}(v_2 \wedge \mathbf{X}[\neg def(max)\mathbf{U}(v_5 \wedge \mathbf{X}[\neg def(max)\mathbf{U}(v_6 \wedge \mathbf{F}v_6)])])])$
$[d(y, v_1), u(y, v_4), d(max, v_4), u(max, v_5), d(max, v_5), u(max, v_6)]$:
$\qquad \mathbf{F}(v_1 \wedge \mathbf{X}[\neg def(y)\mathbf{U}(v_4 \wedge \mathbf{X}[\neg def(max)\mathbf{U}(v_5 \wedge \mathbf{X}[\neg def(max)\mathbf{U}(v_6 \wedge \mathbf{F}v_6)])])])$
$[d(z, v_1), u(z, v_5), d(max, v_5), u(max, v_6)]$:
$\qquad \mathbf{F}(v_1 \wedge \mathbf{X}[\neg def(z)\mathbf{U}(v_5 \wedge \mathbf{X}[\neg def(max)\mathbf{U}(v_6 \wedge \mathbf{F}v_6)])])$

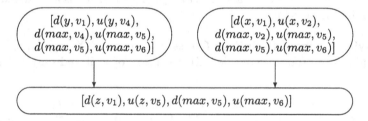

Fig. 9. All-IO-df-chains coverage criterion for Figure 1

4.5   Ordered Definition Contexts

Laski and Korel[11] emphasize that a vertex or arc may contain uses of several different variables, where each use may be reached by several different definitions. Let w be a vertex or arc and $u(x_1, w), ..., u(x_n, w)$ be the uses occurring at w.

– For a set X of variables, we use $d(X, v)$ to denote the set $\{d(x, v) \mid x \in X\}$ of definitions.
– An *ordered definition context* of w is a sequence $[d(X_1, v_1), ..., d(X_m, v_m)]$ of sets of definitions such that $X_1 \cup ... \cup X_m = X$ and there is a path $v_1\pi_1...v_m\pi_m w$, called *ordered context path*, satisfying the following property: for every $1 \leq i \leq m$, $v_i\pi_i...v_m\pi_m w$ is a definition-clear path from v_i to w with respect to every variable x in X_i.

$[d(\{x\}, v_1)]$ of v_2: $\mathbf{F}(v_1 \wedge \mathbf{X}[\neg def(x)\mathbf{U}(v_2 \wedge \mathbf{F}v_6)])$
$[d(\{x, y\}, v_1)]$ of (v_3, v_4): $\mathbf{F}(v_1 \wedge \mathbf{X}[(\neg def(x) \wedge \neg def(y))\mathbf{U}(v_3 \wedge \mathbf{X}(v_4 \wedge \mathbf{F}v_6))])$
$[d(\{x, y\}, v_1)]$ of (v_3, v_5): $\mathbf{F}(v_1 \wedge \mathbf{X}[(\neg def(x) \wedge \neg def(y))\mathbf{U}(v_3 \wedge \mathbf{X}(v_5 \wedge \mathbf{F}v_6))])$
$[d(\{x\}, v_1)]$ of v_4: $\mathbf{F}(v_1 \wedge \mathbf{X}[\neg def(x)\mathbf{U}(v_4 \wedge \mathbf{F}v_6)])$
$[d(\{z\}, v_1), d(\{max\}, v_2)]$ of v_5:
    $\mathbf{F}(v_1 \wedge \mathbf{X}[\neg def(z)\mathbf{U}(\neg def(z) \wedge v_2 \wedge \mathbf{X}[(\neg def(z) \wedge \neg def(max))\mathbf{U}(v_5 \wedge \mathbf{F}v_6)])])$
$[d(\{z\}, v_1), d(\{max\}, v_4)]$ of v_5:
    $\mathbf{F}(v_1 \wedge \mathbf{X}[\neg def(z)\mathbf{U}(\neg def(z) \wedge v_4 \wedge \mathbf{X}[(\neg def(z) \wedge \neg def(max))\mathbf{U}(v_5 \wedge \mathbf{F}v_6)])])$
$[d(\{max\}, v_5)]$ of v_6: $\mathbf{F}(v_5 \wedge \mathbf{X}[\neg def(max)\mathbf{U}(v_6 \wedge \mathbf{F}v_6)])$

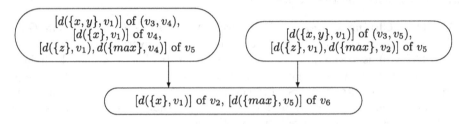

Fig. 10. Ordered contexts coverage criterion for Figure 1

In Figure 1, consider the vertex v_5 that has two uses $u(z, v_5)$ and $u(max, v_5)$. We observe that $[d(\{z\}, v_1), d(\{max\}, v_2)]$ and $[d(\{z\}, v_1), d(\{max\}, v_4)]$ are ordered definition contexts of v_5 which have $v_1v_2v_3v_5$ and $v_1v_2v_3v_4v_5$ as their ordered context path, respectively. For another example, consider the edge (v_3, v_4) that has two uses $u(x, v_3, v_4)$ and $u(y, v_3, v_4)$. $[d(\{x, y\}, v_1)]$ is an ordered definition context of the edge.

Identifying Ordered Definition Contexts. Let $\lambda = [d(X_1, v_1), ..., d(X_m, v_m)]$. By definition, λ is an ordered definition context of w if and only if for every $1 \le i \le m$,

- for every variable $x \in X_1 \cup ... \cup X_{i-1}$, x is not defined at v_i,
- for every variable $x \in X_1 \cup ... \cup X_i$, there is a definition-clear path from v_i to v_{i+1} with respect to x.

This leads to a recursive algorithm for identifying the set of ordered definition contexts.

Ordered Contexts Coverage Criterion. We say that a test sequence π exercises an ordered definition context λ if π is of the form $\pi_1 \cdot \pi_2 \cdot \pi_3$, where π_2 is an ordered context path of λ. A test suite Π satisfies *ordered contexts coverage criterion* if for every vertex or arc w of a flow graph, every ordered definition context of w is exercised by a test sequence in Π. For an ordered definition context λ of w, we associate an LTL formula inductively defined by

- $\mathbf{ltl}(\lambda) = \mathbf{F}\,ltl(\lambda, true)$,
- if λ is $[d(X, v)]\cdot\lambda'$, then $ltl(\lambda, nodef) = (nodef \wedge v \wedge \mathbf{X}[nodef'\mathbf{U}\,ltl(\lambda', nodef')])$, where $nodef' = nodef \wedge \bigwedge_{x \in X} \neg def(x)$,

- if λ is empty and $w = v'$, then $ltl(\lambda, nodef) = (v' \land \mathbf{F}v_f)$,
- if λ is empty and $w = (v', v'')$, then $ltl(\lambda, nodef) = (v' \land \mathbf{X}(v'' \land \mathbf{F}v_f))$.

By induction on the number of definitions in λ, it can be shown that a test sequence π exercises λ if and only if $\pi \models \mathbf{ltl}(\lambda)$. Figure 10 shows the ordered definition contexts, their LTL formulas, and the reduced subsumption graph for the flow graph in Figure 1.

5   Conclusions and Future Work

We have presented a method for reducing the cost of test generation for structural testing. We investigated a family of control flow and data flow oriented coverage criteria and reduced the problem of finding subsumption relations to the problem of LTL model checking. We illustrated the method using the flow graph model of a simple program module.

Our method can be applied to more accurate models of programs. Traditionally, test generation has been performed upon flow graphs. Since a flow graph preserves only the control flow and ignores the values of data variables, it is often the case that the size of state space is not a concern. However, test generation is increasingly performed upon more accurate models that respect the values of data variables such as reachability graphs and abstract state graphs obtained by abstract interpretation. In this case, the size of state space is the primary concern and model checking has been proven to be effective for controlling the state explosion problem. We plan to conduct case studies to see how large and complex programs can be handled by our method when reachability graphs or abstract state graphs are used.

Our method can also be applied to requirements specifications written in state-based specification languages such as extended finite state machines, statecharts, and SDL. Optimal test generation from such specifications is more complicated than that from program modules because it is necessary to cope with a rich set of language constructs for modeling hierarchy, concurrency, and communications. Our method is language-independent in that the temporal logic formulas employed in the method can be immediately used for various specification languages. In fact, differences between specification languages (for example, synchronous computational model in statecharts versus asynchronous computational model in SDL and communications through event broadcasting in statecharts versus communications through unbounded queues in SDL) only affect the rules for translating them into input to model checkers.

Acknowledgements

This research is supported in part by Natural Sciences and Engineering Research Council (NSERC) of Canada under grant OGP 976.

References

1. H. Agrawal, "Dominators, Super Blocks, and Program Coverage," *Proc. of the 21st ACM Symposium on Principles of Programming Languages*, pp. 25-34, 1994.
2. A.V. Aho, R. Sethi, and J.D. Ullman, *Compilers, Principles, Techniques, and Tools*, Addison-Wesley, 1986.
3. A. Bertolino, "Unconstrained Edges and Their Application to Branch Analysis and Testing of Programs," *The Journal of Systems and Software*, 20(2):125-133, Feb. 1993.
4. A. Bertolino and M. Marré, "Automatic Generation of Path Covers Based on the Control Flow Analysis of Computer Programs," *IEEE Transactions on Software Engineering*, 20(12):885-899, Dec. 1994.
5. A. Bertolino and M. Marré, "How Many Paths are Needed for Branch Testing?" *The Journal of Systems and Software*, 35(2):95-106, Nov. 1996.
6. T. Chusho, "Test Data Selection and Quality Estimation Based on the Concept of Essential Branches for Path Testing," *IEEE Transactions on Software Engineering*, 13(5):509-517, May 1987.
7. R. Dssouli, K. Saleh, E. Aboulhamid, A. En-Nouaary, and C. Bourhfir, "Test Development for Communication Protocols: towards Automation," *Computer Networks*, 31(7):1835-1872, June 1999.
8. R. Gupta and M.L. Soffa, "Employing Static Information in the Generation of Test Cases," *Software Testing, Verification and Reliability*, 3(1):29-48, 1993.
9. H.S. Hong, I. Lee, O. Sokolsky, and H. Ural, "A Temporal Logic Based Theory of Test Coverage and Generation," *TACAS '02*, Vol. 2280 of LNCS, pp. 327-341, Springer-Verlag, 2002.
10. H.S. Hong, S.D. Cha, I. Lee, O. Sokolsky, and H. Ural, "Data Flow Testing as Model Checking," *Proc. of the 25th International Conference on Software Engineering*, pp. 232-242, 2003.
11. J.W. Laski and B. Korel, "A Data Flow Oriented Program Testing Strategy," *IEEE Transactions on Software Engineering*, 9(5):347-354, May 1983.
12. Z. Manna and A. Pnueli, *The Temporal Logic of Reactive and Concurrent Systems: Specification*, Springer-Verlag, 1992.
13. M. Marré and A. Bertolino, "Unconstrained Duas and Their Use in Achieving All-uses Coverage," *Proc. of the International Symposium on Software Testing and Analysis*, pp. 147-157, 1996.
14. M. Marré and A. Bertolino, "Reducing and Estimating the Cost of Test Coverage Criteria," *Proc. of the 18th International Conference on Software Engineering*, pp. 486-494, 1996.
15. S.C. Ntafos, "On Required Element Testing," *IEEE Transactions on Software Engineering*, 10(11):795-803, Nov. 1984.
16. S. Rapps and E.J. Weyuker, "Selecting Software Test Data Using Data Flow Information," *IEEE Transactions on Software Engineering*, 11(4):367-375, Apr. 1985.
17. S. Tasiran and K. Keutzer, "Coverage Metrics for Functional Validation of Hardware Designs," *IEEE Design and Test of Computers*, 18(4):36-45, July/Aug. 2001.
18. H. Ural and B. Yang, "A Test Sequence Generation Method for Protocol Testing," *IEEE Transactions on Communications*, 39(4):514-523, Apr. 1991.
19. H. Ural, K. Saleh, and A. Williams, "Test Generation Based on Control and Data Dependencies within System Specifications in SDL," *Computer Communications*, 23(7):609-627, Mar. 2000.
20. H. Zhu, P.A. Hall, and J.H.R. May, "Software Unit Test Coverage and Adequacy," *ACM Computing Surveys*, 29(4):366-427, Dec. 1997.

Specifying and Generating Test Cases Using Observer Automata

Johan Blom, Anders Hessel, Bengt Jonsson, and Paul Pettersson

Department of Information Technology, Uppsala University,
P.O. Box 337, SE-751 05 Uppsala, Sweden
{johan, hessel, bengt, paupet}@it.uu.se

Abstract. We present a technique for specifying coverage criteria and a method for generating test suites for systems whose behaviours can be described as extended finite state machines (EFSM). To specify coverage criteria we use observer automata with *parameters*, which monitor and accept traces that cover a given test criterion of an EFSM. The flexibility of the technique is demonstrated by specifying a number of well-known coverage criteria based on control- and data-flow information using observer automata with parameters. We also develop a method for generating test cases from coverage criteria specified as observers. It is based on transforming a given observer automata into a bitvector analysis problem that can be efficiently implemented as an extension to an existing state-space exploration such as, e.g. SPIN or UPPAAL.

1 Introduction

Model based test case generation has in recent years been developed as a prominent technique in testing of reactive software systems. A model serves both the purpose of specifying how the system should respond to inputs from its environment, and of guiding the selection of test cases, e.g., using suitable coverage criteria. Typical notations for such models are state machines in some form, often extended with data variables. Test cases can be selected as individual "executions" of the model, checking that the outputs from the system under test (SUT) conform to those specified by the model.

There is a large literature and several tools (e.g., [4, 17, 24, 18, 3]) for generation of test cases from extended state machine models (EFSMs). In typical approaches, the selection of test cases follows some particular coverage criterion, such as coverage of control states, edges, etc., or using an explicitly given set of test purposes [5, 23]. When the model contains data variables, constraint solving techniques can be used to find actual values of input parameters that drive the execution in a desired direction [17, 21, 19].

Since different coverage criteria are suitable in different situations, and satisfy different constraints on fault detection capability, cost, information about where potential faults may be located, etc., it is highly desirable that a test generation tool is able to generate test suites in a flexible manner, for a wide variety of different coverage criteria. In other words, a test generation tool should accept

J. Grabowski and B. Nielsen (Eds.): FATES 2004, LNCS 3395, pp. 125–139, 2005.
© Springer-Verlag Berlin Heidelberg 2005

a simple specification of a coverage criterion, given in a language that can easily specify a large set of coverage criteria, and be able to generate test suites accordingly.

In this paper, we present a technique for specifying coverage criteria in a simple and flexible manner, and a method for generating test cases according to such coverage criteria. The technique fits well as an extension of a state-space exploration tool, such as, e.g., SPIN [11] or UPPAAL [16], which performs enumerative or symbolic state-space exploration. It can also be used to generate monitors that measure the coverage of a specific test suite by monitoring the test execution.

In our technique, a coverage criterion is given as a set of *coverage items*, each of which represents an interesting structural property of the EFSM which should be examined by a test suite. A coverage item can state that a particular state, edge, or similar, should be visited, it can be an explicit test purpose, etc. Each coverage item is specified by an *observer*, which observes the execution of a test case, and reports acceptance when the test case has *covered* the coverage item that it specifies. For instance, a coverage item stating that a control state l of an EFSM model should be visited simply observes how the EFSM executes and reports acceptance when it enters l.

A typical coverage criterion is given as a (often rather large) set of coverage items. An important mechanism to facilitate specification of many coverage criteria is to allow *parameterization* of observers. In this way, one can specify a set of coverage items parameterized over, e.g., control states, data variables, edges, etc. of the EFSM model. Using this simple and general mechanism, we can specify most of the coverage criteria that have been used in the literature, and also tailor coverage to specific features of a particular SUT. For instance, if a particular interface is very error prone, we can specify a coverage criterion which requires all possible interleavings of interactions on that interface to be exhibited in a test suite.

A specification of a coverage criterion can be used for test suite generation using a state-space exploration tool. First, we superpose the coverage observers onto the EFSM, then we search for a test sequence or set of test sequences in which as many observers as possible report acceptance. For parameterized observers, we can record the achieved coverage by a (typically small) set of bitvectors, indexed by parameter values, which concisely represent the states of a large set of parameterized observers, in analogy with bitvector analysis in data-flow analysis, e.g., [20]. The same machinery can also be used to monitor the achieved coverage of a certain test suite.

The remainder of the paper is structured as follows. We present EFSMs in the next section, and observers in Section 3. In Section 4, we show how our definitions of coverage can be used for test case generation, and report on a partial implementation of the technique. Section 5 concludes the paper.

Related Work. Most related work on test case generation from models of reactive systems employ some rather specific selection of coverage criteria. Explicitly given test purposes have been considered, both enumerative [5] and symbolic [23].

Test purposes in these works can in some sense be regarded as coverage observers, but are not used to specify more generic coverage criteria and do not make us of parameterization, as in our work. For finite-state machines and EFSMs, several approaches focus on particular coverage criteria, e.g., Bouquet and Legeard [1] synthesize test cases corresponding to combinations of choices of control flow and boundary values of state variables, Nielsen and Skou [21] generate test cases that cover reachable symbolic states. These coverage criteria can be specified as observers in our framework.

Some approaches present more flexible techniques for specifying a variety of coverage criteria. Hong et al [13, 12] describe how flow-based coverage criteria can be expressed in temporal logic. A particular coverage item is expressed in CTL, and a model checker generates a trace which covers the coverage item. In our approach, we use observers instead of temporal logic, which avoids some of the limitations of temporal logic [26]. Friedman et al [6] specifies coverage by giving a set of projections of the state space (e.g., on individual state variables, components of control flow) that should be covered, possibly under some restrictions. Our approach generalizes this one, by allowing to define observers. Also, we can let one pass of a state-space exploration tool generate a test suite that covers a large set of coverage items, whereas the above approaches invoke a run of a model checker for each coverage item.

Constraint Logic Programming for model based test case generation has been used, e.g., by Marre and Arnould [18], by Meudec [19], by Pretschner et al. [22]. These approaches typically compile the specification into a constraint logic programming language, in which test cases can be extracted using symbolic execution.

2   Extended Finite State Machines

We assume that the specification of a module to be tested is given as an extended finite state machine in some syntax. In this section, we present a generic way to describe EFSMs, but our work can be adapted to more specific EFSM notations such as, e.g., UML Statecharts [7] or SDL [14].

We assume that a System Under Test (SUT) interacts with its environment through events. Whenever the SUT receives an input event, it responds by performing some local computation and emitting an output event. To a given SUT, we associate a set A of *event types*, each with a fixed *arity*. An *event* is a term of form $a(d_1, \ldots, d_k)$ where a is an event type of arity k and $d_1, \ldots, d_k$ are the parameters of the event. The set A of event types is partitioned into *input event types* and *output event types*. A *trace* is a finite sequence

$$a_1(\overline{d}_1)/b_1(\overline{d'}_1) \quad a_2(\overline{d}_2)/b_2(\overline{d'}_2) \quad \cdots \quad a_n(\overline{d}_n)/b_n(\overline{d'}_n)$$

of input/output event pairs. Intuitively, the trace represents a behavior where the SUT, starting from its initial state, receives the input event, $a_1(\overline{d}_1)$ and responds with the output event $b_1(\overline{d'}_1)$. Thereafter, it receives the input event $a_2(\overline{d}_2)$ and so on. An *input sequence* is a finite sequence of input events.

Assume a set A_I of input event types, and a set A_O of output event types. An *Extended Finite State Machine* (EFSM) over (A_I, A_O) is a tuple $\langle L, l_0, \overline{v}, E \rangle$ where

- L is a finite set of *locations* (aka control states).
- $l_0 \in L$ is the *initial location*.
- $\overline{v}$ is a finite set of *state variables*.
- E is a finite set of *edges*, each of which is of form

$$ e: \quad \bigcirc_{l} \xrightarrow{a(\overline{w}), g \;\rightarrow\; \overline{u} := \overline{expr} / b(\overline{expr'})} \bigcirc_{l'} $$

where

- e is the name of the edge,
- l is the source location, and l' is the target location,
- $a \in A_I$ is an input event type, and $\overline{w}$ is a tuple of formal parameters of a,
- g is a guard,
- $\overline{u} := \overline{expr}$ is an assignment of new values to a subset $\overline{u} \subseteq \overline{v}$ of the state variables, and
- $b(\overline{expr'})$ is an expression which evaluates to an output event.

g, $\overline{expr}$, and $\overline{expr'}$ may depend on the formal parameters $\overline{w}$ of the input event and the state variables $\overline{v}$.

Intuitively, an edge of the above form denotes that whenever the EFSM is in location l and receives an event of form $a(\overline{w})$, then, provided that the guard g is satisfied, it can perform a computation step in which it updates its state variables by $\overline{u} := \overline{expr}$, emits the output event $b(\overline{expr'})$ and moves to location l'. We require the EFSM to be *deterministic*, i.e., that for any two edges with the same source location l and parameterized input event $a(\overline{w})$, the corresponding guards are inconsistent.

A *system state* is a tuple $\langle l, \sigma \rangle$ where l is a location, and σ is a mapping from $\overline{v}$ to values. We can extend σ to a partial mapping from expressions over $\overline{v}$ in the standard way. The *initial system state* is the tuple $\langle l_0, \sigma_0 \rangle$ where l_0 is the initial location, and σ_0 gives a default value to each state variable. A *computation step* is of the form $\langle l, \sigma \rangle \xrightarrow{a(\overline{d}) / b(\overline{d'})} \langle l', \sigma' \rangle$ consisting of system states $\langle l, \sigma \rangle$ and $\langle l', \sigma' \rangle$, an input event $a(\overline{d})$, and an output event $b(\overline{d'})$, such that there is an edge of the (above) form $l \xrightarrow{a(\overline{w}), g \rightarrow \overline{u} := \overline{expr} / b(\overline{expr'})} l'$, for which $\sigma(g[\overline{d}/\overline{w}])$ is true, $\sigma' = \sigma[\overline{u} \mapsto \sigma(\overline{expr}[\overline{d}/\overline{w}])]$, and $\overline{d'} = \sigma(\overline{expr'}[\overline{d}/\overline{w}])$. A *run* of the EFSM over a trace $a_1(\overline{d}_1)/b_1(\overline{d'}_1) \cdots a_n(\overline{d}_n)/b_n(\overline{d'}_n)$ is a sequence of computation steps

$$ \langle l_0, \sigma_0 \rangle \xrightarrow{a_1(\overline{d}_1)/b_1(\overline{d'}_1)} \langle l_1, \sigma_1 \rangle \xrightarrow{a_2(\overline{d}_2)/b_2(\overline{d'}_2)} \cdots \xrightarrow{a_n(\overline{d}_n)/b_n(\overline{d'}_n)} \langle l_n, \sigma_n \rangle $$

labelled by the input-output event pairs of the trace.

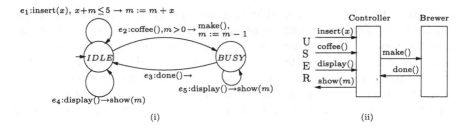

Fig. 1. An EFSM specifying the controller of a simple coffee machine

Example 1. In Fig. 1 an EFSM (from [13]) specifying the behavior of the controller of a simple coffee machine which interacts with a user and a brewer unit
is shown. The controller has $L = \{IDLE, BUSY\}$, $l_0 = IDLE$, $\bar{v} = \{m\}$, $A_I =$
$\{insert, coffee, display, done\}$, $A_O = \{show, make\}$, and $E = \{e_1, e_2, e_3, e_4, e_5\}$.
The parameter x and the variable m take values that are integers in the range
$[0 \ldots 5]$.

An EFSM can be used to check that a trace of a SUT conforms to its specification, by checking that each output event produced by the SUT conforms to
the corresponding output event prescribed in the EFSM. For test generation,
the output events will not be significant, and we will therefore omit them in the
rest of the paper, thus writing an edge of an EFSM as $l \xrightarrow{a(\bar{w}), g \rightarrow \bar{u} := \overline{expr}} l'$. We can
also consider specifications that are parallel compositions of EFSMs, but omit
such a treatment in this version of the paper.

3   Observers

In this section, we present how to use observers to specify coverage criteria
for test generation or test monitoring. A coverage criterion typically consists of
a (long) list of items that should be "covered" or "visited". For instance, the
criterion of "full location coverage" stipulates that a test suite should visit all
locations of a given EFSM. We will use the term *coverage item* for an item
that should be "covered" or "visited". Letting a test sequence be represented
as a trace, we can use standard techniques from model-checking and run-time
verification [25, 8] to represent a coverage item by an *observer*, which monitors a
trace and "accepts" whenever the coverage item has been covered. An observer
observes how an EFSM executes a run over a trace, and "remembers" some
chosen aspects of the EFSM execution. The observer can observe the events of
the trace, as well as syntactical components of edges that the EFSM traverses in
response to observed events, but should not interfere with the execution of the
system.

Typical coverage criteria consist not only of a single coverage item, but of
a large set of coverage items. We therefore extend the notion of observers by a

parameterization mechanism so that they can specify a *set of* coverage items. Parameterized observers are simply observers, in which locations and edges may be parameterized by parameters that range over given domains. Each choice of parameter values gives a certain observer location or edge. For each specified coverage item, the observer has an *accepting* (possibly parameterized) location which (for convenience) we give the name of the corresponding coverage item. When the accepting location is entered, the trace has covered the corresponding coverage item.

As a very simple example, the coverage item *"visit location l of the EFSM"* can be represented by an observer with one initial state, and one accepting location, named $loc(l)$, which is entered when the EFSM enters location l. The coverage criterion *"visit all locations of the EFSM"* can be represented by a parameterized observer with one initial state, and one parameterized accepting location, named $loc(L)$, where L is a parameter that ranges over locations in the EFSM. For each value l of L, the location $loc(l)$ is entered when the EFSM enters location l.

Formally, an *observer* is a tuple (Q, q_0, Q_f, B) where

- Q is a finite set of *observer locations*
- q_0 is the *initial observer location.*
- $Q_f \subseteq Q$ is a set of *accepting observer locations*, whose names are the corresponding coverage items.
- B is a set of edges, each of form

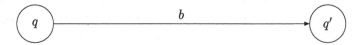

where b is a predicate that can depend on the input event received by the SUT, the mapping from state variables of EFSM to their values after performing the current computation step, and the edge in the EFSM that is executed in response to the current input event.

Intuitively, at any specific instant during test execution the observer is in one of its locations, q say. At each occurrence of an event, the observer traverses an outgoing edge from q, whose predicate is satisfied for this event, and the corresponding transition performed by the EFSM. Note that, in contrast to EFSMs, observers may be non-deterministic, since a coverage item in general can be covered in several ways.

In many cases, the initial location q_0 has an edge to itself with the predicate *true*. We use the symbol • to represent q_0 together with such a self-loop. Similarly, we assume that each $q_f \in Q_f$ has an edge to itself with the predicate *true*. We use the symbol ⊙ to represent accepting locations. In section 3.2, we discuss the effect of these self-loops in more detail. Intuitively, the one in q_0 is often used to allow the observer to non-deterministically start monitoring at any point of an EFSM run. The loop in each q_f is used to allow an observer to stay in an accepting location.

In order for observers to specify coverage criteria consisting of several coverage items, we allow locations and edges to be parameterized. Each parameter has a finite domain, which could be the set of EFSM locations, edges, state variables, or similar. We use uppercase letters in typewriter font for parameters. A parameterized location represents the collection of locations obtained by instantiating its parameters, and similarly for edges.

3.1   Observer Predicates

In the following we introduce a more specific syntax for the predicates b occurring on observer edges. The predicates will use a set of predefined *match variables* that are given values at the occurrence of

- an event $a(\overline{d})$,
- an edge $e : l \xrightarrow{a(\overline{w}),g \to \overline{u}:=\overline{expr}} l'$ of the EFSM, traversed in response to $a(\overline{d})$,
- the computation step $\langle l, \sigma \rangle \xrightarrow{a(\overline{d})} \langle l', \sigma' \rangle$ generated in response to $a(\overline{d})$.

For a traversed EFSM edge we use the following match variables (with associated meaning):

event_type	is the event type a of the occurring event
event-pars	is the list $\overline{d}$ of parameters of the event
edge	is the name e
target_loc	is the target location l'
guard	is the guard expression g
assignments	is the set $\overline{u} := \overline{expr}$ of assignments
target_val	is the function from EFSM state variables to values, s.t. $val(u)$ is the value $\sigma'(u)$ of variable u just after the computation step.

Similarly, we also define *source_loc* for the source location and *source_val* for the value $\sigma(u)$ of variable u just before the computation step. To be able to express more interesting properties we also introduce a set of operations that can be used together with the match variables:

- *lhs* is a function to get the left hand side expression of an assignment. A left hand side expressions is always assumed to be a variable.
- *rhs* is a function to get the right hand side expressions of an assignment. The right hand side expression, *expr*, uses the vocabulary defined for the EFSM specification.
- *vars* is a function such that $vars(Exp)$ returns a set with all variables found in *Exp*. *Exp* is a set that contains the result of applying *rhs* to each assignment in *assignments*, or a *guard* expression.
- *affect* is a function such that $affect(A, Var_1, Var_2)$ returns the assignment it is being applied to, A, if $Var_1 \in vars(rhs(A)) \wedge Var_2 = lhs(A)$ otherwise the empty set is returned.
- *map* is a function such that $map(Fun, Set)$ applies the function, *Fun* on each element in the set *Set* and returns the set of the results.

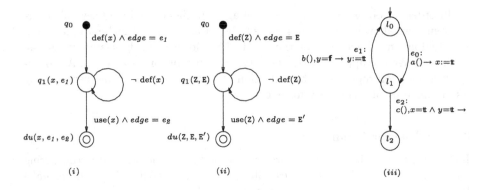

Fig. 2. Examples of (i) observer monitoring definition (on edge e_1) and use (on edge e_2) of variable x, (ii) a parameterized observer, and (iii) a simple EFSM

With the match variables and operations above we define new functions that can be used as tests in the observer. In this paper, we shall make use of:

- $def(v)$, which is true iff the variable v is defined by the transition in the EFSM. This can be expressed as:

$$v \in map(lhs, assignments)$$

- $use(v)$, which is true iff the variable v is used (in a guard or assignment) by the transition in the EFSM. This can be expressed as:

$$v \in vars(map(rhs, assignments)) \lor v \in vars(guard)$$

- $da(v_1, v_2)$, which is true iff the variable v_1 is on the right hand side and variable v_2 is on the left hand side of the same assignment in the EFSM specification. The function can intuitively be understood to be true if v_1 directly affects v_2. This can be expressed as:

$$map(affect(v_1, v_2), assignments) \neq \emptyset$$

Example 2. The (non-parameterized) observer in Fig. 2(i) specifies definition-use pair coverage for a specific variable m, and specific edges e_1 and e_2. Fig. 2(ii) shows a corresponding (parameterized) observer that specifies definition-use pair coverage for *any* EFSM variable Z, and EFSM edges E and E'. This is done by parameterizing the location q_1 with any variable and any edge, and the accepting location du with any variable and any two edges. The edges are parameterized in a similar way. For example, there is one observer edge from location $q_1(z, e)$ to location $du(z, e, e')$ for each EFSM variable z, and each pair e, e' of EFSM edges.

3.2   How Observers Monitor Coverage Criteria

In test case generation or when monitoring test execution of a SUT, an observer observes the events of the SUT, and the computation steps of the EFSM. Reached accepting locations correspond to covered coverage items. We formally define the execution of an observer in terms of a composition between an EFSM and an observer, which has the form of a *superposition* of the observer onto the EFSM. Each state of this superposition consists of a state of the EFSM, together with a *set* of currently occupied observer locations.

Say that a predicate b on an observer edge is satisfied by a computation step $\langle l, \sigma \rangle \xrightarrow{a(\bar{d})} \langle l', \sigma' \rangle$ of an EFSM, denoted $\langle l, \sigma \rangle \xrightarrow{a(\bar{d})} \langle l', \sigma' \rangle \models b$ if b holds for the event $a(\bar{d})$, the computation step $\langle l, \sigma \rangle \xrightarrow{a(\bar{d})} \langle l', \sigma' \rangle$, and the edge e : $l \xrightarrow{a(\bar{w}), g \to \bar{u} := \overline{expr}} l'$ from which the computation step is derived.

Formally, the superposition of an observer (Q, q_0, Q_f, B) onto an EFSM $\langle L, l_0, \bar{v}, E \rangle$ is defined as follows.

- *States* are of the form $\langle \langle l, \sigma \rangle \parallel Q \rangle$, where $\langle l, \sigma \rangle$ is a state of the EFSM, and Q is a set of locations of the observer.
- The *initial state* is the tuple $\langle \langle l_0, \sigma_0 \rangle \parallel \{q_0\} \rangle$, where $\langle l_0, \sigma_0 \rangle$ is the initial state of the EFSM, and q_0 is the initial location of the observer.
- A *computation step* is a triple $\langle \langle l, \sigma \rangle \parallel Q \rangle \xrightarrow{a(\bar{d})} \langle \langle l', \sigma' \rangle \parallel Q' \rangle$ such that $\langle l, \sigma \rangle \xrightarrow{a(\bar{d})} \langle l', \sigma' \rangle$ and

$$Q' = \left\{ q' \mid q \xrightarrow{b} q' \text{ and } q \in Q \text{ and } \langle l, \sigma \rangle \xrightarrow{a(\bar{d})} \langle l', \sigma' \rangle \models b \right\}$$

- A state $\langle \langle l, \sigma \rangle \parallel Q \rangle$ of the superposition *covers* the coverage item represented by the location $q_f \in Q_f$ if $q_f \in Q$.

Note that the way the set Q is updated essentially results in an (on-the-fly) subset construction of the parameterised observer. Initially, Q contains only the initial observer location q_0. In the subsequent computation steps, Q contains the set of all occupied observer locations, representing already covered and partially covered coverage items. In each computation step, the set of occupied observer locations Q' is obtained by generating all possible successors to the locations in Q, i.e. all q' such that there exists a $q \in Q$ and an edge $q \xrightarrow{b} q' \in B$ with b satisfied by the computation step of the EFSM.

Recall that both the initial and all accepting observer locations have implicit self-loops with predicate *true*. This means that in the superposition of the observer onto an EFSM, the initial observer location q_0 is always occupied and all reached accepting observer locations (representing covered coverage items) are guaranteed to remain in Q. The fact that q_0 is always occupied can be intuitively understood as allowing for the observer to non-deterministically start monitoring an EFSM (or a SUT) at *any* computation step of an run (or at any point during test execution).

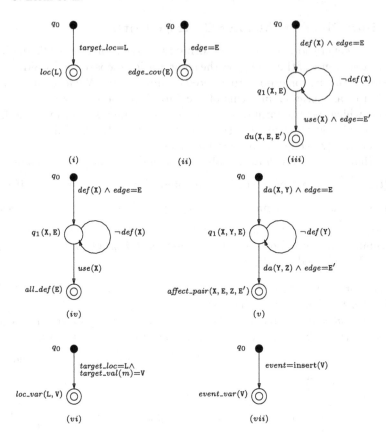

Fig. 3. Seven examples of coverage criteria expressed as observers

Example 3. If the observer in Fig. 2(*ii*) is superposed onto the EFSM in Fig. 2(*iii*), the following computation steps can be taken $\langle\langle l_0, \{x = \mathbf{ff}, y = \mathbf{ff}\}\rangle \parallel \{q_0\}\rangle \overset{a()}{\leadsto}$ $\langle\langle l_1, \{x=\mathbf{tt}, y=\mathbf{ff}\}\rangle \parallel \{q_0, q_1(x, e_0)\}\rangle \overset{b()}{\leadsto} \langle\langle l_0, \{x=\mathbf{tt}, y=\mathbf{tt}\}\rangle \parallel \{q_0, q_1(x, e_0), q_1(y, e_1)\}\rangle$ $\overset{a()}{\leadsto} \langle\langle l_1, \{x = \mathbf{tt}, y = \mathbf{tt}\}\rangle \parallel \{q_0, q_1(x, e_0), q_1(y, e_1)\}\rangle \overset{c()}{\leadsto} \langle\langle l_2, \{x = \mathbf{tt}, y = \mathbf{tt}\}\rangle \parallel \{q_0, q_1(x, e_0), q_1(y, e_1), du(x, e_0, e_2), du(y, e_1, e_2)\}\rangle$. Thus, the two possible definition-use pairs are covered.

3.3   Examples of Observers

Fig. 3 shows observers specifying a number of coverage criteria described in the literature [2].

The *all-locations* coverage criteria is specified by the observer shown in Fig. 3(*i*), where the parameter L is any location in an EFSM. If the observer is superposed onto the EFSM of Fig. 1, we have that L = {*IDLE, BUSY*} and the edge of the parameterized observer represents two edges, one guarded by

$target\_loc = IDLE$ with target location $loc(IDLE)$ $target\_loc(BUSY)$, and the other guarded by $target\_loc = BUSY$ with target location $loc(BUSY)$. The set of possible coverage items is thus $\{loc(IDLE), loc(BUSY)\}$.

The *all-edges* coverage observer in Fig. 3(*ii*) is similar to the all-location coverage observer. The edges of the EFSM in Fig. 1 is E=$\{e_1, \ldots, e_5\}$, and thus the set of possible coverage items when the observer is superposed onto the EFSM is $\{edge\_cov(e_i) \mid e_i \in \text{E}\}$.

The *all-definition use-pairs* (all-uses [2]) coverage observer in Fig. 3(*iii*) has an accepting location $du(\text{X}, \text{E}, \text{E}')$, where X is a variable name, E is an edge on which X is defined, and E' an edge on which X is used. Variable X may not be redefined in the trace between E and E'. If the observer is superposed onto the EFSM the complete set of coverage items is $\{du(m, e_1, e_1)$, $du(m, e_1, e_2)$, $du(m, e_1, e_4)$, $du(m, e_2, e_1)$, $du(m, e_2, e_2)$, $du(m, e_2, e_4)$, $du(m, e_2, e_5)\}$. The definition-use pair $du(m, e_1, e_5)$ can not be covered since m is always redefined on edge e_2 in between e_1 and e_5.

The *all-definitions* coverage observer of Fig. 3(*iv*) is similar to the all-definition use-pairs coverage except that only the defining edges are required to be covered. When the observer is superposed with the EFSM in Fig. 1 the set of accepting locations is $\{all\_def(e_1), all\_def(e_2)\}$.

The *all affect-pairs* (Nafos' required k-Tuples [2]) coverage observer shown in Fig. 3(*v*) accepts whenever a variable x affects a variable z via another variable y. In this case we require that x directly affects y which, without redefinition, directly affects z. No such affect pairs are possible in the EFSM of Fig. 1.

The *context coverage* criteria observer in Fig. 3(*vi*) covers all values of a given variable m. We use $target\_val(m)$, to denote the value of m at the target *EFSM-state*. The observer has an accepting location $loc\_var(\text{L}, \text{V})$, where V is the value domain of variable m. E.g. $loc\_var(IDLE, 0)$ and $loc\_var(BUSY, 1)$ are accepting locations. The observer in Fig. 3(*vii*) is similar, but covers the possible values the event parameter at transitions labelled with the event $insert(x)$.

4   Test Case Generation

4.1   Algorithms

At test case generation, we use the superposition of an observer onto an EFSM, and views the test case generation problem as a search exploration problem. To cover a coverage item q_f is then the problem of finding a trace

$$tr = \langle\langle l_0, \sigma_0\rangle \parallel \{q_0\}\rangle \overset{a(\overline{d})}{\leadsto} \ldots \overset{a'(\overline{d}')}{\leadsto} \langle\langle l, \sigma\rangle \parallel \mathcal{Q}\rangle \text{ such that } q_f \in \mathcal{Q}$$

We will use $\omega(tr) = a(\overline{d}) \ldots a'(\overline{d}')$ to denote the *word* of the trace tr, or just ω whenever tr is clear from the context. In general, a single trace tr may cover several accepting locations of the observer. We say that the trace tr covers n accepting observer states if there are n accepting states in $\mathcal{Q}$, and we use $|Q_f \cap \mathcal{Q}|$ to denote the number of accepting states in $\mathcal{Q}$.

We are now ready to present the test case generation algorithm. We shall limit the presentation to an algorithm generating a single trace. The same technique can be used to produce sets of traces to cover many coverage items. Alternatively, the EFSM model can be annotated with edges that reset the EFSM to its initial state. A generated trace can then be interpreted as a set of test cases separated by the reset edges [9].

An abstract algorithm to compute test case is shown in Fig. 4. To improve the presentation, we use s to denote a system of the form $\langle l, \sigma \rangle$, s_0 to denote the initial system state $\langle l_0, \sigma_0 \rangle$, and a to denote an input action $a(\bar{d})$. The algorithm computes the maximum number of coverage items that can be visited (MAX), and returns a trace with maximum coverage (ω_{max}). The two main data structures WAIT and PASS are used to keep track of the states waiting to be explored, and the states already explored, respectively.

> PASS:= $\emptyset$, MAX := 0, ω_{max} := ω_0
> WAIT:= $\{\langle\langle s_0 \parallel \{q_0\}\rangle, \omega_0\rangle\}$
> **while** WAIT$\neq \emptyset$ **do**
>   select $\langle\langle s \parallel \mathcal{Q}\rangle, \omega\rangle$ from WAIT
>   **if** $|Q_f \cap \mathcal{Q}| >$ MAX **then**
> ω_{max} := ω, MAX := $|Q_f \cap \mathcal{Q}|$
>   **if** for all $\langle s \parallel \mathcal{Q}'\rangle$ in PASS: $\mathcal{Q} \not\subseteq \mathcal{Q}'$ **then**
>   add $\langle s \parallel \mathcal{Q}\rangle$ to PASS
>   for all $\langle s'' \parallel \mathcal{Q}''\rangle$
>   such that $\langle s \parallel \mathcal{Q}\rangle \overset{a}{\rightsquigarrow} \langle s'' \parallel \mathcal{Q}''\rangle$:
>   add $\langle\langle s'' \parallel \mathcal{Q}''\rangle, \omega a\rangle$ to WAIT
> **return** ω_{max} and MAX

Fig. 4. An abstract breadth-first search exploration algorithm for test case generation

Initially, the set of already explored states is empty and the only state waiting to be explored is the extended state $\langle\langle s_0 \parallel \{q_0\}\rangle, \omega_0\rangle$, where ω_0 is the empty trace. The algorithm then repeatedly examines extended states from WAIT. If a state $\langle s \parallel \mathcal{Q}\rangle$ found in WAIT is included in a state $\langle s \parallel \mathcal{Q}'\rangle$ in PASS, then obviously $\langle s \parallel \mathcal{Q}\rangle$ does not need to be further examined. If not, all successor states reachable from $\langle s \parallel \mathcal{Q}\rangle$ in one computation step are put on WAIT, with their traces extended with the input action of the computation step from which they are generated. The state $\langle s \parallel \mathcal{Q}\rangle$ is saved in PASS. The algorithm terminates when WAIT is empty

The variables ω_{max} and MAX are initially set to the empty trace and 0, respectively. They are updated whenever an extended state is found in WAIT which covers a higher number of coverage items than the current value of MAX. Throughout the execution of the algorithm, the value of MAX is the maximum number of coverage items that have been covered by a single trace, and ω_{max} is one such trace. When the algorithm terminates, the two values MAX and ω_{max} are returned.

4.2   Bitvector Implementation

In order to efficiently represent and manipulate the set $\mathcal{Q}$ of observer locations we shall use bitvector analysis [15]. Let the set $\mathcal{Q}$ be represented by a bitvector where each bit represents an observer location q'. Then each bit is updated by the following function

$$f_{q'}(q') = \bigvee_{\langle b,q\rangle\in\ in(q')} q \wedge b$$

where $in(q') = \{ \langle b,q\rangle \mid q \xrightarrow{b} q' \in B \}$ is the set of pairs of predicates b and source locations q of the edges ingoing to the location q'. That is, given a state of the superposition $\langle\langle l,\sigma\rangle \parallel \mathcal{Q}\rangle$ and an EFSM-transition $\langle l,\sigma\rangle \xrightarrow{a(\bar{d})} \langle l',\sigma'\rangle$ the bit representing q' is set to 1 if there is an observer edge $q \xrightarrow{b} q' \in B$, such that $q \in \mathcal{Q}$ and $\langle l,\sigma\rangle \xrightarrow{a(\bar{d})} \langle l',\sigma'\rangle \models b$. Otherwise the bit representing q' is set to 0. It should be obvious that this corresponds precisely to the semantics of an observer superposed onto an EFSM, described in Section 3.2.

Example 4. When the observer in Fig. 2(ii) is superposed onto the EFSM in Fig. 2(iii), we have $\mathsf{E} = \mathsf{E}' = E = \{e_0, e_1, e_2\}$ and $\mathsf{Z} = \bar{v} = \{x, y\}$. Thus, we have that

$$Q = \{ q_0 \} \cup \{ q_1(z, e_a) \mid z \in \bar{v} \wedge e_a \in E\} \cup \{ du(z, e_a, e_b) \mid z \in \bar{v} \wedge e_a, e_b \in E\}$$

Any enumeration of the set can be used as index in the bitvector. As the observer has three locations with parameters we get three types of bitvector functions:

$$f_{q_0}(q_0) = q_0 \wedge \mathtt{tt} \tag{1}$$

$$f_{q_1(v_i,e_j)}(q_1(v_i, e_j)) = (\ q_0 \wedge def(v_i) \wedge (edge = e_j)\ ) \vee$$
$$(\ q_1(v_i, e_j) \wedge \neg def(v_i)\ ) \tag{2}$$

$$f_{du(v_i,e_j,e_k)}(du(v_i, e_j, e_k)) = (\ q_1(v_i, e_j) \wedge use(v_i) \wedge (edge = e_k)\ ) \vee$$
$$(\ du(v_i, e_j, e_k) \wedge \mathtt{tt}\ ) \tag{3}$$

There is one function of type (1), six of type (2), and 18 of type (3). Note that (1) is always true and that (3) will remain true once it becomes true, due to implicit self-loops in these locations.

4.3   Implementation Efforts

Some of the techniques presented in this paper have been implemented in a prototype version of the model-checking tool UPPAAL [16], extended for test case generation [10]. The current implementation uses the bitvector implementation described above, but is limited to a number of predefined coverage criteria. For a given coverage criteria (a set of) test cases can be generated from system specifications described as DIEOU-timed automata [9]. We are currently in progress with a larger case-study in collaboration with Ericsson where this tool will be applied.

We are also developing a tool operating on a subset of the functional language Erlang, also using the techniques presented in this paper. The tool will be applied in a case-study in collaboration with Mobile Arts.

5 Conclusions

We have presented a technique for specifying coverage criteria in a simple and flexible manner using observer automata with parameters. Observers have shown to be a flexible tool in model checking and run-time monitoring, and by this paper we have shown that they are a versatile tool for specifying coverage criteria for test case generation and test monitoring. In particular the parameterization mechanism, as used in this paper, allows a succinct specification of several standard generic coverage criteria. In this way, test case generation can be transformed into a reachability problem, which can be attacked by a standard state-space reachability tool.

In previous works, we have implemented special cases of this test case generation technique, using UPPAAL, indicating that the approach is practical. We are currently working on a general implementation of the observer concept, and plan to apply it in a larger case study.

References

1. F. Bouquet and B. Legeard. Reification of executable test scripts in formal specification-based test generation: The java card transaction mechanism case study. In *FME 2003*, volume 2805 of *Lecture Notes in Computer Science*, pages 778–795. Springer Verlag, 2003.
2. Lori A. Clarke, Andy Podgurski, Debra J. Richardsson, and Steven J. Zeil. A formal evaluation of data flow path delection criteria. *IEEE Trans. on Software Engineering*, SE-15(11):1318–1332, Nov 1989.
3. L. du Bousquet, S. Ramangalahy, S. Simon, C. Viho, A. Belinfante, and R.G. de Vries. Formal test automation: The conference protocol with tgv/torx. In H. Ural, R.L. Probert, and G. von Bochmann, editors, *IFIP 13th Int. Conference on Testing of Communicating Systems(TestCom 2000)*. Kluwer Academic Publishers, 2000.
4. L. du Bousquet and N. Zuanon. An overview of Lutess, a specification-based tool for testing synchronous software. In *Proc. 14th IEEE Intl. Conf. on Automated SW Engineering*, October 1999.
5. J.-C. Fernandez, C. Jard, T. Jéron, and C. Viho. An experiment in automatic generation of test suites for protocols with verification technology. *Science of Computer Programming*, 29, 1997.
6. G. Friedman, A. Hartman, K. Nagin, and T. Shiran. Projected state machine coverage for software testing. In *Proc. ACM SIGSOFT International Symposium on Software Testing and Analysis*, pages 134–143, 2002.
7. Stefania Gnesi, Diego Latella, and Mieke Massink. Modular semantics for a UML statechart diagrams kernel and its extension to multicharts and branching time model-checking. *Journal of Logic and Algebraic Programming*, 51(1):43–75, 2002.
8. K. Havelund and G. Rosu. Synthesizing monitors for safety properties. In J.-P. Katoen and P. Stevens, editors, *Proc. TACAS '02*, 8th Int. Conf. on Tools and Algorithms for the Construction and Analysis of Systems, volume 2280 of *Lecture Notes in Computer Science*, pages 324–356. Springer Verlag, 2002.

9. Anders Hessel, Kim G. Larsen, Brian Nielsen, Paul Pettersson, and Arne Skou. Time-Optimal Real-Time Test Case Generation using UPPAAL. In Alexandre Petrenko and Andreas Ulrich, editors, *Proc. of 3rd International Workshop on Formal Approaches to Testing of Software*, number 2931 in Lecture Notes in Computer Science, pages 136–151. Springer Verlag, 2003.
10. Anders Hessel and Paul Pettersson. A test generation algorithm for real-time systems. To appear in Proc. of 4th Int. Conf. on Quality Software, Sept. 2004.
11. G.J. Holzmann. The model checker SPIN. *IEEE Trans. on Software Engineering*, SE-23(5):279–295, May 1997.
12. H.S. Hong, S.D. Cha, I. Lee, O. Sokolsky, and H. Ural. Data flow testing as model checking. In *ICSE'03: 25th Int. Conf. on Software Enginering*, pages 232–242, May 2003.
13. H.S. Hong, I. Lee, O. Sokolsky, and H. Ural. A temporal logic based theory of test coverage. In J.-P. Katoen and P. Stevens, editors, *Proc. TACAS '02*, 8th *Int. Conf. on Tools and Algorithms for the Construction and Analysis of Systems*, volume 2280 of *Lecture Notes in Computer Science*, pages 327–341. Springer Verlag, 2002.
14. ITU, Geneva. *ITU-T, Z.100, Specification and Description Language (SDL)*, Nov 1999.
15. J. Knoop, B. Steffen, and J. Vollmer. Parallelism for free: Efficient and optimal bitvector analyses for parallel programs. *ACM Transactions on Programming Languages and Systems*, 18(3):268–299, 1996.
16. K.G. Larsen, P. Pettersson, and W. Yi. UPPAAL in a nutshell. *Software Tools for Technology Transfer*, 1(1-2), 1997.
17. D. Lugato, C. Bigot, and Y. Valot. Validation and automatic test generation on UML models: the AGATHA approach. In *Proc. 7th Int. Workshop on Formal Methods for Industrial Critical Systems (FMICS 02), Electronic Notes in Theoretical Computer Science*, volume 66, 2002.
18. B. Marre and A. Arnould. Test Sequence Generation from Lustre Descriptions: GATEL. In *Proc. 15th IEEE Intl. Conf. on Automated Software Engineering (ASE'00)*, Grenoble, 2000.
19. C. Meudec. ATGen: Automatic test data generation using constraint logic programming and symbolic execution. In *Proc. 1st Intl. Workshop on Automated Program Analysis, Testing, and Verification*, Limerick, 2000.
20. Steven S. Muchnick. *Advanced Compiler Design and Implementation*. Morgan Kaufmann, 1997.
21. Brian Nielsen and Arne Skou. Automated test generation from timed automata. *International Journal on Software Tools for Technology Transfer*, 5:59–77, 2003.
22. A. Pretschner. Classical search strategies for test case generation with constraint logic programming. In *Proc. Formal Approaches to Testing of Software, FATES '01*, pages 47–60, Aalborg, Denmark, August 2001.
23. V. Rusu, L. du Bousquet, and T. Jéron. An approach to symbolic test generation. In *Int. Conf. on Integrating Formal Methods*, volume 1945 of *Lecture Notes in Computer Science*, pages 338–357. Springer Verlag, 2000.
24. M. Schmitt, A. Ek, J. Grabowski, D. Hogrefe, and B. Koch. Autolink - putting sdl-based test generation into practice. In *11th Int. Workshop on Testing of Communicating Systems (IWTCS'98)*, Tomsk, Russia, Sept. 1998.
25. M. Y. Vardi and P. Wolper. An automata-theoretic approach to automatic program verification. In *Proc. LICS '86*, 1st *IEEE Int. Symp. on Logic in Computer Science*, pages 332–344, June 1986.
26. P. Wolper. Temporal logic can be more expressive. In *Proc. 22nd Annual Symp. Foundations of Computer Science*, pages 340–348, 1981.

Semi-formal Development of a Fault-Tolerant Leader Election Protocol in Erlang

Thomas Arts[1], Koen Claessen[2], and Hans Svensson[2]

[1] IT University in Göteborg, Box 8718, 402 75 Göteborg, Sweden
thomas.arts@ituniv.se
[2] Chalmers University of Technology, Göteborg, Sweden
{koen, hanssv}@cs.chalmers.se

Abstract. We present a semi-formal analysis method for fault-tolerant distributed algorithms written in the distributed functional programming language Erlang. In this setting, standard model checking techniques are often too expensive or too limiting, whereas testing techniques often do not cover enough of the state space.

Our idea is to first run instances of the algorithm on generated stimuli, thereby creating *traces* of events and states. Then, using an abstraction function specified by the user, our tool generates from these traces an abstract state transition diagram of the system, which can be nicely visualized and thus greatly helps in debugging the system. Lastly, formal requirements of the system specified in temporal logic can be checked automatically to hold for the generated abstract state transition diagram. Because the state transition diagram is abstract, we know that the checked requirements hold for a lot more traces than just the traces we actually ran.

We have applied our method to a commonly used open-source fault-tolerant leader election algorithm, and discovered two serious bugs. We have also implemented a new algorithm that does not have these bugs.

1 Introduction

The company Ericsson has developed a telecommunication switch called the AXD 301 [7]. The control software of this switch is written in the distributed functional programming language Erlang [2]. A major challenge in the development of the switching software is to get the almost one million lines of code tested in the relatively short time between releases of the product. A typical time consuming and difficult activity is testing fault-tolerance properties. The particular fault-tolerance we investigate here is the effect of taking down parts of a switch (because of maintenance or hardware problems) and restart them later in time.

We report on our case study to take away part of the testing load by analyzing a critical part of the code by semi-formal methods. The part we looked at is a *leader election* protocol. In the AXD 301, a module of about 2000 lines of code implements both a leader election protocol and a resource manager. In

J. Grabowski and B. Nielsen (Eds.): FATES 2004, LNCS 3395, pp. 140–154, 2005.

order to be able to deal with the complexity of this module, Ericsson's engineers rewrote the module in two parts, separating the resource manager and the leader election protocol. The simplified resource manager has been formally verified in earlier work by using a model checking approach [3]. The slightly generalized and cleaned up leader election protocol contains about 800 lines of code and is available as open source [21].

The leader election problem is a well-known and extensively studied problem. The objective of the protocol is for the processes among themselves to establish a designated process, called the *leader*. Leader election protocols have been designed for many different settings. In our case, we are interested in a solution that is fault-tolerant. Fault-tolerance is based on communication links breaking or on processes that may die or revive again at any point in time. If the currently elected leader dies or is disconnected, the surviving processes need to elect a new leader amongst them. However, during the election process, other processes may cease to work. We consider asynchronous communication with buffered messages. Among the many articles published on the leader election protocol [9, 6, 16, 17, 1], we know of only few that address all these problems. It was actually hard to find a paper describing exactly the setting that Erlang uses: asynchronous message passing, reliable communication channels between every pair of processes, possible failure and/or revival of a process at any point in time and a reliable notification mechanism of when processes die.

The algorithm used in the leader election protocol implementation we analyzed was an adaptation of a previously published algorithm [16]. There is a fixed set of processes that can die arbitrarily, and they have to negotiate a leader among them. The first process that comes up has priority to become leader, in order to have a selected leader as soon as possible. Only when the current leader dies, a new leader should be elected.

There are two basic properties that the leader election implementation needs to obey: (1) **Safety** — it is never the case that there are two or more leaders at the same time; (2) **Liveness** — in a stable situation (i.e. processes stop dying for a while), a leader will eventually be elected.

We have considered using model checking techniques to formally verify these properties. However, we found that dealing with the fault-tolerance lead to state-space explosion in the used model checkers, which severely limited the number of processes we could deal with. More informal methods based on testing seemed to be necessary.

The Erlang runtime system has built-in support for generating *traces* of the events occurring during execution. With simple means, one can specify what one considers an event (sending a message, receiving a message, a process dying, a function call, etc.). Tracing can be switched on and off on demand. Studying the traces reveals not only that an error occurred, but can also demonstrate the chain of events that lead to the error.

We have developed a methodology for semi-formal analysis of such traces of distributed systems (c.f. [5]). The idea is to first produce traces of the system by generating stimuli, as in testing. Then, we build *abstractions* of the traces with the help of an *abstraction function* specified by the user. An abstraction function basically maps data structures in the events and states to different (simpler) representations. An abstraction reduces the number of states, by mapping the actual concrete states onto a set of abstract states. This also allows us to detect cyclic behaviour in the trace, since different concrete states can be mapped to the same abstract state. The accompanying abstract state transition diagram concisely indicates the different abstract states visited during an execution, together with the messages sent and received during the transitions. A path through such a state diagram represents a trace, but it is not necessarily the case that the trace is a possible trace for the system since the diagram is really a diagram for an abstracted model of the system.

We propose to generate traces of simple instances of the software first, such as a reduced number of processes or executing only one possible scenario. For these traces it is easy to define abstraction functions. The same functions can be used for more complicated instances of the software.

The generated abstractions are used in two ways: (1) They increase understanding of the system, and can help to more easily spot the causes of bugs (as explained in Section 2.4); (2) We can formally verify properties of the abstraction, thus ensuring that the desired properties actually hold for *all* paths through the abstract state diagram (as explained in Section 2.7).

When we applied our methodology on the implementation of the leader election algorithm, we discovered two serious bugs. Failing to correct the bugs in an efficient way, we also tried to implement a different algorithm for leader election. This implementation is based on [17] and was tested with the methodology described in this paper without finding any errors.

2   Methodology

In this section, we describe our methodology in more detail. We do this by concretely following the analysis of a leader election algorithm in chronological order. We start by describing the original algorithm, how we generate stimuli to obtain system traces, and how we use abstractions to find bugs. Then, we describe our own implementation of leader election, where all of our analyses failed to find any errors, and discuss coverage issues related to our method.

2.1   Fault-Tolerant Leader Election Version 1

The Erlang code for the algorithm we started with is publicly available on the web [21]. However, for simplification purposes we actually analyze a cut-down version of this code here. All code we used in this case study is available on the web [18].

The implementation is loosely based on a fault-tolerant leader election algorithm described in [16], but with an adaptation in order to deal with faults being dying processes instead of failing communication links.

The participating processes behave as follows. When the protocol is started each process is given a list of all the participation processes; the position in this list is also the priority order for the processes. A process always plays one of the following four roles: *candidate, captured, surrendered* or *elected*. When a process is started it is always a candidate to become a leader. The first thing it does is to try to capture all the other processes, by broadcasting a 'capture'-message. If another candidate-process receives a 'capture'-message, the receiving process will take action based on the priority; it will ignore messages from processes with lower priority, and accept messages from processes with higher priority by sending an 'accept'-message. After accepting, the process changes its role to being captured. A captured process will ignore 'capture'-messages and forward 'accept'-messages to the process that has captured it. Whenever a candidate has captured more than half of the participating living processes, it will announce itself as the leader by broadcasting an 'elect'-message. If a process receives an 'elect'-message it will immediately surrender.

Whenever the leader dies (processes discover this since the Erlang runtime system will send a 'DOWN' message to all interested processes), a new election round is started. Whenever a process revives, this process will be notified of the (possible) presence of a leader via an 'elect'-message as a reply from the leader to the 'capture'-message sent when the process revived.

When we got the algorithm, it was said that it would always eventually choose a leader if more than 50% of the processes are alive and if the system is stable for long enough. (It is though possible that a leader is elected with fewer processes alive.) The algorithm is not supposed to elect a new leader unless the leader dies.

2.2   Generating Stimuli and Tracing

The Erlang Runtime System (ERTS) has built in functionality for tracing running processes. The tracing can be switched on or off at any given time, without interfering with the execution. It is possible to trace sent and received messages, function calls, process related events, process scheduling and garbage collection. In a distributed environment there exists functionality for redirecting trace messages to a central collection process, in order to collect all trace data into the same log file.

Stimuli for Leader Election Implementation. In order to generate traces of the leader election protocol, a set of nodes is started, and a leader election process is started on each node. The stimuli for a leader election system is killing and reviving processes. A simulation process then randomly selects which process to kill/revive by sending messages to the control processes. How many processes can be dead at the same time is configured in the simulator process.

In order to further test the robustness of the leader election protocol, we implemented a variant where we also delay messages between nodes in a random way. The idea is that this simulates slow and/or overloaded connections. Note that this is not tested in a standard setting where one runs all nodes on the same hardware, since communication delays will be rather static in such a setting.

Tracing the Implementation. We first collected trace data for the simplified version of the leader election protocol, without using message delays. When running a leader election system with three processes, everything worked fine,

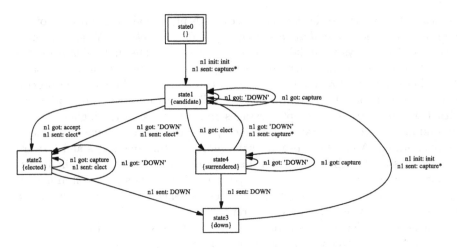

Fig. 1. Abstract trace for one process in a three node setting

but when running with five processes something was obviously wrong; there were two processes simultaneously announcing themselves as leader! In the search for this error, we focused on the trace data for one of the nodes which was elected as leader. The raw trace data contained roughly 120 states and 200 message events, a bit too many for easy overview. The problem here is that it is easy to spot where in the trace the fault happened (two leaders are elected), but not where in the trace the event happened that triggered the fault (the first illegal state).

2.3   Abstractions

It is clear that in order to understand larger traces of systems, one has to reduce the information in the trace to a relevant subset of all information. One way of doing this is by using an *abstraction* (c.f. [5]). Abstractions are made by applying an *abstraction function* that converts each concrete state in the trace to an abstract state, which contains less information. Several different concrete states from the trace might actually be mapped to the same abstract state. Thus, we can redisplay the trace by means of a state transition diagram, where each abstract state occurs only once, and transitions occur between two abstract states if there exists a transition in the trace between two corresponding concrete states. However, by doing this we also lose some context, for example a state visited exactly N times in the actual trace is represented by a loop, and thus potentially infinitely visits, in the abstract trace. Moreover, we can also make the sent and received messages more abstract by applying a message abstraction function.

An example of an abstract state transition diagram of the leader election protocol is displayed in Fig. 1. Our tool automatically generates this diagram, given an abstraction function specified by the user. The original trace used for this diagram is a trace of a correct execution with three leader election processes.

Here, the abstraction function on states is tracking the state of only one process, abstracting away the states of the other processes. Moreover, it has removed all other information in the concrete state, but for the role a process is playing. This diagram shows that with help of an abstraction, one can get an understanding for the basic parts of the algorithm, since it is easy to follow how the process moves between the different roles. We call the transition diagram generated from a trace and an abstraction function an *abstract trace*.

Common Abstraction Function Building Blocks. We have implemented a library of common abstraction function building blocks. Commonly used functions are: removing parts of state data, replacing a list by its length, focusing on the state of one process, merging states of two processes into one state, etc. This library makes it easy to quickly define new abstraction functions.

2.4   Abstractions for Bug Finding

The idea is now to find an abstraction function which clearly helps us to establish where in the code the bug is located. It is hard to give a general approach on how to come up with an appropriate abstraction. Most of the time, the programmer has some sort of intuition about what parts of the states and which events influence a particular bug.

In the case of our bug, we have applied the following principles. Some of the state data, such as the list of participating nodes, is the same in all states, and such data can often be abstracted from. In the state data there are also two lists, containing the references to monitored nodes and the nodes which are down. The contents of these lists are not really useful, it is enough to know how many elements there are in the lists. So, we abstract away from these lists by remembering their length, but not their content. Concerning the events, most of the message data can be abstracted away, only keeping the type of a message.

The above abstraction reduces the state space from 120 to 23 states, which is small enough to overview. It is now possible to spot the bug by just looking at the abstract trace (Fig. 2). The state where the process is elected as leader is dark shaded in the figure (it is in the lower left half). This state is part of a long almost non-forking path, and it is likely that the first illegal state is to find at the top of this path. This is indeed the case and if we zoom in on two lightly shaded states in the upper left part of Fig. 2 the result can be seen in Fig. 3.

Let us examine closer what happens in the bug-containing trace. The state data contains three fields: the role, the number of nodes that are down, and the number of monitored nodes. In the state labeled 'state9' we can see that the list of dead processes contain one process, and the list of monitored processes contain four processes. Since processes should not monitor themselves, this is clearly one process too many.

This bug turned out to be a mistake we made ourselves, when implementing the cut-down version of the algorithm. We had been uncareful in the implementation and mixed up variable names. It shows, however, the usefulness and simplicity of the approach.

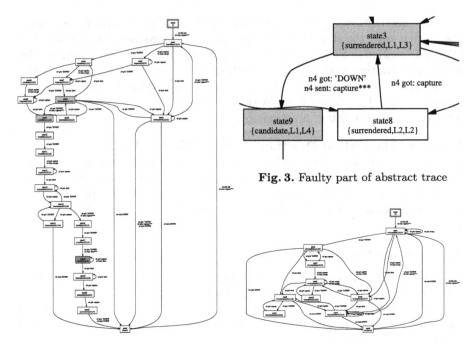

Fig. 2. Abstract trace containing bug

Fig. 3. Faulty part of abstract trace

Fig. 4. Bug-free abstract trace

If we compare the abstract trace in Fig. 2 where the bug is present with an abstraction made from a trace where the bug is fixed in Fig. 4, one can clearly see from the graph structure that the erroneous behaviour is gone.

The First Serious Bug. After correcting this bug, we collected a new set of traces. This time we initially observed no obvious faulty behaviour, we therefore activated the random delaying of messages in the generation of stimuli. Now we could observe a faulty behaviour, this time in a leader election system with only three nodes, and again it was a violation of the safety property: Two nodes simultaneously announced themselves as leaders. Again we turned to abstract traces in the search for an explanation. In this case we found the error to be present in situations where many nodes failed simultaneously.

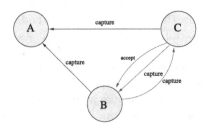

Fig. 5. Deadlock situation in leader election protocol

Consider the situation in Fig. 5, where initially only process A is alive and the priority of the processes is A > B > C. If then B and C revive more or less simultaneously and the present leader (A) is suffering from slow connections, it is possible that the newly revived processes will agree on a leader before the present leader is able to announce its presence.

This is indeed a serious bug, and this bug is present also in the original Erlang code. But it is also the case that this situation will not occur if the system is simulated in such a way as to always have more than half of the processes alive. So, we continued the analysis of the protocol with less aggressive stimuli.

2.5   Sanity Checks on Abstractions

We call an abstract trace *sufficient* if all real traces of the system are embedded in it. Note that by construction, it is guaranteed that at least the original trace is embedded in the abstract trace. If all possible traces of the system are embedded, we cover all possible executions of the system. If an abstract trace is sufficient and a property holds for this abstract trace, then it also holds for all real traces. However, in general we do not know whether an abstract trace is sufficient. This is related to coverage and is discussed in Sect. 2.8.

No Quiescent States. There are other problematic states where the system can get stuck. Remember that we stimulate the system by taking down and reviving processes arbitrarily during tracing. If there exist a state in an abstract trace that has only one outgoing arc labeled with a 'DOWN'-message of a process, something is wrong as well. This means that the system is in a state where the only way to get out is for a process to die. Since there are no guarantee that processes eventually will die, the system is stuck in that state.

There might be two reasons for this. One is that the abstract trace is insufficient (which means that we should have chosen a different abstraction function, or collected more trace data). The other is that the system has a deadlock in that state (which could indicate an error). Our tool automatically reports such quiescent states.

The Second Serious Bug. When we investigate quiescent states for our leader election algorithm, there is a warning for some potential deadlock nodes. Most of those can immediately be discarded, since these are states in which there is a leader elected and hence are not problematic states.

But there is indeed a quiescent state which indicates a real deadlock! In some cases when the leader process dies, the remaining processes end up in a state where a process is waiting for a message that is not going to be sent. Consider the situation in Fig. 6, where all the processes are initially alive, A is the leader and the priority of the processes is A > B > C. Then if A is killed, B and C are notified of this and each receive a 'DOWN'-message. Now, if the message to B is faster than the message to C, it is possible for B to start a new election round and send a 'capture'-message to C before C receives the original 'DOWN'-message. In that case C will simply ignore the 'capture'-message, since C (falsely) thinks that A is alive and will answer the 'capture'-message on behalf of C. When C finally gets the 'DOWN'-message, and starts its new election round B will ignore the

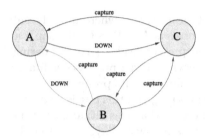

Fig. 6. Deadlock situation in leader election protocol

'capture'-message from C with the motivation that B is higher prioritized than C, which means that C should reply to B's 'capture'-message instead. Therefore we end up in a situation where B is waiting for a message that C is not going to send. This deadlock situation is not broken until another node dies or revives.

Thus we have discovered yet another bug in the leader election algorithm, this bug is also present in the original, non-simplified, implementation! The error would probably never occur when all nodes run on similar hardware, however, our addition of delays in messages reveals a very tricky error that may show up in very rare circumstances or when the protocol is used with nodes on different hardware.

2.6   Fault-Tolerant Leader Election Version 2

At this point, we had discovered two serious bugs in the original leader election implementation. We were unable to repair the implementation. So, we decided to try to implement and analyze another algorithm for leader election. Our new algorithm is based on 'The Bully Algorithm for Synchronous Systems' in [17], but again we were forced to make some modifications in order to adapt the algorithm to our setting.

The algorithm is quite simple and it is easy to understand how it works. When a process comes up, it first checks whether any process of higher priority is alive. If there is, it waits for one of these processes to become leader. If not, the process itself decides to try to become leader. It then checks that all other processes of lower priority either are aware of its existence, or are dead. If so, it announces itself as leader.

The main change we made to the algorithm in the paper was to avoid restarting the election process each time a process revives. This is inefficient and not applicable to the situation where our leader election protocol is supposed to be used. We made the change in two steps, first we changed the algorithm such that no new election would be started if a process with lower priority than the leader revived and later we took care of the situation where a process with higher priority than the leader revived. This second change was surprisingly complex. We also made some changes that did not affect the functionality, but which reduced the number of messages sent by the system. The code is available on the web [18].

After making the changes, we collected a new set of traces. We created some different abstractions, under which the system seems to be working correctly.

2.7   Abstractions for Verification

So far, we have been able to spot errors exhibited by our abstractions either visually or by means of simple sanity checks. However, when the abstractions or desired properties get more complicated, to be sure that an abstract trace obeys a given property, an automated technique is needed. Our idea is to simply formally check properties of the abstract traces using a model checker.

LTL Properties. We formulate the properties that we want to verify in linear time logic (LTL). In the introduction we mentioned two basic properties for a leader election protocol: (1) There are never two elected leaders at the same time; (2) If the system is stable, eventually a leader will be chosen. For a leader election situation with 3 nodes, the first property can be expressed in LTL as follows:

$$\Box(\neg((l_1 \wedge l_2) \vee (l_1 \wedge l_3) \vee (l_2 \wedge l_3))). \tag{1}$$

Here, l_i is defined to be true exactly when the leader election process running on node i is the elected leader. So, the property can be read as: "It is never the case that node 1 and 2 are leader at the same time, or node 1 and 3, or node 2 and 3."

The second property can be expressed as follows:

$$\Box(\Box(\neg l_1 \wedge \neg l_2 \wedge \neg l_3) \Rightarrow \Box\Diamond(d_1 \vee d_2 \vee d_3)). \tag{2}$$

Here, l_i is defined as above, and d_i is true exactly when node i dies. This property can be read as: "The only traces where no leader is chosen are those traces where process die infinitely often."

Checking if the above properties hold for a given abstract trace is done using standard LTL model checking techniques [10].

Improper Cycles. Since we are modeling asynchronous message passing using transition systems, the information needed to represent the real state of our system consists of more than simply the state of the transition diagram. We also need to know what messages have been sent that have not arrived yet. This problem is illustrated by some counter examples we get of our properties. A cycle in a counter example that contains a message M that is being received by a transition on the cycle, but not sent by a transition of the cycle can of course never represent a real run of the system. We call such a cycle an *improper cycle*.

An example is displayed in Fig. 7, which displays a situation that can not correspond to an actual trace, since such a trace only consumes 'accept'-messages. This could not be an infinite chain of events, since that would mean that an infinite number of 'accept'-messages has to be produced. So, when we search for counter examples in the LTL model checking algorithm, we also have to check

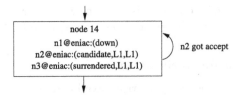

Fig. 7. Loop which is not a possible trace

that found cycles contain the production of all messages that are consumed. Our property checker automatically rejects runs that contain such improper cycles.

Results. We have checked that both properties 1 and 2 hold for abstract traces of our new implementation of the leader election algorithm, for up to N processes. We have done most of the testing with $N = 3$ and $N = 5$, but has also used larger N ($N = 7$ and $N = 10$). Note that this does not mean that we have formally verified the above properties for the system; only that all generated abstract traces satisfied the properties.

2.8   Coverage

When discussing test-based methods, the issue of coverage is central. Coverage methods should provide some sort of measure of how much of the system one has exercised, and this is important for evaluating the result of the testing. In general, coverage methods can warn of potential situations where we have *not* tested enough; very seldom we can know that we have indeed tested enough. Therefore, it is good practice to apply as many different coverage measures as possible.

Code Coverage. Erlang has a built-in module, `cover`, for various basic kinds of coverage analysis. It is a very standardized set of tools, which basically provides information of how many times each executable line of code has been accessed. The limitations of point-coverage are well-known. For our new leader election algorithm, we have traced the system such that we exercised all lines of the code that were supposed to be run.

Abstract Trace Coverage. Instead of looking at how the actual generated traces have exercised the different parts of the system, we can investigate coverage properties of the abstract traces.

A simple way of doing this is to specify quantitative properties of expected events in the abstract traces. For example, for each node, how many states exist where that node has been elected as leader? For each state and each process, how often is it possible to reach a state where that process is dead? How much of the theoretically reachable state space is actually reached?

For our new leader election algorithm, coverage results are of course affected by how much tracing is done, and how the stimuli are chosen. It is interesting to study what will happen with coverage numbers for different amount of tracing. The measures that we considered here are the percentage of reached states and the percentage of the states which could be left via a 'DOWN'-transition. The results are not very surprising, the number of reached states as well as the number of nodes with an outgoing 'DOWN'-transition increased with the length of the traces. The numbers are quickly rising for small amounts of tracing, but levels out after further tracing. In the longest traces we reached 87% of the states in the complete state space (it is not entirely clear that all of the states could indeed be reached). About 30% of states had an outgoing 'DOWN'-transition, a somewhat low number. This could be explained by the fact that the stimuli system was not fast enough, so in many situations a killing could not happen with our simulation technique. It is possible that this can be improved with better stimuli generation.

3   Related Work

The leader election protocol has been extensively studied. There are many variations of this algorithm with different assumptions about the network topology and other constraints. Published leader election algorithms are often proved correct on paper, but implementations tend to divert a bit from the actual algorithm, after which correctness is no longer guaranteed. This happened for example with both implementations we studied, which were based on published algorithms [16, 17].

Formal verification and formal testing are supplementary techniques. We deal with real code, whereas there have been other approaches to deal with models of leader election algorithms. For example, the formal verification of the IEEE 1394 leader election protocol [14] has results that cannot directly be applied to our leader election protocol, since different assumptions are made on the network topology and detection of faults.

The two other model checking approaches that we are aware of [11, 12] deal with algorithms that have constraints that differ from our case. Model checking is possible because the algorithms that are verified are essentially less complex than the one we consider.

Different from formal testing, we do not have a formal model of the software to generate test cases (e.g. [8, 19, 20]). We more or less construct an incomplete model from the real traces. This model is on one hand shown to the engineers for visual verification and on the other hand input to our model checking approach. Given that we call all our traced events observable, we obtain an abstraction in which all real traces are observable in the abstract trace, however, not vice versa. We use executions of the software to obtain a model for the software with a good coverage and apply model checking techniques on the model to test the software.

Compared to the initial work on trace analysis for Erlang [5], we went further than visualizing the traces as graphs, but we actually performed model checking on those graphs. We improved the trace collection mechanism to simulate delays in communication and to be able to handle events that occur quickly after that tracing starts (events that we missed in the earlier setting). The latter was necessary to be able to deal with re-starting processes.

Another project working with trace analysis is the Java PathExplorer [13]. With this tool it is possible to specify properties for Java programs in temporal logic. The program is instrumented to emit events when executed. The properties are then checked for the event stream. The related tool Java Multi-PathExplorer [15] takes the concept a bit further by also being able to generate more possible traces from a single observed trace. This is done by reordering of unrelated events. This technique could be complementary to our method that uses abstractions to generate more possible traces.

4   Conclusions and Future Work

In this paper we describe a case-study in which we use abstraction of traces to analyze a complex software component. By using this technique, we were able to identify two errors in the code. We re-designed the code and verified it by the same technique of trace abstraction, not finding any errors this time.

The described methodology of analysis and abstraction of traces is generally applicable to Erlang programs, in particular to the kind of software that is written in industrial projects. The primitives necessary to create a trace are part of the standard Erlang runtime system. Generating traces is rather common testing technology for engineers working with Erlang software. However, so far, engineers look at the output traces as a textual long list of events. By the possibility of visual verification, i.e. inspection of the graphs obtained from an abstracted trace, motivation is created to write those abstraction functions [5]. Compared to writing extra code for testing Erlang code, writing the abstraction functions really is a minor job, since they only address data conversion of state and messages.

The first thing we achieve by using abstracted traces instead of analyzing the real traces, is that there is less 'noise' in the output. With manual inspection of a trace, it makes a difference whether one looks at 2000 long events or a few dozens of short events. The second advantage is that the abstraction allows us to detect cyclic behaviour, which need not necessarily be cyclic behaviour in the original trace. For example, if one abstracts from a time stamp, one would be able to see a certain message repetitively been sent from a certain state, whereas with the time stamp, it occurs as non-cyclic in the trace. The additional cycles not only make the trace shorter, but they also give extra insight in the behaviour of the software. Third, one can prove properties over the abstract traces, which then hold for many more than just the original trace. A property proved for an abstract trace holds for all traces that result in the same abstraction. In that way, we achieve a larger coverage by only looking at a few traces.

Since the methodology of generating traces in general cannot guarantee full coverage, we use it for identifying errors instead of proving correctness. By proving properties that should hold, we know that something is wrong if we get a counter example. If we cannot exhibit the found error in the actual trace, we might have used an inadequate abstraction. For example, the abstract state space may contain cycles that do not correspond to a cycle in the real code.

Thus, we can detect errors in the code, but we pay the price of possibly seeing some false negatives. However, these false negatives can also result in a better understanding of the system.

As mentioned in the introduction, part of the AXD 301 software was verified by using a model checking approach. Is the same approach applicable here? First of all, the tool to generate the state space of an Erlang program [4] could not be directly applied to the code. The tool abstracts away from process failures, thus we could only verify all runs in which none of the processes died. Here we could confirm that indeed a leader was selected on all branches.

It is ongoing work to add process failure and recovery to the tool. We added it by hand to the model we obtained from the tool, immediately spotting two major problems. First, there is the obvious state space explosion problem, resulting from the explosion in possible events that can happen in different orders. Second, the way message passing is modeled by the tool is too restrictive and excludes particular orders of events that could happen in reality. Thus, with the present available technology, it is a real challenge to verify the properties we are interested in with a model checker. Therefore we think that one should first apply the much cheaper tracing technology to find errors in the code. In case one cannot find any error, it might be beneficial to generate the whole state space and use the same abstraction functions to reduce the model and prove the properties of interest.

Future Work. Possible future work includes automating the creation of the used abstraction functions. We have also considered developing a design document that helps software engineers to quickly create useful abstraction functions.

We would also like to see if it is possible to integrate our abstraction functions with standard model checking techniques based on abstraction. In order to increase the capacity (e.g. number of participating processes) of model checking techniques even more, we probably even need to use symmetry reduction or symbolic model checking.

References

1. M.K. Aguilera, C. Delporte-Gallet, and H. Fauconnier. Stable leader election. In *Distributed Computing, 15th International Conference DISC2001*, volume 2180 of *Lecture Notes in Computer Science*. Springer-Verlag, October 2001.
2. J. Armstrong, M. Williams, C. Wikstrom, and R. Virding. *Concurrent Programming in Erlang*. Prentice-Hall, Englewood Cliffs, New Jersey, USA, second edition, 1996.
3. T. Arts, C. Benac Earle, and J. Derrick. Development of a verified Erlang program for resource locking. *Int. J. on Software Tools for Technology Transfer*, 2004. to appear.
4. T. Arts, C. Benac Earle, and J. J. Sánchez Penas. Translating Erlang to mCRL. In *Fourth International Conference on Application of Concurrency to System Design*, Hamilton (Ontario), Canada, June 2004. IEEE computer society.
5. T. Arts and L.-Å. Fredlund. Trace analysis of Erlang programs. In *Proceedings of the 2002 ACM SIGPLAN workshop on Erlang*, pages 16–23. ACM Press, 2002.

6. N. Bjørner, U. Lerner, and Z. Manna. Deductive verification of parameterized fault-tolerant systems: A case study. In *Proceedings of the 2nd International Conference on Temporal Logic*. Kluwer, 1997.

7. S. Blau and J. Rooth. AXD 301 - A new generation ATM switching system. *Ericsson Review*, 1:10–17, 1998.

8. E. Brinksma. A theory for the derivation of tests. *Protocol Specification, Testing and Verification*, VIII:63–74, 1988.

9. J.J. Brunekreef and S. Mauw J.-P. Katoen, R. Koymans. Design and analysis of dynamic leader election protocols in broadcast networks. *Distributed Computing*, 9(4):157–171, 1996.

10. E. M. Clarke, O. Grumberg, and D. A. Peled. *Model Checking*. The MIT Press, 2000.

11. L-Å. Fredlund, J.F. Groote, and H. Korver. Formal verification of a leader elction protocol in process algebra. *Theoretical Computer Science*, 177(2):459–486, 1997.

12. H. Garavel and L. Mounier. Specification and verification of various distributed leader election algorithms for unidirectional ring networks. *Science of Computer Programming*, 29(1-2):171–197, 1996.

13. K. Havelund and G. Roşu. An overview of the runtime verification tool Java PathExplorer. *Formal Methods in System Design*, 24(2):189 – 215, March 2004.

14. J.M.T. Romijn. A timed verification of the IEEE 1394 leader election protocol. *Formal Methods in System Design*, 19(2):165–194, 2001. special issue of FMICS 1999.

15. K. Sen, G. Roşu, and G. Agha. Runtime safety analysis of multithreaded programs. In *Proceedings of the 9th European software engineering conference held jointly with 10th ACM SIGSOFT international symposium on Foundations of software engineering*, pages 337–346. ACM Press, 2003.

16. G. Singh. Leader election in the presence of link failures. In *IEEE Transactions on Parallel and Distributed Systems, Vol 7*. IEEE computer society, 1996.

17. S.D. Stoller. Leader election in distributed systems with crash failures. Technical Report 481, Computer Science Dept., Indiana University, May 1997. Revised July 1997.

18. H. Svensson. Various material related to the paper. http://www.cs.chalmers.se/ ~hanssv/ erlang_testing.

19. J. Tretmans. *A Formal Approach to Conformance Testing*. PhD thesis, University of Twente, Enschede, The Netherlands, 1992.

20. J. Tretmans and A. Belinfante. Automatic testing with formal methods. In *EuroSTAR'99: 7th European Int. Conference on Software Testing, Analysis & Review*, Barcelona, Spain, November 8–12, 1999. EuroStar Conferences, Galway, Ireland.

21. U. Wiger. Fault tolerant leader election. http://www.erlang.org/.

An Automata-Theoretic Approach for Model-Checking Systems with Unspecified Components*

Gaoyan Xie and Zhe Dang

School of Electrical Engineering and Computer Science,
Washington State University, Pullman, WA 99164, USA
{gxie, zdang}@eecs.wsu.edu

Abstract. This paper introduces a new approach for the verification of systems with unspecified components. In our approach, some model-checking problems concerning a component-based system are first reduced to the emptiness problem of an oracle finite automaton, which is then solved by testing the unspecified components on-the-fly with test-cases generated automatically from the oracle finite automaton. The generated test-cases are of bounded length, and with a properly chosen bound, a complete and sound solution is immediate. Particularly, the whole verification process can be carried out in an automatic way. In the paper, a symbolic algorithm is given for generating test-cases and performing the testings, and an example is drawn from an TinyOS application to illustrate our approach.

1   Introduction

In recent years, component-based software development [20, 6] has gained enormous popularity where large systems are built by assembling software components previously developed by the same organization, customized by third-party software vendors, or even purchased as commercial-off-the-shelf (COTS) products. This development method, however, has also posed one serious challenge to the quality assurance issue of component-based software—externally obtained components could be a new source of system failures. And the response to this challenge is greatly complicated by some intrinsic characteristics of component-based software: 1) for copyright or patent reasons, source codes or design details of externally obtained software components are usually not available to system developers; 2) software components are generally built with multiple sets of functionality [15] and with huge state space in their interfaces; 3) in many applications, software components are used for dynamic upgrading or extending running systems [30] that are too expensive or not supposed to be stopped at all. For instance, in practice, testing is almost the most natural resort to solve the problem; and when integrating a component into a system, developers may choose to either extensively test the component in isolation or hook the component with the system and conduct integration testing. The problem with the first choice, however, is that it is usually difficult to know when the testing over the component is adequate, and indiscriminately testing all the functionality of a software component is not only expensive but sometimes also

---

* The research was supported in part by NSF Grant CCF-0430531.

J. Grabowski and B. Nielsen (Eds.): FATES 2004, LNCS 3395, pp. 155–169, 2005.

infeasible due to the second characteristic. The second choice is not always applicable due to the third characteristic. On the other hand, for safety-critical and mission-critical systems, formal verification techniques, like model-checking [9], are usually desired over the testing techniques to establish the solid confidence for a reliable component. Yet, existing formal verification techniques are not always applicable either, due to the first characteristic.

Clearly, this problem plagues both component-based software systems and modularized hardware systems that contain externally obtained components. Generally, we call such systems as *systems with unspecified components* (in spite of the fact that in many cases, the components are partially specified, our approach still applies). In this paper, we study some model-checking problems, i.e., *reachability*, *safety*, and *LTL Model-checking problems*, for systems with unspecified components.

Most of the current work addresses this problem from the viewpoint of component developers, i.e., how to ensure the quality of components before they are released [33, 29, 24, 34]. This view, however, is fundamentally insufficient: an extensively tested component (by the vendor) may still not perform as expected in a specific deployment environment, since the deployment environments of a component could be quite different and diverse such that they may not be thoroughly tried by the vendor. We approach this problem from system developers' point of view: how to ensure that a component functions correctly in a host system where the component is deployed. The idea of our approach is simple: with respect to certain requirements about a system, derive and test the expected behaviors for the unspecified components. Specifically, we first reduce the model-checking problems concerning systems with unspecified components to the emptiness problem of *oracle finite automata* [35], which are finite automata augmented with query tapes and the ability of querying some external oracles during its computation. This is similar to the conventional automata-theoretic approaches for model-checking [32]. The difference, however, is that decision problems in conventional automata-theoretic model-checking approaches generally have analytic solutions, while the emptiness problem of an oracle finite automaton can only be resolved by querying the oracles with query strings of length bounded by some B. Since each query in the oracle automaton is equivalent to running a test-case corresponding to the query string over an unspecified component, so essentially the solution to solve the emptiness problem is a testing process. But the key point is the generation of test-cases. In this paper, we give an efficient testing algorithm that only generates test-cases that are useful to solve the problem, and performs testing on the fly. Moreover, with an appropriately chosen bound B, our approach is both sound and complete.

2 Preliminaries

2.1 The System Model

In this paper, we consider systems consisting of a host system and a collection of components whose design details are not given. Such a system is denoted by

$$Sys = \langle M, X_1, ..., X_k \rangle \tag{1}$$

for some $k \geq 1$, where M is the host system and each X_i, $1 \leq i \leq k$, is an unspecified component. Both the host system M and all the unspecified components X_i's are finite-state transition systems and they communicate synchronously via a finite set of input and output symbols.

Formally, a component X_i can be viewed as a quintuple

$$\langle S_i, s_{init}^i, \Sigma_i, \nabla_i, R_i \rangle, \tag{2}$$

where S_i is a finite set of states, $s_{init}^i \in S_i$ is the initial state, Σ_i is a finite set of input symbols, ∇_i is a finite set of output symbols, and $R_i \subseteq S_i \times (\Sigma_i \cup \nabla_i) \times S_i$ is the transition relation. Transitions in $S_i \times \Sigma_i \times S_i$ are called *input transitions*, while those in $S_i \times \nabla_i \times S_i$ are called *output transitions*. Since X_i is unspecified, its states set S_i and transition relation R_i are not supposed to be given. But we can assume that its sets of input and outputs symbols, Σ_i and ∇_i as well as an upper bound m_i for X_i's number of states $|S_i|$ are always given, we also assume that a special input symbol (not in Σ_i) "reset" always makes X_i return to its initial state s_{init}^i regardless of its current state. Furthermore, for each unspecified component X_i, we assume that it is *input-deterministic*, i.e., for any $\alpha \in \Sigma_i$, if $(s, \alpha, t) \in R_i$ and $(s, \alpha, t') \in R_i$ then $t = t'$; we also assume that X_i is *output-deterministic*, i.e., for any $\beta \in \nabla_i$ and $\beta' \in \Sigma_i \cup \nabla_i$, if $(s, \beta, t) \in R_i$ and $(s, \beta', t') \in R_i$ then $\beta = \beta'$ and $t = t'$. These two latter assumptions ensure that black-box testing can be efficiently performed on X_i. A *behavior* of X_i is a sequence of symbols in $\Sigma_i \cup \nabla_i$: $c_0 c_1 ...$, such that there is a sequence of states $s_0 s_1 ...$ with $s_0 = s_{init}^i$ and $(s_j, c_j, s_{j+1}) \in R_i$ for each $j \geq 0$.

The host system M, formally, is also defined as a tuple $\langle S, \Gamma, R_{env}, R_{comm}, s_{init} \rangle$, where

- S is a finite set of states;
- Γ is a finite set of event symbols;
- $R_{env} \subseteq S \times \Gamma \times S$ defines a set of *environment transitions*, where each transition $(s, a, s') \in R_{env}$ makes M move from state s to state s' upon receiving an event (symbol) $a \in \Gamma$ from the outside environment[1];
- $R_{comm} \subseteq S \times \bigcup_{1 \leq i \leq k} (\Sigma_i \cup \nabla_i) \times S$ defines a set of *communication transitions*, where each transition $(s, \alpha, s') \in R_{comm}$ with $\alpha \in \Sigma_i$ (called an *output transition*) makes M move from state s to state s' as well as send α to the unspecified component X_i, while each transition $(s, \beta, s') \in R_{comm}$ with $\beta \in \nabla_i$ (called an *input transition*) makes M move from state s to state s' upon receiving β from X_i; and,
- $s_{init} \in S$ is M's initial state.

For the Sys defined above, we assume that the set Γ, all Σ_i's and ∇_i's are pairwise disjoint. This assumption excludes broadcasting communications in our system model. For simplicity's sake, we also require that each unspecified component X_i is *closed*[2] in

---

[1] We assume that Γ always includes a special symbol ϵ such that (s, ϵ, s') makes M move from state s to state s' without receiving any event symbol.

[2] Note that this assumption does not limit the expressiveness of our model, since two communicating components can be regarded as one component.

the sense that it communicates only with the host system M; i.e., X_i only receives input symbols sent by M and sends output symbols only to M. Finally, it is worthwhile to notice that the system model defined here covers both systems that are sequential compositions of components and systems that are just collections of concurrently running components. This model is also flexible enough to characterize the two-way communications between the host system and a component in the form of function calls or in the form of synchronized events.

A *behavior* of the system Sys is a sequence τ of symbols in $\Gamma \cup \bigcup_{1 \le i \le k} (\Sigma_i \cup \nabla_i)$: $c_0 c_1 \ldots$ such that: 1) there exists a sequence θ of states $s_0 s_1 \ldots$, where $s_0 = s_{init}$ and $(s_j, c_j, s_{j+1}) \in R_{env}$ (resp.$(s_j, c_j, s_{j+1}) \in R_{comm}$) if $c_j \in \Gamma$ (resp. $c_j \in \Sigma_i \cup \nabla_i$ for some $1 \le i \le k$); 2) for each $1 \le i \le k$, let τ_i denote the subsequence of τ consisting of symbols only in Σ_i and ∇_i, then τ_i is a behavior of X_i. The combination of the behavior τ and the state sequence θ is also a sequence: $s_0 c_0 s_1 c_1 s_2 \ldots$, called a *computation* of Sys. For any given state $s \in S$, we say that the system Sys can *reach* s iff Sys has a computation on which s appears (i.e., $s_0 c_0 s_1 c_1 \ldots s$). Note that, in the case when X_i is fully specified, the system can be regarded as an I/O automaton [23]. As

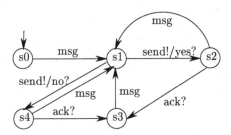

Fig. 1. A simple communication system

an illustrating example, we consider a simple system $Sys = \langle M, X \rangle$ that has only one unspecified component X. In this system, M keeps receiving messages from the outside environment and then transmits the message through X. The unspecified component X accepts only one input symbol *send*, but has three output symbols *yes*, *no* and *ack*. The transition graph of M is depicted in Figure 1, where a suffix ? denotes an input transition (e.g., *ack?*), a suffix ! denotes an output transition (e.g. *send!*), and an infix / is an abbreviation (to save space) for a pair of consecutive output/input transitions (e.g., *send!/yes?*), while a symbol without any suffix denotes an event transition (e.g. *msg*).

2.2   Black-Box Testing

Black-box testing is a technique to test a system without knowing its internal structure. The system is regarded as a "black-box" in the sense that its behavior can only be determined by observing (i.e., testing) its input/out sequences. Each unspecified component X_i defined in the previous subsection can be regarded as a "black-box". But, our definition of an unspecified component in (2) is not the Mealy machine as used in traditional black-box testing. So, for the purpose of testing over X_i, we assume that whenever X_i

is sent an input symbol in Σ_i, it immediately outputs a special output symbol (not in ∇_i) "yes" or "no" to indicate whether the input symbol is accepted or not. Also we assume that X_i has a special input symbol (not in Σ_i) "probe" that always makes M_i execute an output transition $(s, \beta, s') \in R_i$ if s is its current state, or just output the special symbol "no" if there are no such transitions. Let π^j denote the j-th element of a string π, then the following algorithm **BlkBoxTest**(X_i, π) is used in this paper to test whether π is an behavior of X_i:

Algorithm 1   **BlkBoxTest**(X_i, π)
1: send "reset" to X_i;
2: **for**($j := 0, j < |\pi|, j + +$)
3:      **if** π^j is an input symbol $\alpha \in \Sigma_i$
4:          **if** send(X_i, α)="No"
5:              **return** "No";
6:      **else if** π^j is an input symbol $\beta \in \nabla_i$
7:          **if** send$(X_i,$ "probe")$\neq \beta$
8:              **return** "no";
9: **return** "yes";

3 Oracle Finite Automata

In a recent paper [35], we studied oracle finite automata that are finite automata augmented with queries to some oracles. In that paper, we show that, in many cases, the emptiness problems (whether an oracle finite automaton accepts an empty language) are bounded testable; i.e., one can calculate a number B (called query bound) such that querying the oracles with query strings not longer than B is sufficient to solve the emptiness problems. We have obtained computable query bounds B for various classes of oracles for various restricted forms of oracle finite automata (e.g., regular oracles, context-free oracles, commutative semilinear oracles, etc.). However, efficient algorithms for solving the problem were not given in [35]. In this section, after we recall some basic definitions on oracle finite automata, we given an efficient dynamic testing algorithm to solve the emptiness problem of oracle automata, which in turn will be used to solve the model-checking problems concerning systems with unspecified components in the next section.

3.1 Definitions

An oracle automaton is a finite automaton augmented with a finite number of query tapes (that are initially empty) and the power of querying some oracles during its computation. Let $\mathcal{O}$ be a class of languages over alphabet Σ. An oracle O is a language in $\mathcal{O}$ whose definition is unknown, but querying the oracle with a word w on Σ (i.e., $w \in \Sigma^*$) always gives a definite "yes" or "no" answer (depending on whether w is a word of O). Formally, an *oracle finite automaton* (OFA) with k oracles drawn from $\mathcal{O}$ (written as $M^{\mathcal{O}}$), is a tuple

$$\langle S, \Sigma, R, s_{\text{init}}, F, k \rangle, \tag{3}$$

where Σ is the given alphabet, S is a finite set of *states* with s_{init} being the *initial state* and $F \subseteq S$ being a set of *accepting states*. R is a (finite) set of *transitions*, each of which is one of the following:

- a *input transition*, $s \xrightarrow{a} s'$, which makes M move from state s to state s' after reading an input symbol a;
- a *write transition*, $s \xrightarrow{\text{write}(i,a)} s'$, which makes M move from state s to state s' after appending a symbol a to the end of the i-th query tape;
- a *positive-query transition*, $s \xrightarrow{\text{query}(i)} s'$, which makes M move from state s to state s' when querying the i-th oracle (with the i-th query tape content as the query string) returns a "yes" answer;
- a *negative query transition*, $s \xrightarrow{\neg\text{query}(i)} s'$, which makes M move from state s to state s' when query(i) returns a "no" answer;
- or a *reset transition*, $s \xrightarrow{\text{reset}(i)} s'$, which makes M move from state s to state s' and resets the i-th query tape content to be empty,

where $s, s' \in S$, $a \in \Sigma$, and $1 \leq i \leq k$. Note that the syntactical definition of $M^{\mathcal{O}}$ does not include any definition of its oracles, except that they should be drawn from $\mathcal{O}$. So $M^{\mathcal{O}}$ actually defines a collection of OFAs, and in the following, we shall use $M^{\mathcal{O}}(O_1, \ldots, O_k)$ to denote the specific OFA associated with k oracles $O_1, \ldots, O_k$ drawn from $\mathcal{O}$.

The semantics of an oracle finite automaton $M^{\mathcal{O}}(O_1, \ldots, O_k)$ can be defined as usual. A word w is *accepted* by $M(O_1, \ldots, O_k)$ if there is an accepting run over w. The language accepted by $M^{\mathcal{O}}(O_1, \ldots, O_k)$, $L(M^{\mathcal{O}}(O_1, \ldots, O_k))$, is the set of all words accepted by $M^{\mathcal{O}}(O_1, \ldots, O_k)$.

Syntactically, an *oracle Buchi automaton* (ω-OFA) $M_{\omega}^{\mathcal{O}}$ is an oracle finite automaton $M^{\mathcal{O}}$ in (3). But they are semantically different. An ω-word $w_{\omega} \in \Sigma^{\omega}$ is *accepted* by $M_{\omega}^{\mathcal{O}}(O_1, \ldots, O_k)$ if there is an ω-run on w_{ω} such that some accepting state in F appears infinitely often. The ω-language $L_{\omega}(M_{\omega}^{\mathcal{O}}(O_1, \ldots, O_t))$ is still the set of ω-words accepted by the ω-OFA $M_{\omega}^{\mathcal{O}}(O_1, \ldots, O_t)$.

3.2   Testability of the Emptiness Problem

For the OFAs and ω-OFAs defined in the previous subsection, various decision problems can be considered. In this paper, we study the *emptiness problem*, which is to decide whether an OFA $M^{\mathcal{O}}(O_1, \ldots, O_k)$ accepts an empty language. In the next section, we will show that this emptiness problem is closely related with some model-checking problems for systems with unspecified components. Obviously, since the behavior of an OFA depends on the query results with its oracles and the definitions of the oracles are unknown, we can not analytically solve the problem only from the definition of M itself.

Recall that an oracle O is a language drawn from some class of languages $\mathcal{O}$. Suppose that $\mathcal{O}$ is the class of languages accepted by deterministic finite automata (DFA) with at most m states. Then a finite automaton (without oracles) T can be constructed to solve the emptiness problem of the OFA $M^{\mathcal{O}}(O_1, \ldots, O_k)$ as follows:

1. for each oracle O_i, $\mathcal{T}$ constructs a DFA $\mathcal{A}_i$ that accepts exactly the language O_i by querying O_i with all words on Σ with length less than $2m - 1$ [31], and saves each $\mathcal{A}_i$ on its working tape;

2. $\mathcal{T}$ starts to faithfully simulate M except that when M queries an oracle O_i with a query string w, $\mathcal{T}$ runs the DFA $\mathcal{A}_i$ on its working tape (whose length is bounded by $2m - 1$) with w as $\mathcal{A}_i$'s input, and the query is considered successful if $\mathcal{A}_i$ accepts w, or vice versa.

Obviously, $M^{\mathcal{O}}(O_1, \ldots, O_k)$ accepts an empty language iff $\mathcal{T}$ accepts an empty language. Since the emptiness problem of $\mathcal{T}$ can be analytically solved (after $\mathcal{T}$ constructs all the $\mathcal{A}_i$'s.), so does the the emptiness problem of $M^{\mathcal{O}}(O_1, \ldots, O_k)$. Additionally, because the above construction involves pre-querying all oracles with query strings not longer than $2m - 1$, which can be viewed as a testing process, we also say that the emptiness problem of $M^{\mathcal{O}}(O_1, \ldots, O_k)$ is $(2m - 1)$-testable.

Let $\mathrm{OFA}^{\mathrm{DFA}(m)}$ denote the OFAs whose oracles are drawn from the class of languages accepted by deterministic finite automata (DFA) with at most m states. Then we have the following conclusion:

Theorem 1. *The emptiness problem for* $\mathrm{OFA}^{\mathrm{DFA}(m)}$ *is* $(2m - 1)$-*testable.*

Similarly, let $\mathrm{OFA}_\omega^{\mathrm{DFA}(m)}$ denote a oracle Buchi automata whose oracles are drawn from the class of languages accepted by deterministic finite automata (DFA) with at most m states. Then we have the following conclusion:

Theorem 2. *The emptiness problem for* $\mathrm{OFA}_\omega^{\mathrm{DFA}(m)}$ *is* $(2m - 1)$-*testable.*

Clearly, not every OFA's emptiness problem can be solved in this way; i.e., not every OFA's emptiness problem is testable. For instance, OFAs associated with oracles from context-free languages are proved to be not testable (for a detailed exposition about the testability of oracle automata, see [35]).

3.3   A Dynamic Testing Algorithm

The solution to the emptiness problem for $\mathrm{OFA}^{\mathrm{DFA}(m)}$ and $\mathrm{OFA}_\omega^{\mathrm{DFA}(m)}$ in the previous subsection involves pre-querying the oracles indiscriminately with all possible strings with length shorter than $2m - 1$. This would be extremely inefficient in practice, considering the fact that there are an exponential number ($|\Sigma|^{2m-1}$) of such strings.

In this subsection, we introduce a more efficient algorithm to solve the emptiness problem for $\mathrm{OFA}^{\mathrm{DFA}(m)}$ and $\mathrm{OFA}_\omega^{\mathrm{DFA}(m)}$. The new algorithm only queries the oracles with query strings that could be "generated" by the OFAs. Since each query to an oracle can also be viewed as a test over the oracle where the query string is a test-case, this algorithm can also be viewed as a dynamic testing process where test-cases are generated on-the-fly.

Suppose that $M^{\mathrm{DFA}(m)}$ is an OFA as defined in (3). Without loss of generality, we assume that M is associated with only one oracle (i.e., $k = 1$); generalization to multiple oracles is straightforward. Consequently, there will be only one query tape in M. Then we write instructions $\mathrm{reset}(i)$, $\mathrm{write}(i, a)$, $\mathrm{query}(i)$, and $\neg\mathrm{query}(i)$ as reset, $\mathrm{write}(a)$, query, and $\neg\mathrm{query}$, respectively. A transition relation r is a subset of

$S \times S$, where S is the state set of M. We use $r_1 \circ r_2$ to denote the relation obtained from composing relation r_1 with relation r_2, Intersect to denote the intersection operator, and TransClosure(r) to denote the transitive closure of a relation r, respectively. We also use Empty(r) to test whether a relation r is empty. Then, from the definition of M, we define the following transition relations:

$$r_{\texttt{input}} = \{\langle s, s' \rangle : \exists a, s \overset{a}{\to} s' \in R\},$$
$$r_{\texttt{reset}} = \{\langle s, s' \rangle : s \overset{\texttt{reset}}{\to} s' \in R\},$$
$$r_{\texttt{write}(a)} = \{\langle s, s' \rangle : s \overset{\texttt{write}(a)}{\to} s' \in R\},$$
$$r_{\texttt{query}} = \{\langle s, s' \rangle : s \overset{\texttt{query}}{\to} s' \in R\},$$
$$r_{\neg\texttt{query}} = \{\langle s, s' \rangle : s \overset{\neg\texttt{query}}{\to} s' \in R\}.$$

We first present the algorithm, **TestEmptiness**(B), for testing the emptiness of $M^{\mathrm{DFA}(m)}$, where the query strings are not longer than B. Later, we will describe an algorithm for testing the emptiness of $M_\omega^{\mathrm{DFA}(m)}$.

Algorithm 2 TestEmptiness(B)
1: $l := 0$;
2: $\Theta := \{(\{\langle s, s \rangle : s \in S\}, \Lambda)\}$;
3: $E = \{\langle s_{\texttt{init}}, s_{\texttt{init}} \rangle\}$;
4: $\Theta' := \Theta$;
5: **for each** (r, w) in Θ with $|w| = l$
6:      $r' := r \circ \texttt{TransClosure}(r_{\texttt{input}})$;
7:      **if** $\neg\texttt{Empty}(r' \circ r_{\texttt{query}})$ or $\neg\texttt{Empty}(r' \circ r_{\neg\texttt{query}})$
8:          query the oracle with query string w;
9:          **if** the query returns yes
10:             $r' := r \circ \texttt{TransClosure}(r_{\texttt{input}} \cup r_{\texttt{query}})$;
11:         **if** the query returns no
12:             $r' := r \circ \texttt{TransClosure}(r_{\texttt{input}} \cup r_{\neg\texttt{query}})$;
13:     replace the entry (r, w) in Θ with (r', w);
14:     $r'' := r' \circ r_{\texttt{reset}}$;
15:     **if** $\neg\texttt{Empty}(r'')$
16:         $E := \texttt{TransClosure}(E \cup r'' \cup r_{\texttt{input}})$;
17:     **for each** $a \in \Sigma$
18:         $r'' := r' \circ r_{\texttt{write}(a)}$;
19:         **if** $\neg\texttt{Empty}(r'')$
20:             add (r'', wa) to Θ;
21: $l := l + 1$;
22: **for each** (r, w) in Θ
23:      $r' := \texttt{Intersect}(E \circ r, \{s_{\texttt{init}}\} \times F)$;
24:      **if** $\neg\texttt{Empty}(r')$
25:          **return** "unsuccessful";
26: **if** Θ' and Θ are equal or $l > B$
27:      **return** "successful";
28: **goto** 4;

The **TestEmptiness** algorithm works as follows. We maintain a finite set Θ of pairs of a relation r and a word w. For two states s and s', $\langle s, s' \rangle$ is in r iff, starting from state s and with empty query tape, there is some input word such that state s' is reached (after running M on the input) with the query tape content w, during which no reset occurs. The algorithm also maintains a relation E: for two states s and s', $\langle s, s' \rangle$ is in E iff, starting from state s and with empty query tape, there is a run of M that brings to state s' and also with empty query tape. After initializing Θ and E, the entire algorithm works as a loop from statement 4 to statement 28 and back. In the l-th round (l starts with 0), the algorithm updates an element (r, w) in Θ with $|w| = l$, realized by changing w into wa (i.e., $\texttt{write}(a)$ on the query tape). However, transitions like reading input symbols and querying the oracle can happen before this write, and obviously, the query result matters. This is shown in statements 6–13 where an updated version (r', w) of (r, w) is replaced in Θ (i.e., statement 13). Notice that, a query is performed when necessary shown in statement 8. Then, $\texttt{write}(a)$ is implemented in statements 17–20 to add longer query strings wa into Θ. Clearly, w can also be changed into an empty string through a $\texttt{reset}$, which causes an update on E (recalling the meaning of E mentioned earlier) shown in statements 14–16. Finally in the round, statements 22–27 are used to check whether M accepts an empty language. Clearly, according to the semantics of Θ, if it has a (r, w) where r contains the pair of the initial state and an accepting state, then obviously M accepts a nonempty language — an "unsuccessful" is returned as the result of statements 23–25. If the set Θ does not change in the round (so further rounds are not necessarily) or the level l is higher than the given bound B, then M must accept an empty language (i.e., returns "successful" as in statement 27).

It's not hard to show that the above algorithm is both sound and complete, if one chooses a bound $B \geq m \cdot |M|$. It shall also be noted that the algorithm can be implemented symbolically. This is because a relation can be represented symbolically as a Boolean formula whose satisfying assignments can be further encoded with a BDD [7]. Operations like $\texttt{TransClosure}$, $\texttt{Intersect}$, $\circ$, $\texttt{Empty}$ are all standard operations in existing BDD libraries [28].

We can construct another algorithm ω-**TestEmptiness** for testing the emptiness problem of $M_\omega^{\mathrm{DFA}(m)}$, using **TestEmptiness**. This algorithm works as follows. It first constructs an OFA M' from the ω-OFA M that works as follows. M' first guesses an accepting state in F (the set of accepting states in the ω-OFA M) and faithfully simulates M. M' accepts an input word if M enters the guessed accepting state for m times. Clearly, M' is an OFA (instead of an ω-OFA), and it is not hard to show that M' accepts an empty language iff the ω-OFA M does. Then ω-**TestEmptiness** calls algorithm **TestEmptiness**(B) running on M' with $B \geq |F| \cdot |M| \cdot m^2$. One can also show that the algorithm ω-**TestEmptiness** is both sound and complete.

4   The Model-Checking Problems

As mentioned in Section 1, this paper studies some model-checking problems, i.e., the reachability, safety, and LTL model-checking problems for systems with unspecified components. In this section, we show that these model-checking problems can be first reduced to the emptiness problem of oracle finite automata, and then be solved by testing the unspecified components with the algorithms defined in the previous section.

Suppose that $Sys = \langle M, X_1, ..., X_k \rangle$ is defined in (1). Let $m = \max_{1 \le i \le k} m_i$ (recall that m_i is an upper bound for the number of states in X_i). The *reachability problem* is to decide: starting from its initial state, whether Sys can reach some state in a given set Bad of states; i.e., whether Bad is reachable in Sys (in practice, Bad may specify some "bad" states that are not supposed to be reached).

To solve this problem, we first construct an OFA, $M_{\mathrm{OFA}}^{\mathrm{DFA}(m)}(O_1, \ldots, O_k)$ in (3) from the definition of Sys as follows:

1. for each $1 \le i \le k$, let oracle O_i denote the set of behaviors of the unspecified component X_i (remember that an oracle is a language without detailed definition);
2. let M_{OFA} have the same set of states and same initial state as M;
3. let M_{OFA}'s Σ be the union of Γ and all Σ_i's and ∇_i's in Sys;
4. let Bad be M_{OFA}'s accepting states;
5. for each transition (s, a, s') in M with $a \in \Gamma$, add a transition $(s \xrightarrow{a} s')$ to M_{OFA};
6. for each transition (s, α, s') in M with $\alpha \in \Sigma_i$ for some $1 \le i \le k$, add a transition $(s \xrightarrow{\mathtt{write}(\alpha,i)} s')$ to M_{OFA};
7. for each transition (s, β, s') in M with $\beta \in \nabla_i$ for some $1 \le i \le k$, add a new state s'', as well as two transitions $(s \xrightarrow{\mathtt{write}(\beta,i)} s'')$ and $(s'' \xrightarrow{\mathtt{query}(i)} s')$ to M_{OFA}.

For instance, from the system depicted in Figure 1, we can construct an OFA as shown in Figure 2 (since this OFA has only one query tape, in Figure 2, we write instructions $\mathtt{write}(i, a)$ and $\mathtt{query}(i)$ as $\mathtt{write}(a)$ and $\mathtt{query}$ respectively).

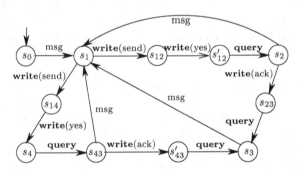

Fig. 2. An oracle finite automaton

Now it is easy to see that Bad is not reachable in the system Sys iff the constructed M_{OFA} accepts a nonempty language. Then we have,

Theorem 3. *The reachability problem for the system Sys is testable.*

The *safety problem* is to decide whether every behavior of the system Sys is contained in a given regular language R. Assume that the complement of R can be accepted by a finite automaton M_R and let $\bar{M}$ be the Cartesian product of M_R and M. Notice that each state in $\bar{M}$ is a pair of states in M_R and M respectively and $\bar{M}$ totally has $|M_R| \cdot |M|$

number of states; i.e. $|\bar{M}| = |M_R| \cdot |M|$. Let F denote the set of states in $\bar{M}$, each of which contains a final state of M_R. Similar to the construction in the reachability problem (except that F would be the OFA's accepting states), we can construct an OFA, $\bar{M}_{\mathrm{OFA}}^{\mathrm{DFA}(m)}(O_1, \ldots, O_k)$ from this $\bar{M}$ as well as the unspecified components X_i, $1 \le i \le k$. Then it shall be noticed that the safety problem is true iff the constructed $\bar{M}_{\mathrm{OFA}}$ accepts an empty language. Hence we have,

Theorem 4. *The safety problem for the system Sys is testable.*

Next, we consider the model-checking problems concerning ω-behaviors of the system Sys; i.e., the LTL model-checking problem.

The linear-time temporal logic (LTL) views the behaviors of a finite-state system as a set of paths, i.e., infinite words on an alphabet Σ. And LTL formulas, which are interpreted over paths, are defined as follows:

$$\phi ::= a \mid \neg\phi \mid \phi \wedge \phi \mid X\phi \mid \phi U\phi,$$

where $a \in \Sigma$ is an *atomic proposition*. X is the *next* operator, and U is the *until* operator. We interpret each atomic proposition a as the singleton set $\{a\}$. Intuitively, a path σ satisfies an atomic proposition a if the first symbol of σ is symbol a. A path σ satisfies $X\phi$ if σ^1 (by deleting the first symbol in σ) satisfies ϕ. σ satisfies $\phi U\psi$ if there is a suffix σ^i (by deleting the first i symbols) of σ such that (1). the suffix satisfies ψ and (2). ϕ is consistently satisfied on each σ^j with $0 \le j < i$. Notice that our treatment of atomic propositions here is essentially equivalent to a standard LTL definition [10] (though the appearance of ours is a little different). LTL is capable of expressing many interesting properties of a reactive system. For instance, the property "the pump is on for infinitely many times" can be expressed as $\Box\Diamond\mathtt{pumpOn}$ (where $\Diamond\phi$ (eventually ϕ) is an abbreviation for $\mathtt{true}\ U\ \phi$, and $\Box\phi$ (always ϕ) stands for $\neg\Diamond\neg\phi$.). We use $[f]$ to denote the set of ω-words that satisfy f. It is known that $[f]$ can be accepted by a Buchi automaton (an ω-OFA without the query tapes) with $O(2^{|f|})$ number of states, where $|f|$ is the length of f).

The *LTL model-checking* problem is to decide whether every ω-behavior of the system Sys satisfies a given LTL formula f. Similar to the standard LTL model-checking approach [32], we define $\bar{M}$ to be the Cartesian product of M and the Buchi automaton that accepts $[\neg f]$. Similar as before, we construct an ω-OFA, $\bar{M}_{\omega}^{\mathrm{DFA}(m)}(O_1, \ldots, O_k)$ from this $\bar{M}$ as well as the unspecified components X_i s. Observe that the LTL model-checking problem is equivalent to checking the emptiness of $\bar{M}_{\omega}^{\mathrm{DFA}(m)}(O_1, \ldots, O_t)$. Hence, we have the following result:

Theorem 5. *The LTL model-checking problem for the system Sys is testable.*

Note that in the above constructions, the oracles actually characterize the behaviors of the unspecified components. Therefore, when we apply the **TestEmptiness** algorithm to the constructed OFAs (OFA$_\omega$s), line 8 of **TestEmptiness**, i.e., "query the oracle with string w" should be replaced with **BlkBoxTest**(X, w). That is, the model-checking problems for the systems Sys are finally reduced to testings over the unspecified components in Sys.

Remark. As we have seen from the above reductions from the model-checking problems on Sys to the emptiness problems for the constructed M_{OFA}s, there are no reset and negative query transitions in M_{OFA}. This implies that the reduction and the algorithms still work when we understand each m_i, instead of being the number of states in component X_i, to be the number of states in a *nondeterministic* finite automaton that accepts the behaviors of X_i. This will greatly bring down the bound B for query strings for the algorithms **TestEmptiness** and ω-**TestEmptiness**. Also, the above argument still applies, if we further allow "reset" to be an ordinary input symbol of X_i, i.e., "reset" can appear on a transition in Sys. Clearly, the transition containing a "reset" in sys corresponds to a reset transition in the OFA to which Sys is reduced.

5   Applications

In this section, we consider a TinyOS application. TinyOS is a lightweight operating system for networked sensors [18]. It is designed with a highly modularized architecture such that a specific application can be easily built by assembling just the software components required to synthesize the application from the hardware components. In a TinyOS application, components are glued together through *interfaces*. An interface consists of a set of commands and a set of events, and each component declares the interfaces it provides to other components and the interfaces it shall use from other components. The provider of an interface must implement a command handler for each command in the interface; and the user of an interface must implement an event handler for each event in the interface. The command handlers return a boolean value indicating a success or failure. A TinyOS application is event-driven; i.e., it executes by synchronizing events and commands between its components.

For instance, consider a data acquirement application which periodically transmits the reading of a photo sensor via some underlying communication network. This application consists of a host system and three components: *timer*, *photo* and *comm* whose

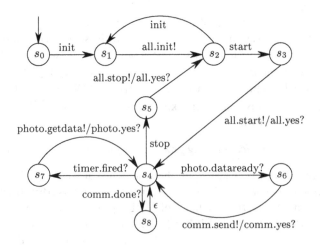

Fig. 3. A data acquirement system

functionality are as implied by their names. All three components respond to three standard commands: *init*, *start*, and *stop*. Particularly, the timer component also signals an event *fired* when the time interval set runs out. The photo component always responds to a command *getdata*, but it signals an event *dataready* only when the sensor's reading is ready. The comm component always responds to a command *send*, but it signals an event *done* only when the data is successfully sent.

Suppose the internal specifications of the three components are not available, but we know they are all finite state transition systems. Then each of them can be treated as an unspecified component in (2), and the system can be viewed as a system in (1). The transition graph of the host system is depicted in Figure 3, where s_0 is the initial state, suffix "?" is used to denote an event coming from a component, suffix "!" is used to denote a command sent to a component, infix "/" is used as an abbreviation (to save space) for a pair of consecutive command and event, symbols without any suffix denote commands from the outside world, and ϵ denotes an empty symbol. Notice that, in Figure 3, we use two additional events "yes" and "no" to indicate the return value of a command handler (i.e., the success or failure of a command), and we also used "all" as an abbreviation for all of the three components. [3]

Then we can consider the following LTL model-checking problem for the system Sys (which can be expressed in the LTL formalism defined earlier):

- $Sys, s_0 \models AG(s_6 \rightarrow X((\neg s_6)\ U\ s_7))$, i.e., on all computations of Sys, no two *photo.dataready* outputs can be sent without receiving a *photo.getdata* message.

From the results presented in this paper, this LTL model-checking problems can be reduced to the emptiness problem of an ω-OFA constructed from the system. And the emptiness problem of the ω-OFA can be solved by querying (testing) the oracles (unspecified components) with strings of bounded length.

6   Related Work

In the formal verification area, there has been a long history of research on verification of systems with modular structure (called modular verification [27]). A key idea [21, 17] in modular verification is called the *assume-guarantee* paradigm: A module should guarantee to have the desired behavior once the environment with which the module is interacting has the assumed behavior. There have been a variety of implementations for this idea (see, e.g., [1]). However, the assume-guarantee idea does not fit with our problem setup since it requires users to have clear assumptions about a module's environment. Although Giannakopoulou et. al.[14] introduced a novel approach to generate assumptions that characterize exactly the environment in which a component satisfies its property. Their donot generalize to systems with unspecified components where a purely formal method is not applicable.

In the past decade, there also has been some research on combining model-checking and testing techniques for system verification, which can be classified into a broader class

---

[3] This example comes from the TinyOS distribution [4], and we abstracted its original nesC source code into this automaton form.

of techniques called specification-based testing. But most of the work [8, 19, 11, 13, 3, 5, 2] just utilizes model-checkers' ability of producing counter-examples from a system's specification to generate test-cases against an implementation. In spirit, our work is closely related with the series of work by Peled et. al. [26, 16, 25] where they studied the issue of checking a black-box against a temporal property (called black-box checking). But our problem setup is on the verification of component-based systems, and we focus on how to derive test-cases for unspecified components from the host system. Their approach requires a clearly-defined property (LTL formula) about the black-box, which is not always possible in component-based systems. Fisler et. al. [12, 22] introduced an idea of deducing a model-checking condition for extension features from the base feature to study model-checking feature-oriented software designs. Unfortunately, their approach relies totally on model-checking techniques; their algorithms have false negatives and do not handle LTL formulas.

References

1. Rajeev Alur, Thomas A. Henzinger, Freddy Y. C. Mang, Shaz Qadeer, Sriram K. Rajamani, and Serdar Tasiran. MOCHA: Modularity in model checking. In *CAV'98*, volume 1427 of *LNCS*, pages 521–525. Springer, 1998.
2. Paul Ammann, Paul E. Black, and Wei Ding. Model checkers in software testing. NIST-IR 6777, National Institute of Standards and Technology, 2002.
3. Paul Ammann, Paul E. Black, and William Majurski. Using model checking to generate tests from specifications. In *ICFEM'98*, page 46, 1998.
4. UC Berkeley. Tinyos 1.1.0, Sep. 2003. http://webs.cs.berkeley.edu/tos/download.html.
5. Paul E. Black, Vadim Okun, and Yaacov Yesha. Mutation operators for specifications. In *ASE'00*, page 81, 2000.
6. A.W. Brown and K.C. Wallnau. The current state of CBSE. *IEEE Software*, 15(5):37–46, Sep/Oct 1998.
7. Randal E. Bryant. Symbolic Boolean manipulation with ordered binary-decision diagrams. *ACM Computing Surveys*, 24(3):293–318, 1992.
8. J. Callahan, F. Schneider, and S. Easterbrook. Automated software testing using model checking. In *Proceedings 1996 SPIN Workshop*, 1996.
9. E. M. Clarke and E. A. Emerson. Design and synthesis of synchronization skeletons using branching time temporal logic. In *Workshop of Logic of Programs*, volume 131 of *LNCS*. Springer, 1981.
10. E.A. Emerson. Temporal and modal logic. In *Handbook of Theoretical Computer Science*, pages 997–1072. Elsevier, 1990.
11. A. Engels, L.M.G. Feijs, and S. Mauw. Test generation for intelligent networks using model checking. In *TACAS'97*, volume 1217 of *LNCS*, pages 384–398. Springer, 1997.
12. Kathi Fisler and Shriram Krishnamurthi. Modular verification of collaboration-based software designs. In *ESEC/FSE'01*, pages 152–163. ACM Press, 2001.
13. Angelo Gargantini and Constance Heitmeyer. Using model checking to generate tests from requirements specifications. In *ESEC/FSE'99*, volume 1687 of *LNCS*, pages 146–163. Springer, 1999.
14. Dimitra Giannakopoulou, Corina S. P¿s¿reanu, and Howard Barringer. Assumption generation for software component verification. In *ASE'02*, page 3. IEEE Computer Society, 2002.

15. Ian Gorton and Anna Liu. Software component quality assessment in practice: successes and practical impediments. In *ICSE'02*, pages 555–558. ACM Press, 2002.
16. Alex Groce, Doron Peled, and Mihalis Yannakakis. Amc: An adaptive model checker. In *CAV'02*, volume 2404 of *LNCS*, pages 521–525. Springer, 2002.
17. Thomas A. Henzinger, Shaz Qadeer, and Sriram K. Rajamani. You assume, we guarantee: Methodology and case studies. In *CAV'98*, volume 1427 of *LNCS*, pages 440–451. Springer, 1998.
18. Jason Hill, Robert Szewczyk, Alec Woo, Seth Hollar, David E. Culler, and Kristofer S. J. Pister. System architecture directions for networked sensors. In *Architectural Support for Programming Languages and Operating Systems*, pages 93–104, 2000.
19. G. J. Holzmann. The model checker SPIN. *IEEE Transactions on Software Engineering*, 23(5):279–295, May 1997. Special Issue: Formal Methods in Software Practice.
20. W. Kozaczynski and G. Booch. Component-based software engineering. *IEEE Software*, 15(5):34–36, Sep/Oct 1998.
21. Leslie Lamport. Specifying concurrent program modules. *ACM Transactions on Programming Languages and Systems (TOPLAS)*, 5(2):190–222, 1983.
22. Harry Li, Shriram Krishnamurthi, and Kathi Fisler. Verifying cross-cutting features as open systems. *ACM SIGSOFT Software Engineering Notes*, 27(6):89–98, 2002.
23. N. Lynch and M. Tuttle. Hierarchical correctness proofs for distributed algorithms. Proc. 6th ACM Symp. on Principles of Distributed Computing, pp. 137–151, 1987.
24. A. Orso, M. J. Harrold, and D. Rosenblum. Component metadata for software engineering tasks. *LNCS*, 1999:129–144, 2001.
25. Doron Peled. Algorithmic testing methods. In *CAV'03*, volume 2725 of *LNCS*. Springer-Velag, july 2003.
26. Doron Peled, Moshe Y. Vardi, and Mihalis Yannakakis. Black box checking. In Jianping Wu, Samuel T. Chanson, and Qiang Gao, editors, *FORTE/PSTV'99*, pages 225–240. Kluwer, 1999.
27. A. Pnueli. In transition from global to modular temporal reasoning about programs, 1985. In K.R. Apt, editor, Logics and Models of Concurrent Systems, sub-series F: Computer and System Science.
28. F. Somenzi. Cudd: Cu decision diagram package release, 1998.
29. J. Stafford and A. Wolf. Annotating components to support component-based static analyses of software systems, September 2000. In Grace Hopper Celebration of Women in Computing, Hyannis, Massachusetts.
30. C. Szyperski. Component technology: what, where, and how? In *ICSE'03*, pages 684–693. IEEE Computer Society Press, 2003.
31. B. A. Trakhtenbrot and Ya. M. Barzdin. *Finite automata; behavior and synthesis*. North-Holland Pub. Co., 1973.
32. M. Y. Vardi and P. Wolper. An automata-theoretic approach to automatic program verification (preliminary report). In *LICS'86*, pages 332–344. IEEE Computer Society Press, 1986.
33. J. Voas. Developing a usage-based software certification process. *IEEE Computer*, 33(8):32–37, August 2000.
34. J. Whaley, M. C. Martin, and M. S. Lam. Automatic extraction of object-oriented component interfaces. In *ISSTA'02*, July 2002.
35. Gaoyan Xie, Cheng Li, and Zhe Dang. Testability of oracle automata, 2004. To Appear in the Proceedings of CIAA'04.

Test Patterns with TTCN-3

Alain Vouffo-Feudjio and Ina Schieferdecker

Fraunhofer FOKUS, Berlin, Germany
{vouffo, schieferdecker}@fokus.fraunhofer.de

Abstract. Patterns are used in various engineering disciplines to represent common aspects of a set of solutions to a (set of) common problem(s). This paper discusses main concepts of test patterns, provides a characterization of test patterns and describes the use of test patterns in the test development process. Test patterns can be used to support the vertical reuse between different testing phases and testing kinds, horizontal reuse between different product version and historical reuse between different product versions. Specification means for test patterns will be analysed and compared with the language features of the Testing and Test Control Notation (TTCN-3) [8].

1 Introduction

Test patterns represent a form of reuse in test development in which the essences of solutions and experiences gathered in testing are extracted and documented so as to enable their application in similar contexts that might arise in the future. Test patterns aim at capturing test design knowledge from past projects in a canonical form, so that future projects would benefit from it. In this paper we will describe different views on the concept of test patterns and discuss methodological aspects such as notation, test pattern mining and test pattern application. The concept of patterns as it is currently known in the software development community originates from the works of Alexander [1], a building architect who had the basic idea of recording design wisdom in a canonical form. He defines a pattern as "both a description of a thing which is alive, and a description of the process which will generate that thing". It soon became obvious that the concept of patterns introduced by Alexander for the buildings architecture domain could also apply to nearly any design and engineering field. As [2] pointed out: "A pattern is the result of abstracting from a given (set of) problem-solution pair(s) and distilling common factors, which can be reused to solve other problems".

In analogy to the patterns for urban architecture, software designers acknowledged the existence of patterns in software architecture and the need for identifying and describing them in such a way that they would possibly be reused wherever the context might require it. Therefore, [3] defines a software architecture pattern as both a part of a software system and a description of how to build that part. The purpose of software architecture patterns is to identify and specify abstractions above level of single instances or components in a software system, as well as to document existing

J. Grabowski and B. Nielsen (Eds.): FATES 2004, LNCS 3395, pp. 170–179, 2005.

well proven design experiences, software architectures and guidelines. Also software patterns provide a common vocabulary and understanding for design principles and well-proven experiences.

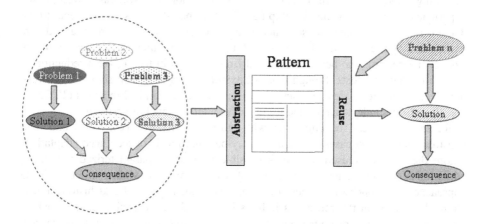

Fig. 1. Pattern Extraction and Reuse: The process of extracting the essence of a set of problem-solution-benefit combinations is displayed in the left hand part of the figure, whereas on the right-hand side, the reverse process of producing a solution for a similar problem-benefit pair by applying the previously identified pattern is illustrated

However some severe debates also emerged around patterns and how they relate to existing software methodologies. As described in [2], emphasis must be put on the fact that patterns can and should not be viewed as solution for all possible software engineering problems and one should not attempt to force patterns reuse in situations where they simply would not fit. Patterns should rather be viewed as a complementary approach to existing methodologies. Also patterns should harmonize with the fundamental principles of software construction commonly known as "enabling techniques", which are independent of a specific software development method such as Abstraction, Encapsulation, Information Hiding, Modularization, Separation of Concerns, Coupling and Cohesion, Sufficiency, Completeness and Primitiveness, Separation of Policy and Implementation, Separation of Interface and Implementation, Single Point of Reference, and Divide-and-conquer.

While some patterns address some of those concepts explicitly, it is important to make sure that patterns do not affect those principles. This also applies for the usual non-functional requirements on software systems, i.e. changeability, interoperability, efficiency, reliability, testability and reusability. It should be kept in mind, that while some patterns will aim at enhancing some of those requirements and help in achieving them, it is also possible that a given pattern affect some of the non-functional requirements negatively. For example, the broker pattern, which is the base of many middleware architectures such as CORBA, eases testing of individual client or server components in a distributed system. However it decreases the testability of client-server systems by introducing additional elements between the client and the server.

Test systems and more specifically TTCN-3 test systems are a special type of software systems and with their growing complexity, the need for cataloguing good practices with regard to design, architecture, implementation and execution is becoming more and more urgent. Just as for "normal" software, well-proven experiences gathered while developing TTCN-3 based test systems need to be documented to ease their reuse. Therefore we define a test pattern as a software pattern that applies specifically to the testing domain. Similarly to general software system engineering, the benefits expected from patterns in testing are a reduction of time-to-market and costs through reuse of existing test artefacts. It should be pointed out here, that the term "test artefacts" in this context is not limited to actual (TTCN-3) code but also include concepts and principles at a higher level of abstraction.

Reuse of tests can be compared with reuse of software. Test suites and their constituents (like test cases or test data) may be reused as is or may need adaptations before they can be reused. E.g. it is possible to develop parameterized test cases, which enables their adaptation to different testing contexts. Mainly, three different approaches are important for test reuse: the vertical, horizontal and historic reuse. Vertical reuse is on the reuse possibilities between different testing phases such as requirements testing, prototype testing, module testing, integration testing, system testing, and acceptance testing. Another approach is between different types of testing, e.g. tests developed for functional testing could be reused for performance or scalability testing [5]. The horizontal reuse addresses the reuse of tests between various products and within product families. The historical reuse addresses test reuse between product generations. Historical and horizontal reuses are similar as "different products" in horizontal reuse could be considered as "different product versions" in historical reuse. The differences in products/product families and product versions will show in different testing parts being reused for testing.

2   Categories of Test Patterns

The issue of patterns in general and specifically that of test patterns has very often been a source of some misunderstanding among experts. This stems from the generality of the concept and the fact that depending on the aspect of test engineering on which focus is laid, apparently different definitions and classifications might emerge. In our current work we've identified the following views on test patterns:

- The scope-based view: The nature of the test development process may vary a lot, depending on the scope or target of those tests. It is obvious, that the techniques for generating, specifying, executing and evaluating the tests can be totally different, whether unit testing, integration testing or system testing is being performed. Examples of patterns for unit testing have been provided by [11] , whereas some others for component testing of object oriented software as described in [12] and in [7].
- The management-based view: In some cases such as [13], the issues of patterns in test development is discussed at a higher level of abstraction, which involves aspects such as the management of test projects and test organizations, the strategies for achieving higher efficiency in testing etc.

We chose to adopt a scope-based approach and focus on the process of developping a test system based on a formal notation such as TTCN-3 or the UML 2.0 test profile (U2TP). Therefore in the coming section we will go through the different phases of developing a TTCN-3 based test system and discuss which type of test patterns could be identified and possibly reused to ease or improve that phase of the process.

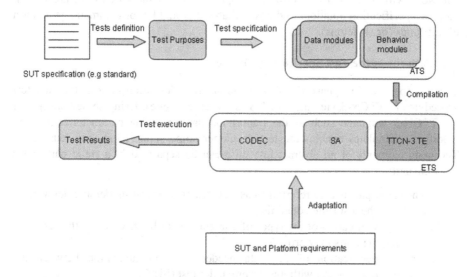

Fig. 2. Above illustrates the process of TTCN-3 based test development, going from a specification of the system under test (SUT) to an executable test suite which can be run to provide the required test results. To obtain a complete executable test suite (ETS), elements related to the SUT and the test platform, such as the encoder/decoder (CODEC) and the system adapter (SA) must be developed and combined to the TTCN-3 test executable (TE) generated automatically from the abstract test suite (ATS) through compilation

2.1 Patterns in the Test Definition Phase

Test definition is the first phase in building a TTCN-3 based test system. It consists of extracting test purposes from the SUT's specification, depending on what the test goals are. Further analysis is required to try to identify possible patterns in this process, for example along certain families of SUTs. Questions are e.g.

- Do generic patterns exist for extracting test purposes from SUT specification?
- Which test purposes are more prone to detect failures in a given SUT domain such as a telecommunication protocol and should therefore always be present in test suites for that domain?
- For SUTs specified in a formal language, could generic patterns for extracting test purposes for such systems be identified and made available for reuse?

With the process of deriving TTCN-3 test cases from test purposes being quite costly and error-prone, the need for formalizing how test purposes are described has arisen. In the Pattern for Test Development (PTD) group setup by the European Telecommunications Standards Institute (ETSI) some patterns have been proposed for that purpose [4]. One long term goal is to enable automatic derivation of test cases from such formalized and machine processable test purposes. One of the purposes of our work will be to analyze, how that approach fits in the current picture of test purpose specification notations and how suitable it would be for automatic generation of test suites (or skeletons).

2.2 Patterns in the Test Specification Phase

The test specification phase deals with the abstract definition of test data and test procedures in TTCN-3 yielding an ATS (abstract test suite). Using some concepts of the TTCN-3 language such as the import mechanism, value parameterization and modifiable templates enables the test developer some support for code reusability. The main elements of an abstract test suite can be separated in a static part and a dynamic part:

- The static part is also referred to as test structure or test model and describes a model of the test suite containing
  - A specification of the types of components to be involved in the test suite and the ports they provide.
  - A specification of the data needed for communication between the components and with the system under test (SUT).
- The dynamic part specifies
  - how test components of the types specified in the static part are created and connected with each other or the SUT to build a test configuration or a test architecture, and
  - the message flow between the elements of the test architecture and the mechanisms for verdict assignment for each test case.

Following the path above, TTCN-3 test patterns can be classified in 4 basic categories depending on their application area:

- Architectural patterns
  Architectural patterns address solutions as to how test systems could be configured to solve or avoid specific recurring problems and to ensure that the fundamental principles mentioned in the introduction to this document are not jeopardized. This also includes patterns for the coordination and synchronization of test components in a test system.
- Behavioural patterns
  Behavioural patterns provide ways for defining the behaviour of elements in a test suite. Behaviour patterns might apply for single elements of that test suite, as well as for the interaction of test components with each other or with a given SUT.

- Data patterns
  Data patterns are test patterns describing reusable concepts and approaches for specifying and generating test data.
- Test reuse patterns
  Test reuse patterns describe strategies for reusing existing TTCN-3 tests
    - for evaluating different aspects of the SUT. E.g. proven approaches for using tests originally defined for conformance or functional testing to test the SUT with regard to load management (scalability) or performance, or
    - along the SUT's product lifecycle, i.e. how to ensure that major modifications on the test suite would not be required as new versions of the SUT are developed.

2.3 Patterns in the Test Adaptation Phase

After completing the abstract specification of the test suite, the test adaptation phase of the test development process starts. In this phase, the ATS is extended with the test runtime interface (TRI) [9] and test communication interfaces (TCI) [10] adaptors to build the fully executable test suite (ETS) which can actually be run to assess the SUT's correctness. Typically, the system adaptor (SA), the platform adaptor (PA) and the codec (CD) are to be modified. Some of the questions which need to be answered in that phase are:

- What are the patterns for encoders/decoders for TTCN-3 test systems?
- What are the patterns to test encoders/decoders on proper functioning?
- What are the Do's and Don'ts to be followed when writing a TTCN-3 system adapter?
- Which well proven techniques and experiences can one rely on in that process?

2.4 Patterns in Test Execution

In the test execution phase, two key aspects are to be considered for possible patterns. Test management patterns cover solutions for ensuring that test suites are executed in a way that their results are relevant for the SUT in that they enable error detection on the system and provide the person executing the tests with means for identifying which parts of the system does not function as required. This includes tracing and logging approaches during test execution, avoiding memory leaks during test execution etc. Test execution automation patterns focus on methods for effectively automating the test execution process, independently of the scale of the test suite.

3 Methodological Aspect of Test Patterns

A methodology for test patterns should not only address the various kinds of test patterns for the different approaches of test reuse, but also define how a test pattern is to be defined, identified, selected and applied. In the following we shortly discuss a test pattern template for the definition of test patterns, aspects of test patterns mining and of the application of test patterns.

3.1 Test Pattern Template

To unify the pattern definition process and to avoid misunderstandings between developers discussing patterns, a template providing a guideline is needed. Taking the test pattern template provided by [7] as basis, we propose a more refined test pattern template adapted to the TTCN-3 testing domain. Further analysis will be made, to assess how appropriate that template would also be for other test approaches based on formal notation.

3.2 Test Pattern Mining

Test pattern mining is the process of abstracting from existing problem-solution-benefit triples in the test developing process, to obtain patterns suitable for reuse in future contexts. Although the process of going through existing test artefacts and trying to identify patterns for later reuse might appear costly and unrewarding at the first sight, we believe in long term it could effectively help in shortening the test development lifecycle and hence reduce costs.

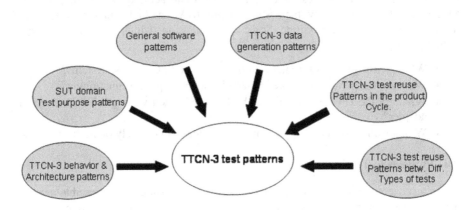

Fig. 3. Elements of Test Patterns can be provided from several activities in and around the Test Developing Process

3.3 Test Pattern Reuse

Reuse of test patterns should basically be independent of the implementation language used for specifying the ATS or for implementing the adaptation to the system and platform environment. However, in a TTCN-3 based test development process the definition of test patterns in TTCN-3 (and extensions thereof) provides several benefits. TTCN-3 test patterns

- Are expressed formally
- Provide means for patterns in the three phase of test system development and for the different approaches of test reuse
- Are defined already in the language of the target test system specification

TTCN-3 provides some concepts for test patterns such as the import mechanism, value parameterization and modifiable templates. Object-based concepts providing further means for the specification and application of test patterns do not exist, but are currently discussed as whether and how they could be included into TTCN-3. Then, better test pattern definitions would be possible. In the meantime we are using specific annotations to TTCN-3 so as to differentiate the generic parts and specific parts of a test pattern. The generic parts are annotated with <> and are to be replaced when applying the test pattern. The specific parts are not annotated. They constitute the essence of that test pattern and should remain untouched when applying that pattern). These annotations are used in the following example.

4 An Example TTCN-3 Test Pattern

To illustrate the ideas presented in the sections above, this section presents an example of a TTCN-3 test pattern. It is a behavioral test pattern for a watch dog on SUT responses.

Name	Timer on transmission
Class	Behaviour
Testing phases	Specification
Testing goals	All
Application domain	Any
Intend	Avoid deadlock situation when transmitting data from test component
Context	For the testing of reactive systems tested typically via interfaces
Parameter	Timer duration
Roles	test component, source port, destination port
Detailed description	After calling a method from a test component or sending a message on a given port, a timer should be started to avoid deadlock in case the SUT does not reply to the function call or to the transmitted message

Example	`function timedSend (template <outMessageType> <outMsg>, <OutPortType> <outPort>, timer <t>, template <inMessageType> <inMsg>, <InPortType> <inPort>) returns verdicttype {`
	`        <outPort>.send (<outMsg>); <t>.start;`
	`alt {`
	`        []<inPort>.receive (<inMsg>) {`
	`        <t>.stop; return pass;}`
	`        []<t>.timeout{return fail;}}}`

Consequences	None
Related patterns	Default pattern
Known uses	Protocol testing

5 Conclusions

This paper discusses that developing reusable tests is similar to developing reusable software components and therefore the same techniques and methods can be applied. Requirements for reusable tests were presented on a general level based on past studies as well as new requirements were identified and illustrated using TTCN-3 language.

In addition to the three dimensions of software reuse (granularity, scope and target) presented in [6], test reuse addresses three approaches for reuse. Additionally to domain analysis traditionally required in software reuse, vertical, horizontal or historical reuse is to be considered. Vertical reuse should be considered when the test reuse is applied on an individual product or software component and the interfaces are likely to remain intact. However, if this product is a part of product family or is likely to be a basis for future updates (interfaces are likely to change), horizontal and historical reuse will provide bigger savings in the long run.

The discussed aspects of test patterns can be used as guidelines when designing and implementing reusable tests. Applying these guidelines into practice demands careful consideration to identify the best possible way to utilize and combine them. However, one should notice that striving for the best reusability by combining as many guidelines as possible, will not always produce the best results in terms of usefulness and functionality. Finding the balance between reusability and usability requires consideration. Nevertheless, one of the major strengths of test reuse is that it provides high quality and maintainable tests that are sometimes hard to come up with otherwise. Therefore, test reusability should be an obvious issue when developing tests.

In the ongoing work we will continue to develop test patterns and to apply/propose language extensions for TTCN-3 in order to enable the specification of test pattern. Tool support for these language extensions is also considered.

References

[1] Ch. Alexander: The Timeless Way of Building, Oxford University Press 1979.
[2] F. Buschmann, R. Meunier, H. Rohnert, P. Sommerlad, M. Stal: Pattern-Oriented Software Architecture, A System of Patterns, Volume 1, Wiley Series in Software Design Patterns, ISBN 0 471 95869 7, 1996-2001.
[3] I. Jacobson, M. Griss, P. Johnsson: Software Reuse - Architecture, Process and Organisation for Business Success. New York, USA: Addison-Wesley, 1997.
[4] ETSI Draft Report: Methods for Testing and Specification (MTS) M. Frey et al,: Pattern for Test Development (PTD), March 2004.
[5] I. Schieferdecker, T. Vassilou-Gioles:. Tool Supported Test Framworks in TTCN-3. Electronic Notes in Theoretical Computer Science 80. 10 p. http://www.elsevier.nl/locate/entcs/volume80.html, 2003
[6] E.-A. Karlsson:. Software Reuse. A Holistic Approach. New York, NY. John Wiley & Sons. 1995.
[7] Robert V. Binder, Testing Object Oriented Systems: Models, Patterns and Tools, Addison Wesley, 1999
[8] ETSI ES 201 873 01, Methods for Testing and Specification (MTS); The Testing and Test Control Notation version 3; Part1: TTCN-3 Core Language; ETSI Standard, Feb. 2003

[9] ETSI ES 201 873 05, Methods for Testing and Specification (MTS); The Testing and Test Control Notation version 3; Part5: TTCN-3 Runtime Interface (TRI); ETSI Standard, Feb. 2003

[10] ETSI ES 201 873 06, Methods for Testing and Specification (MTS); The Testing and Test Control Notation version 3; Part6: TTCN-3 Control Interfaces; ETSI Standard, Feb. 2003

[11] M. Clifton, Advanced Unit Tests; Part V; Unit Test Patterns; An introduction to the Concept of Unit Test Patterns http://www.codeproject.com/gen/design/autp5.asp, March 2004

[12] John Mc. Gregor, A Parallel Architecture for Component Testing of Object Oriented Software; http://www.cs.clemson.edu/%7Ejohnmc/new/pact/qwpaper.html ,

[13] D. Delano, L. Rising, System Test Pattern Language, AG Communication Systems http://www.agcs.com/supportv2/techpapers/patterns/papers/systestp.htm#TestersMoreImportant

High-Level Restructuring of TTCN-3 Test Data

Antal Wu-Hen-Chang[1], Dung Le Viet[1], Gabor Batori[1], Roland Gecse[2], and Gyula Csopaki[1]

[1] Department of Telecommunications and Media Informatics,
Budapest University of Technology and Economics*,
H-1117, Magyar tudósok körútja 2, Budapest, Hungary
Phone: (36) 1-463-2225, Fax: (36) 1-463-3107
[2] Conformance Laboratory, Ericsson Hungary Ltd.,
P.O.B.107, H-1300 Budapest, Hungary
Phone: (36) 1-437 7618, Fax: (36) 1-437 7767
{wuhen, leviet, batori, csopaki}@tmit.bme.hu
Roland.Gecse@ericsson.com

Abstract. TTCN-3 (Testing and Test Control Notation 3) [1, 2, 3] test suites developed for testing complicated systems contain a large number of test data definitions. These definitions are often redundant and lengthy, which leads to compilation and run-time inefficiencies. Our intention is to provide remedy for this problem, by proposing a method that restructures the test data definitions of an already existing TTCN-3 module. In this paper we introduce a model for TTCN-3 test data and a method for its optimization. The results of an empirical study using our approach is presented as well.

1 Introduction

Telecommunication software provides the foundation of the communication infrastructure. These systems must be reliable, efficient and compatible with systems from different vendors. Consequently, their development must be accompanied by quality assurance activities, thus testing plays a vital role during the development process of each telecommunication system. The purpose of testing is to find all errors and shortcomings of the system. This is a very resource-demanding and time-consuming task, because it requires the manual effort of many well-trained developers. Therefore, its support is an important challenge.

TTCN-3 (Testing and Test Control Notation 3) is the new industry-standard test specification language that was developed and standardized by the European Telecommunication Standards Institute (ETSI). It is a very powerful language that has been tried out on different application areas of testing. It can be applied for all kinds of black-box testing for reactive and distributed systems and it is suitable to test virtually any system including telecommunication and mobile systems, Internet and CORBA based protocols. The general testing process with TTCN-3 includes the following main steps: the

---

* This research is supported by Inter-University Centre for Telecommunications and Informatics (ETIK).

J. Grabowski and B. Nielsen (Eds.): FATES 2004, LNCS 3395, pp. 180–194, 2005.
© Springer-Verlag Berlin Heidelberg 2005

developed test suite is compiled and extended with an adaptor that provides the connection between the tested system and the executable test suite. Then, the executable test suite is executed against the system under test. Finally, the results are evaluated.

TTCN-3 has a special language element – the template – that provides sophisticated means for describing test data. In order to test complicated systems, the TTCN-3 templates can be created either in a manual or in an automatic way, but in neither case is the result optimal, since developers cannot cope with the enormous number of huge data structures, and automatic methods focus primarily on the generation problem. According to our empirical experiences test data definition occupies at least 60-70 percent of a complete test specification, and they are highly redundant. Consequently, these modules are unnecessarily large that leads to several problems. In case of very large TTCN-3 modules the compilation time can be surprisingly long, which sets back the development process. It is not uncommon, that the compilation of the test specification takes more than an hour on an average computer, and complicated test suites consist of several different modules. Besides, executable test suites derived from large modules have performance drawbacks, that makes it harder to develop performance or scalability test suites, where performance is a critical issue. Furthermore, we must take into account, that the development process of a test suite is cyclic, therefore these problems appear repeatedly.

By eliminating the redundant and unused data structures, the quality of the generated implementation code can be significantly improved, but the compilers available on the market do not address the problem of test data optimization. In our paper, we introduce a re-engineering method that can be applied without human intervention to test data templates defined in TTCN-3. The approach analyzes and restructures [4, 5] an already existing TTCN-3 template specification, so that it becomes more compact, redundancy-free and the compilation time is reduced. Naturally, the alterations retain semantical correctness, only syntactical changes are introduced. The reason for operating at the formal description level is that we want our method to be compiler independent, but our approach can be utilized to implement an optimizer in a compiler.

The paper is organized as follows. In Section 2 we define the TTCN-3 template model, Section 3 proposes an edit distance function for templates. Section 4 introduces our method and an execution example. In Section 5, we present the results and findings of the empirical analysis of the presented method, and finally we summarize our work in Section 6.

2   TTCN-3 Template Model

The main idea of our approach is to detect similarities among the different test data structures, because the description of the similar structures can be abbreviated by using inheritance, parameterization and references. To be able to compare the data structures, a graph-based model was defined for TTCN-3 templates.

2.1   Template Trees

In TTCN-3, templates are used either to transmit a set of distinct values or to test whether a set of received values matches the template specification.

Formally, a TTCN-3 template can be modeled as a directed, multi-labeled tree $T = (V, E)$, where each node $n \in V$ corresponds to a field in the template and each directed edge $e \in E$ represents an aggregation relationship of two nodes.[1] The parent node of an edge symbolizes a complex data structure that carries a field, which is modeled by the connected child node. The nodes are labeled with several attributes:

- $f(n)$: Name of the field.
- $v(n)$: The field can carry values, ranges and matching attributes, which is modeled by this function. In case of parameterized templates, the function can denote that the node is a *parameter*.
- $t(n)$: The type of the field.
- $s(n)$: The edges can be ordered and unordered. Each node contains complementary information about how its children behave:
  - *record*: Fixed ordering of children is expressed using the record construct.
  - *set*: Arbitrary ordering of children can be expressed with the set construct.
  - *union*: Unions express a choice of alternative types.
  - *simple*: If the node doesn't have any children.
- $o(n)$: denotes whether the field is mandatory or optional.

Type definitions provide the rules that determines the structure of the templates. Therefore, the tree for a template is built according to the template definition and the corresponding type definition. The references to other templates and entities are resolved, so that every leaf node in the tree is entirely specified.

Example 1 (Template Model). In the following simple example we show how the templates are mapped to the tree model:

```
type record ConferenceType {      template DateType today := {
    charstring location,              9, 22
    DateType begin,               };
    DateType end
};                                template ConferenceType conf:=
type record DateType {            { begin := today,
    integer month,                  end := tomorrow,
    integer day                     location := "Linz"
};                                };

template DateType tomorrow modifies today:= {
    day := 23
};
```

Figure 1 depicts the template trees produced from the TTCN-3 code fragment shown above. Every box represents a node with its most important attributes. The field name is in the top left corner, the name of the corresponding type is placed in the middle. In the bottom right corner the value can be found. The references to the "today" and "tomorrow" templates are extracted.

---

[1] In the definitions and function descriptions we let T denote a template tree as well as the root node of a template tree T for simplification purposes.

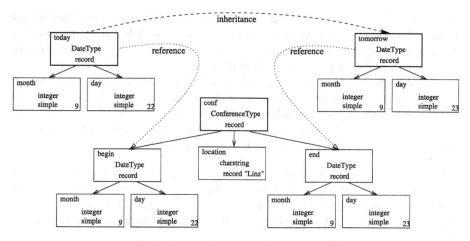

Fig. 1. Example for the template tree model

2.2   Template Relationships

TTCN-3 templates provide the following possibilities to organize and re-use test data:

- already defined structures can be included in a new template via *references*
- Simple form of *inheritance* is present using modified templates
- *Parameterization* of templates is allowed using template and value formal parameters

The template model must be extended to cope with these concepts as well. Since they can be modeled as relationships of two template (sub-)trees, new edge sets were defined for each.

Template References. Templates can contain references to other templates. Although, we showed in our previous example (Fig. 1) that these references are resolved in the template tree, we must be able to track the inclusion relationship of the entities. For this purpose we defined a set of directed edges, where the edges act as a pointer. The originating point is always a tree of a template, while the arrow-head of the edge points to the node, where the tree is included.

An example is shown in Fig. 1, where the "today" and "tomorrow" templates are referenced from "conf". As a graphical notation we use arrows with dotted line.

Modified Templates. Templates provide a simple form of inheritance. This enables the adaptation of templates to different testing situation and avoids the duplication of similar test data. Normally, a template specifies a set of values or matching symbols for each and every field defined in the appropriate definition. New templates can be derived from previously defined templates, rather than having to be defined from scratch. A modified template describes modifications to particular fields of the original template, either directly or indirectly. If a template field and its corresponding value or matching symbol is specified in the modified template, then the specified value or matching symbol replaces the one specified in the parent template. If a template field and its corresponding value or matching symbol is not specified in the modified template, then the value or matching symbol in the parent template shall be used.

Template modification can be resembled with the inheritance concept of object-orientation. Between the root nodes we keep track of the inheritance hierarchy with the help of the directed edge set defined exactly for this purpose. As a notation we use dashed arrows. Figure 1 provides an example of the notation for the "today" and "tomorrow" templates given in the code fragment of the previous example.

Parameterized Templates. Templates for both sending and receiving operations can be parameterized. The formal parameters of a template may include templates, functions and special matching symbols. In our model parameterization is handled by the $v()$ function of the nodes in the template trees. It is set to *parameter*, if the actual field is declared as a parameter.

Inline Templates. Inline (and inline modified) templates are treated as ordinary templates in our approach. The only difference is that, they are created in the dynamic part of the TTCN-3 module and they have no explicit names.

Definition 1 (Template Model). *The template model is a 3-tuple: $M = (S, R, I)$ where S, R and I are the finite set of template trees, directed reference edges and directed inheritance edges respectively.*

3   Edit Distance

Since our algorithm seeks for similar test data structures, a measure is needed that makes it possible to compare two templates to each other, and provides an objective number that describes how strongly they are related. That is why our method is established on a distance definition for TTCN-3 test data.

In order to compute the distance of two templates, first the specific test data structures are mapped to trees, then these trees are compared to each other. The distance is proportional to the difficulty of transforming the trees into each another by using edit operations. The general approach to edit distance problems has been to define a sequence of primitive operations that can be applied to one object to produce another, and to define the distance between two objects as a function computed on a sequence of such operations. Each operation is assigned a cost that represents the difficulty of making that change to the object. When the edit distance is calculated the cost of the operations is considered, and the lowest cost sequence that provides a solution is chosen.

There is considerable related work in the field of edit distance algorithms for trees [6, 7, 8].

3.1   Operators

A necessary precondition for defining an edit distance is to clearly specify its basis, i.e. which edit operations are available and to formally define them. We defined several operators and the corresponding cost functions, so that the distance of two templates is equal to the number of required value assignments in the modified template if one is derived from the other. TTCN-3 offers several ways to produce a derived template from an other, the set of operations must reflect to these possibilities. Each tree operation defined here models modifications permitted in TTCN-3. We provide their mathematical definition, and the corresponding cost function as well.

Definition 2. $\phi(T)$ *is equal to the number of nodes residing in the T tree.*

Definition 3. $\gamma()$ *is the cost function.*

Operator 1 (Node Relabeling). *If two trees differ only in some carried values and both trees have the same structure, then this operator should be used to determine the number of necessary changes. Each time the operator is applied the value of a node can be changed to a new one.*

- $Relabel(T, n, l_{new})$ *is a relabel operator applied to the root node $n \in T$, where T is a template tree. The operation yields T', where $v(n) = l_{new}$.*
- *Cost:* $\gamma(Relabel(T, n, l_{new})) = 1$.

Operator 2 (Choice). *This operator chooses a different alternative union branch from the one that already exists. This involves deleting the old sub-tree, and creating a new one according to the type definition.*

- $Choice(T, n, T_{new})$ *is a choice operator applied to the node $n \in T$, $s(n) =$ union, where T is a template tree. The operation yields T', where T_{new} is the new sub-tree connected to n.*
- *Cost:* $\gamma(Choice(T, n, T_{new})) = \phi(T_{new})$.

Operator 3 (Sub-tree Insertion). *This operator inserts a new sub-tree (or a single node) to a node. For example a new sub-tree element can be introduced at an optional node that was omitted earlier, or at nodes that model "set of" and "record of" TTCN-3 constructs.*

- $Addtree(T, n, T_{new})$ *is the tree insertion operator applied to the node $n \in T$. The operator yields T', where T_{new} is a new sub-tree inserted as a child of n.*
- *Cost:* $\gamma(Addtree(T, n, T_{new})) = \phi(T_{new})$.

Operator 4 (Sub-tree Deletion). *At optional elements a whole sub-structure can be omitted from the actual template.*

- $Deltree(T, n)$ *is the tree deletion operator applied to the node $n \in T$. The operator yields T', without the node n and its sub-tree.*
- $\gamma(Deltree(T, n)) = 1$.

type definitions	original specification	original tree	operator	target tree	modified specification

type union number {
  integer whole,
  complex comp
};
	template number first :={
	  whole := 1
	};
		number
		○
		whole
		(1)
			Relabel
			⟶
			cost=1
				number
				○
				whole
				(2)
					template number second
					  modifies first := {
					  whole :=2
					};

type record complex {
  integer real,
  integer imag
};
 	
type record pair {
  integer num,
  complex comp optional
};
	template number first :={
	  whole := 1
	};
		number
		○
		whole
		(1)
			Choice
			⟶
			cost=3
				number
				○
				comp
				(1) (2)
					template number second
					  modifies first := {
					  comp :={ real:=1, imag:=2}
					};

	template pair first :={
	  num:=1, comp:=omit
	};
		pair
		num comp
		(1) (omit)
			Sub–tree insertion
			⟶
			cost=3
				pair
				num comp
				(1) (1) (2)
					template pair second
					  modifies first :={
					  comp := { real:=1, imag:=2 }
					};

	template pair first := {
	  num:=1,
	  comp := { real:=1, imag:=2 }
	};
		pair
		num comp
		(1) (2)
			Sub–tree deletion
			⟶
			cost=1
				pair
				num comp
				(1) (omit)
					template pair second
					  modifies first := {
					  comp:=omit
					};

Fig. 2. Example for the application of the edit operators

Example 2 (Applying operators). Figure 2 demonstrates some examples of the application of the operators. The first column contains the necessary type definitions for the sample templates. Each line of the remaining columns is dedicated to one of the four operators. Next to the original specifications the corresponding trees are shown. The trees of the target templates are hold in the target tree column. The operator column describes the required operator and the cost of the transformation that converts the original to the target tree. The modified specification that produces the target template from the original is given in the last column.

3.2   Computing Edit Distance

Our proposed algorithm for determining the minimum edit distance of two template trees is recursive. The first invocation of the algorithm is given the root nodes of two trees, the original and the target trees; it then invokes the algorithm on each child of the first root paired with each child of the other root.

   The method can be divided to three main if-else branches. The first examines, whether the types of the two nodes are equal. If it is not the case, it is no worth continuing the comparison because there is no valid operator sequence that transforms a template to a template of another type. The second branch is for the leaf nodes, where the degree[2] of the node is zero. Here, the two label functions for the values are compared. If a change is detected, the function returns with the cost of the relabel operator, or with zero if the values are equal. The third branch is for nodes that can be regarded as roots of subtrees. First of all, the optionality of the nodes is checked. Whether a part of the data structure is omitted in the template, the *Addtree, Deltree* operator pair should be applied. Otherwise, the distance of two nodes is calculated by invoking the *EditDistance* function for their children. The *CorrespondingNode* function is used to locate the corresponding

---

[2] The degree of a node is equal to the number of its child nodes.

children for the ith child node of n_A among the child nodes of n_B. We could not avoid this function, because sometimes the edges are not ordered. The corresponding nodes, where the field function and the type function are equal, always must be present. There is one exception however: the union construct expresses a choice of alternative types. To address this problem we added the lines where the *Choice* operator is applied when two union nodes can be found.

Function 1 (Pseudo-code for computing edit distance).

```
EditDistance(n_A, n_B)
   //Branch for type checking:
   if t(n_A) ≠ t(n_B)
      return ∞
   //Branch for leaf nodes:
   if Degree(n_A)=Degree(n_B)=0
      if v(n_A) ≠ v(n_B)
         return γ(Relabel(n_A, v(n_B)))
      else
         return 0;
   //Branch for sub-tree nodes:
   else
      if n_A and n_B are optional
         if n_B is omitted
            return γ(Deltree(T_{n_A}, n_A))
         if n_A is omitted
            return γ(Addtree(T_{n_A}, n_A, n_B))
      distance ⇐ 0;
      for i ⇐ 1 to Degree(n_A)
         if ∃CorrespondingNode(n_A[i])
            distance ⇐ distance +
               EditDistance(n_A[i], CorrespondingNode(n_A[i]))
         else
            if n_A and n_B are unions
               return γ(Choice(T_{n_A}, n_A, n_B)
         else
            return ∞
      return distance;
```

4   Proposed Method

We have defined a method that alters the template description part of an already existing TTCN-3 module, so that it becomes more compact and redundancy-free.

4.1   The Scenario

Figure 3 shows the scheme of our method. The input is an already existing TTCN-3 module, which is processed by the Filter component. This component extracts the test data

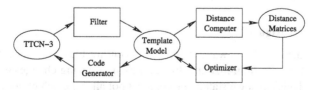

Fig. 3. The scenario of the method

definitions and projects them to trees, thus the Template Model is produced. This projection converts the wildcards of receive templates and the range definitions to character strings. Henceforth, they appear as simple string values. Next, the distance computer compares each tree to the others, and the acquired distances are stored in matrices. The optimizer introduces compressing alterations to the tree model: based on the distance matrices new inheritance hierarchies are created and the data patterns that appear in a repeated fashion are extracted and referenced. Finally, the TTCN-3 description of the tree models is generated according to the implemented mappings and is woven back into the original test suite.

4.2   Estimation of the Specification's Size

The method utilizes a measurement that estimates the size of the resulting template description. The basis of this measurement is the number of field assignments residing in a TTCN-3 template specification. This can be computed using the template model, because an unambiguous projection can be defined between the model and the corresponding TTCN-3 template specification.

Definition 4 (Size function for the template model). *The size of the template model M is the summary of the sizes of the contained template trees:* $F_{\text{size}}(M) = \sum_{\forall T_i} \text{size}(T_i)$.

Function 2 (Pseudo-code for calculating $F_{\text{size}}()$).

```
Size(T)
   if T is derived from Tbase
      MarkCommonNodes(T,Tbase)
   for all Tref, where Tref is referenced from nx ∈ T
      MarkCommonNodes(nx,Tref)
   return the number of not marked nodes in T

MarkCommonNodes(nA, nB)
   if v(nA) = v(nB)
      Mark nA
      for i ⇐ 1 to Degree(nA)
         if ∃CorrespondingNode(nA[i])
            MarkCommonNodes(nA[i],CorrespondingNode(nA[i]))
```

By default, the size of the template is equal to the number of nodes in the template tree. If the template inherits some fields from an other, that is, there is an edge in the set of modify edges I, whose target hyper-node is the actual template tree T, then it is clear that we do not need to count the inherited nodes, therefore we mark them by the help of the *MarkCommonNodes* function. If some parts of the template tree are referenced, the cost must be decreased by the size of the referenced part, again by marking the referenced parts. Finally, the required number of assignments can be calculated by summarizing the nodes that were not marked.

4.3   Optimizer Algorithms

After the cost function $F_{\text{size}}()$ was defined, we can outline the algorithm of the optimizer component that tries to minimize this function by introducing changes to the template model. These changes, as we stated before, must not alter the behavior of the TTCN-3 module. The algorithm can be summarized in the following steps:

Algorithm 1. *Optimizer Algorithm*

1. *A template model M and the distance matrices are the input of the algorithm.*
2. *Based on the distances:*
   (a) *A new inheritance hierarchy is generated for the model. (Algorithm 2)*
   (b) *The model is made more compact by using references for the repeated data structures. (Algorithm 3)*

The generation of a new inheritance hierarchy and the introduction of references are described in the following algorithms:

Algorithm 2 (Inheritance hierarchy). *This algorithm determines the minimal cost inheritance structure of the template model.*

```
00  Input: Template model M = (S, R, I)
01  The template trees Tᵢ are grouped by the type function
    of the root node t(Tᵢ) into distinct sets Sₖ ∈ S.
02  for all Sₖ
03    for all (i, j)
04      Dₖ(i, j) ⇐ EditDistance(Tᵢ ∈ Sₖ, Tⱼ ∈ Sₖ)
05  for all Dₖ
06    A weighted and directed edge set Eᵃ is created
      from the distances of the Dₖ matrix³.
07    i ⇐ 1; E₀ˢ ⇐ {}; k_cost ⇐ F_size(M(Sₖ, R, E₀ˢ))
08    Select an edge eᵢ ∈ Eᵃ of minimum value not in E_{i-1}ˢ
      such that Gᵢ ⇐<Sₖ, E_{i-1}ˢ ∪{eᵢ}> is acyclic.
09    if eᵢ exists
10      Eᵢˢ ⇐ E_{i-1}ˢ ∪{eᵢ}
11      Eᵃ ⇐ Eᵃ \ eᵢ
12    else goto 20.
13    if F_size(M(Sₖ, R, Eᵢˢ)) < k_cost
14      k_cost ⇐ F_size(M)
15      Every edge, whose target node is equal to the
        target node of eᵢ is dropped from Eᵃ.
        /* Because it is no worth producing the same       *
         * template again from another. For similar reasons: */
16      Delete the reverse pair of the edge e.
17    else
18      Eᵢˢ ⇐ E_{i-1}ˢ
19    i ⇐ i + 1; goto 8.
20  I ⇐ I ∪ E_{i-1}ˢ
```

The input of the algorithm is a template model $M = (S, R, I)$. The template trees of the model are organized in distinct S_k sets according to their type function. In steps 2-4, with the help of Func. 2, that computes the edit distance between two templates, a distance matrix D_k is produced for each set: every template tree is compared to one another and the acquired distances are stored in a matrix. In step 5, a new inheritance hierarchy is created for each S_k. The template trees are regarded as hyper-nodes and a weighted edge set is created based on the corresponding D_k distance matrix (step 6). With the help of the Kruskal algorithm [9], we produce a minimum spanning tree that will substitute the old set of inheritance edges (steps 7-19). In each iteration a new edge is selected from the edge set and the new value of the cost function $F_{size}(M)$ is compared to the old. The selected edge is put into the I set only if the new size of the model is smaller than the old one.

---

[3] The indices in E^a and E^s stand for "available" and "selected", respectively.

Algorithm 3 (Reference Introduction). *This algorithm seeks for data structure frag-ments that occur in the template model in a repeated fashion.*

```
00  Input: Template model M = (S, R, I)
01  for all Ti ∈ S
02     All possible sub-tree T_{i,j}^{sub} ∈ Ti is produced.
03     The sub-trees are grouped into distinct sets S_l^{sub}
          by the type of their root node.
04     The sets are ordered according to the level of the
          contained sub-trees.
          /* The level of a sub-tree is equal to the number of edges that *
           * must be traversed in order to get from the root node of the  *
           * original tree to the root node of the extracted sub-tree     */
05  kcost ⇐ Fsize(M)
06  for all S_l^{sub}
07     Compute the distance matrix D_l^{sub}.
08     A weighted and directed edge set E^a is created
          from the distances of the D_l^{sub} matrix.
09     According to the Kruskal algorithm, select an
          edge < Ti, Tj >∈ E^a of minimal value.
10     if < Ti, Tj > exits
11        S ⇐ S ∪ {Ti, Tj}
12        I ⇐ I ∪ < Ti, Tj >
13        e_{ref1} ⇐< Ti, Parent(Ti) >
14        e_{ref2} ⇐< Tj, Parent(Tj) >
15        R ⇐ R ∪ {e_{ref1}, e_{ref2}}
16     else stop
17     if Fsize(M(S, R, I)) < kcost
18        kcost ⇐ Fsize(M(S, R, I))
19     else
20        S ⇐ S \ {Ti, Tj}
21        I ⇐ I \ < Ti, Tj >
22        R ⇐ R \ {e_{ref1}, e_{ref2}}
23     goto 9.
```

The input of Alg. 3 is the template model. In the first step, all possible sub-tree $T_{i,j}^{sub} \in T_i$ is produced from the template trees of the model, where $T_i \in S$, $\forall i$. The j index runs from zero to the number of the nodes in tree T_i, whose degree is larger than zero. Then, in step 3, the sub-trees are organized into distinct sets S_k^{sub} by the type of their root nodes, and the sets are ordered according to the level of the contained sub-trees. Thus, a set consisting of first level sub-trees will lead the list of the sets. The rationale of this ordering is that, it is more profitable to extract and to reference a few large structures than many smaller ones. The sub-trees, whose original trees are described as a modified template according to the model are dropped from the sets, because extracting parts of those trees is not prosperous.

The remaining part of the procedure (from step 6) is based on the Kruskal algorithm. First, a directed and weighted edge set is created from the distances and the edges of a minimum spanning tree are selected one by one (step 9). After the next edge e of the spanning tree is determined, we put the two nodes of the edge into the set of template trees of the model (step 10). Then the edge is inserted into the inheritance edge set $I \in M$. Furthermore, two reference edges are created in the reference edge set $R \in M$ between the nodes of e and their parent trees, where they are referenced from. Next, in step 17, the size of the model is checked using the $F_{size}(M)$ function. If it is less than it was, the alterations made to the model M are valid. Otherwise, we undo the previous changes to the model.

It is important to note that we do not deal with generating parameterized templates. Although their introduction would not reduce the required number of assignments in the template description, the total number of templates could be reduced remarkably. Therefore, the application of parameterized templates is inevitable and in our future work we intend to extend our procedure.

Besides, we have to mention, that deep inheritance hierarchies spoil readability because of multiple inheritances. This side effect can be avoided if the depth of the inheritance hierarchies generated by Alg. 2 is limited.

4.4   Execution Example

On behalf of promoting deeper understanding about how the method works, we include a simple execution example in this section.

We have three template messages, two connection requests, and a data indication:

```
type union PDU {                 template PDU connect1 := {
    ConnectReq conreq,               conreq := {
    DataInd datind                       addr := {
};                                           subsystem := 1,
                                             pointcode := 2 },
type record ConnectReq {             connectid := 0 }
    Address addr,                };
    integer connectid            template PDU connect2 := {
};                                   conreq := {
                                         addr := {
type record DataInd {                    subsystem := 1,
    Address addr,                        pointcode := 3 },
    charstring data                  connectid := 0 }
};                               };
                                 template PDU data := {
type record Address {                datind := {
    integer subsystem,               addr := {
    integer pointcode                    subsystem := 1,
};                                       pointcode := 2 },
                                     data := "Hello" }
                                 };
```

The template trees generated from the TTCN-3 template specification part can be seen in Fig. 4. These trees constitute the first and only template tree set $S_1 = \{connect1, connect2, data\}$. The inheritance and reference sets are initially empty: $I = \{\}, R = \{\}$. The distance matrix D_1 is generated for the set and the initial size of the template model is computed: $F_{size}(M) = 6 + 6 + 6 = 18$.

The next step produces a new inheritance hierarchy. The Kruskal algorithm is applied to generate the minimum spanning tree for the hyper-nodes, the steps are depicted in Fig. 5.

The smallest element in the distance matrix is one, and the first occurrence of this value is located at $D_1(0, 1)$. Therefore, the first step of the Kruskal algorithm selects the edge <connect1, connect2> with weight one. This edge is than inserted into the inheritance set I, thus, the connect2 template is derived from the connect1 base template. According to the altered model the new cost is calculated: $F_{size}(M) = 14$.

Before the second step, the reverse of the previously chosen edge ($D_1(1, 0)$) and the edges that would produce an other derived template of connect2: ($D_1(0..2, 1)$) are dropped from the available edge set. Naturally, the already chosen $D_1(0, 1)$ element cannot be selected again. This leads the algorithm to select the edge <connect1, data>,

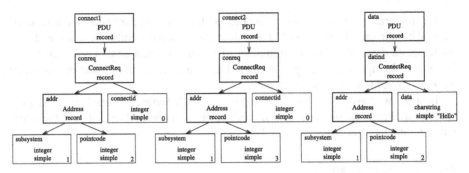

Fig. 4. Template trees

which is put into the set I. The size of the new model will be $F_{\text{size}}(M) = 14$, which is not smaller than the value we got from the previous step, therefore this iteration is canceled, and the Kruskal algorithm stops.

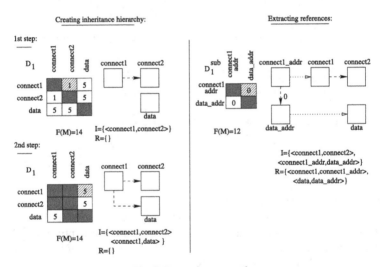

Fig. 5. Execution example

The next task of the method is to extract data structures that appear repeatedly in the template model. For this purpose every possible sub-tree is produced from the template trees of the S_1 set except the tree of *connect2*, because it is a modified template. The resulting trees are grouped together by the type of their root node, consequently the following sets are created: $S_1^{\text{sub}} = \{T_{\text{conreq part of connect1}}\}$, $S_2^{\text{sub}} = \{T_{\text{datind part of data}}\}$, $S_3^{\text{sub}} = \{T_{\text{addr of connect1}}, T_{\text{addr of data}}\}$. Since in $S_1^{\text{sub}}, S_2^{\text{sub}}$ there is only one element, they are not taken into consideration. For S_3^{sub} the distance matrix D_3^{sub} is computed as it is shown in Fig. 5.

With the help of the Kruskal algorithm the edge <*connect1_addr,data_addr*> is selected and put into the inheritance edge set I. It is worth mentioning, that the two nodes can be contracted because the distance between them is zero, that is, the two sub-trees are exactly the same. Additionally, the two extracted nodes are referenced from their parents, therefore the edges <*connect1, connect1_addr*> and <*data, data_addr*> are inserted into the set of reference edges R. The final size of the model is $F_{size}(M) = 12$.

According to the template model, the following TTCN-3 template definitions can be generated:

```
template PDU connect1 := {        template Address connect1_addr:={
  conreq:= {                        subsystem :=1,
    addr:= connect1_addr,           pointcode:=2
    connectid:=0                  };
  }
};                                template PDU data := {
template PDU connect2                datind:= {
  modifies connect1 := {              addr:= connect1_addr,
    conreq:={                         data:="Hello"
      addr:={pointcode:=3}          }
    }                             };
};
```

5 Empirical Experiences

To implement our method we developed a software system [10, 11] that performs a high level restructuring that operates on the formal description of a TTCN-3 test suite. We used a sample TTCN-3 test module to investigate the presented method. The test module contained templates for RANAP [12] messages. RANAP is a core building block at the heart of every 3G network that provides all the necessary signaling control for network access and channels communications between mobile terminal entities (handsets, PDAs etc) and the 3G network.

Table 1. Data from the case study

	Template#	Assignments#	Generated C++ Code	Compile Time	Object Code Size
Original	37	160	59Kbyte	7155ms	403Kbyte
Restructured	26	85	33Kbyte	3902ms	219Kbyte

The original template description consisted of 26 simple, 11 parameterized templates and a supporting function. In aggregate the description embodied 160 assignments. To generate the template model we extracted the sent and received top level messages according to the dynamic description of the TTCN-3 module. This way we acquired 12 large template definitions with 138 assignments. The algorithm was able to reduce the number of the assignments to 85, which is only 53% of the extracted data. As the data shows (Table 1) the size of the generated C++ code, the compile time, and the object code size changed according to the assignment ratio[4]. Only a small fluctuation could be noticed.

---

[4] The experiment was done on a PC equipped with Intel PIII-450 processor and 256M of RAM.

6   Conclusion

Testing is a vital part of the software development process and TTCN-3 is a powerful and wide-spread formal language for describing complex test scenarios. In the practice the test data definition part of the TTCN-3 modules are usually redundant, which leads to compile-time and run-time inefficiencies. In this paper we presented a method and a tool focusing on the problem of TTCN-3 template restructuring. By means of the proposed method, it is possible to compress TTCN-3 template descriptions, which has a beneficial influence on the executable test suite.

We elaborated an edit distance and introduced a model for describing TTCN-3 templates. For the edit distance problem we used a special set of operators considering the specialties of the TTCN-3 language. An algorithm was defined for making the template specifications more compact. Based on the method a tool was developed, and was used for a simple case study.

Our future work includes case studies on real world test suites and the extension of the approach, so it will be able to generate parameterized templates.

References

1. ISO 9646-3: Information Technology - Conformance Testing Methodology and Framework; Part 3: The Tree and Tabular Combined Notation (TTCN).
2. ETSI ES 201 873-1 V2.2.1 (2002-08): Methods for Testing and Specification (MTS); The Testing and Test Control Notation Version 3; Part1: TTCN-3 Core Language.
3. J. Grabowski, D. Hogrefe, Gy. Rethy, I. Schieferdecker, A. Wiles, C. Willcock: An introduction to the testing and test control notation (TTCN-3) Comput. Networks Vol. 42(3):375-403, 2003.
4. E.J. Chikofsky, J.H. Cross: Reverse Engineering and Design Recovery: A Taxonomy. IEEE Software, Vol 7(1):13-17, 1990.
5. T. Mens, T. Tourwe: Survey of Software Refactoring. IEEE Trans. on Software Engineering, Vol. 30(2):126-139, 2004.
6. R.A. Wagner, M.J.Fisher: The String-to-string Correction Problem. Journal of the ACM, Vol. 21:168-173, 1974.
7. D. Barnard, G. Clarke, N. Duncan: Tree-to-tree Correction for Document Trees. Technical Report 95-375, Queen's University, January 1995.
8. A. Nierman, H. V. Jagadish: Evaluating Structural Similarity in XML Documents. Proc. of the Fifth International Workshop on the Web and Databases. WebDB '02, Madison, Wisconsin, USA, 2002.
9. T. Cormen, C. Leiserson, R. Rivest: Introduction to Algorithms. The MIT Press, 2001.
10. A. Wu-Hen-Chang, D. Le Viet, R. Gecse and Gy. Csopaki: Representing and Processing Formally Defined Data Structures. Proc. of Eunice '03, 2003.
11. R. Gecse, S. Dibuz: An Intuitive TTCN-3 Data Presentation Format. Testcom, 2003.
12. 3GPP TS 25.413 V6.1.0: UTRAN Iu interface Radio Access Network Application Part (RANAP). 2004.

Ordering Mutants to Minimise Test Effort in Mutation Testing

Kalpesh Kapoor[1,*] and Jonathan P. Bowen[2]

[1] Dhirubhai Ambani Institute of Information and Communication Technology,
Near Indroda Circle, Gandhinagar (Gujarat) 382 007, India
kalpesh_kapoor@da-iict.org
[2] Centre for Applied Formal Methods,
London South Bank University,
103 Borough Road, London. SE1 0AA. UK
bowenjp@lsbu.ac.uk

Abstract. Mutation testing is a fault-based testing approach based on the competent programmer, and coupling effect hypotheses. One of the main difficulties faced in practice is due to the large number of mutants that can be generated for a given implementation. Earlier research to solve this problem has suggested variants of mutation testing, and finding an effective set of mutation operators. This paper presents an alternative approach for reducing the cost of testing by the identification of hierarchies among first-order mutants. The theory described here is also applicable to the quantitative assessment of testing effort and can be used to guide successive testing steps in fault-based testing.

1 Introduction

Fault-based testing [12] is a sound methodology to assess the quality of a test set. It helps in evaluating their ability to reveal hypothesised faults that can occur in an implementation. A fault in a program is a defect that can result in an observable failure on execution of the program. Unlike other testing approaches that attempt to only discover faults by test runs, fault-based testing also aims to show the absence of faults on successful execution of the program.

Mutation testing [1,3] is a powerful fault-based unit and component testing technique based on the competent programmer hypothesis. For a given program, P, to be tested, mutation testing requires the consideration of all possible 'nearby' programs that differ from P in a well-specified way. The nearby pro-

* Work undertaken while at London South Bank University. This research has benefited from participation in and discussions with colleagues on the UK EPSRC FORTEST Network on Formal Methods and Testing (URL: http://www.fortest.org.uk). Financial support for travel is gratefully acknowledged (EPSRC Grant no. GR/R43150/01). The authors also wish to express thanks to Dr. Martin Woodward for sending hard copies of papers [17,26,5,24].

J. Grabowski and B. Nielsen (Eds.): FATES 2004, LNCS 3395, pp. 195–209, 2005.

grams, called *first-order mutants*, are generated from the implemented program by applying *mutation operators* that cause a single syntactic change in P.

Given a test set, its effectiveness is measured by computing the ratio of first-order mutants that it can identify to be different from P and the total number of mutants. A mutant is said to be *killed* by a test set if it can distinguish the mutant to be different from the implemented program. Since some of the mutants could be functionally equivalent to P, they have to be identified manually or by other methods [13] and their number is reduced from the total number of mutants before computing the effectiveness.

The second hypothesis that is assumed to hold in mutation testing is the *coupling effect* [3], according to which the higher order mutants (i.e., programs) that can be obtained by applying more than one application of mutation operators, need not be considered. This is because it is expected that if a test set can kill all (non-equivalent) first-order mutants, it is also likely to kill the higher order mutants.

A test set, T, is said to be mutation-adequate if for each first-order mutant, P', that is not functionally equivalent to the program under test, P, there is at least one test case in T for which execution of P and P' results in different behaviour. Then if P is correct on a test set T having this property, it is concluded that P is correct with respect to faults represented by the mutation operators. Thus a mutation-adequate test set is good at distinguishing a program from its mutants and, if the program is faulty, the test set is also likely to be good at distinguishing the program from a correct program [7].

Thus, mutation testing provides a practical and effective means of evaluating a test criteria and test sets. However, with the increase in size of implementation, it is computationally expensive or infeasible to consider all possible mutants that can be hypothesised [26, 24, 11, 14, 15].

The number of possible mutants is proportional to the product of the number of data references and the number of data objects [23, 14]. Offutt and Pan [13] have given statistics such as the number of statements and mutants for various programs; the statistics include a program 'Cal' with 29 statements for which 3,010 mutants were considered. A consequence of the generation of a large number of possible mutant programs is that they need to be executed in each step of the testing phase till an adequate test set is obtained.

To overcome this problem, a number of approaches have been suggested, such as finding an effective set of mutation operators [14] and variants of mutation testing [8, 11, 25]. A short survey is presented in [15]. The original idea, as described above, is referred to as *strong mutation testing*.

This paper presents an alternative method to improve mutation testing by identifying fault and mutant hierarchies in order to reduce the test effort. For example, let P be an implemented program, and P' and P'' be two first-order mutants of P. It is possible to reduce test effort by considering only P' if it can be deduced that any test set which can distinguish P from P' is also be guaranteed to distinguish P to be different from P''.

1.1   Related Work

A similar approach, but complementary to that presented in this paper, has been suggested in [26, 17, 5], involving the determination of an optimal ordering for the relational operators. The key idea can be stated as follows. Let P be a given program and P' and P'' be two mutants that are obtained by replacing a relational operator, say RO, in P by other relational operators, RO_1 and RO_2 respectively, where RO_1 is higher in the optimal ordering relation than RO_2 [26]. Then, for a given input, if P' remains live then P'' will also remain live. Thus, when attempting to kill mutants, P' should be tried before P''. However, Woodward in [24] has shown a fallacy in the above argument by providing a counter example.

The rest of the paper is organised as follows. The next section presents the theoretical foundation for the work. Section 3 discusses the properties and conditions for ordering mutants. The implementation aspects and applicability of existing infrastructure is presented in section 4. Finally, conclusions are presented in section 5.

2   Theoretical Underpinning

Let P be an implemented program that represents a function, $p : D \twoheadrightarrow R$, where '$p$' is the semantic (possibly partial) function represented by the program P. The domain and range (D and R, respectively) could be finite or infinite sets.

A state is a function from a set of variables to their (assignable) values. Two states are equal if they represent the same function. A state may also associate an (abstract) failure attribute, represented by $\perp$, to one or more variables. Consider for example, an assignment statement, $x := y + z$. If the addition of the current values of variables y and z results in an overflow then an (incorrect) value will be assigned to the variable x and a $\perp$ attribute will be associated with x.

Any operation that involves variables with the $\perp$ attribute might not propagate $\perp$ and may also result in correct output at the termination of program execution. This is because internal failures may get masked during successive steps of the execution [12]. Note that the $\perp$ attribute is also considered while checking the equality of two states. A program is said to fail externally if the final state includes one or more variables with the $\perp$ attribute.

A *test case* is an input state. For convenience, a test case will be considered as an element of the input domain of a given program. Therefore, the notation $t \in D$, where D is some input domain, would actually mean that the test case is obtained by assigning values to variables by choosing an element from D. A *test set* is a set of test cases.

Let P be a program that is being tested. A mutation operator can be defined to be a rule for generating mutants by making a single syntactic change in P for example, changing operator '+' to '−' (see [9] for a list of mutation operators). A mutant that can be obtained by a single application of mutation operator on P is referred to as first-order mutant. Unless otherwise stated, first-order mutants will be simply referred to as mutants in the rest of the paper.

Definition 1 (Distinguishing Test Case). *A test case, t, is said to distinguish[1] a program P from its mutant P' if $P(t) \neq P'(t)$, where $P(t)$ and $P'(t)$ are final states obtained on executing P and P', respectively, with input t.*

Thus, a distinguishing test case identifies that the program and its mutant represent two distinct functions. It may happen that one of the programs fails while the other does not, in which case they are obviously distinguishable (as per the definition of state equality given earlier). The problem of automatic computation of a distinguishing test case is undecidable, in general, for an arbitrary pair of programs. However, in practice it is often possible to find such test cases using approximation techniques.

In strong mutation testing, the programs are distinguished by considering the final states, whereas other variants, weak [8] and firm [25] mutation testing, allow to distinguish two programs by observing their internal states. The analysis stated in this paper also holds if Definition 1 is modified to allow the distinction of programs on the basis of internal states as in weak or firm mutation testing. However, there are limitations of such an approach (see Theorem 1 for an explanation).

A partial order between mutant programs can be defined using the following relation.

Definition 2 (Relation Between Mutants). *Let P' and P'' be two mutants of P then P' is said to be stronger than P'' denoted by $P \vdash P' \geq_m P''$ if*

$$\forall t \in D \cdot t \; distinguishes \; P, P' \Rightarrow t \; distinguishes \; P, P''$$

where t is a test case and D is the input domain of P.

The above relationships can also be stated in terms of test sets i.e. for all test sets the above property must hold. The $\geq_m$ relationship among mutants can be used to minimise the test effort by identifying strong mutants in a set of possible mutant programs.

Again in common with a number of program analysis problems, identifying every possible $\geq_m$ relation is undecidable in general. Nevertheless, in the restricted setup of mutation testing it may be possible to find the relationship between some, if not all, mutant programs. The consequence of any technique being inherently incomplete is that it may not always be able to deduce the $\geq_m$ relation between two given mutants. However, this is not harmful except that both mutants need to be considered during testing.

The notation $\not\geq_m$ will be used to indicate that either $\geq_m$ relationship is not known or it does not exist between a given pair of programs. For a pair of mutants, P' and P'', of P if both $P \vdash P' \not\geq_m P''$ and $P \vdash P'' \not\geq_m P'$ hold then both P' and P'' must be considered during mutation testing. The notation $P = P'$ will be used to signify that P is semantically equivalent to P'.

The programs under consideration in this paper are assumed to be written in a typical imperative programming language whose semantics is available and

---

[1] This is the same as *killing* a mutant.

which provides constructs such as branch and loop. A countable set of variables, numerals and labels is assumed. The labels (also referred to as locations) are used to *uniquely* identify the program segments in order to facilitate the analysis. Figure 1 shows the abstract syntax of the programming language and the rules for labelling the statements. The entities with superscripts L are given a unique label.

$$
\begin{array}{lll}
stmt & ::= [\ var := expr\ ]^L \\
& |\ \ \textbf{if}\ [\ bool\ ]^L\ \ \textbf{then}\ stmt\ \textbf{else}\ stmt\ \textbf{end} \\
& |\ \ \textbf{while}\ [\ bool\ ]^L\ \ \textbf{do}\ \ stmt\ \textbf{end} \\
& |\ \ stmt\ ;\ stmt\ \ |\ \ [\text{skip}]^L \\
bool & ::= \textbf{true}\ |\ \textbf{false}\ |\ bool\ logicOperator\ bool \\
& |\ \ \neg\ bool\ \ |\ \ relationalExpression\ \ |\ \ (\ bool\ )
\end{array}
$$

Fig. 1. Partial abstract syntax for the programming language

The Boolean conditions (i.e., *bool*) are used solely for deciding the branch to be followed in the next step of the execution and therefore are assumed not to modify the state of the program. A label when given to a Boolean condition is said to be a *p-location*, otherwise it is said to be a *c-location*. Note that a condition in an **if** or **while** statement is given a unique label (i.e., different from the labels that are given to statements that appear inside the **then-else** or body of a **while** statement, respectively).

An operational view of a program execution will give a sequence of states, called a trace, representing the execution sequence of the program's statements. Since some statements (e.g. **skip**) may not change the state, the trace may have repeating consecutive entries. A trace is generated as follows: the start state is the input state and is given the index 0; for every labelled statement that the execution passes through, the state after that label is added to the trace. The final state corresponds to the end of program execution.

Let $\downarrow$ be an infix operator that gives the ith element of a given trace. Let *Labs* be a function that takes a statement, S, (i.e., *stmt* above) and returns the set of labels that appear in S. Further, let $\mathcal{L}$ be a function that takes a trace, tr, of length n and an integer i ($1 \leq i \leq n$), and returns the label of the statement that resulted in the state $tr \downarrow i$; formally: $\mathcal{L} : Trace \times Integer \rightarrow Label$.

To analyse a given program, we will also use the concept of symbolic execution which has been used in a wide variety of problems, such as, test data generation [4] and detecting equivalent mutants [13]. In symbolic execution, a program is executed with the symbolic values representing arbitrary values, instead of actual input values. Such an execution results in a tree in which every node consists of symbolic values of the variables and the path constraint that must be true to reach that node.

3   Ordering Mutants

Let P be an implemented program and P' be a first order mutant that differs from P at location l. A test case, t, can distinguish P from P' provided the following necessary and sufficient conditions hold on executing P and P' with starting state t [11, 21, 16, 13]:

a. the execution must reach location l (*reachability*);
b. the evaluation of expressions at location l in P and P' must result in different values at least once (*infection*);
c. the final states on termination of execution of P and P' must be different (*propagation*).

Condition (b) (i.e., infection) has been referred to as *necessity* in [13], and the *original state failure condition* in [16] consisting of an *origination condition* and *computational transfer conditions*. The above conditions (a) and (b) can be stated formally as follows.

Proposition 1. *Let P' be a mutant of a program P which is obtained by applying mutation operator at location l. Further, let tr and tr' be the traces that are obtained by executing P and P' with a test case t, respectively. Then the following properties holds:*

a. *The reachability condition holds iff*
$$\exists i \; \mathcal{L}(tr, i) = \mathcal{L}(tr', i) = l;$$
b. *If l is a c-location then the infection condition holds iff*
$$\exists i \cdot (\mathcal{L}(tr, i) = l \wedge \mathcal{L}(tr', i) = l \wedge tr \downarrow i \neq tr' \downarrow i$$
$$\wedge \, (\forall j \cdot j < i \Rightarrow tr \downarrow j = tr' \downarrow j))$$
c. *If l is a p-location that refers to a condition in an **if** statement as shown in Figure 2(a) then the infection condition holds iff*
$$\exists \; i \cdot (\mathcal{L}(tr, i) = l \wedge \mathcal{L}(tr', i) = l \wedge$$
$$(\mathcal{L}(tr, i + 1) \in Labs(S_t) \wedge \mathcal{L}(tr', i + 1) \in Labs(S_e))$$
$$\vee \, (\mathcal{L}(tr, i + 1) \in Labs(S_e) \wedge \mathcal{L}(tr', i + 1) \in Labs(S_t)))$$
d. *If l is a p-location that refers to a condition in a **while** statement as shown in Figure 2(b) then the infection condition holds iff*
$$\exists \; i \cdot (\mathcal{L}(tr, i) = l \wedge \mathcal{L}(tr', i) = l \wedge$$
$$(\mathcal{L}(tr, i + 1) \in Labs(S_w) \wedge \mathcal{L}(tr', i + 1) \notin Labs(S_w) \vee$$
$$\mathcal{L}(tr, i + 1) \notin Labs(S_w) \wedge \mathcal{L}(tr', i + 1) \in Labs(S_w)))$$

Proof. Properties (a) and (b) follow by observing that the location must be reached and in the case of a c-location the two executions must result in two different states if they are to be distinguished.

Other than reachability, the main condition in (c) and (d) is that at some point during the execution of programs the paths followed after reaching location l must be different. This is because if two conditional expressions at location l always evaluate to the same value in P and P', the resultant end states will also remain the same.

l:	**if** ($cond$) **then**	l:	**while** ($cond$) **do**
	S_t		S_w
	else		**end**
	S_e		
	end		
	(a)		(b)

Fig. 2. Structures for proposition 1(c) & (d)

In the case of an **if** statement, the different evaluation of conditions will result in the execution of *then* and *else* branches; whereas in the case of **while** statement it will result in unequal number of executions of the **while** loop.   □

Let D be the input domain of program P, and P' be a mutant of P obtained by applying a mutation operator at location l. Using the terminology of [13], let subdomain $D_r^{l,P'} \subseteq D$ be the set of inputs which reaches location l; similarly, $D_n^{l,P'} \subseteq D$ be the set of inputs that can cause the original and mutated expression to result in different values and $D_s^{l,P'} \subseteq D$ be the set that causes P and P' to result in different final outcomes.

Fact 1. A test case, t, will distinguish P from P' iff $t \in D_s^{l,P'}$ which implies $t \in D_r^{l,P'} \cap D_n^{l,P'}$ and $D_s^{l,P'} \subseteq D_r^{l,P'} \cap D_n^{l,P'}$ [13].

Note that there may be test cases in $D_n^{l,P'}$ that does not satisfy the reachability condition. The computation of both $D_r^{l,P'}$ and $D_n^{l,P'}$ is undecidable, in general. However, in practice it is easier to compute the set $D_n^{l,P'}$ as it only requires analysis of the expressions at location l which are often simple. On the other hand, computation of $D_r^{l,P'}$ is more expensive and complex as it requires analysis of the paths that can reach location l.

Proposition 2. $P \vdash P' \geq_m P'' \Leftrightarrow D_s^{l',P'} \subseteq D_s^{l'',P''}$, *where* P' *and* P'' *are mutants obtained by applying mutation operators at location* l' *and* l'' *in* P, *respectively.*

Proof. The proof follows from the definitions.   □

A straightforward method to identify $\geq_m$ relation is by checking if $D_s^{l',P'} \subseteq D_s^{l'',P''}$. It is also possible to restrict the test cases to be from the set $S = D_s^{l',P'} \cap D_s^{l'',P''}$, provided that the set S is not empty, in which case distinguishing P' will also guarantee the same for P''.

The sets $D_s^{l',P'}$ and $D_s^{l'',P''}$ can be computed by using symbolic execution techniques, which give a constraint on inputs that must be satisfied by a distinguishing test case. Such an approach of computing the detection conditions for hypothesised faults has been extensively studied, for example, in *constraint-based testing* [4] and computation of failure conditions in [12, 16]. Let C_1^s and C_2^s be two constraints that correspond to the subdomains $D_s^{l',P'}$ and $D_s^{l'',P''}$ respectively. Then, $C_1^s \Rightarrow C_2^s$ will also guarantee that $P \vdash P' \geq_m P''$.

Remark 1. The benefit obtained in using the above procedure may be comparably less as it still requires complete symbolic analysis of all the mutants, which may be expensive for complex programs.

The objective of this paper is not only to reduce the storage space for mutants but also to reduce the number of executions of implemented program and its mutants. Therefore, if possible, the $\geq_m$ relation between mutants should be established during their generation itself, thereby only producing the strongest mutants. This approach is an improvement over the method where mutants are first generated explicitly and then an attempt to establish a partial order among them is made.

However, generating the set of strongest mutants may lead to problems due to the presence of equivalent mutants already in the set. Note that the property $P \vdash P' \geq_m P''$ holds trivially for any P'' if P is equivalent to P' (i.e., when $D_s^{l,P'} = \emptyset$). The statistics, as reported in [13], indicate that the number of equivalent mutants is typically in the range of 7 to 12% of the total number of mutants and the automatic detection rate using symbolic execution varies from 12 to 84% of the total number of equivalent mutants.

Thus, although explicit generation of all mutants may not be required, the information regarding them must still be maintained. This information about $P \vdash P' \geq_m P''$ will be required whenever it is deduced or suspected that $P = P'$, for example when a significant amount of effort is spent in killing P' without success (such as, large size of the test set and large number of times reachability and infection conditions are met). The required information about all mutants can effectively be stored using the schemata approach described in [20]. However, the instantiation order for mutants will be guided by the hierarchies among them.

Let l' and l'' be two locations in P that are mutated to obtain mutants P' and P'' respectively. These mutants will be known as *intra-location* mutants of P if $l' = l''$, otherwise they will be referred to as *inter-location* mutants.

3.1   Intra-location Mutants

Let P be an implemented program and P' and P'' be two intra-location mutants of P that are obtained by applying mutation operator at location l in P. Let C_1 and C_2 be the predicates that correspond to the sets $D_n^{l,P'}$ and $D_n^{l,P''}$, respectively.

Now consider the example program shown in Figure 3(a). The mutants fun' and fun'' are shown in boxes and are obtained by applying mutation operator at location $L2$, where $<=, <$ and $>$ are relational operators. The conditions[2] C_1 and C_2, in this case, are x = 4 and **true** respectively. In other words, C_1 and C_2 are necessary (but not sufficient), at location $L2$, to distinguish P from P' and P'' respectively. Note that C_1 implies C_2. In [16], it is concluded that in such cases it is sufficient to consider only C_1 (see page 543 and Table X in [16]).

---

[2] Obtained by taking exclusive-or of two expressions, e.g., $C_1 \equiv x <= 4 \oplus x < 4$, where $\oplus$ is exclusive-or operator.

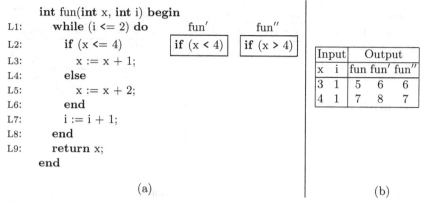

Fig. 3. (a) A counter example for mutations of an **if** statement. (b) Input and output for the program

However, in general, this argument is neither valid for a p-location nor a c-location. Figure 3(b) gives the output of two test cases for the program and its two mutants that are shown in Figure 3(a). The first row shows that the mutants are not equivalent to the original program, whereas the second row shows that the above conjecture is not true. The following theorem gives formal reasoning for the above observation.

Theorem 1. *Let P be a program and P' and P'' be its two intra-location mutants obtained by mutating a statement at location l then, $D_n^{l,P'} \subseteq D_n^{l,P''}$ does not guarantee $P \vdash P' \geq_m P''$.*

Proof.
$$D_s^{l,P'} \subseteq D_r^{l,P'} \cap D_n^{l,P'} \quad \text{(fact 1)}$$
$$D_s^{l,P''} \subseteq D_r^{l,P''} \cap D_n^{l,P''} \quad \text{(fact 1)}$$
$$D_r^{l,P'} = D_r^{l,P''} \qquad \text{(intra-location mutants)}$$
$$D_n^{l,P'} \subseteq D_n^{l,P''} \qquad \text{(given)}$$

The most favourable conclusion that can be drawn from the above statements is that both $D_s^{l,P'}$ and $D_s^{l,P''}$ are subsets of $D_r^{l,P'} \cap D_n^{l,P'}$. But this does not guarantee $D_s^{l',P'} \subseteq D_s^{l'',P''}$ (as required by Proposition 2). □

Example. Figure 4(a) shows a concrete example that illustrates the above theorem for a c-location.

Consider the two mutants, Comp' and Comp'', obtained by applying mutation operator at location $L1$ in Comp (see Figure 4(a)). The D_n sets for both mutants is the whole input domain D since the mutated statements would result in different values for any integer input. In other words, the conditions C_1 and C_2 are *true*. However, input x = 8 will distinguish only Comp from Comp'; whereas input x = 3 will distinguish Comp from Comp'' (see Figure 4(b)). Thus, mutants Comp' and Comp'' are not related under $\geq_m$.

```
int Comp(int x) {        Comp'              Comp''
L1:  x := x + 1;     [ x := x - 1; ]    [ x := x + 2; ]
L2:  if (x = 5 ∨ x = 7)
        x := 9;
     else
        x := 6;
     return x;
}
```

Input	Output		
(x)	Comp	Comp'	Comp''
8	6	9	6
3	6	6	9

	Comp'	Comp''
D_n	D	D
D_s	$\{4,8\}$	$\{3,4,5,6\}$

(a)   (b)

Fig. 4. (a) An example program for Theorem 1. (b) Input, output and subdomains for the program

Corollary 1. *Let P, P', P'' and l be the entities as stated in Theorem 1. Then,*

$$D_n^{l,P'} \cap D_n^{l,P''} = \emptyset \Rightarrow (P = P' \vee P \vdash P' \not\geq_m P'')$$

Proof. The first three conditions are identical with the proof for Theorem 1.

$$D_n^{l,P'} \cap D_n^{l,P''} = \emptyset \qquad \text{(given)}$$
$$\Rightarrow D_s^{l,P'} \cap D_s^{l,P''} = \emptyset \qquad \text{(set theory)}$$
$$\Rightarrow D_s^{l,P'} = \emptyset \vee D_s^{l,P'} \not\subseteq D_s^{l,P''} \quad \text{(set theory)}$$
$$\Leftrightarrow P = P' \vee P \vdash P' \not\geq_m P'' \qquad \text{(fact 1 and Proposition 2)}$$

□

Note that the above corollary also holds for the implication $P = P'' \vee P \vdash P'' \not\geq_m P'$ and confirms that the hierarchy does not hold if the set $D_n^{l,P'} \cap D_n^{l,P''}$ is empty. This is particularly helpful in *isolating* those mutants that definitely need to be considered during testing.

However, a hierarchy can be established between mutants under certain conditions. These conditions are discussed below.

Theorem 2. *Let P be a given program and l be a p-location that corresponds to a condition, c. Further, let c be mutated to c' and c'' giving mutants P' and P'', respectively. Then, $(c' \Leftrightarrow c'') \Rightarrow P \vdash P' \geq_m P''$.*

Proof. As per Proposition 1 (c) and (d), P and P' (P'') must follow different paths after reaching location l (sometime during an execution) in order to be distinguished.

The condition $(c' \Leftrightarrow c'')$ ensures that condition c' and c'' always evaluate to the same Boolean value. Thus, for a given test case, the path followed by P' and P'' will always be the same, ensuring that whenever the infection and propagation conditions hold for P', they will hold for P'' as well. □

The above condition in Theorem 2 is a very strong requirement and at first sight it may appear to be less useful. However, the following section will illustrate that such a property can be helpful in reducing the test effort.

Remark 2. Why do we need such a strong condition to hold in general? To answer this question, let us consider the two mutants P' and P'', obtained by mutating a condition for a **while** loop of P. For a given test case, let $i_p, i_{p'}$ and $i_{p''}$ be the number of times the **while** loop is executed in P, P' and P'', respectively. Thus, the necessary conditions for killing P' and P'' are $i_p \neq i_{p'}$ and $i_p \neq i_{p''}$ respectively. To establish $P \vdash P' \geq_m P''$, one of the following properties must hold:

a. $i_{p'} = i_{p''}$ or
b. the resulting states must be the same after executing the body of **while** loop $i_{p'}$ and $i_{p''}$ times.

The condition in Theorem 2 is equivalent to (a) above. However, the condition (b) is equally acceptable, but requires analysis of the program segment to guarantee that it holds for any test case that distinguishes P from P'; this may be difficult to establish. It is also possible to weaken the requirement in Theorem 2 under certain conditions as described by the following theorem.

Theorem 3. *Let P be a given program and l be a p-location that corresponds to a condition, c, in an **if** statement in P. Further, let c be mutated by two operators to c' and c'' giving mutations P' and P'', respectively. Then, a test case t will guarantee $P \vdash P' \geq_m P''$ provided the following conditions hold:*

a. *there exists a unique i such that $\mathcal{L}(tr, i) = \mathcal{L}(tr', i) = l$, where tr and tr' are the traces obtained on executing P and P' respectively, with test case t.*
b. *$(c \oplus c') \Rightarrow (c \oplus c'')$, where $\oplus$ is exclusive-or operator;*

Proof. As per Proposition 1 (c) and (d), P and P' (P'') must follow different paths after reaching location l (sometime during an execution) in order to be distinguished.

The condition (a) ensures that the **if** statement is executed exactly once, whereas condition (b) guarantees that P'' will follow the same path as P' after executing l, if P' execution differs from that of P. This is achieved by the condition $(c \oplus c') \Rightarrow (c \oplus c'')$ which ensures that if condition c and c' are different then c and c'' will also be different.

The necessity for the condition (a) can be explained as follows. Assume that the **if** statement is executed twice and c' differs from c in second execution. However, it is possible that only c'' may differ from c in the first initial execution (as it is allowed by the condition (b)), in which case it is not guaranteed that killing P' will also ensure the same for P''. $\square$

Thus, Theorem 2, Remark 2 and Theorem 3 give three different possibilities and also present the reasoning for the conditional requirements associated with them.

Note that in Theorem 3, c and c'' may differ, but c and c' may evaluate to the same values, in which case P'' may be detected but P' will not. Thus P'' could be detected by more test cases than P'. This can also be observed by noting that

$c \oplus c'$ defines the subdomain $D_n^{l,P'}$ and considering the implication as a subset relation.

Some programming languages also allow variables of type Boolean that can appear in assignment statements such as $a := b \vee c$ where a, b and c are of type Boolean. For the special case of Boolean variables Theorem 1 can be refined as follows:

Corollary 2. *Let l correspond to a computation statement of the form var $:= c$, where var and c are of type Boolean. If c is mutated to c' and c'' then $P \vdash P' \geq_m P''$ holds, provided the conditions specified in Theorem 3 hold.*

Proof. The proof is similar to that for Theorem 3 with the observation that *var* can take only two values.   □

3.2   Inter-location Mutants

Let P' and P'' be two inter-location first order mutants of a program P that are obtained by mutating location l' and l'' respectively. Consider the set $R = D_r^{l',P'} \cap D_r^{l'',P''}$.

If $R = \emptyset$, there is no relationship between P' and P'' and both of them must be considered during mutation testing. The checking of condition $R = \emptyset$ does not necessarily require explicit computation of the reachability sets. In fact, various control-flow, data-flow and other analysis techniques used in program optimisation, etc., can also be applied to discover if $R = \emptyset$ holds. An example where the condition $R = \emptyset$ holds is when l' and l'' appear in **then** and **else** branches of an **if** statement.

Consider the other case when $R \neq \emptyset$; i.e., there may be an execution that passes through both l' and l''. In this case in order to find if the two mutants are related, it is necessary to evaluate the impact of mutation at l' at location l'' (or vice versa). If this analysis succeeds then the process of identifying the hierarchy between inter-location mutants is identical to that for intra-location mutants.

Such an analysis, in which the effect of a fault is propagated, is extensively studied in the literature in terms of propagation conditions. For example, the local propagation of origination conditions is referred to as transfer conditions in [16].

The following section will further illustrate the approach suggested in this section.

4   Theory to Practice

The analysis required to check the conditions discussed in the previous section can be undertaken using existing program analysis tools. In particular, we will use symbolic evaluation and assume that the symbolic execution of the program under test is done once to obtain the symbolic execution tree. This requirement may be relaxed if program transformation techniques such as those mentioned in [6] are applied to make the program more testable.

Remark 3. Let C be a first-order quantifier-free logical formula that we want to test to determine if it holds at location l in program P. There are three possibilities for the property to hold: (a) C holds in general; (b) C is not valid; (c) C is not valid in general but it holds in the restricted context of P.

In the case (c) above, if the simplified formula is not false, it can give a hint for generating test data for a conditional hierarchy. This is particularly helpful in the context of Theorem 1, which implies that mutations of c-locations are not directly comparable. However, it is still possible to analyse intra or inter-location mutants by propagating the mutation at a c-location to a p-location and then checking for the hierarchy.

Consider, for example, the program shown in Figure 4(a) earlier. Observe that x is defined before and after $L2$; therefore it is safe to propagate the mutations of $L1$ to location $L2$ and then attempt to check the properties using Theorem 3. Let x_1 be the value of x before executing the statement at location $L1$. After execution of the statement at location $L1$, the value of variable x will be $x_1 + 1$, $x_1 - 1$ and $x_1 + 2$ for the programs Comp, Comp$'$ and Comp$''$, respectively. Thus, in this case c, c' and c'' are as follows:

$$c \equiv x_1 + 1 = 5 \lor x_1 + 1 = 7 \quad \Leftrightarrow \quad x_1 = 4 \lor x_1 = 6$$
$$c' \equiv x_1 - 1 = 5 \lor x_1 - 1 = 7 \quad \Leftrightarrow \quad x_1 = 6 \lor x_1 = 8$$
$$c'' \equiv x_1 + 2 = 5 \lor x_1 + 2 = 7 \quad \Leftrightarrow \quad x_1 = 3 \lor x_1 = 5$$

Also,

$$c \oplus c' \equiv x_1 = 4 \lor x_1 = 8$$
$$c \oplus c'' \equiv 3 \le x_1 \le 6$$

Therefore, if mutant Comp$'$ can be killed using a test case such that the value of the variable x before executed $L1$ is 4 then it is guaranteed that it will also kill Comp$''$. This shows that by doing local analysis it is also possible to identify a potential test case that can kill two mutants.

The deductions mentioned in Remark 3 can be done automatically using existing tools such as the Cooperating Validity Checker (CVC) [2], which can check the validity of quantifier-free first-order formulas over several interpreted theories including real linear arithmetic, arrays, uninterpreted functions and constants, abstract data types, etc.

```
x, y, z : REAL;
f : [REAL -> REAL];
QUERY (f(x + y) <= z XOR f(x - y) <= z)
   => (f(x + y) <= z XOR f(x + y) > z);
```

Fig. 5. CVC input

Consider, for example, a condition $c \equiv f(x + y) <= z$ that appears in an **if** statement of a program, where f is a function from $real \to real$. Let c' and c'' be the two mutants of c obtained by mutating $+$ to $-$ and $<=$ to $>$, respectively. Assume that a test case executes the **if** statement only once (such statistics can be collected during the execution of the program). Then CVC can be used to check if $c \oplus c' \Rightarrow c \oplus c''$ (see Theorem 3) by giving the input shown in Figure 5. In this case CVC returns the result to be valid for any f.

The analysis of Boolean expressions has been extensively studied in the literature; see for example [18, 22]. In [10, 19], a hierarchy between different types of faults that can arise in Boolean specifications is analysed. These results are applicable in the context of Theorem 3. Similarly, Corollary 1 and $R = \emptyset$ (section 3.2) can be used to identify those mutants that are guaranteed to have the $\not\geq_m$ relationship.

5   Conclusions and Future Work

Mutation testing is a powerful testing approach that can not only ensure the checking of hypothesised faults but also the generation of test data satisfying common structural coverage criteria. The main difficulty faced in mutation testing is due to the large number of mutant programs that can be generated for a given implemented program. We have given a strategy that suggests the ordering of the mutants such that if a mutant is stronger than another, then killing the stronger will automatically kill the weaker. This approach can significantly reduce the cost of mutation testing.

We have presented various conditions to identify the relationship between mutants that can be analysed locally and thus can be evaluated in a effective way.

As the kind of analysis required to establish hierarchies is already part of various program analysis and transformation tools, and also tools like CVC [2] are already available, the given approach should be practical. However, an extensive empirical study, ideally on industrial-scale examples, is required to verify that this is indeed the case. We hope and believe that this theoretical paper will provide a good basis for such a study.

References

1. T. A. Budd, R. A. DeMillo, R. J. Lipton, and F. G. Sayward. Theoretical and Empirical Studies on using Program Mutation to Test the Functional Correctness of Programs. In *7th Symposium on Principles of Programming Languages*, pages 220–233. ACM, 1980.
2. Cooperating Validity Checker, Stanford University, USA. http://verify.stanford.edu/CVC/ (last accessed: 14 August 2004).
3. R. A. DeMillo, R. J. Lipton, and F. G. Sayward. Hints on Test Data Selection: Help for the Practicing Programmer. *IEEE Computer*, 11(4):34–41, April 1978.
4. R. A. DeMillo and A. Jefferson Offutt. Constraint-Based Automatic Test Data Generation. *IEEE Transactions on Software Engineering*, 17(9):900–910, September 1991.
5. I. M. M. Duncan and D. J. Robson. Ordered Mutation Testing. In *ACM SIGSOFT Software Engineering Notes*, volume 15, pages 29–30, April 1990.
6. M. Harman, L. Hu, R. Hierons, J. Wegener, H. Sthamer, A. Baresel, and M. Roper. Testability Transformation. *IEEE Transactions on Software Engineering*, 30(1):3–16, 2004.

7. R. M. Hierons. Comparing Test Sets and Criteria in the Presence of Test Hypotheses and Fault Domains. *ACM Transactions on Software Engineering and Methodology*, 11(4):427–448, October 2002.

8. W. E. Howden. Weak Mutation Testing and Completeness of Test Sets. *IEEE Transactions on Software Engineering*, 8:371–379, July 1982.

9. K. N. King and A. J. Offutt. A Fortran Language System for Mutation-Based Software Testing. *Software Practice and Experience*, 21(7):685–718, 1991.

10. D. R. Kuhn. Fault Classes and Error Detection Capability of Specification-based Testing. *ACM Transactions on Software Engineering and Methodology*, 8(4):411–424, October 1999.

11. B. Marick. The Weak Mutation Hypothesis. In *International Symposium on Software Testing and Analysis*, pages 190–199, 1991.

12. L. J. Morell. A Theory of Fault-based Testing. *IEEE Transactions on Software Engineering*, 16(8):844–857, August 1990.

13. A. J. Offutt and J. Pan. Automatically Detecting Equivalent Mutants and Infeasible Paths. *Software Testing, Verification and Reliability*, 7(3):165–192, September 1997.

14. A. J. Offutt, G. Rothermel, R. H. Untch, and C. Zapf. An Experimental Determination of Sufficient Mutant Operator. *ACM Transactions on Software Engineering and Methodology*, 5(2):99–118, April 1996.

15. A. J. Offutt and R. H. Untch. Mutation 2000: Uniting the Orthogonal. In W. E. Wong, editor, *Mutation Testing in the Twentieth and the Twenty First Centuries*, pages 45–55. Kluwer, October 2000.

16. D. J. Richardson and M. C. Thompson. An Analysis of Test Data Selection Criteria using the RELAY Model of Fault Detection. *IEEE Transactions on Software Engineering*, 19(6):533–553, June 1993.

17. I. J. Riddell, M. A. Hennell, M. R. Woodward, and D. Hedley. Practical Aspects of Program Mutation. Technical report, University of Liverpool, UK, 1982.

18. K.-C. Tai. Theory of Fault-based Predicate Testing for Computer Programs. *IEEE Transactions on Software Engineering*, 22(8):552–562, August 1996.

19. T. Tsuchiya and T. Kikuno. On Fault Classes and Error Detection Capability of Specification-based Testing. *ACM Transactions on Software Engineering and Methodology*, 11(1):58–62, January 2002.

20. R. H. Untch, A. J. Offutt, and M. J. Harrold. Mutation Analysis Using Mutant Schemata. In *International Symposium on Software Testing and Analysis*, pages 139–148, 1993.

21. J. M. Voas. PIE: A Dynamic Failure-Based Technique. *IEEE Transactions on Software Engineering*, 18(2):717–727, August 1992.

22. E. Weyuker, T. Gorodia, and A. Singh. Automatically Generating Test Data from a Boolean Specification. *IEEE Transactions on Software Engineering*, 20(5):353–363, May 1994.

23. W. E. Wong and A. P. Mathur. Reducing the Cost of Mutation Testing: An Empirical Study. *Journal of Systems and Software*, 31(3):185–196, December 1995.

24. M. R. Woodward. Concerning Ordered Mutation Testing of Relational Operators. *Software Testing, Verification and Reliability*, 1(3):35–40, October 1991.

25. M. R. Woodward and K. Halewood. From Weak to Strong, Dead or Alive? An Analysis of some Mutation Testing Issues. In *2nd Workshop on Software Testing, Verification, and Analysis*, pages 152–158, July 1988.

26. M. R. Woodward, M. A. Hennell, and D. Hedley. A Limited Mutation Approach to Program Testing. Technical report, University of Liverpool, UK, May 1980.

Testing COM Components Using Software Fault Injection and Mutation Analysis, and Its Empirical Study[**]

Hoijin Yoon[1], Eunhee Kim[2], Joo Young Seo[3], and Byoungju Choi[3,*]

[1] College of Computing, Georgia Institute of Technology, USA
hjyoon@know.cc.gatech.edu
[2] Software Center, Samsung Electronics Co. Ltd, Korea
eunhee2.kim@samsung.com
[3] Department of Computer Science and Engineering,
Ewha Women's University, Korea
{jyseo, bjchoi}@ewha.ac.kr

Abstract. CBSD needs to customize and compose components. Customization and composition can cause faults which are hard to detect by existing testing techniques, since components have different structures from traditional programs. This paper proposes a testing technique for customization and composition, and then it tailors the technique to COM component architecture. Since CBSD aims to reduce development cost, testing should consider the cost of testing. Effective test data will help reduce testing cost. Therefore, an empirical study shows that the technique proposed in this paper selects effective test data.

1 Introduction

The issues in CBSD are seen from two perspectives: that of the component provider and that of the component user. One key factor that distinguishes the two perspectives is the availability of the component source code; the component providers have access to the source code, whereas the component users typically do not [1]. The lack of the source code limits the testing that the component user can perform [2], and a new component testing technique is needed that takes the view of the component user.

CBSD has two main activities from the standpoint of the component user; one is 'Customization,' [3] and the other is 'Composition.' Customization is for tailoring pre-built components to the current development domain, and composition is for merging the customized components to component-based software. Testing should be performed just after the customization and the composition, in order to keep components error-free in the current system.

Souza defined component customization [4]. Specifically, the component hides its internal behavior, yet provides an interface whereby the component user can change

---

[*] Corresponding Author.

[**] This work was partially supported by grant No.R04-2003-000-10139-0 from the Basic Research Program of the Korea Science & Engineering Foundation. This work was partially supported by University IT Research Center Project.

J. Grabowski and B. Nielsen (Eds.): FATES 2004, LNCS 3395, pp. 210–224, 2005.

the component's behavior or its methods. Component customization includes every activity to modify the existing component for reuse. It includes adding new domain-specific functions as well as simple modifications to attributes.

Component customization testing tests the faults occurring through component customization. Customization could cause faults through modifying the interface of a component. The faults exist in the interface, but the faults are executed through the interaction between the interface and the core part of a component. Thus, the faults from the customization can be detected by the integration testing, not by the unit testing of the interface. The two parts of the integration testing have different characteristics; the interface is a white-box, and the core part is a black-box. The integration testing of both a white-box and a black-box requires a new technique, since most of the existing integration testing techniques consider either white-box programs or black-box programs. This paper proposes an integration testing technique of these two parts as the customization faults.

The components are composed in an application, and the process composing components is called "Composition." Composition can be performed by various operators depending on component architecture. For example, EJB composes components by calling methods in the other component.

The composition could cause faults through linking two components. The components composed are pre-built components or domain components. Even if the pre-built components work perfectly in a certain system, they could work incorrectly in another system. An example is the Ariane 5's lesson [5]. A component that worked well in Ariane 4 causes faults in Arian 5, and thus Ariane 5 was derailed.

We have proposed a technique for detecting faults that occur through customization and composition demonstrated in our earlier papers [6]. The testing technique was based on the general characteristics of the components, and thus we have tailored the technique to EJB component architecture [6]. Now, this paper customizes the technique to the Component Object Model (COM) that is one of the most popular component architectures. With the COM-based testing technique, an empirical study shows the effectiveness of the test data selected by this technique. The effectiveness of test data is a particularly important issue, since the purpose of CBSD is to reduce the cost of development. Testing with effective test cases will save testing cost.

The remainder of the paper is organized as follows. In Section 2, a customization testing technique and a composition testing technique are described, and then they are tailored to COM in Section 3. Section 4 analyzes the effectiveness of the proposed technique through an empirical study. Section 5 presents some concluding remarks.

2 Technique for Customization Testing and Composition Testing

2.1 A Customization Testing Technique

The component customization testing is a form of integration testing of the two parts of a component, and the two parts were defined as a Black-box class and a White-box class [7]. The customization testing defined which part of a component could be a Black-box class and which part of a component could be a White-box class, and then selected some specific parts where faults were injected. With the specific parts, it used fault-injected versions of a customized component in order to select test cases that differentiate fault-injected versions from a customized version. The following terms [7] were defined to describe the customization testing technique.

Definition 1. Black-box class (*B*)
The black-box class is a part of the component where the source code is not disclosed and therefore cannot be modified for customization. This is denoted as *B*. The component provider creates *B*, and *B* has the execution code of a component.

Definition 2. White-box class (*W*)
The white-box class is a part of the component where the source code is open to the component user and can be modified for the customization. The white-box class is denoted as *W*. Usually the component provider creates *W*, and the component user modifies *W* for customization. The customized interface is denoted as *cW* and the fault-injected into *cW* is denoted as *fW*.

Definition 3. Component (*BW*)
The component is a combination of *B* and *W*, and so is denoted as *BW*. *BW* with the customized *W* is denoted as *cBW* and the fault injected into *BW* is denoted as *fBW*.

Definition 4. Fault Injection Target (*FIT*)
This is the specific part into which a fault is injected. More effective test data can be selected by injecting a fault only into the *FIT*.

Definition 5. Fault Injection Operator (*FIO*)
FIO is an operator that defines how to inject a fault without causing syntax errors.

A *FIT* is a constituent unit of *cW*, for instance, a single XML element for EJB. The *cBW* executes the behavior customized to current domain requirements by referring to the elements in *cW*. This does not mean that *B* directly refers to all elements of *cW*. *B* refers to a specific element in *cW*, say *x*, and then indirectly refers to another element, say *y*, by directly referring to *x* related to *y*.

Definition 6. Directly Referred Element (*DRE*)
DRE is an element of the interface that *B* refers to directly.

Definition 7. Indirectly Referred Element (*IRE*)
IRE is an element of the interface that a *DRE* refers to and *B* refers to indirectly through the *DRE*. The set of indirect reference elements related to *DRE*, say *d*, is denoted as an *IRE(d)*.

When there are faults in *IRE* of *cBW* from customization, these faults influence *B* through *DRE*. Therefore, the test cases must detect the faults both in *DRE* and in the relevant *IRE*. Identifying *DRE* as the *FIT* is under the assumption that "the test cases selected by injecting a fault into *DRE* can detect the faults in *DRE* and in relevant *IRE*."[6]

For testing the customized component *cBW* in Figure 1 (a), the technique creates a *fBW* by injecting a fault into the *FIT* of *cW* as shown in Figure 1 (b). The fault injection operator is called *FIO*. *FIT*s are selected in consideration of the interaction between *B* and *cW* as described above, so it is the *FIT* that enhances the effectiveness of test cases in this paper.

Once *fBW* is generated, the technique selects test data by following Definition 8.

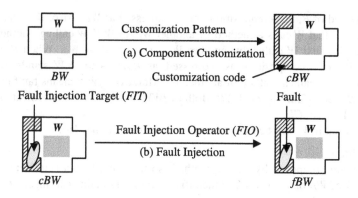

Fig. 1. Component customization and fault injection

Definition 8. Test data selection for component customization:
A test data for component customization is a sequence of method calls that differentiate *fBW* from *cBW*. *TC* is a set of these test cases.

$$TC = \{\ x \mid cBW(x) \neq fBW(x),\ \text{where } x \text{ is a method sequence.}\}$$

Definition 8 looks similar to the mutation test case selection technique [8], but it does not select the test cases with the mutants made by mutating all the elements of *cBW* as mutation testing does. It uses the mutants made by mutating only the *FIT*, based on the interaction between *B* and *cW*.

2.2 A Composition Testing Technique

All of the components of an application in CBSD are not pre-built components. Some components of an application should be developed since they can not be found in component repositories or anywhere else. Therefore, an application developed in CBSD consists of reused-components and in-house-components that are developed for the application itself. The composition should consider these two different types of components. These are defined as follows in this paper.

Definition 9. Black box component ($\bar{B}$)
Black box component means a component that was developed by another component developer or in another system and that is reused in the current system. The component users do not know the source codes of the black box component. The black box component is described simply as $\bar{B}$.

Definition 10. White box component ($\bar{W}$)
White box component means a component that is newly developed in the current application. Therefore, the developer can control the contents of the white box component. The white box component is expressed simply as $\bar{W}$.

Definition 11. Composition Unit (*CU*)
Composition Unit means a unit generated by composing two components, $\bar{B}$ or $\bar{W}$. We call the Composition Unit as *CU* simply. $\bar{W}\bar{B}$, $\bar{W}\bar{W}$, $\bar{B}\bar{B}$, and $\bar{B}\bar{W}$ are *CU*s. When

$\overline{W}$ calls a method of $\overline{B}$, this composition unit is expressed as $\overline{W}\overline{B}$. Also, $\overline{W}\overline{W}$ stands for the composition that $\overline{W}$ calls a method of another $\overline{W}$. In $\overline{W}\overline{W}$, $\overline{W}$ calling another $\overline{W}$ is expressed as $\overline{W}_s$ and $\overline{W}$ called by another $\overline{W}$ is expressed as $\overline{W}_d$. When $\overline{B}$ calls a method of $\overline{B}$, this composition is expressed as $\overline{B}\,\overline{B}$. Also, $\overline{B}\,\overline{W}$ stands for the composition that $\overline{B}$ calls a method of another $\overline{W}$. Moreover, $f\overline{W}\overline{W}$ means fault injected $\overline{W}\overline{W}$ and $f\overline{W}\overline{B}$ means fault injected $\overline{W}\overline{B}$. Both of $f\overline{W}\overline{W}$ and $f\overline{W}\overline{B}$ are fault injected *CUs*, so $f\overline{W}\overline{W}$ and $f\overline{W}\overline{B}$ are *fCU*.

To define what in $\overline{W}$ will be *FIT*, following definitions are needed.

Definition 12. *P*
Components are composed by calling method, so there must be a statement calling methods in $\overline{W}$ of $\overline{W}\overline{B}$ or $\overline{W}_s$ of $\overline{W}\overline{W}$. *P* identifies parameters in that calling sentence.

Definition 13. *R*
There must be calling sentences in $\overline{W}_s$ of $\overline{W}\overline{W}$ and methods called by them in $\overline{W}_d$ of $\overline{W}$ $\overline{W}$ when the composition is through calling methods. *R* refers to a return variable in a called method of $\overline{W}_d$.

Definition 14. *ref(x)*
ref(x) means statements that make a change in a value of *x*. *ref(P)* and *P* are located in the same $\overline{W}_s$. *ref*(R) and *R* are located in same $\overline{W}_d$.

Components are composed to *CU*, and the kind of components that are in a *CU* depends on the composition pattern, as shown in Figure 2 (a). Figure 2 (b) shows this fault injection process. *FIT*s are selected in consideration of the interaction between components of *CU*, and it is the *FIT* that enhances the effectiveness of test cases in this technique.

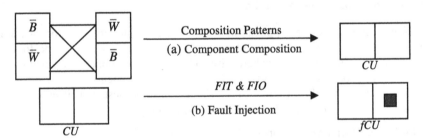

Fig. 2. Component composition and fault injection

There are several patterns in building *CU* through component composition as shown in Figure 2 (a), and the locations and the operations of injecting a fault into *CU* depend on these patterns. After creating *fCU* by injecting a fault into the *FIT* with the *FIO*, the test data are selected as described in Definition 15.

Definition 15. Test data for the component composition
A test data for component customization is a sequence of method calls that differentiate *fCU* from *CU*. *TD* is a set of these test data.

$$TD = \{\, x \mid CU(x) \neq fCU(x), \text{ where } x \text{ is a method sequence.} \}$$

3 Testing Technique for COM Components

The technique in Section 2 has a similar structure of a component, which consists of *W* and *B*. *W* and *B* of the technique are illustrated in Figure 3.

Fig. 3. Structure of the testing technique

As a component, the technique can be customized by specifying *W*, in which Patterns, *FIT*s, and *FIO*s are.   In this section, the technique is customized to COM by specifying the patterns, *FIT*, and *FIO*.

3.1 Customization Testing in COM

COM Customization Patterns. A COM component consists of an object and its interfaces.   An object consists of classes that constitute the main functions of a component.   It could be *B* since it doesn't open its source code and it has the main code of its functions.   An interface of a COM component is accessible from outside, so it is *W* in COM.   Customization patterns of COM should be defined first before selecting *FIT* and *FIO* in COM. Table 1 shows the COM customization patterns.

Table 1. Customization Patterns in COM

Pattern	Definition
Pattern 1	A pattern which sets the values of properties by changing the interface
Pattern 2	A pattern which sets the values of properties by making a new interface.
Pattern 3	A pattern which adds new functions by changing the interface
Pattern 4	A pattern which adds new functions by making a new interface
Pattern 5	A pattern which modifies functions by inserting a new sequence to an interface
Pattern 6	A pattern which modifies functions by making a new interface and by inserting a new sequence into the new interface

***FIT*s and *FIO*s of Customized COM.** Once the customization patterns in COM are categorized, *FIT* and *FIO* in every pattern should be defined according to Definition 4 and Definition 5.   *FIT* is a specific part of *W* which communicates with *B* directly. It's not a modified part through customization. In order to select *FIT* of COM component, many practical COM components should be considered, and COM components coded with VB are analyzed in this paper.   *FIT*s in every pattern are selected by analyzing VB COM components as shown in Table 2.

Table 2. *FIT*s and *FIO*s in VB COM

Patterns	FITs	FIOs
Pattern 1	*Dim* : A property declared with Dim	*MDim* : Modify the value of the property declared with "Dim"
	Form : A property declared with Form	*MForm* : Modify the value of the property of a "Form"
Pattern 2	*DimN* : A property declared with Dim in a new Interface	*MDimN* : Modify the value of the property declared with "Dim" in a new Interface
	FormN : A property declared with Form in a new Inteface	*MFormN* : Modify the value of the property of a "Form" in a new Interface
Pattern 3	*PublicSub* : A function declared with *Public Sub*	*RSub*: Replace a function with a new component
		CSub: Create a new function
	PublicFunction : A function declared with *Public Function.*	*RFnt*: Replace a function with a new component
		MPrm: Modify the value of the parameter of a new function
Pattern 4	*PublicSubN* : A function declared with *Public Sub* in a new Interface	*RSubN*: Replace a function with a new component in a new Interface
		CSubN: Create a new function in a new Interface
	PublicFunctionN : A function declared with *Public Function* in a new Interface	*RFntN*: Replace a function with a new component in a new Interface
		MPrmN: Modify the value of the parameter of a new Function in a new Interface
Pattern 5	*PublicSub :* A function declared with *Public Sub*	*CSubS*: Create a new function including a new sequence
	PublicFunction : A function declared with *Public Function.*	*MPrmS*: Modify the value of the parameter of a new function including a new sequence
Pattern 6	*PublicSubN* : A function declared with *Public Sub* in a new Interface	*CSubSN*: Create a new function including a new sequence in a new Interface
	PublicFunctionN : A function declared with *Public Function* in a new Interface	*MPrmSN*: Modify the value of the parameter of a new Function including a new sequence in a new Interface

3.2 Composition Testing in COM

COM Composition Patterns. Software that is developed in EJB or COM consists of $\bar{B}$s and $\bar{W}$s. Components of COM are composed by calling methods. Hence, the composition patterns with $\bar{B}$ and $\bar{W}$ are in Table 3.

Table 3. Composition patterns

Patterns	Definitions
$\overline{B}\overline{B}$	A pattern in which $\bar{B}$ calls a method of $\bar{B}$
$\overline{B}\overline{W}$	A pattern in which $\bar{B}$ calls a method of $\bar{W}$
$\overline{W}\overline{B}$	A pattern in which $\bar{W}$ calls a method of $\bar{B}$
$\overline{W}\overline{W}$	A pattern in which $\bar{W}$ calls a method of $\bar{W}$

The composition of $\overline{B}\overline{B}$ pattern was already built by a component provider since the component users cannot access $\bar{B}$ in the composition testing. This composition cannot and need not be considered because it is presumed to be error-free in CBSD. The composition of $\bar{B}\bar{W}$ pattern is also built by the component provider of $\bar{B}$ because the component users cannot access the composition code in $\bar{B}$ as it is not open to him according to Definition 9. Therefore, the composition testing needs to handle $\bar{W}\bar{B}$ pattern and $\bar{W}\bar{W}$ pattern. *FIT*s and *FIO*s for $\bar{W}\bar{B}$ pattern and $\bar{W}\bar{W}$ pattern will be defined for the composition testing.

***FIT*s and *FIO*s of Composed COM.** In $\bar{W}\bar{B}$ pattern of COM, there might be errors in $\bar{W}$ because $\bar{B}$ cannot be modified by a current developer for a composition. Thus, a fault will be injected in $\bar{W}$. However, we inject a fault not into entire $\bar{W}$ but only *FIT* of $\bar{W}$ which could lead to the selection of more highly effective test data. Since a composition is made by method calling in COM, we can first consider *ref(P)* as *FIT*. Nevertheless, we select only *P*, which is smaller than *ref(P)*, as *FIT*. This is under an assumption that "Test cases selected by injecting a fault only to *P* can detect the errors that exist not only in *P* but also in the *ref(P)* in $\bar{W}$"[6]. To delete or to add as the *FIO* is impossible, because *P* needs to keep a signature of the called method. According to Definition 4, $f\bar{W}\bar{B}$ also needs to be executable. Therefore, only an operator that replaces *P* with another variable or constant is possible to be *FIO*. We call this *FIO* as *Replace(P)*.

In $\bar{W}\bar{W}$ pattern of COM, there might be errors in $\bar{W}_s$ and $\bar{W}_d$. In COM, we select *P* of $\bar{W}_s$ and *R* of $\bar{W}_d$ as *FIT* with the assumptions that "Test cases selected by injecting a fault only to *P* can detect the errors that exist not only in *P* but also in the *ref(P)* in $\bar{W}$" and "Test cases selected by injecting a fault only to *R* can detect the errors that exist not only in *R* but also in the *ref(R)* in $\bar{W}_d$"[6]. To delete and to add are impossible to be *FIO* because *P* and *R* need to keep a signature of the called method. From Definition 4, $f\bar{W}\bar{W}$ also need to be executable, so only an operator that replaces *P* or *R* to another variable or constant is possible to be *FIO*. We call each *FIO* as *Replace(P)* and *Replace(R)* respectively.

Table 4 shows *FIT*s and *FIO*s for each composition pattern in COM.

Table 4. *FIT*s and *FIO*s of COM

Patterns	*FIT*	*FIO*	Description
$\bar{W}\bar{B}$	*P*	*Replace(P)*	to replace *P* of $\bar{W}$ to another variable or constant
$\bar{W}\bar{W}$	*P*	*Replcae(P)*	to replace *P* of $\bar{W}_s$ to another variable or constant
	R	*Replcae(R)*	to replace *R* of $\bar{W}_d$ to another variable or constant

4 An Empirical Study

The empirical study shows that the test data has sufficient effectiveness to detect the faults through customization and composition. A set of test data with high effectiveness with a small number of mutants or *fBW*s could reduce the testing cost by reducing the testing time, and thus it coincides with the purpose of CBSD, the reduction of development cost. This section evaluates the effectiveness of test cases in terms of two criteria; Eff_1 and Eff_2.

Eff_1 = (The number of faults detected by the set of test cases / The total number of faults) * 100
Eff_2 = (The number of test cases with fault detection / The total number of test cases) * 100.

Eff_1 measures how many faults are detected for the set of test data [9]. Eff_2 measures how many test cases detect faults out of the selected test cases [10]. This section evaluates Eff_1 and Eff_2 through an empirical study. The results of four domains will be analyzed to demonstrate the merit of the technique by evaluating the following items: Eff_1, Eff_2, the number of $fBWs$, and Eff_2 per one fBW.

4.1 Comparisons

The empirical study compares the testing technique of this paper with three existing testing techniques. They are the interface mutation, the mutation testing, and the data flow testing. The technique of this paper is named FIT/FIO for the convenience of description in the empirical study.

Interface Mutation. The interface mutation was proposed by Delamaro [11] as a integration testing technique of modules of a structural program. It mutates only the interface of the modules instead of the entire program code. The idea of the interface mutation was applied to a distributed component system [12]. The approach applied the interface mutation only to the interface part of a distributed component system, and made the mutation operator for CORBA IDL. This empirical study uses the mutation operators for COBRA IDL except *Replace*[12], which is an operator for replacing an occurrence of one of "in", "out" and "inout" with another in the list.

The interface mutation and FIT/FIO test components through only the interface. In addition, test data of the technique generated in our technique and the interface mutation is a form of method-calls implemented in a server. The difference lies in which part of the interface is mutated for testing. FIT/FIO mutates the *FITs* defined by the patterns, while the interface mutation mutates the entire interface. In case of CORBA, it applies the mutation operators to the entire IDL file. In the empirical study, the interface mutation is called IM for short.

Mutation Testing. Mutation testing is an error-based testing adequacy criterion proposed by DeMillo et al. [8], initially with the name "Mutation Analysis." In practice, the criterion is applied by creating the set of alternative programs called mutants of a program P. The mutants differ from P only on simple syntactic changes determined by a set of mutant operators. To assess the adequacy of a test set T, each mutant, as well as the program P, has to be executed against the test cases in T. According to the concept of mutation testing, the empirical study mutates components that are built with Visual Basic by modifying all the variables and the operators one by one.

FIT/FIO mutates only *FIT* of the interface of a component, while the mutation testing mutates the entire component. Mutation testing may generate too many test data compared to FIT/FIO. The size of the test data of the mutation testing is not appropriate to the testing of CBSD, since CBSD aims to reduce development cost, including testing cost. This bottleneck problem of mutation testing is reflected in Eff_2 through the empirical study. In the empirical study, the original mutation testing is called OM for short.

White-Box Testing : Dataflow. There exist various techniques for white-box testing. Most of them perform tests based on program codes, but the white-box part of a component is different from ordinary program codes and the white-box part alone doesn't work. The white-box part of a component is made with a special language such as IDL or XML. Therefore, it is not reasonable to apply the existing code-based white-box testing techniques to components. Data flow testing technique which is neither the mutation-based technique nor the code-based technique is compared with the component testing techniques in the empirical study. Of the criteria defined in the data flow technique, all-defs is similar to the process by which the *FIT* is defined. In the empirical study, the data flow testing with all-defs criteria is called DataFlow for the convenience of description.

4.2 The Empirical Study on the Customization Testing Under COM

Customized COM Applications. The five COM components of Table 5 have been used for this empirical study. AppStack was selected from the sample codes of [9]. AppZipcode and AppVoting came from [10]. The others were developed in Visual Basic 6.0. They each have their own customized versions. FIT/FIO, IM, OM, and DataFlow are applied to the customized versions to test them. For evaluating their effectiveness, it is assumed that the customized versions of Table 5 have faults through the customization.

Table 5. COM applications used in the empirical study of COM customization testing

COM applications	Sizes	Patterns	Description
AppStack	95 lines	Pattern 4	It pushes and pops data that a user inputs
AppOperator	88 lines	Pattern 1	It calculates two values with an operator. The user inputs two values and an operator.
AppBooking	103 lines	Pattern 6	It shows tables in a restaurant, and the user picks one. It generates a reservation number, and saves it on DB.
AppZipcode	54 lines	Pattern 3	It searches a zip code with an address the user inputs.
AppVoting	97 lines	Pattern 5	The user selects an example of a question. It shows how many users selected the item so far.

Customization Faults Inside the COM Applications. The empirical study inserts the customization faults into the customization code for the customization patterns. The customization code is the interface W, and W of VB COM components is the class module. Therefore, the customization code exists in the class module. The COM customization pattern 1, 3, and 5 add the customization code to the interface. The COM customization pattern 2, 4, and 6 add the customization code to a new interface.

The interface of COM defines the abstract functions of the classes. W calls the classes defined in B through the interaction between B and W. Therefore, the customization code can be tested by the integration testing of W and B. The faults included in the COM applications of the empirical study exist in the customization code, thus the faults should be tested by integration testing, which is the customization testing technique developed in this paper. Another significant point is that the customization faults of the empirical study are not related to *FIT* at all. They are the result of the customization itself.

Result. The results of the empirical study are in Table 6. An analysis will be made describing Eff_1, Eff_2, the number of *fBWs* or mutants, and Eff_2 per one *fBW* or mutant.

Table 6. The values from the empirical study of COM customization testing

		App Stack	App Operator	App Booking	App Zipcode	App Voting	Average
Eff_1	FIT/FIO	100.00%	100.00%	100.00%	100.00%	100.00%	**100.00%**
	IM	50.00%	50.00%	33.33%	66.67%	66.67%	**53.33%**
	OM	100.00%	100.00%	100.00%	100.00%	100.00%	**100.00%**
	DataFlow	100.00%	50.00%	33.33%	100.00%	33.33%	**63.33%**
Eff_2	FIT/FIO	85.00%	100.00%	100.00%	80.00%	100.00%	**93.00%**
	IM	50.00%	50.00%	35.00%	30.00%	90.00%	**51.00%**
	OM	75.00%	100.00%	55.00%	75.00%	100.00%	**81.00%**
	DataFlow	75.00%	100.00%	55.00%	55.00%	50.00%	**67.00%**
fBWs or mutatns	FIT/FIO	2	1	2	1	2	**1.60**
	IM	1	4	2	2	2	**2.20**
	OM	16	24	22	22	26	**22.00**
Eff_2 per one *fBW* or mutant	FIT/FIO	42.50%	100.00%	50.00%	80.00%	50.00%	**64.50%**
	IM	50.00%	12.50%	17.50%	15.00%	45.00%	**28.00%**
	OM	4.69%	4.17%	2.50%	3.41%	3.85%	**3.72%**

Analysis. Eff_1 is measured by the formula, Eff_1 = (The number of faults detected by the set of test cases / The total number of faults) * 100. Eff_1 of FIT/FIO and OM is 100%. That is because FIT/FIO is based on *FIT*s defined to be sensitive to the customization faults, and OM selects the test data as many as it generates the mutants of the entire COM application, rather then the specific part of a component. FIT/FIO generates fewer *fBWs* during testing.

The empirical study has measured Eff_2 by the formula, Eff_2 = (The number of test cases with fault detection / The total number of test cases) * 100. Eff_2 of FIT/FIO is 93% in average for the five customized COM applications. The average Eff_2 of OM is 81% and the average Eff_2 of FIT/FIO is 93%. Eff_2 of OM is smaller than that of FIT/FIO, while Eff_1 of OM is the same as that of FIT/FIO. It means that the test data of FIT/FIO is more sensitive to the customization faults than the test data of OM. Although the mutation operators of IM and FIT/FIO are developed under the same interface concept, they have varying degrees of effectiveness, depending on whether it focuses on the component system or the distributed system.

The large number of mutants or *fBWs* creates a higher testing cost due to the cost of managing and handling the *fBWs* during testing. OM generates an average of 22 mutants. It is excessively larger than FIT/FIO's 1.60 or IM's 2.20. That is because OM doesn't define the restrictions to generating mutants. It mutates the entire COM applications not like FIT/FIO and IM. Considering the testing cost, OM is not proper to CBSD testing because it must handle too many mutants and test data.

The difference between FIT/FIO and OM is bigger in Eff_2 per one *fBW* or mutant than in Eff_2. This means that FIT/FIO generates more effective test data with fewer faults compared to the others. This is because it generates fewer *fBWs* due to identifying the customization patterns, and also because it selects the test data that is sensitive to the customization faults due to defining *FIT*s based on the interaction between *B* and *W*.

4.3 The Empirical Study on the Composition Testing Under COM

Composition Units of COM Applications. Table 7 shows the COM applications including the composition units tested in this empirical study. It is assumed that the composition units of the COM applications have faults through the composition. The composition testing technique that was tailored to COM in Section 3 tests the composition units to detect their faults.

Table 7. COM applications used in the empirical study of COM composition testing

Applications	Components of *CU*s	Sizes	Patterns	Description of Composition
App Stack	$(\overline{W})$COM_Stack $(\overline{W})$COM_Pop	102	$\overline{W}\overline{W}$	COM_Stack calls the method, pop() of COM_Pop
App Operator	$(\overline{W})$COM_Operator $(\overline{B})$COM_Operation	96	$\overline{W}\overline{B}$	COM_Operator calls the methods, OperSum(), OperSub(), OperDiv(),OperMult() of COM_Operation.
App Booking	$(\overline{W})$COM_Booking $(\overline{B})$COM_MkReg	110	$\overline{W}\overline{B}$	COM_Booking calls the method, MakeRegNum() of COM_MkReg
App Zipcode	$(\overline{W})$COM_SearchZip $(\overline{W})$COM_AddZip	62	$\overline{W}\overline{W}$	COM_SearchZip calls the method, AddZip() of COM_AddZip
App Voting	$(\overline{W})$COM_Voting $(\overline{B})$COM_ProcessVoting	114	$\overline{W}\overline{B}$	COM_Voting calls the method, calResult() of COM_ProcessVoting

Composition Faults Inside the COM Applications. The faults caused by the composition are exposed through the interaction between two components of *CU*. If a fault can be detected by testing only the unit, $\overline{W}$ or $\overline{B}$, it can not be said to be a composition fault. Therefore, the empirical study should require that the COM applications include faults that can not be exposed by unit testing but exposed by integration testing. The composition testing of this paper is an integraion testing of two components of *CU*.

The fauls in the composition code of $\overline{W}_s$ of $\overline{W}\overline{W}$ pattern or $\overline{W}$ of $\overline{W}\overline{B}$ pattern can be detected only by the integration testing. However, the faults existing in the composition code of $\overline{W}_d$ of $\overline{W}\overline{W}$ pattern can be tested by the unit testing of $\overline{W}_d$. The composition code existing in $\overline{W}_d$ is related to the return variables, and it resides inside $\overline{W}_d$ not with $\overline{W}_s$. Consequently, the faults existing in $\overline{W}_s$ of $\overline{W}\overline{W}$ pattern or $\overline{W}$ of $\overline{W}\overline{B}$ pattern should be tested only by integration testing, which is the composition testing technique of this paper, and thus the empirical study inserts the composition faults in $\overline{W}_s$ of $\overline{W}\overline{W}$ pattern and $\overline{W}$ of $\overline{W}\overline{B}$ pattern. Another point is that the composition faults of the emprical study are not related to *FIT* at all. They are caused by the composition itself.

Result. Table 8 was calculated with the values that the testing techniques have generated in this empirical study. They are Eff_1, Eff_2, the number of fBWs or mutants, and Eff_2 per one fCU or mutant.

Table 8. The values from the empirical study of COM composition testing

		App Stack	App Operator	App Booking	App Zipcode	App Voting	Average
Eff_1	FIT/FIO	100.00%	100.00%	66.67%	100.00%	100.00%	93.33%
	IM	100.00%	100.00%	66.67%	33.33%	66.67%	73.33%
	OM	100.00%	100.00%	100.00%	100.00%	100.00%	100.00%
	DataFlow	100.00%	100.00%	33.33%	66.67%	66.67%	73.33%
Eff_2	FIT/FIO	90.00%	85.00%	100.00%	100.00%	85.00%	92.00%
	IM	50.00%	85.00%	95.00%	90.00%	100.00%	84.00%
	OM	48.89%	62.50%	40.00%	44.44%	25.00%	44.17%
	DataFlow	80.00%	75.00%	25.00%	65.00%	60.00%	61.00%
fCUs or mutatns	FIT/FIO	2	1	1	2	1	1.40
	IM	1	4	2	4	2	2.60
	OM	30	32	40	24	24	30.00
Eff_2 per one fCU or mutant	FIT/FIO	45.00%	85.00%	100.00%	50.00%	85.00%	73.00%
	IM	50.00%	21.25%	47.50%	22.50%	50.00%	38.25%
	OM	1.63%	1.95%	1.00%	1.85%	1.04%	1.49%

Analysis. Eff_1 measures how many faults are detected for the set of the test data. FIT/FIO and OM have the great Eff_1s. OM has 100% Eff_1 for every application. This is because OM select lots of test data through mutating the entire component, and thus the test data are enough to detect the faults included in the COM applications. Eff_1 does not care how many test data are generated. That is why the empirical study measures Eff_2 as well as Eff_1.

Eff_2 measures how many test data detect faults out of the total test data. It focuses on the number of the test data generated by a testing technique. Since the testing cost is important in CBSD, the number of the test data a tester should handle is also important. Eff_2 is calculated with the number of test data that detected faults. Eff_2 The difference between FIT/FIO and OM gets bigger in 'Eff_2' than in 'Eff_1.' The average of FIT/FIO is 92%. It is larger than Eff_2 of OM while Eff_1 of FIT/FIO is smaller than Eff_1 of OM. The difference between FIT/FIO and OM in Eff_1 is 6.67% and the difference in Eff_2 is 29.16% in average. FIT/FIO select the test data that is sensitive to the composition faults since it uses FIT that is based on the interaction between $\bar{B}$ and $\bar{W}$, and the composition faults occur in the interaction, not in the unit.

OM also has a large number of mutants, which are 30 mutants in average, compared to the others because OM mutates the entire $\bar{W}$ of CU. Not like OM, FIT/FIO and IM have their own method for injecting faults to generate mutants or fCUs.

The difference between FIT/FIO and IM is bigger in "Eff_2 per one fBW or mutant" than in "Eff_2." It means that FIT/FIO generates more effective test data with fewer fBWs compared to the others, since it generates fewer fCUs due to identifying the composition patterns. It also selects the test data that is sensitive to the composition faults due to defining FITs based on the interaction between two components of CU.

5 Concluding Remarks

The lack of the source code of components makes it difficult for component users to test components. This paper has tailored the component customization testing technique [7] to COM components. It has also evaluated the effectiveness of the test cases with COM components. This paper has the following three advantages:

First, it enables the component user to test faults occurring in interactions between the implementation part, which is closed, and the interface part, which is available to the component user, although the component user can access only the source code of the interface of the components.

Second, it is applicable to 'real' component architectures. The specific FITs and FIOs were developed for COM in Section 3. It is possible to apply the technique of this paper to various component architectures, because the definitions of the B, W, FIT, and FIO came from the component's general characteristics and can be tailored to any specific component architecture as shown on COM in this paper and EJB[16].

Third, it selects effective test cases. The empirical study evaluated effectiveness with the two definitions of effectiveness: Eff_1 and Eff_2. The results and the analysis of the empirical study were showed in Section 4. The effectiveness is one of the important requirements in CBSD. The effective test cases can save testing time, consistent with the purpose of component-based software, namely, a major reduction in the cost of software development. The empirical study showed that the FIT generates a reasonable number of fBWs, selecting effective test cases, which leads to increased effectiveness.

The technique of this paper can be applied to other component architectures by customizing the patterns, FIT, and FIO, since the technique consists of B and W like a component as shown in Figure 3. We have already done an empirical study on EJB component in an earlier paper [6]. It showed that this technique applied to EJB components produces more effective test data, as measured by Eff_1 and Eff_2.

Finally, this paper has customized the testing technique to COM components, and the empirical study of Section 4 showed that this technique applied to COM components also contributes to greater effectiveness. The testing techniques of this paper will match the component-based development as shown in the empirical study of COM and EJB.

A tool has been built for EJB components. It tests EJB components automatically using the technique tailored to EJB, and it was used in the empirical study with EJB [6]. A tool for COM components can be built now. Moreover, the approach in this paper will be applied to test web-based software engineering, which seems to be very popular these days.

References

1. Mary Jean Harrold: Testing : A Roadmap. Proceeding of the Future of Software Engineering of the 22nd International Conference on Software Engineering, Jun. (2000)
2. Mary Jean Harrold, Donglin Liang, and Saurabh Sinha: An Approach To Analyzing and Testing Component-Based Systems. Proceeding of the First International ICSE Workshop on Testing Distributed Component-Based Systems, May. Los Angeles, CA. (1999)
3. Paul Allen. Practical Strageties for Migration to CBD. IT Journal Distributed Component Systems. (1999)
4. Desmon F.D'Souza and A.C.Wills: Object, Components, and Frameworks with UML. Addison-Wesley. (1998)
5. J.M.Jezequl and David Sussman: Design by Contract : The Lessons of Ariane. Computer, Jan. (1997) 129-130
6. Hoijin Yoon, Byoungju Choi: Effective Test Case Selection for Component Customization and Its Application to EJB. The Software Testing, Verification, and Reliability Journal, to appear on Vol.14 No.2 June (2004)
7. Hoijin Yoon and Byoungju Choi: Component Customization Testing Technique Using Fault Injection Technique and Mutation Test Criteria. Proceeding of Mutation 2000, Oct. San Jose, USA.(2000) 71-78
8. R.A.DeMillo, R.J.Lipton, and F.G.Sayward: Hints on Test Data Selection: Help for the Practicing Programmer. IEEE Computer, Vol. 11, No. 4. (1978) 34-41
9. W. Eric Wong, Joseph R. Horgan, Aditya P. Mathur, and Alberto Pasquini: Test Set Size Minimization and Fault Detection Effectiveness: A Case Study in a Space Application. Proceeding of COMPSAC'97. Washington D.C., USA, (1997) 522-529
10. Aditya P. Mathur and W. Eric Wong: Comparing the Fault Detection Effectiveness of Mutation and Data Flow Testing: An Empirical Study. SERC-TR-146-P, Purdue University. (1993)
11. Marcio E. Delamaro, Jose C. Maldonado, and Aditya P. Mathur: Interface Mutation: An Approach for Integration Testing. IEEE Transactions on Software Engineering, Vol. 27, Vo. 3. (2001) 228-247
12. S. Ghosh: Testing Component-Based Distributed Applications. Ph. D Dissertation, Department of Computer Science in Purdue University. (2000)

Author Index

Lecture Notes in Computer Science

For information about Vols. 1–3315

please contact your bookseller or Springer

Vol. 3361: S. Bengio, H. Bourlard (Eds.), Machine Learning for Multimodal Interaction. XII, 362 pages. 2005.

Vol. 3360: S. Spaccapietra, E. Bertino, S. Jajodia, R. King, D. McLeod, M.E. Orlowska, L. Strous (Eds.), Journal on Data Semantics II. XI, 223 pages. 2005.

Vol. 3359: G. Grieser, Y. Tanaka (Eds.), Intuitive Human Interfaces for Organizing and Accessing Intellectual Assets. XIV, 257 pages. 2005. (Subseries LNAI).

Vol. 3358: J. Cao, L.T. Yang, M. Guo, F. Lau (Eds.), Parallel and Distributed Processing and Applications. XXIV, 1058 pages. 2004.

Vol. 3357: H. Handschuh, M.A. Hasan (Eds.), Selected Areas in Cryptography. XI, 354 pages. 2004.

Vol. 3356: G. Das, V.P. Gulati (Eds.), Intelligent Information Technology. XII, 428 pages. 2004.

Vol. 3355: R. Murray-Smith, R. Shorten (Eds.), Switching and Learning in Feedback Systems. X, 343 pages. 2005.

Vol. 3353: J. Hromkovič, M. Nagl, B. Westfechtel (Eds.), Graph-Theoretic Concepts in Computer Science. XI, 404 pages. 2004.

Vol. 3352: C. Blundo, S. Cimato (Eds.), Security in Communication Networks. XI, 381 pages. 2005.

Vol. 3351: G. Persiano, R. Solis-Oba (Eds.), Approximation and Online Algorithms. VIII, 295 pages. 2005.

Vol. 3350: M. Hermenegildo, D. Cabeza (Eds.), Practical Aspects of Declarative Languages. VIII, 269 pages. 2005.

Vol. 3349: B.M. Chapman (Ed.), Shared Memory Parallel Programming with Open MP. X, 149 pages. 2005.

Vol. 3348: A. Canteaut, K. Viswanathan (Eds.), Progress in Cryptology - INDOCRYPT 2004. XIV, 431 pages. 2004.

Vol. 3347: R.K. Ghosh, H. Mohanty (Eds.), Distributed Computing and Internet Technology. XX, 472 pages. 2004.

Vol. 3346: R.H. Bordini, M. Dastani, J. Dix, A.E.F. Seghrouchni (Eds.), Programming Multi-Agent Systems. XIV, 249 pages. 2005. (Subseries LNAI).

Vol. 3345: Y. Cai (Ed.), Ambient Intelligence for Scientific Discovery. XII, 311 pages. 2005. (Subseries LNAI).

Vol. 3344: J. Malenfant, B.M. Østvold (Eds.), Object-Oriented Technology. ECOOP 2004 Workshop Reader. VIII, 215 pages. 2005.

Vol. 3343: C. Freksa, M. Knauff, B. Krieg-Brückner, B. Nebel, T. Barkowsky (Eds.), Spatial Cognition IV. Reasoning, Action, and Interaction. XIII, 519 pages. 2005. (Subseries LNAI).

Vol. 3342: E. Şahin, W.M. Spears (Eds.), Swarm Robotics. IX, 175 pages. 2005.

Vol. 3341: R. Fleischer, G. Trippen (Eds.), Algorithms and Computation. XVII, 935 pages. 2004.

Vol. 3340: C.S. Calude, E. Calude, M.J. Dinneen (Eds.), Developments in Language Theory. XI, 431 pages. 2004.

Vol. 3339: G.I. Webb, X. Yu (Eds.), AI 2004: Advances in Artificial Intelligence. XXII, 1272 pages. 2004. (Subseries LNAI).

Vol. 3338: S.Z. Li, J. Lai, T. Tan, G. Feng, Y. Wang (Eds.), Advances in Biometric Person Authentication. XVIII, 699 pages. 2004.

Vol. 3337: J.M. Barreiro, F. Martin-Sanchez, V. Maojo, F. Sanz (Eds.), Biological and Medical Data Analysis. XI, 508 pages. 2004.

Vol. 3336: D. Karagiannis, U. Reimer (Eds.), Practical Aspects of Knowledge Management. X, 523 pages. 2004. (Subseries LNAI).

Vol. 3335: M. Malek, M. Reitenspieß, J. Kaiser (Eds.), Service Availability. X, 213 pages. 2005.

Vol. 3334: Z. Chen, H. Chen, Q. Miao, Y. Fu, E. Fox, E.-p. Lim (Eds.), Digital Libraries: International Collaboration and Cross-Fertilization. XX, 690 pages. 2004.

Vol. 3333: K. Aizawa, Y. Nakamura, S. Satoh (Eds.), Advances in Multimedia Information Processing - PCM 2004, Part III. XXXV, 785 pages. 2004.

Vol. 3332: K. Aizawa, Y. Nakamura, S. Satoh (Eds.), Advances in Multimedia Information Processing - PCM 2004, Part II. XXXVI, 1051 pages. 2004.

Vol. 3331: K. Aizawa, Y. Nakamura, S. Satoh (Eds.), Advances in Multimedia Information Processing - PCM 2004, Part I. XXXVI, 667 pages. 2004.

Vol. 3330: J. Akiyama, E.T. Baskoro, M. Kano (Eds.), Combinatorial Geometry and Graph Theory. VIII, 227 pages. 2005.

Vol. 3329: P.J. Lee (Ed.), Advances in Cryptology - ASIACRYPT 2004. XVI, 546 pages. 2004.

Vol. 3328: K. Lodaya, M. Mahajan (Eds.), FSTTCS 2004: Foundations of Software Technology and Theoretical Computer Science. XVI, 532 pages. 2004.

Vol. 3327: Y. Shi, W. Xu, Z. Chen (Eds.), Data Mining and Knowledge Management. XIII, 263 pages. 2005. (Subseries LNAI).

Vol. 3326: A. Sen, N. Das, S.K. Das, B.P. Sinha (Eds.), Distributed Computing - IWDC 2004. XIX, 546 pages. 2004.

Vol. 3325: C.H. Lim, M. Yung (Eds.), Information Security Applications. XI, 472 pages. 2005.

Vol. 3323: G. Antoniou, H. Boley (Eds.), Rules and Rule Markup Languages for the Semantic Web. X, 215 pages. 2004.

Vol. 3322: R. Klette, J. Žunić (Eds.), Combinatorial Image Analysis. XII, 760 pages. 2004.

Vol. 3321: M.J. Maher (Ed.), Advances in Computer Science - ASIAN 2004. Higher-Level Decision Making. XII, 510 pages. 2004.

Vol. 3320: K.-M. Liew, H. Shen, S. See, W. Cai (Eds.), Parallel and Distributed Computing: Applications and Technologies. XXIV, 891 pages. 2004.

Vol. 3319: D. Amyot, A.W. Williams (Eds.), System Analysis and Modeling. XII, 301 pages. 2005.

Vol. 3318: E. Eskin, C. Workman (Eds.), Regulatory Genomics. VII, 115 pages. 2005. (Subseries LNBI).

Vol. 3317: M. Domaratzki, A. Okhotin, K. Salomaa, S. Yu (Eds.), Implementation and Application of Automata. XII, 336 pages. 2005.

Vol. 3316: N.R. Pal, N.K. Kasabov, R.K. Mudi, S. Pal, S.K. Parui (Eds.), Neural Information Processing. XXX, 1368 pages. 2004.